Burials
at
Wauwatosa
Cemetery

Milwaukee County
Wisconsin

Elizabeth Doherty Herzfeld, CGRS

HERITAGE BOOKS
2015

HERITAGE BOOKS

AN IMPRINT OF HERITAGE BOOKS, INC.

Books, CDs, and more—Worldwide

For our listing of thousands of titles see our website
at
www.HeritageBooks.com

Published 2015 by
HERITAGE BOOKS, INC.
Publishing Division
5810 Ruatan Street
Berwyn Heights, Md. 20740

International Standard Book Numbers
Paperbound: 978-0-7884-1966-9
Clothbound: 978-0-7884-6147-7

INTRODUCTION

Wauwatosa Cemetery is bordered by Wauwatosa Avenue (76th St.), between North Avenue and Wright Street. Much of it is visible from Wauwatosa Ave. It is not laid out in a normal grid pattern, so it was hard to arrange the list of names precisely; though the families may have been buried in the same plot the stones are in different rows. I'm certain that in some cases their names will not appear next to each other in this work. Some stones are illegible or missing and many graves in the Potter's Field area are not marked. In other cases it was also hard to decipher names and other information, due to the way the information was placed on the stone. For instance, if there was no surname, was it the same as the main family listed on the stone? What about the stones with only a given name, is that person related to the people buried next to them? When there is only one date, was this a baby who was born and died in the same year? Another thing I noticed was that many times the death date is missing, because no one notified the monument company from which they purchased the stone to have it done. This is usually the case when the last person listed on the stone died.

The earliest burial was 1820. The cemetery was originally located one mile south of it's present location and in 1866 the cemetery association obtained permits to relocate the burials to the new location. The cemetery office does not have records of many babies that died in the late 1800s and early 1900s. This book contains the names of approximately 4500 people

Historically Wauwatosa Cemetery is quite interesting. There are two Revolutionary soldiers buried there, James Morgan and Samuel Riddle. There are also many Civil War soldiers, as well as memorial stones for those Civil War soldiers who died while they were in the army. Many of the town's leading citizens are buried here. James Morgan also has the earliest birth date of the known burials, 5 Apr 1748.

Some inscriptions are quite interesting. Many times the maiden name of the woman is inscribed on the stone, but unless that name was specifically noted as the maiden name by saying "nee" or "geb" I did not classify it as the maiden name, that is, put it in parenthesis and capitalize it. Sometimes a middle name may look like a maiden name, but it is actually a middle name. Occasionally the birth place is also noted on the headstone; one stone even lists the place of marriage. Marriage dates and names of children also appear on some stones. When the inscriptions were in another language, I copied them as they appear on the stone. There may be some errors, since some of the stones are quite worn.

Some people have two stones, perhaps old stones with newer stones placed next to them, or a military stone and a regular stone.

The listed information starts with the section, followed by the surname, given name(s), maiden name if any, birth date, birth place, death date, death place, inscription, and comments. When a ? appears it means the information is unknown or questionable. Not all of this information appears for each person. Sometimes there are no dates, places of birth or death, or inscriptions. I also added some pieces of information found elsewhere, such as Civil War service information. An asterisk follows some records marking some of the names found in my book, *Genealogical Abstracts from the Wauwatosa News, 1899-1904*, that I abstracted, and which was published by Heritage Books, Bowie, MD. 1999.

I wish to thank Betty Mainguth, who is the secretary for Wauwatosa Cemetery, for all her help.

ABBREVIATIONS

b..............................born
c/o.........................child of or children of
d..............................day(s) and died
d/o.........................daughter of
DAR.......................Daughters of the American Revolution
DOD.......................date of death
fam.........................family
GAR.......................Grand Army of the Republic
leg..........................Legion
m.............................month(s)
p/o.........................parents of
SAR.......................Sons of the American Revolution
s/o.........................son of
y.............................. year(s)
w/o.........................wife of

COMMON GERMAN WORDS

Dez..........................Dec.
Liebling...................darling
Mai..........................May
Mutter......................mother
Okt..........................Oct.
Ruhe Sanft...............Rest Easy
Sohn.........................son
Tochter....................daughter
Vater........................father

WAUWATOSA
CEMETERY
OFFICE ← 2ND FLOOR

WRIGHT STREET

ENTER
NORTH ENTRANCE

N

WAUWATOSA AVE (76TH ST)

NORTH SUB.

NORTH SUB.

NEOE

NE

NW

SW

SE

SEOE

ZEMK LANE

EXIT
SOUTH ENTRANCE

AUTO WAY

NORTH AVE

LONGFELLOW SCHOOL PARKING

LONGFELLOW MIDDLE SCHOOL

NORTH SUB.

NW 2

POTTER'S FIELD NW
ALL 1800'S
BURIED BY ROWS
1-1   1-13

SECTION 11

SEC 7

SEC 6

SEC 8

CHAPEL

SEC 9

FENCE

DUMP
AREA

SECTION 10

TREE

HILL

FENCE

SE SELEY Edwin H. b.1819-d.1868; Cushing-Seley plot, w/Lucinda, Ellen M. & Harry R. Seley, Walter & Eloisa Cushing

SE SELEY Lucinda b.1822-d.1858, "His Wife (Edwin H.)", Cushing-Seley plot, w/ Edwin H., Ellen M. & Harry R. Seley, Walter & Eloisa Cushing

SE SELEY Ellen M. b.1842-d.1885, Cushing-Seley plot, w/Edwin H., Lucinda & Harry R. Seley, Walter & Eloisa Cushing

SE SELEY Harry R. b.1858-d.1859, Cushing-Seley plot, w/Edwin H., Lucinda & Ellen M. Seley, Walter & Eloisa Cushing

SE CUSHING Walter b.1796-d.1856, Cushing-Seley plot, w/Edwin H., Lucinda, Ellen M.& Harry R.Seley & Eloisa Cushing

SE CUSHING Eloisa b.1797-d.1886, "His Wife (Walter)" Cushing-Seley plot, w/Edwin H., Lucinda, Ellen M.& Harry R.Seley & Walter Cushing

SE CUSHING John Henry b.1830-d.1918, w/ Clara Fisher Cushing, n/t Cushing- Seley Plot

SE CUSHING Clara Fisher b.1844-d.1927, w/ John Henry Cushing, n/t Cushing- Seley Plot

SE ZIMMERMANN John b.1826-d.1915, w/ Wilhelmina, n/t John C. & Ph. W., Margaretha & Phillip Zimmermann

SE ZIMMERMANN Wilhelmina b.1836-d.1910, w/ John, n/t John C. & Ph. W., Margaretha & Phillip Zimmermann

SE ZIMMERMANN John C. b.31Oct1857-d.19Jul1869, "11y 8m 19d" w/ Ph. W.; n/t John, Wilhelmina, Margaretha & Phillip Zimmermann

SE ZIMMERMANN Ph. W. b.23Dec1800-d.7Jun1874, w/ John C., n/t John, Wilhelmina, Margaretha & Phillip Zimmermann

SE ZIMMERMANN Margaretha b.1800-d.1880, n/t John, Wilhelmina, John C., Ph. W. & Phillip Zimmermann

SE ZIMMERMANN Phillip b.1800-d.1874, n/t John, Wilhelmina, John C., Ph. W. & Margaretha Zimmermann (probably a second stone for Ph. W.)

SE NIENEMANN Wilhelm b.3Sep1818-d.29Jan1894, n/t Christine Nienemann

SE NIENEMANN Christine b.23Oct1821-d.2Jan1903, n/t Wilhelm Nienemann

SE BASSLER Phillip d.23Feb1882?, "age 65y 3m 21d" w/ Soloma Frank Bassler

SE BASSLER Soloma Frank d.18Jul1871, "w/o Phillip Bassler, aged 51y 4m 12d" w/ Phillip Bassler

SE DUTCHER Hazel A. b.1908-d.1977

SE ZIMMERMANN John b.31Oct1857-d.19Jul1859, n/t Emma & Rosetta Zimmermann

SE ZIMMERMANN Emma b.1866-d.1918, n/t John & Rosetta Zimmermann

SE ZIMMERMANN Rosetta b.1854-d.1911, n/t John & Emma
Zimmermann
SE WINTERS Emma H. b.1857-d.1931, "Mother" n/t John W. Winters
SE WINTERS John W. b.8Feb1861-d.17Dec1916, "Father" n/t Emma H.
Winters
SE CABBOTT W. H. d.20Nov?1867, "21y 11m 10d"
SE CHURCH George b.21Aug1825-d.21Nov1889, n/t Minnie, Arthur P
& Hattie S. Church
SE CHURCH Minnie b.16Nov1858-d.1Apr1902, "w/o C.L. Church" n/t
George, Arthur P & Hattie S. Church; C.L. Church is not buried in this
cem.
SE CHURCH Arthur P. b.1883-d.1956, n/t George, Minnie & Hattie S.
Church
SE CHURCH Hattie S. b.1883-d.1974, n/t George, Minnie & Arthur P.
Church; DAR Emblem on stone
SE MOWER Timothy d.4Jan1853, "77 yrs." n/t Eunice Mower
SE MOWER Eunice d.20Apr1860, "77 yrs." n/t Timothy Mower
SE HOWARD Mary M. Chapin b.11Mar1809-d.22Mar1842, "w/o L.T.
Howard" n/t Eliza Jane Briggs, Luther T. & Emily Cheeseman Howard
SE HOWARD Eliza Jane Briggs b.31Jul1821-d.25Feb1856, "w/o L.T.
Howard" n/t Mary M. Chapin, Luther T. & Emily Cheeseman Howard
SE HOWARD Emily Cheeseman b.16Jan1820-d.27Sep1904, "Mother,
w/o L.T. Howard" n/t Mary M. Chapin, Luther T. & Eliza Jane Briggs
Howard
SE HOWARD Luther T. b.17Jul1808-d.1Dec1892, "Father" n/t Mary M.
Chapin, Emily Cheeseman & Eliza Jane Briggs Howard; L. T. Howard
was an early settler of Wauwatosa
SE SCHMIDT Phillip b.1830-d.1922, w/ Minnie, Maria, Peter, Minnie,
Bertha & John Schmidt
SE SCHMIDT Minnie b.1842-d.1905, w/ Phillip, Maria, Peter, Minnie,
Bertha & John Schmidt
SE SCHMIDT Minnie b.1884-d.1966, w/ Phillip, Maria, Peter, Minnie,
Bertha & John Schmidt
SE SCHMIDT Maria b.1806-d.1876, w/ Phillip, Minnie,Peter, Minnie,
Bertha & John Schmidt
SE SCHMIDT Peter b.1803-d.1868, w/ Phillip, Minnie,Maria, Minnie,
Bertha & John Schmidt
SE SCHMIDT Bertha b.1873-d.1874, w/ Phillip, Minnie, Maria, Peter,
Minnie & John Schmidt
SE SCHMIDT John b.1861-d.1861, w/ Phillip, Minnie, Maria, Peter,
Minnie & Bertha Schmidt

SE BURR Mary d.16Nov1861, "w/o James Burr, 66y 8m 12d" w/ Dexter
Burr; James Burr is not buried at this cemetery

SE BURR Dexter d.30Mar1861, "s/o James & Mary Burr, 40y 9m 17d"
w/ Mary Burr

SE QUIRK Homer b.1895-d.1947, n/t Margaret Quirk

SE QUIRK Margaret b.1874-d.1956, n/t Homer Quirk

SE DAVIDSON Edith V. b.1883-d.1966, "Mother" w/ Alexander Davidson
and possibly others

SE DAVIDSON Alexander b.1885-d.1959, "Father" w/ Edith V. Davidson
and others; Masonic Emblem

SE METCALF Minnie A. b.19Dec1873-d.3Feb1948, "Mother" w/ George
D. Metcalf

SE METCALF George D. b.1874-d.20Feb1965, "Father" w/ Minnie A.
Metcalf; death date not completed, death date from cemetery records;
cemetery records show birth date as 1875

SE DUMEZ Lillian b.1891-d.1979, w/ Lester I. Dumez & Myrtle B.
Crudim, MD

SE DUMEZ Lester I. b.1887-d.1966, w/ Lillian Dumez & Myrtle B.
Crudim, MD

SE CRUDIM Myrtle B. b.1892-d.1955, "M.D." w/ Lillian & Lester I.
Dumez

SE WIEGAND Nancy b.1931-d.1948, "Daughter" w/ Nona & Phillip
Wiegand

SE WIEGAND Nona b.1907-d.1972, "Mother" w/ Nancy & Phillip
Wiegand

SE WIEGAND Phillip b.1900-d.1972, "Father" w/ Nancy & Nona
Wiegand

SE YUNK Theresa b.1884-d.1962, "Mother" w/ Frank X. Yunk

SE YUNK Frank X. b.1878-d.1963, "Father" w/ Theresa Yunk

SE LIPMAN Ralph L. b.8Sep1903-d.21Dec1995, w/ Ruth E. Lipman

SE LIPMAN Ruth E. b.14Apr1907-d.24Feb1998, w/ Ralph L. Lipman
death date from cemetery records

SE NEITZKE Bertha A. b.1908-d.1993, w/ Richard C. Neitzke

SE NEITZKE Richard C. b.1903-d.1964, w/ Bertha A. Neitzke

SE BABICH Stephanie b.1885-d.1967, w/ Sam Babich

SE BABICH Sam b.1886-d.1988, w/ Stephanie Babich

SE JACOBSEN Pearl E. b.1915-d.1983, w/ William L. Jacobsen

SE JACOBSEN William L. b.1917-d.1998, w/ Pearl E. Jacobsen

SE HINZ Lucile I. b.1Feb1902-d.30May1988, w/ Herbert H. Hinz

SE HINZ Herbert H. b.6Jun1899-d.29Jun1953, w/ Lucile I. Hinz

SE WELKE Mary Hudson Dunn b.2Dec1897-d.1Jun1993, "Beloved Poet
"Our Marney"" w/ Stanley John Welke

SE WELKE Stanley John b.23Apr1892-d.2Nov1954, "Soldier, Patriot, Gentleman" w/ Mary Hudson Dunn Welke

SE MELENDY Samuel d.18Apr1849, "34y 8m 18d" w/ Amelia Springer & William E. Melendy & M. A. Margaret Santais

SE MELENDY Amelia Springer d.6Nov1862, "40y 7m 21d" w/ Samuel & William E. Melendy & M. A. Margaret Santais

SE MELENDY William E. d.23Aug1847, "6m 13d, s/o S & A S Melendy" w/ Samuel & Amelia S. Melendy & M. A. Margaret Santais

SE SANTAIS M. A. Margaret (MELENDY) b.1845-d.2Sep1900, Veulettes, France; w/ Samuel, Amelia S. & William E. Melendy

SE READER Wm. J. b.16Mar1807-d.7Aug1884, w/ Sophia H. Reader

SE READER Sophia H. b.2Feb1824-d.8Oct1886, "w/o Wm. J. Reader" w/ Wm. J. Reader

SE EITENEIER Charles b.1871-d.1931, n/t Julia & William Eiteneier, Catharina Nass & other Nass's, Nass family plot

SE EITENEIER Julia (NASS) b.1840-d.1917, "Mother" n/t Charles & William Eiteneier, Catharina Nass & other Nass's, Nass family plot

SE EITENEIER William b.1833-d.1917, "Father" n/t Julia & Charles Eiteneier, Catharina Nass & other Nass's, Nass family plot

SE NASS Catharina b.22Sep1831-d.7Jun1903, n/t Elizabeth, Charles & Emilius Nass & Charles, Julia & William Eteneier, family Plot

SE NASS Elizabeth b.3Mar1829-d.7Apr1892, n/t Catharina, Charles & Emilius Nass & Charles, Julia & William Eteneier, family Plot

SE NASS Charles b.20Nov1833-d.20Oct1880, n/t Catharina,Elizabeth & Emilius Nass & Charles, Julia & William Eteneier, family Plot

SE NASS Emilius b.4Apr1794-d.19Sep1869, n/t Catharina,Elizabeth & Charles Nass & Charles, Julia & William Eteneier, family plot

SE BROCKWAY Lafayette b.1847-d.1917, w/ Mary B., Mary F., Bessie, Addie, Walter H., Gilbert H. & other Brockways

SE BROCKWAY Mary B. b.1849-d.1889, w/ Lafayette,Mary F., Bessie, Addie, Walter H., Gilbert H. & other Brockways

SE BROCKWAY Mary Francis b.1848-d.1936, w/ Lafayette, Mary B., Bessie, Addie, Walter H., Gilbert H. & other Brockways

SE BROCKWAY Bessie b.1882-d.1882, w/ Lafayette, Mary B., Mary F., Addie, Walter H., Gilbert H. & other Brockways

SE BROCKWAY Addie b.1873-d.1896, w/ Lafayette, Mary B., Mary F., Bessie, Walter H., Gilbert H. & other Brockways

SE BROCKWAY Walter H. b.1874-d.1900, w/ Lafayette, Mary B., Mary F., Bessie, Addie, Gilbert H. & other Brockways

SE BROCKWAY Gilbert H. b.1876-d.1900, w/ Lafayette, Mary B., Mary F., Bessie, Addie, Walter H. & other Brockways

SE BROCKWAY Mildred b.1879-d.1967, w/ Lafayette, Mary B., Mary F., Bessie, Addie, Walter H. & other Brockways

SE BROCKWAY Arthur W. b.1885-d.1970, w/ Lafayette, Mary B., Mary F., Bessie, Addie, Walter H. & other Brockways

SE BROCKWAY Beulah V. b.1899-d.1989, w/ Lafayette, Mary B., Mary F., Bessie, Addie, Walter H. & other Brockways

SE BROCKWAY Robert C. b.1929-d.1957, w/ Lafayette, Mary B., Mary F., Bessie, Addie, Walter H. & other Brockways

SE VAN VRANKEN Ida A. b.1859-d.1930, n/t La Mont E. Van Vranken

SE VAN VRANKEN La Mont E. b.1856-d.1923, n/t Ida A. Van Vranken

SE FELLOWS Jane M. b.1869-d.1930

SE WLETSCHAK Elsie C. b.1895-d.1985, "Mother" w/ Frank E. Wletschak

SE WLETSCHAK Frank E. b.1895-d.1955, "Father" w/ Elsie C. Wletschak

SE ASZMANN Lillian M. b.1887-d.1953, w/ Edward W. Aszmann

SE ASZMANN Edward W. b.1885-d.1966, w/ Lillian M. Aszmann

SE HACKWORTHY Louise D. b.1902-d.1994, w/ Clement R. Hackworthy

SE HACKWORTHY Clement R. b.1894-d.1952, w/ Louise D. Hackworthy

SE CARTER Lavinia Andrews b.1824-d.1860

SE OWEN Edmond Pendleton b.1873-d.1951, "Husband" w/ Anna Owen

SE OWEN Anna b.1877-d.1978, "Wife" w/ Edmond P. Owen

SE CUNNINGHAM Mary b.12Oct1871, New Foundland-d.2May1952, Wauwatosa; "Thy Word is a Light Unto My Path" n/t Helen M. & Jesse Jay Davis

SE DAVIS Helen M. (CUNNINGHAM) b.26Jun1903-d.8Nov1994, "Long May Your Big Jib Draw" n/t Mary Cunningham & Jesse Jay Davis; picture of sail boat on stone

SE DAVIS Jesse Jay b.2Nov1897-d.4Jul1967, "Wis 1st Sgt Co K 20 Inf WWI" n/t Mary Cunningham & Helen M. Davis

SE HULLINGER Mary R. b.1935-d.1984, w/ David P. Hullinger

SE HULLINGER David P. b.1928-d.no date, w/ Mary R. Hullinger; Masonic Emblem

SE HOFFMAN Florence E. b.1897-d.1992, w/ John R. & John G. Hoffman

SE HOFFMAN John R. b.1892-d.1977, w/ Florence E. & John G. Hoffman

SE HOFFMAN John G. b.1926-d.1986, "Son" w/ John R. & Florence E. Hoffman

SE BROWN Jonathan b.1Aug1891-d.27Feb1892, n/t Mathilda, Oscar W., Virginia, Mary Ann, Lucy Minnie, Sarah M. & other Browns

SE BROWN Mathilda b.27Jul1867-d.15Apr1900, "w/o Jonathan Brown" n/t Jonathan, Oscar W., Virginia, Mary Ann, Lucy Minnie, Sarah M. & other Browns

SE BROWN Oscar W. b.1912-d.1914, w/Virginia; n/t Jonathan, Mathilda, Mary Ann, Lucy Minnie, Sarah M. & other Browns

SE BROWN Virginia b.1913-d.1914, w/ Oscar W; n/t Jonathan, Mathilda, Mary Ann, Lucy Minnie, Sarah M. & other Browns

SE BROWN Mary Ann b.1906-d.1924, n/t Jonathan, Mathilda, Virginia, Oscar W., Lucy Minnie, Sarah M. & other Browns

SE BROWN Lucy Minnie b.1914-d.1926, n/t Jonathan, Mathilda, Virginia, Oscar W., Mary Ann, Sarah M. & other Browns

SE BROWN Sarah M. d.7Oct1849, "w/o Jonathan Brown, 33y 7m" w/ Jonathan, Martha J., Lincoln, Abbie A., n/t Jonathan & other Browns M

SE BROWN Jonathan b.16Mar1813-d.24Oct1900, w/ Sarah M., Martha J., Lincoln, Abbie A., n/t Jonathan & other Browns

SE BROWN Martha J. b.5Dec1820-d.4Apr1891, "w/o Jonathan Brown" w/ Sarah M., Jonathan, Lincoln, Abbie A., n/t Jonathan & other Browns

SE BROWN Lincoln d.8Jan1890, "s/o J & M.J.B., 19y 6m" w/ Sarah M., Jonathan, Martha J., Abbie A., n/t Jonathan & other Browns

SE BROWN Abbie A. b.1863-d.1926, w/ Sarah M., Jonathan, Martha J.,Lincoln, n/t Jonathan & other Browns

SE BROWN Jonathan b.1852-d.1928, n/t Sarah M., Jonathan, Martha J., Abbie A., Lincoln, Mathilda & other Browns

SE COWLES Mary A. b.1833-d.1912, n/t Elon Cowles

SE COWLES Elon b.1831-d.1865, n/t Mary A. Cowles

SE BROWN Leonard b.18May1803-d.11Oct1882, "Father" n/t Amanda F. Brown; GAR Emblem

SE BROWN Amanda F. b.7Jun1806-d.8Jul1886, "Mother" n/t Leonard Brown

SE CONNELL Anna G. b.1855-d.1925, n/t M. E., L. S., F. G., Theresa M., & William I. Connell

SE CONNELL M. E. b.1848-d.1923, n/t Anna G., L. S., F. G., Theresa M., & William I. Connell

SE CONNELL L. S. b.1873-d.1945, n/t Anna G., M. E., F. G., Theresa M., & William I. Connell

SE CONNELL F. G. b.1875-d.1968, n/t Anna G., M. E., L. S., Theresa M., & William I. Connell

SE CONNELL Theresa M. b.1820-d.1907, "Mother" n/t Anna G., M. E., L. S., F. G. & William I. Connell

SE CONNELL William I. b.1815-d.1851, "Father" n/t Anna G., M. E., L. S., F. G. & Theresa M. Connell

SE MANNING Walter J. b.3Nov1905-d.10Feb1998, "Beloved Husband of Alice E. 1911-1985"; Alice E. is not buried here, she donated her body to science.

SE KELLY Herbert John b.20Nov1893-d.3Mar1988, "Sgt US Army WWI" n/t Elfrieda Dorothea & Judith Ann Kelly

SE KELLY Elfrieda Dorothea b.18Jul1907-d.17Jul1997, "Dear Generous Fritzi;Bel.Wife & Mother" n/t Herbert John & Judith Ann Kelly

SE KELLY Judith Ann b.4Jan1937-d.6Feb1996, "Bel. daughter & Sister; La Belle Artiste" n/t Herbert John & Elfrieda Dorothea Kelly

SE LELAND Joshua W. b.no date-d.no date, old stone, P. Carr Sec.? not listed in cemetery records

SE GARVENS Evelyn H. b.1902-d.1956, w/ Arvine A. Garvens, n/t Arvine R. Wales & other Wales

SE GARVENS Arvine A. b.1900-d.1983, w/ Evelyn H. Garvens, next to Wales family

SE WALES Gideon d.16Nov1861, "63y 15d" w/ Polly, Allen A., Arvine R., & Mary C. Wales, n/t Evelyn H. & Arvine A. Garvens; Gideon Wales was an early settler of Wauwatosa.

SE WALES Polly d.1Jun1888, "7y 2m 22d" w/ Gideon, Allen A., Arvine R., & Mary C. Wales, n/t Evelyn H. & Arvine A. Garvens

SE WALES Allen A. d.20Oct1868, "16y 5m 20d" w/ Gideon, Polly, Arvine R., & Mary C. Wales, n/t Evelyn H. & Arvine A. Garvens

SE WALES Arvine R. d.9Mar1850, "16y 9m 9d" w/ Gideon, Polly, Allen A., & Mary C. Wales, n/t Evelyn H. & Arvine A. Garvens

SE WALES Mary C. b.1848-d.1915, w/ Gideon, Polly, Allen A., & Arvine R. Wales, n/t Evelyn H. & Arvine A. Garvens

SE WATSON Willis E. b.1846-d.1915, n/t Jennie M. & Mary E. Browne Watson

SE WATSON Jennie M. b.1854-d.1917, n/t Willis E. & Mary E. Browne Watson

SE WATSON Mary Everts Browne b.1820-d.1892, "w/o George Watson" n/t George, Willis E., Jennie E. & Henry Eugene Watson & Mabel Everts

SE WATSON Henry Eugene d.6Aug1849, "1y 4m" w/ George, & Mary E. Browne Watson & Mabel Everts, n/t Willis & Jennie Watson

SE EVERTS Mabel d.3May1869, "4y 18d" w/ George, Mary E. Browne & Henry Eugene n/t Willis E. & Jennie M. Watson

SE WATSON George b.8Jan1814-d.14Oct1873, w/ Mary E. Browne, & Henry E. Watson & Mable Everts, n/t Willis E. & Jennie M. Watson

SE BROWNE Ella b.1859-d.1871, w/ Maria L., Elizabeth M., Henry W.,
& Levi H. Browne & Charles R. & Mary F. Staples
SE BROWNE Maria L. d.29Jun1860, "? 1m? (hard to read) d/o HW & LA
Browne" w/Ella, Elizabeth M., Henry W., & Levi H. Browne & Charles
R. & Mary F. Staples
SE BROWNE Elizabeth M. d.3Oct1849, "11m 26d, d/o HW & LA
Browne" w/ Ella, Maria L., Henry W., & Levi H. Browne & Charles R.
& Mary F. Staples
SE BROWNE Henry W. b.1821?-d.1863, "(hard to read)" w/ Ella, Maria
L., Elizabeth M., & Levi H. Browne & Charles R. & Mary F. Staples
SE BROWNE Levi H. d.1855, "1y 5m 12d (hard to read)" w/ Ella, Maria
L., Elizabeth M., & Henry W. Browne & Charles R. & Mary F. Staples
SE STAPLES Charles Ray b.21Apr1866-d.2May1893, w/ Ella, Maria L.,
Elizabeth M., Henry W. & Levi H. Browne & Mary F. Staples
SE STAPLES Mary Frances b.29Jun1863-d.19Jul1895, w/ Ella, Maria L.,
Elizabeth M., Henry W. & Levi H. Browne & Charles R. Staples
SE STADLER Henrietta E. b.no date-d.11Jun1941, only one date
SE WRIGHT Frederick M. b.1859-d.1926
SE SMITH Martha Johnson b.1855-d.1942, w/ Rev. Oliver H. P. Smith
SE SMITH Oliver H. P. b.1851-d.1912, "Rev." w/ Martha Johnson Smith
SE SMITH S. Compton b.1814-d.1876?, "Dr." w/ Evalina Wheeler? Smith;
stone is an open Bible in Marble, very worn
SE SMITH Evalina Wheeler? b.1827-d.1906, w/ Dr. S. Compton Smith;
stone is an open Bible in Marble, very worn
SE METER Martha (MUELLER) b.3Mar1874-d.25Oct1928, w/ Mathias
Meter
SE METER Mathias b.21Sep1877-d.28Nov1955, w/ Martha Meter
SE GREEN Lydia A. b.1830-d.1917
SE TRUESDELL Ellen W. b.1859-d.1941
SE HANKS Nancy b.15Apr1839-d.14Apr1867, "w/o Augustus Hanks" old
stone lying flat, broken, can't read age; name on stone looks like
Shanks, but cemeter records have no Shanks in their records
SE HANKS L. P. d., "Co. E 24th Wisconsin Infantry" military stone,
probably Civil War; Lorin P. Hanks of Granville enlisted in the army
5 Aug 1862 and served until 28 Feb 1863 when he became disabled [1]
SE HANKS Amos d.29Apr1866, "age 59" old stone, lying flat, broken
SE PETERSEN Hans b.1859-d.1937, n/t Anna K., Lily Henrietta, Margaret Helen, and Elna Marie Petersen

1 *Roster of Wisconsin Volunteers, War Of The Rebellion, 1861-1865, Compiled by Authority*
Of The Legislature, Under The Direction Of Jeremiah M. Rusk, Govenor and Chandler P.
Chapman, Adjutant General, published by Madison Democrat Printing Co. state
printers, 1886 (hereafter called Roster of Wisconsin Volunteers, War Of The Rebellion,
1861-1865)

SE PETERSEN Anna K. (NIELSON) b.1870-d.1943, n/t Hans, Lily Henrietta, Margaret Helen, and Elna Marie Petersen

SE PETERSEN Lily Henrietta b.1892-d.1952, n/t Hans, Anna K., Margaret Helen, and Elna Marie Petersen

SE PETERSEN Margaret Helen b.1898-d.1961, n/t Hans, Anna K., Lily Henrietta, and Elna Marie Petersen

SE PETERSEN Elna Marie b.1890-d.1983, n/t Hans, Anna K., Lily Henrietta, and Margaret Helen Petersen

SE BRIGGS Franklin P. d.24Mar1855, "aged 31 years" old stone lying flat, broken

SE JACOBS Jennie A. d.7May1875, "d/o C.H. & J.R. Jacobs, 12y 2m 15d" n/t Charles, Jane & Fannie Jacobs

SE JACOBS Fannie d.17Nov1861, "d/o C.H. & J.R. Jacobs, aged 3m" n/t Charles, Jane & Jennie A. Jacobs

SE JACOBS Charles H. b.1836-d.1886, w/ Jane A., n/t Fannie & Jennie A. Jacobs

SE JACOBS Jane A. b.1827-d.1897, w/ Charles, n/t Fannie & Jennie A. Jacobs

SE KREBS Earle K. b.1903-d.1957, n/t Birdelle R. Krebs

SE KREBS Birdelle R. b.1905-d.1973, n/t Earle K. Krebs

SE VINYARD Charlotte N. b.1903-d.1969, w/ Clarence Vinyard

SE VINYARD Clarence b.1898-d.1968, w/ Charlotte N. Vinyard

SE HAYNES Mary Frances (CORRAO) b.1958-d.1991, w/ John Donald & Don Haynes

SE HAYNES John Donald b.no date-d.no date, w/ Mary Frances & Don Haynes

SE HAYNES Don d.28Jan1980, w/ Mary Frances & John Donald Haynes; only one date

SE LOOKER Glen W. b.1932-d.1990,

SE KOHN Ethel M. b.1904-d.1984, w/ Douglas R. Kohn

SE KOHN Douglas R. b.1903-d.1988, w/ Ethel M. Kohn

SE MILNE Nancy Ritter b.2Jan1928-d.27Jul1991, "(Ric)" w/ Charles Robert Milne

SE MILNE Charles Robert b.27Apr1926-d.no date, "(Bob)" w/ Nancy Ritter Milne

SE COLEMAN William A. b.2Apr1852-d.25Dec1904, w/ Frances C. Cleveland Coleman, large stone near road on south side of section

SE COLEMAN Frances C. Cleveland b.18Feb1848-d.18Dec1888, "w/o W. A. Coleman", w/ William A. Coleman, large stone near road on south side of section

SE BARRETT Marie A. b.1914-d.1919
SE BROWN Clarence Henry d.24Mar1869, "s/o Geo. W. & M.L. Brown, 3y 5m 3d?" w/ Geo. W., Lorette C.,Julia M. & Marie? Brown, marble stone, very worn
SE BROWN Geo. W. d.6Jul1881, "58y 11m 6d" w/ Clarence H., Lorette C., Julia M. & Marie? Brown, marble stone, very worn
SE BROWN Lorette Caemelt? d.16Mar1856, "w/o Geo. W. Brown, 24y 22d" w/ Clarence H., Geo. W., Julia M. & Marie? Brown, marble stone, very worn
SE BROWN Julia M. b.1858-d.1934, "Daughter" w/ Clarence H., Geo. W., Lorette & Marie? Brown, marble stone, very worn
SE BROWN Marie? d.1889, "w/o Geo. W. Brown, 66y 11m 22d?" w/ Clarence Henry, Geo. W., Lorette & Julia M. Brown, marble stone, very worn
SE ADAMS Oliver b.26Mar1915-d.11Jun1998
SE KASS George C. b.1902-d.1980, "Beloved Father" n/t Sylvia M. Kass
SE KASS Sylvia M. b.1905-d.1971, "Beloved Mother" n/t George C. Kass
SE REBHOLZ Richard A. b.24Jun1919-d.7Apr1996, "1st Lt. US Army WWII" n/t Elizabeth Reholz, military stone; there are 2 stones for Richard
SE REBHOLZ Elizabeth Ann b.1920-d.no date, "m. 14 Feb 1942" w/ Richard Andrew Rebholz
SE REBHOLZ Richard Andrew b.1919-d.1996, "m. 14 Feb 1942" w/ Elizabeth Ann Rebholz; there are 2 stones for Richard
SE MILLER Charles J. b.1894-d.1964
SE GROVER Ebenezer Jaruis b.3Sep1829-d.14Jul1890, "Father" n/t Helen Permella, Celina D., & Salmon, Jr. Grover
SE GROVER Helen Permella b.5Dec1832-d.2Jun1864, "Mother" n/t Ebenezer Jarius,Celina D., & Salmon, Jr. Grover
SE GROVER Celina D. b.29Oct1806-d.17Aug1864, "Grandma" n/t Ebenezer Jarius, Helen P., & Salmon, Jr. Grover
SE GROVER Salmon, Jr. b.7Sep1803-d.13Sep1884, "Grandpa" n/t Ebenezer Jarius, Helen P., & Celina D. Grover
SE KERR Ivy W. b.1897-d.1990, "Mother, m. 1917" w/ Kenneth W. Kerr
SE KERR Kenneth W. b.1895-d.1975, "Father, m. 1917" w/ Ivy W. Kerr
SE RING James Hilton b.17Feb1923-d.27Mar1990, "m. 28 Sep 1947" w/ Helen Wilson Ring
SE RING Helen Wilson b.16Sep1924-d.no date, "m. 28 Sep 1947" w/ James Hilton Ring
SE SHELDON John b.30Mar1813-d.8Aug1880, n/t Mary & Ida M. Sheldon

10

SE SHELDON Mary b.1817-d.1908, n/t John & Ida M. Sheldon
SE SHELDON Ida M. b.14Mar1850-d.28May1901, n/t John & Mary
  Sheldon
SE CORNWALL Cynthia b.1792?-d.1871, w/ Eber, Nathaniel & John S.
  Cornwall & Cynthia M. & Edwin T. Wilson
SE CORNWALL Eber b.1Aug1792-d.11Jul1880, w/ Cynthia, Nathaniel &
  John S. Cornwall & Cynthia M. & Edwin T. Wilson
SE CORNWALL Nathaniel O. or D. b.1821-d.1885, w/ Cynthia, Eber &
  John S. Cornwall & Cynthia M. & Edwin T. Wilson
SE CORNWALL John S. b.8Aug1815-d.9Feb1841, "27y 4m" w/ Cynthia,
  Eber & Nathaniel D. Cornwall & Cynthia M. & Edwin T. Wilson
SE WILSON Cynthia M. b.2Aug1833-d.2Jun1878, w/ Cynthia, Eber,
  Nathaniel D. & John S. Cornwall & Edwin T. Wilson
SE WILSON Edwin T. b.1833-d.5May1879, w/Cynthia, Eber, Nathaniel D.
  & John S. Cornwall & Cynthia M. Wilson, old stone, hard to read
SE BUELL Bernice M. b.1900-d.1991, w/ Theodore W. Buell
SE BUELL Theodore W. b.1899-d.1961, w/ Bernice M. Buell
SE GOETTELMAN Carlyle A. b.1897-d.1956,
SE WOLTER Anna b.18Dec1882-d.5Jan1976, "Grandma" w/ Emil A.
  Wolter, Eastern Star Symbol
SE WOLTER Emil A. b.25Aug1881-d.4Nov1951, "Grandpa" w/ Anna
  Wolter, Masonic Symbol
SE WELKE Alice I. (WOLTER) b.30Sep1905-d.12May1984, "Mommy"
  w/ Erwin H. Welke
SE WELKE Erwin H. b.23Jul1903-d.14Jan1951, "Daddy" w/ Alice I.
  Welke
SE MORGAN Fanny C. d.14Dec1855, "w/o David Morgan" n/t David &
  James Morgan, stone broken, unable to read date & age
SE MORGAN David d.19Jan1875, "79y" n/t Fanny C. & James Morgan,
  stone broken, hard to read date & age, David was an early settler of
  Wauwatosa., cemetery records show that he was a Civil War Veteran
SE MORGAN James b.5Apr1748-d.3Mar1840, "91y 10m 28d; Col. John
  Evan's VA Troops Rev. War" n/t Fanny C. & David Morgan, 2 stones,
  one is a military stone. The DAR records show James was born in
  Virginia, he married Margaret Joliff and was a private and a spy for
  Virginia, he received a pension.[2] "...Morgan served in Captain James
  Brening's Company of the Virginia Regiment in 1778...he also served
  in the Pennsylvania Regiment led by Captain Samuel Mason and as a
  scout and spy against the Native Americans. He was discharged in

2 DAR Patriot Index Centennial Edition, Part II, page 2074, published by National Society
  Daughters of the American Revolution Centennial Administration, Washington; 1990

11

1796 and lived in virginia until 1829 when he moved to Illinois, he then moved to Wauwatosa in 1830 to be closer to his family." [3]

SE BROWNE Jonathan d.7Aug1855, "Father, Capt.; 69y" w/ Abbey E., Charles E., Martha E., Clarence D.,Edith D. & Ida Isabel Browne, "Johathan was born in New York and served in the New York Militia during the War of 1812, he came to Wauwatosa in 1845 with his wife and youngest son, Edward.[4]

SE BROWNE Abbey Everts d.14Apr1854, "His Wife (Jonathan); 60y" w/ Jonathan, Charles E., Martha E., Clarence D.,Edith D. & Ida Isabel Browne

SE BROWNE Charles E. b.6Jan1816-d.1Oct1895, w/ Jonathan, Abbey E., Martha E., Clarence D.,Edith D. & Ida Isabel Browne

SE BROWNE Martha Everts b.22Sep1823-d.19Dec1886, "His Wife (Charles E.)" w/ Jonathan, Abbey E., Charles E., Clarence D.,Edith D. & Ida Isabel Browne

SE BROWNE Clarence Duane d.31Jul1854, "s/o Charles E. & Martha E. Browne; 22m" w/ Jonathan, Abbey E., Charles E., Martha E., Edith D. & Ida Isabel Browne

SE BROWNE Edith Darrow d.25Sep1860, "d/o Charles E. & Martha E. Browne; 18m" w/ Jonathan, Abbey E., Charles E., Martha E., Clarence D & Ida Isabel Browne

SE BROWNE Ida Isabel b.1854-d.1936, w/ Jonathan, Abbey E., Charles E., Martha E.,Clarence D. & Edith D. Browne

SE ROSS Hiram J. b.10Dec1811-d.2May1893, w/ Hannah, Ann A. & Hubert B. Ross; Hiram J. Ross was an early settler of Wauwatosa

SE ROSS Hannah b.10Apr1817-d.25Apr1886, w/ Hiram J., Ann A. & Hubert B. Ross

SE ROSS Ann A. b.14Feb1845-d.10Jun1847, w/ Hiram J., Hannah & Hubert B. Ross

SE ROSS Hubert B. b.13May1848-d.1Oct1850, w/ Hiram J., Hannah & Ann A. Ross

SE BLACKWELL Bernard b.4Jul1886-d.26Sep1887,

SE WALKER James A. b.19Aug1829-d.3Sep1895, w/ Gratia A. & Winefred Walker, GAR mkr.

SE WALKER Gratia A. b.1838-d.1926, w/ James A. & Winefred Walker

SE WALKER Winefred b.28Dec1866-d.25Sep1867, w/ James A. & Gratia A. Walker

[3] *Wauwatosa Cemetery: The Heritage of a Community,* by Mead & Hunt, Inc., prepared for the Wauwatosa Historic Preservation Commission and the City of Wauwatosa, published by Mead & Hunt, Inc., April 1999 (hereafter called The Heritage of a Community), page 5.

4 The Heritage of a Community, page 5

SE BENKERT Paula b.1891-d.1970, n/t Kathrine Benkert
SE BENKERT Kathrine b.29Jan1886-d.22Apr1976, n/t Paula Benkert, no
  death date on stone, date of death is from cemetery records
SE BUNKE Helen B. b.1901-d.1982, w/ Paul W. Bunke
SE BUNKE Paul W. b.1903-d.1968, w/ Helen B. Bunke
SE HEINEMAN Lucille A. b.29Jan1909-d.4Jul1981, "Wife" w/ Gordon T.
  Heineman
SE HEINEMAN Gordon T. b.2Sep1901-d.6Nov1973, "Husband" w/
  Lucille A. Heineman
SE KLING Henry M. b.8Oct1908-d.24Jul1966, "Wisconsin PFC Coast
  Arty Corps WWII"
SE BARRETT Georgie C. d., "s/o (can't read) & JR Barrett" n/t Gladys
  Arline, Marie A., & Julia Cain Barrett,can't read dates,no cem rec
SE BARRETT Gladys Arline b.6Nov1839-d.6Apr1900, n/t Georgie C.,
  Marie A., & Julia Cain Barrett
SE BARRETT Marie A. b.1914-d.1919, n/t Georgie C., Gladys Arline, &
  Julia Cain Barrett
SE BARRETT Julia Cain b.1858-d.1919, n/t Georgie C., Gladys Arline, &
  Marie A. Barrett
SE JAMES Robert C., Jr. b.1962-d.1997, "US Army"
SE RADTKE David K. b.20Oct1922-d.6Nov1972, "Wis. Cpl. US Army
  WWII" n/t Gertrude & Albert Radtke
SE RADTKE Gertrude b.1901-d.1992, w/ Albert, n/t David K. Radtke
SE RADTKE Albert b.1898-d.1960, w/ Gertrude, n/t David K. Radtke
SE LENTZ Marie b.1862-d.1954, w/ Emil Lentz
SE LENTZ Emil b.1863-d.1944, w/ Marie Lentz
SE KURTZ Evelyn F. b.1918-d.1996, w/ George L. Kurtz
SE KURTZ George L. b.1917-d.no date, w/ Evelyn F. Kurtz
SE LANTZ Katherine L. b.1918-d.1996, w/ Thad-D. Lantz
SE LANTZ Thad D. b.1919-d.1992, w/ Katherine L. Lantz, Kiwanis
  Emblem
SE HILBERT Alice Jean b.23Jun1936-d.1May1989, "Beloved Wife &
  Mother"
SE REINKE Joyce B. b.1938-d.no date, "One Day at a Time" w/ Robert F.
  Reinke
SE REINKE Robert F. b.1934-d.1988, w/ Joyce B. Reinke, American
  Legion mkr.
SE WILSON Eugene b.1914-d.1970, "Brother"
SE RASCHKA Frank C. b.1910-d.1992, w/ Charles Raschka
SE RASCHKA Charles d.1960, "Infant" w/ Frank C. Raschka, only one
  date

SE FARCHMIN Geraldine b.1905-d.1989, w/ Emil, n/t Rudolph Farchmin
SE FARCHMIN Emil b.1893-d.1955, w/ Geraldine, n/t Rudolph Farchmin
SE FARCHMIN Rudolph b.1893-d.1964, n/t Geraldine & Emil Farchmin
SE RAKOS Mary b.1885-d.1953, w/ Mike Rakos
SE RAKOS Mike b.1887-d.1960, w/ Mary Rakos
SE LEDERMANN Mary b.1888-d.1963, w/ George Ledermann
SE LEDERMANN George b.1892-d.1964, w/ Mary Ledermann
SE VAN UXEM Meta b.1878-d.1957, w/ William Van Uxem
SE VAN UXEM William b.1876-d.1952, w/ Meta Van Uxem
SE FISCHER Louise M. b.1872-d.1950, "Mother" w/ Charles R., Viola A.,
    Charles H., & Mayme L. Fischer
SE FISCHER Charles R. b.1869-d.1946, "Father" w/ Louise M., Viola A.,
    Charles H., & Mayme L. Fischer
SE FISCHER Viola A. b.1901-d.1983, w/ Louise M., Charles R., Charles
    H., & Mayme L. Fischer
SE FISCHER Charles H. b.1899-d.1985, "Husband" w/ Louise M.,
    Charles R., Viola A., & Mayme L. Fischer
SE FISCHER Mayme L. b.1901-d.1980, "Wife" w/ Louise M., Charles R.,
    Viola A., & Charles H. Fischer
SE OURAND Joyce L. b.7Oct1924-d.13Mar1995, "Beloved Mother",
    this name could be wrong, there is no cemetery record under this name
SE SCHMIDTILL Helene R. b.1897-d.19—, w/ Louis W. Schmidtill cem
    records do not show her buried here
SE SCHMIDTILL Louis W. b.1887-d.1956, w/ Helene R. Schmidtill
SW ZIRWES Mabel b.1892-d.1985, w/ Jacob Zirwes
SW ZIRWES Jacob b.1885-d.1954, w/ Mabel Zirwes
SW LIPMAN Ethel b.1897-d.1988, "Mother" w/ Elmer L. Lipman
SW LIPMAN Elmer L. b.1893-d.1949, "Father" w/ Ethel Lipman
SW LONGENECKER Caroline b.1875-d.1966, w/ Charles Longenecker
SW LONGENECKER Charles b.1875-d.1953, w/ Caroline Longenecker
SW BARRETT none b.1882-d.24Nov1883?, dates hard to read, could be
    wrong, no cemetery record
SW JUEDES Alvin b.1893-d.1955, n/t Clara Juedes
SW JUEDES Clara b.1897-d.1988, n/t Alvin Juedes
SW CURRENS Elizabeth H. b.1895-d.1968, w/ Arthur D. Currens
SW CURRENS Arthur D. b.1892-d.1954, w/ Elizabeth H. Currens
SW POLLNOW Grace D. b.1915-d.1977, w/ Elmer H. Pollnow
SW POLLNOW Elmer H. b.1916-d.1962, w/ Grace D. Pollnow
SW HALLORAN Wilma D. b.1907-d.1991, w/ John J. Halloran, Sr.
SW HALLORAN John J., Sr. b.1906-d.1975, w/ Wilma D. Halloran
SW NARWOLD Dorothy M. b.29Mar1926-d.22Mar1989, w/ William L.
    Narwold

SW NARWOLD William L. b.13Nov1925-d.no date, w/ Dorothy M. Narwold

SW DEHNEL Nicholas Jay b.6Jul1990-d.30Aug1990, "Our Son"

SW WLETSCHAK Joan b.1936-d.no date, "Wife" w/ George Wletschak

SW WLETSCHAK George b.1927-d.1994, "Husband" w/ Joan Wletschak

SW BUCKMAN C. Arthur b.1897-d.1951, "Husband" n/t Gertrude Buckman

SW BUCKMAN Gertrude b.1897-d.1978, "Wife" n/t C. Arthur Buckman

SW FINCH Phillip A. b.30Jan1890-d.24Aug1950, w/ Edna & Janet Finch

SW FINCH Edna b.1888-d.1982, w/ Phillip A. & Janet Finch

SW FINCH Janet b.1917-d.no date, w/ Phillip A. & Edna Finch

SW BUSCHER Anna b.1884-d.1968, w/ Gustav, n/t Clarence Buscher

SW BUSCHER Gustav b.1884-d.1971, w/ Anna, n/t Clarence Buscher

SW BUSCHER Clarence b.1911-d.1950, "Son" n/t Anna & Gustav Buscher

SW WLETSCHAK Maxine H. b.1922-d.1942, "Daughter" n/t Horton S., Frank, & Faye Wletschak & Donna F. Lonetree

SW WLETSCHAK Frank b.1901-d.1979, "Father" w/ Faye, n/t Horton S., & Maxine H. Wletschak & Donna F. Lonetree

SW WLETSCHAK Faye b.1898-d.1975, "Mother" w/ Frank, n/t Maxine H., & Horton S. Wletschak & Donna F. Lonetree

SW LONETREE Donna F. (WLETSCHAK) b.25Dec1931-d.no date, "Daughter" n/t Maxine H., Frank, Faye, & Horton S. Wletschak

SW WLETSCHAK Horton S. b.29Oct1923-d.4Jan1993, n/t Maxine H., Frank, & Faye Wletschak & Donna F. Lonetree

SW BARRETT Mary b.30Apr1817-d.4Aug1884, "Mother" n/t Benjamin Barrett

SW BARRETT Benjamin b.11Mar1807-d.14Jan1899, "Father" n/t Mary Barrett

SW FARRIES Jessie Leona b.26Jul1877-d.19Feb1879, familyplot w/ Jane Brown & Wm. Farries

SW FARRIES Jane Brown b.3Dec1846-d.18Jun1908, familyplot w/ Jessie Leona & Wm. Farries

SW FARRIES Wm. b.25Dec1842-d.9Dec1921, familyplot w/ Jessie Leona Farries & Jane Brown; Wm. enlisted in the army in Wauwatosa 6 Aug 1862, he was a Corp. and Sergt. in the 24th Infantry Co. E, , wounded at Mission Ridge; Mustered Out 10 Jun 1865[5]

SW BROWN Scott C. b.1Mar1865-d.30Nov1875, "Son" n/t Corolin C. & Malcolm G. Brown

---

5 Roster of Wisconsin Volunteers, War Of The Rebellion, 1861-1865

SW BROWN Corolin C. b.8Aug1832-d.12Mar1901, "Mother" n/t Scott
C. & Malcolm G. Brown
SW BROWN Malcolm G. b.7Dec1831-d.13Sep1908, n/t Scott C. &
Corolin C. Brown
SW METTELMAN Dorothy Howard b.1904-d.1980
SW PARKER Reuben W., d.19Mar1873, "aged 64y 11m 17d" w/ Julius A.
& Susan B. Parker & Lucy B. Converse, date from cemetery record
SW PARKER Julius A., d.28Jun1878, "aged 39y 2m 16d" w/ Reuben W. &
Susan B. Parker & Lucy B. Converse, date from cemetery record
SW PARKER Susan B., d.11Jul1889, "73y" w/ Reuben W. & Julius A.
Parker & Lucy B. Converse, date and age from cemetery record
SW CONVERSE Lucy B., d.7May1883, "aged 60y or 69y" w/ Reuben W.
& Julius A. & Susan B. Parker
SW QUINDT Jeanette b.1918-d.no date, w/ Gustave Quindt
SW QUINDT Gustave b.1912-d.1992, w/ Jeanette Quindt
SW HOLTZ Arnold Paul b.29Dec1924-d.2Aug1992, "US Army WWII" w/
Ellen Janet Holtz
SW HOLTZ Ellen Janet b.18Dec1926-d.no date, w/ Arnold Paul Holtz
SW LOONEY Kyle B. b.2Aug1987-d.28Oct1987, "Our Little Angel"
SW BECHTEL Helena b.9Jun1857-d.27Jan1942, "Mother" n/t John,
Elizabeth, Jacob, Ida, & Margaretha Bechtel
SW BECHTEL John b.5Nov1860-d.29Jan1919, "Father" n/t Helena,
Elizabeth, Jacob, Ida, & Margaretha Bechtel
SW BECHTEL Elizabeth b.17Aug1858-d.31Oct1874, n/t Helena, John,
w/ Jacob, Ida, & Margaretha Bechtel
SW BECHTEL Ida b.4Dez1863-d.11Jan1869, n/t Helena, John, w/ Jacob,
Elizabeth & Margaretha Bechtel
SW BECHTEL Jacob b.11Mai1825-d.23Dec1885, n/t Helena, John, w/
Ida, Elizabeth & Margaretha Bechtel
SW BECHTEL Margaretha b.11Aug1822-d.27Apr1888, n/t Helena, John,
w/ Ida, Elizabeth & Jacob Bechtel
SW SCHWEICKHART George b.11Jul1824-d.30Apr1905, w/ Margaret,
Daniel, Helene & George Schweickhart, one other name unreadable
SW SCHWEICKHART Margaret b.16Apr1830-d.29Aug1872, w/ George,
Daniel, Helene & George Schweickhart, one other name unreadable
SW SCHWEICKHART Daniel b.8Dec1856-d.23Jul1883, w/ George,
Margaret, Helene & George Schweickhart, one other name unreadable
SW SCHWEICKHART Helene b.4Jun1863-d.2Aug1911, w/ George,
Margaret, Daniel & George Schweickhart, one other name unreadable
SW SCHWEICKHART George b.1858-d.1926, w/ George, Margaret,
Daniel & Helene Schweickhart, one other name unreadable

SW SCHWEICKHART Benjamin b.10Aug1860-d.14Mar1862, w/
George, Daniel, Helene & George Schweickhart, this is the name that
is unreadable, information from cemetery records

SW POTTER Charles M. b.1878-d.1953, w/Alice H., Milton B., Jennie,
Hitty W., Charles W., Eliza G. & other Potters

SW POTTER Alice H. b.1880-d.1958, w/Charles M., Milton B., Jennie,
Hitty W., Charles W., Eliza G. & other Potters

SW POTTER Milton B. b.8Jul1845 Wauwatosa, Wis.-d.28Nov1931, w/
Charles M., Alice H., Jennie, Hitty W., Charles W., Eliza G. & other
Potters

SW POTTER Jennie (CHURCH) b.30Nov1849 Wauwatosa-d.13Apr1931,
w/Charles M., Alice H., Milton B., Hitty W., Charles W., Eliza G. &
other Potters

SW POTTER Levi B. b.15Dec1815 Fitzwilliam, NH-d.24Feb1883, w/
Charles M., Alice H., Milton B., Hitty W., Charles W., Eliza G. & other
Potters; L. B. Potter was an early settler of Wauwatosa

SW POTTER Hitty Wenzel b.26Jul1820 Framingham, Mass.-
d.27Oct1884, "w/o L.B. Potter" w/Charles M., Alice H., Milton B.,
Levi B., Charles W., Eliza G. & other Potters

SW POTTER Lucilla T. b.28Jul1842-d.20Aug1842, w/Charles M., Alice
H., Milton B., Levi B., Charles W., Eliza G. & other Potters; dates from
cemetery records

SW POTTER Charles W. b.1861-d.1861, "s/o L.B. & H.W. Potter" w/
Charles M., Alice H., Milton B., Levi B., Hitty W., Eliza G. & other
Potters

SW POTTER Eliza G. b.27Jan1853-d.30Dec1867, w/Charles M., Alice
H., Milton B., Levi B., Hitty W., Henry B. & other Potters

SW POTTER Henry B. b.12Jan1847-d.12Aug1906, "Co. F 5 Wis. Inf." w/
Marion E., Alice H., Milton B., Levi B., Hitty W., & other Potters,
GAR mkr; Henry enlisted in the army in Wauwatosa 3 Jun 1861, he was
in the 5th Infantry Co.F, discharged 28 May 1863, disability[6]

SW POTTER Marion E. b.31Oct1881-d.19Mar1923, "d/o M.B. & J.C.
Potter" w/Jennie C., Alice H., Milton B., Levi B., Hitty W., & other
Potters

SW POTTER John Church b.1879 Wauwatosa, Wis.-d.1926 France, "1st
Lt Sig Corps WW,Pioneer Telephone Engineer in" Spain 1924-1926;
w/ Winifred-D. n/t Levi B. & Hitty W. Potter family

SW POTTER Winifred D. b.29Nov1888-d.30Dec1978, w/ John Church,
n/t Levi B. & Hitty W. Potter family

SW SCHAFER Della H. b.1893-d.1978, w/ Gustave A. Schafer

SW SCHAFER Gustave A. b.1893-d.1978, w/ Della H. Schafer

SW DIGMAN Ora L. b.15May1893-d.6Mar1966, w/ Lorenz H. Digman
dates from cemetery records

SW DIGMAN Lorenz H. b.1889-d.1947, w/ Ora L. Digman

SW BUCKINGHAM Viora V. b.1885-d.1983, "Wife" w/ Frank V.
Buckingham

SW BUCKINGHAM Frank V. b.1886-d.1951, "Husband" w/ Viola V.
Buckingham

SW FALK Fredrick b.1893-d.1948, "Husband"

SW WALKER Mary Jo Wolfe b.1897-d.1982, w/ Olive A. Walker

SW WALKER Olive A. b.1869-d.1948, w/ Mary Jo Wolfe Walker

SW McDONALD Martha Larsen b.1862-d.1958, "Mother" w/ William H.
McDonald

SW McDONALD William H. b.1860-d.1948, "Father" w/ Martha L.
McDonald

SW KUEHN F/O Karl F. b.1Nov1915-d.5Jan1945, w/ Alfred & Lucy B.
Kuehn, I don't know what F/O means

SW KUEHN Alfred b.24Jul1881-d.14Jul1956, w/ Karl F. & Lucy B.
Kuehn

SW KUEHN Lucy B. b.17Jan1890-d.4Mar1968, w/ Karl F. & Alfred
Kuehn dates from cemetery records

SW KRAATZ Katherine b.1871-d.1964, n/t Albert Kraatz

SW KRAATZ Albert b.1894-d.1948, n/t Katherine Kraatz

SW GILLESPIE Robert W. b.1921-d.1983, "MT Sgt US Marine Corps
WWII"

SW RICHARDS Clarence P. b.30Jul1919-d.17Apr1988, "PFC US Army
WWII"

SW ANDERSON Harvey D. b.29Jun1924-d.4May1983, "QM3 US Navy
WWII"

SW NIKORA Alexandria b.1899-d.1990, "Dear Mother of Leo & Alex"

SW TOFTE Arthur R. b.1902-d.1980, "Renaissance Man" w/ Dorothy C.,
Arthur E. & Geneva Tofte

SW TOFTE Dorothy C. b.1916-d.no date, w/ Arthur R., Arthur E. &
Geneva Tofte

SW TOFTE Arthur E. b.1881-d.1968, w/ Arthur R., Dorothy C. & Geneva
Tofte; Masonic Symbol

SW TOFTE Geneva b.1881-d.1968, w/ Arthur R., Dorothy C. & Arthur E.
Tofte; Eastern Star symbol

SW HECHT Inez Bernice b.16Oct1905-d.3Jun1991, "Beloved Wife &
Mother"

SW ENGSTAD Leonora J. b.1905-d.1981

SW BLANK Lydia b.1924-d.1993, w/ Paul Blank

SW BLANK Paul b.1925-d.no date, w/ Lydia Blank
SW SCHEINER Fred b.1885-d.1945, "Father" n/t Adelle Scheiner
SW SCHEINER Adelle b.1892-d.1951, n/t Fred Scheiner
SW BALTES Clara b.9Feb1879-d.8Dec1954, w/ George Baltes
SW BALTES George b.29Aug1877-d.30Oct1944, w/ Clara Baltes
SW UECKE Emil W. b.1882-d.1942, w/ Frieda L. Uecke
SW KEMPFF Elizabeth b.1863-d.1955, "Mother" w/ John M. Kempff
SW KEMPFF John M. b.1861-d.1944, "Father, Pastor" w/ Elizabeth
    Kempff
SW ENGSTROM Frank E. b.4Dec1887-d.11Jan1942, w/ Irma S.
    Engstrom
SW ENGSTROM Irma S. b.5Jan1901-d.29Apr1990, w/ Frank E.
    Engstrom
SW HANKS Fannie F. b.1867-d.1941, "Mother" w/ Byron E. Hanks, may
    be in Farries family plot
SW HANKS Byron E. b.1869-d.1944, "Father" w/ Fannie F. Hanks, may
    be in Farries family plot
SW FARRIES Harriet M. b.19Nov1842-d.11Dec1928, w/ John Farries &
    Carrie F. Noyes
SW FARRIES John b.11May1840-d.5May1915, w/ Harriet M. Farries &
    Carrie F. Noyes
SW NOYES Carrie F. b.25Nov1863-d.16Nov1941, w/ Harriet M. & John
    Farries
SW VAN UXEN Infant d.1883, w/ Adrian, Maria, John & Peter Van Uxen
    & Elizabeth Spalding & Hugo F. Schramm, only one date
SW VAN UXEN Infant d.1884, w/ Adrian, Maria, John & Peter Van Uxen
    & Elizabeth Spalding & Hugo F. Schramm, only one date
SW VAN UXEN Adrian b.1841-d.1937, "Father" w/ Maria, John & Peter
    Van Uxen, & Elizabeth Spalding & Hugo F. Schramm
SW VAN UXEN Maria b.1847-d.1924, "Mother" w/ Adrian, John & Peter
    Van Uxen, & Elizabeth Spalding & Hugo F. Schramm
SW VAN UXEN John b.1875-d.1903, "Son" w/ Adrian, Maria & Peter Van
    Uxen & Elizabeth Spalding & Hugo F. Schramm
SW VAN UXEN Peter b.1889-d.1966, "Son" w/ Adrian, Maria & John Van
    Uxen & Elizabeth Spalding & Hugo F. Schramm
SW SPALDING Elizabeth b.1909-d.1995, w/ Adrian, Maria, Peter & John
    Van Uxen & Hugo F. Schramm
SW SCHRAMM Hugo F. b.1884-d.1922, "Son-in-Law" w/ Adrian, Maria,
    Peter & John Van Uxen & Elizabeth Spalding
SW ROBBINS Annie b.1891-d.1983, w/ Robert E., n/t Edith M., Edward
    S. & Harry S. Robbins, possibly family plot w/ Edward W. & Elsie N.
    Robbins

SW ROBBINS Robert E. b.1890-d.1977, w/ Annie, n/t Edith M., Edward S. & Harry S. Robbins, possibly family plot w/ Edward W. & Elsie N. Robbins

SW ROBBINS Edith M. b.1867-d.1951, w/ Edward S., n/t Annie, Robert

SW UECKE Frieda L. b.1888-d.1971, w/ Emil W. Uecke E. & Harry S. Robbins, possibly family plot w/ Edward W. & Elsie N. Robbins

SW ROBBINS Edward S. b.1868-d.1942, w/ Edith M., n/t Annie, Robert E. & Harry S. Robbins, possibly family plot w/ Edward W. & Elsie N. Robbins

SW ROBBINS Harry S. b.1895-d.1924, n/t Edith M., Annie, Robert E. & Edward S. Robbins, possibly family plot w/ Edward W. & Elsie N. Robbins

SW SORENSON Dorothy Katherine (CAMERON) b.31Jan1918-d.14Feb1995, "Mother"

SW RUDEBUSCH Mary Ann b.no date-d.no date, "p/o Thomas, George, Glenn, Louise, & Alice" w/ Leroy G. Rudebusch

SW RUDEBUSCH Leroy G. b.1928-d.1984, "p/o Thomas, George, Glenn, Louise, & Alice" w/ Mary Ann Rudebusch

SW CARLSON Grace b.1Sep1898-d.4May1994

SW HEIT Irma H. b.13Sep1919-d.no date, w/ Otto & Eva Heit

SW HEIT Otto b.8Feb1907-d.no date, w/ Irma H. & Eva Heit

SW HEIT Eva b.9Mar1944-d.29Oct1983, w/ Irma H. & Otto Heit

SW PUETZ Erika b.1908-d.1995

SW ERKE Julius J. b.8Mar1911-d.no date, w/ John W. & Catherine M. Erke

SW ERKE John W. b.3Nov1946-d.26Mar1992, w/ Julius J. & Catherine M. Erke

SW ERKE Catherine M. b.26Jul1915-d.no date, w/ Julius J. & John W. Erke

SW WARREN Clara B. b.20Mar1845-d.15Apr1859, family plot w/ Luther A. & Anna H. Warren and others

SW WARREN Della M. b.23Oct1847-d.17Feb1849, family plot w/ Luther A. & Anna H. Warren and others

SW WARREN Jon w Albert b.16Sep1850-d.10Jul1878, family plot w/ Luther A. & Anna H. Warren and others

SW WARREN Jonathan M. b.4Feb1810-d.12May1877, family plot w/ Luther A. & Anna H. Warren and others; Johathan Warren was an early settler of Wauwatosa

SW WARREN Lavinia D. b.20Apr1812-d.8Sep1872, family plot w/ Luther A. & Anna H. Warren and others, large granite stone

SW WARREN Luther A. b.1834-d.1903, "Father" w/ Jonathan M. & Lavinia D. Warren, Wade, Nickerson & Nethercut families; L. A.

Warren was an early settler of Wauwatosa *
SW WARREN Anna Hoppin b.1836-d.1924, "Mother" w/ Jonathan M. &
Lavinia D. Warren, Wade, Nickerson & Nethercut families
SW NETHERCUT Helen Warren b.1861-d.1923, w/ Jonathan M. &
Lavinia D. Warren, Wade, Nickerson & Nethercut families
SW NETHERCUT Olive Jean b.5Aug1906-d.5Sep1906, w/ Jonathan M. &
Lavinia D. Warren, Wade, Nickerson & Nethercut families
SW NETHERCUT William Richard b.1859-d.1940, w/ Jonathan M. &
Lavinia D. Warren, Wade, Nickerson & Nethercut families
SW WADE Charles George b.1860-d.1930, w/ Jonathan M. & Lavinia D.
Warren, Wade, Nickerson & Nethercut families
SW WADE Clara Warren b.1859-d.1938, w/ Jonathan M. & Lavinia D.
Warren, Wade, Nickerson & Nethercut families
SW NICKERSON Frances Warren b.1870-d.1937, w/ Jonathan M. &
Lavinia D. Warren, Wade, Nickerson & Nethercut families
SW NICKERSON Harold Webster b.1858-d.1900, w/ Jonathan M. &
Lavinia D. Warren, Wade, Nickerson & Nethercut families
SW PAINTER Robert b.7Mar1812-d.14Aug1888, "Father" w/ Catharine,
James D., Lucetta M. & Robbie Painter; R. Painter was an early settler
of Wauwatosa
SW PAINTER Catharine b.10Dec1815-d.10Sep1892, "Mother, His Wife
(Robert)" w/ Robert, James D., Lucetta M. & Robbie Painter
SW PAINTER James D. b.4Aug1838-d.16Sep1905, "Papa" w/ Robert,
Catharine, Lucetta M. & Robbie Painter
SW PAINTER Lucetta M. b.12Dec1840-d.27Oct1917, "Mamma" w/
Robert, Catharine, James D. & Robbie Painter, dates from cemetery
records
SW PAINTER Robbie d.13Sep1890, "3y" w/ Robert, Catharine, James D.
& Lucetta M. Painter, date from cemetery records
SW LYMAN Edith Stoddard b.1868-d.1950, "Mother" n/t Ernest W., Paul
H. & Louise H. Lyman & Earl S. & Marie L. Caven
SW LYMAN Ernest Walter b.1867-d.1938, n/t Edith S., Paul H. & Louise
H. Lyman & Earl S. & Marie L. Caven
SW LYMAN Paul H. b.1899-d.1980, n/t Edith S., Ernest W., & Louise H.
Lyman & Earl S. & Marie L. Caven
SW LYMAN Louise H. b.1897-d.1985, n/t Edith S., Ernest W., & Paul H.
Lyman & Earl S. & Marie L. Caven
SW CAVEN Earl Samuel b.1884-d.1938, w/ Marie L. Caven, n/t Edith S.,
Ernest W., Paul H. & Louise H. Lyman
SW CAVEN Marie Lyman b.1895-d.1967, w/ Earl S. Caven, n/t Edith S.,
Ernest W., Paul H. & Louise H. Lyman

SW ERWIN Maude Flory b.1888-d.1946, buried in front of Flory Family

SW GUENTHER Katherine b.1848-d.1934, w/ Phillip, n/t Louis, John & Jacob Guenther & Katherina & Rudolph Gunther

SW GUENTHER Phillip b.1848-d.1922, w/ Katherine, n/t Louis, John & Jacob Guenther & Katherina & Rudolph Gunther

SW GUENTHER Louis b.1879-d.1881, n/t Katherine & Phillip, w/ John & Jacob Guenther, n/t Katherina & Rudolph Gunther

SW GUENTHER John b.1890-d.1899, n/t Katherine & Phillip, w/ Louis & Jacob Guenther, n/t Katherina & Rudolph Gunther

SW GUENTHER Jacob b.1879-d.1945, n/t Katherine & Phillip, w/ John & Louis Guenther, n/t Katherina & Rudolph Gunther

SW GUNTHER Katherina (BECHTEL) b.9Jun1819-d.27Jul1877, w/ Rudolph Gunther, n/t Katherine, Phillip, Louis, John & Jacob Guenther; dates from cemetery records; stone worn

SW GUNTHER Rudolph b.15Jan1876-d.5Mar1878, w/ Katherina Gunther, n/t Katherine, Phillip, Louis, John & Jacob Guenther

SW HOLDMAN Friedrich d.7Feb1894, "Father, 68y"

SW HEINEMAN Fred b.1876-d.1934, "Father" n/t Georg & Anna M. Heinemann

SW HEINEMANN Georg b.28Feb1821-d.29Oct1878, "Vater" n/t Ana M. Heinemann & Fred Heineman

SW HEINEMANN Anna M. b.6Aug1837-d.27Jul1893, "Mutter" n/t Georg Heinemann & Fred Heineman

SW CAMERON Katharine (SOMMERS) b.10Feb1897-d.20May1920, "Wife"

SW DAY Fisk Holbrook, Dr. b.11 Mar 1826, Richmond, NY-d.30 May 1903, Lansing, Mich.; w/ Frances W., Marcus W. & Stuart R. Day; Dr. Day settled in Wauwatosa in 1851. His home still stands and occasionally tours are given by the Wauwatosa Historical Society. Dr. Day received his deegree from the Jefferson Medical College in Philadelphia, he practiced in New York State for a few years before moving to Wauwatosa. He was the chief physician at the Milwaukee County Hospital and an amateur geologist and paleontologist. Some of his fossils and geological specimens can be found at the Smithsonian Institution, Harvard University, and Chicago's Field Museum. Dr. Day's house is on the National Register of Historic Places and was named a National Historical Landmark. *[7]

SW DAY Frances W. b.1837-d.1889, w/ Fisk H., Marcus W. & Stuart R. Day

7 The Heritage of a Community, page 8

SW DAY Marcus W. b.1869-d.1870, w/ Fisk H., Frances W. & Stuart R. Day

SW DAY Stuart R. b.1871-d.1872, w/ Fisk H., Frances W. & Marcus W. Day

SW ROBBINS Edward W. b.24Apr1825-d.24Dec1911, w/ Elsie N. Robbins, may be family plot w/ Annie & Robert E. Robbins

SW ROBBINS Elsie N. b.19Jun1829-d.24Jun1907, w/ Edward W. Robbins, may be family plot w/ Annie & Robert E. Robbins

SW HAM Dorothy M. b.1918-d.1983, may be in Robbins family plot

SW ST. GEORGE Irwin H. b.1892-d.1970, w/ Helen M. St. George

SW ST. GEORGE Helen M. b.1891-d.1975, w/ Irwin H. St. George

SW EDWARDS Kenneth George b.no date-d.10Jul1943, "Wis. Pvt. Air Corps" n/t Ellis Eggleston Edwards

SW EDWARDS Ellis Eggleston b.no date-d.14Aug1930, "Ohio 2nd Lt. Air Service" n/t Kenneth George Edwards

SW LONGENECKER George W., Rev. b.1861-d.1951, n/t Emma R. Longenecker

SW LONGENECKER Emma Rosina b.1866-d.1952, n/t George W. Longenecker

SW KOENITZER Christina b.1811-d.1897, "Mother" n/t Wilhelm Koenitzer

SW KOENITZER Wilhelm b.1809-d.1893, "Father" n/t Christina Koenitzer

SW DUNLOP Douglass b.1911-d.1965, n/t Isabelle M., John M. & Donald M. Dunlop & Margaret & Roy Roecker

SW DUNLOP Donald M. b.1903-d.1969, n/t Isabelle M., John M. & Douglass Dunlop & Margaret & Roy Roecker

SW DUNLOP Isabelle M. b.1874-d.1944, w/ John M. n/t Donald M. & Douglass Dunlop & Margaret & Roy Roecker

SW DUNLOP John M. b.1860-d.1930, w/ Isabelle M. n/t Donald M. & Douglass Dunlop & Margaret & Roy Roecker *

SW ROECKER Margaret b.1914-d.1993, w/ Roy Roecker n/t Isabelle M. Donald M. Douglass & John M. Dunlop

SW ROECKER Roy b.1908-d.1982, w/ Margaret Roecker n/t Isabelle M. Donald M., Douglass & John M. Dunlop

SW ANDERSON Frances D. b.1907-d.1982, w/ Leslie A. Anderson, stone faces south

SW ANDERSON Leslie A. b.1907-d.1995, w/ Frances D. Anderson, stone faces south

SW NEEDHAM Arthur E. b.27Jun1876-d.7Jun1942, w/ Anna O., Enoch G., Mary C., Esther A., Emma L. and other Needhams

SW NEEDHAM Anna O. b.3Nov1871-d.29Sep1960, w/ Arthur E., Enoch G., Mary C., Esther A., Emma L. and other Needhams

SW NEEDHAM Enoch Gardner b.1Feb1817 Union, Conn.-d.16Jun1891, w/ Arthur E., Anna O., Mary C., Esther A., Emma L. and other Needhams

SW NEEDHAM Mary Caroline b.31Mar1828-d.10Jan1906, "His Wife (Enoch G.)" w/ Arthur E., Anna O., Enoch G., Esther A., Emma L. and other Needhams

SW NEEDHAM Esther Amelia b.16Sep1862-d.8Sep1919, w/ Arthur E., Anna O., Enoch G., Mary C., Emma L. and other Needhams

SW NEEDHAM Emma Louise b.25Apr1857-d.16Dec1939, w/ Arthur E., Anna O., Enoch G., Mary C., Esther A. and other Needhams

SW NEEDHAM William b.1Nov1855-d.3Aug1856, w/ Arthur E., Anna O., Enoch G., Mary C., Esther A. and other Needhams

SW NEEDHAM Henry Martyn b.27Sep1850-d.22Jun1862, w/ Arthur E., Anna O., Enoch G., Mary C., Esther A. and other Needhams

SW NEEDHAM Amelia b.11Mar1858-d.14Apr1863, w/ Arthur E., Anna O., Enoch G., Mary C., Esther A. and other Needhams

SW NEEDHAM Edward Irving b.10Nov1860-d.15Nov1863, w/ Arthur E., Anna O., Enoch G., Mary C., Esther A. and other Needhams

SW ZIEMER Theresa b.1877-d.1964, w/ Frank Ziemer

SW ZIEMER Frank b.1873-d.1909, w/ Theresa Ziemer

SW WITTE Richard S. b.1864-d.1939, w/ Mabel W., n/t Richard & Frances Witte

SW WITTE Mabel W. b.1868-d.1947, w/ Richard S., n/t Richard & Frances Witte

SW HOYT Miriam b.1872-d.1933, w/ Emerson D., Carrie F., S. Demerit, Alice T., Geneva E. & Emerson D. Hoyt

SW HOYT Emerson D. b.1847, Wauwatosa-d.1924, w/ Miriam, Carrie F., S. Demerit, Alice T., Geneva E. & Emerson D. Hoyt, first mayor of the City of Wauwatosa *

SW HOYT Emerson D. b.1909-d.1985, w/ Miriam, Carrie F., S. Demerit, Alice T., Geneva E. & Emerson D. Hoyt

SW HOYT Carrie F. b.1845-d.1896, w/ Miriam, Emerson D., S. Demerit, Alice T., Geneva E. & Emerson D. Hoyt

SW HOYT S. Demerit b.1875-d.1949, w/ Miriam, Emerson D., Carrie F., Alice T., Geneva E. & Emerson D. Hoyt; Demerit married Alice Hart 22 Oct 1903, d/o Mr. and Mrs. W. A. Hart of Wauwatosa. *

SW HOYT Alice T. b.1877-d.1953, w/ Miriam, Emerson D., Carrie F., S. Demerit, Geneva E. & Emerson D. Hoyt *

SW HOYT Geneva E. b.1916-d.1982, w/ Miriam, Emerson D., Carrie F., S. Demerit, Alice T. & Emerson D. Hoyt

SW BUTTERFIELD Anna M. b.9May1812-d.10Mar1886
SW JOHNSON Mary J. b.13Jun1809-d.30Mar1889, w/ Mary O. & Mark
Johnson
SW JOHNSON Mary Orrilla b.28Dec1852-d.23May1894, w/ Mary J. &
Mark Johnson
SW JOHNSON Mark b.7Jun1814-d.21Aug1866, w/ Mary J. & Mary O.
Johnson
SW BREED Gersham P. b.7Jan1810-d.31Jan1898, n/t Catharine L., Henry
A. & Mary A. Breed
SW Catharine L. b.15Aug1815-d.20Jan1894, "w/o Gersham P. Breed" n/t
Gersham P., Henry A. & Mary A. Breed
SW BREED Henry A. b.10Jul1844-d.5Mar1901, n/t Gersham P.,
Catharine L. & Mary A. Breed
SW BREED Mary A. b.28Mar1816-d.11Dec1871, n/t Gersham P.,
Catharine L. & Henry A. Breed
SW FLORY Joyce S. b.1920-d.1994, w/ A. John, William J., Norma K., &
Arthur C. Flory
SW FLORY A. John b.1915-d.1968, w/ Joyce S., William J., Norma K., &
Arthur C. Flory
SW FLORY William J. b.1954-d.1994, w/ Joyce S., A. John, Norma K., &
Arthur C. Flory
SW FLORY Norma K. b.1885-d.1984, w/ Joyce S., A. John, William J., &
Arthur C. Flory
SW FLORY Arthur C. b.1883-d.1943, w/ Joyce S., A. John, William J., &
Norma K. Flory
SW BRAZEE Alvin C. b.24Jul1855-d.19Jun1910, n/t Alice E. Brazee
SW BRAZEE Alice E. b.1861-d.1935, n/t Alvin C. Brazee
SW ROLTSCH Jane G. b.1912-d.1998, "Daughter"
SW CHANDLER Florence b.1875-d.1960, w/ Charles R. & Phil Chandler
SW CHANDLER Charles T. b.1872-d.1951, w/ Florence & Phil Chandler
SW CHANDLER Phil b.1898-d.1956, w/ Florence & Charles T. Chandler
SW STEVENSON Walter Anson b.1867-d.1947, n/t Adelle W. Stevenson
SW STEVENSON Adelle Wever b.1867-d.1950, n/t Walter A. Stevenson
SW GREENMAN Elizabeth D. b.22Dec1894-d.24Nov1966, w/ William
G. Greenman
SW GREENMAN William G. b.13Mar1891-d.3Mar1992, w/ Elizaberh D.
Greenman
SW OSGOOD Carroll W. b.1898-d.1982, w/ Mildred H. & John S.
Osgood; possibly a doctor, staff symbol on stone
SW OSGOOD Mildred H. b.1902-d.1986, w/ Carroll W. & John S.
Osgood

SW OSGOOD John S. b.1930-d.1953, w/ Carroll W. & Mildred H. Osgood

SE RAGSDALE Elizabeth b.7Jan1911-d.21Jul1932, w/ Virginia, Charles E. & Elizabeth G. Ragsdale & Lucia R. Shantz

SE RAGSDALE Virginia b.31May1906-d.5Jul1939, w/ Elizabeth, Charles E. & Elizabeth G. Ragsdale & Lucia R. Shantz

SE SHANTZ Lucia Ragsdale b.8Jul1907-d.19Jun1987, w/ Elizabeth, Virginia, Charles E. & Elizabeth G. Ragsdale

SE RAGSDALE Charles E. b.13Jan1882-d.17Jan1958, w/ Elizabeth, Virginia, & Elizabeth G. Ragsdale & Lucia R. Shantz

SE RAGSDALE Elizabeth G. b.20Oct1883-d.9Aug1959, w/ Elizabeth, Virginia & Charles E. Ragsdale & Lucia R. Shantz

SE LOOMIS Harriet F. d.6May1884 Ypsilanti, Mich., "w/o Oliver H. Loomes, d/o J.A. & H. F. Warren, aged 26y 4m 15d" n/t J. Albert Loomis

SE LOOMIS J. Albert d.13May1884, "s/o O.H. & H.F. Loomis; aged 11d" n/t Harriet F. Loomis

SE WARREN Sarah H. d.9Apr1864, "d/o Joseph A. & Sarah H. Warren; 21y 3m"

SE HARWOOD Carrie Warren b.27Aug1860-d.30Dec1939, w/ Benjamin E. Harwood, Joseph A., Sarah B. & Harriet F. Warren, next stone illegible

SE HARWOOD Benjamin E. b.11May1861-d.5Nov1923, w/ Carrie W. Harwood, Joseph A., Sarah B. & Harriet F. Warren, another stone illigible

SE WARREN Joseph Alonzo b.17Jan1815-d.24Jun1903, w/ Carrie W. & Benjamin E. Harwood & Sarah B., & Harriet F. Warren; Joseph Warren was an early settler of Wauwatosa

SE WARREN Sarah B. d.30Jan1843, "w/o Joseph A. Warren; 29y 1m" w/ Carrie W. & Benjamin E. Harwood & Joseph A., & Harriet F. Warren; there is another stone, possibly Harwood.

SE WARREN Harriet F. b.29Dec1917-d.28Jan1899, "Native of Windsor, Mass.,w/o Joseph A." Warren"w/ Carrie W. & Benjamin E. Harwood & Sarah B. & Joseph A. Warren

SW GREEN Betsy d.11Apr1867, "aged 77y 8d"

SW WHEELER Jefferson G. b.25Jul1900-d.3Feb1985, "Sgt US Army WWII" n/t Nathan, Lyman G., Mabel G., Lyman E. Naomi L., Lyman & Solome Wheeler

SW POWELL Philip Allen b.27Apr1926-d.14Nov1944

SW SCHROEDER Gerhard b.1889-d.1952, w/ Sophie Y. Schroeder

SW SCHROEDER Sophie Y. b.1896-d.1992, w/ Gerhard Schroeder

SW WHEELER Nathan d.13Sep1859, "aged 77y 10m 19d" n/t Lyman G., Mabel G., Lyman E., Naomi L., Lyman, Salome & Jefferson G. Wheeler; Nathan married 2nd Amorilla Aldrich at Kewaskum and they had one child, Sarah, born 5 Dec 1848, who never married. He moved into a large and comfortable log house on the farm of his son, Lyman, in Wauwatosa. Nathan was almost six feet tall and a strong rugged man. He was born 24 Oct 1781 in Shrewsbury, Mass.[8]

SW WHEELER Lyman Grover b.1863-d.1945, n/t Nathan, Mabel G., Lyman E., Naomi L., Lyman, Salome & Jefferson G. Wheeler. Excerpts that name specific people buried in Wauwatosa Cemetery are included after the name listed in this book. Lyman's middle name, Grover was his Mother's maiden name. In his "Vinyets" he states "We were an active, hearty family and with all our viands lived well." His father, Lyman Wheeler, told his children stories of his early life in Vermont and as a settler in his first log house in the woods, he was a Wauwatosa pioneer. Lyman, Sr. was married twice and Lyman G. Wheeler was from his second family, he was 57 when the younger Lyman was born, then came Lev, 2 1/2 years later (Lev is not buried in Wauwatosa Cemetery) and seven years later, Marion was born on 4 Mar 1870. Lyman G. became engaged to Mabel Gregg prior to the summer of 1883, but they did not marry until he finished his education. He studied at the State University from 1884 until he graduated, 20 June 1890, with a degree in Letters and Science Course and the Law. He married 26 June 1890, their children were Gladys Evelyn b.17 Apr 1891; Warren Gregg b.1 Apr 1897, and twins, Lyman E. and Jefferson G. b.25 Jul 1900. While he was growing up he lived in the vicinity of 50th and North Ave.*[9]

SW WHEELER Mabel b.1866-d.1932, n/t Nathan, Lyman G., Lyman E., Naomi L., Lyman, Salome & Jefferson G. Wheeler; wife of Lyman G. Wheeler and daughter of Jefferson Gregg, she was born 8 Jun 1866 in Brookfield, Wis. Mabel attended classes for 2 or 3 years at the university, however her health was weakened from the intense study and she left school.[10]

SW WHEELER Lyman E., Sr. b.25Jul1900-d.1987, "Capt. US Army WWII" n/t Nathan, Lyman G., Mabel G., Naomi L., Lyman, Salome & Jefferson G. Wheeler; Capt. Lyman Wheeher was the twin brother of Jefferson, Lyman and Jefferson both served in WWI and WWII. They

8 The Wheeler Family in America original text by by Lyman Grover Wheeler in 1923 assembled and edited by Lt. Col. Lyman Edward Wheeler IV, 2000, unpublished (hereafter called The Wheeler Family in America)
9 The Wheeler Family in America
10 The Wheeler Family in America

worked on the Charles Hart ranch in Montana in 1916-1917. Lyman was chief of tire maintenance for the army at the Pentagon in WWII. Prior to entering the Army in 1942, he was head of the War Production Board in Milwaukee.[11]

SW WHEELER Naomi L. b.1902-d.1991, "Beloved w/o Lyman Wheeler" n/t Nathan, Lyman G., Mabel G., Lyman E., Lyman, Salome & Jefferson G. Wheeler; Naomi was born in Carol County, Iowa just outside Ralston, she met her husband at Iowa State University where he graduated.[12]

SW WHEELER Lyman b.1806-d.1887, "Wisconsin Pioneer 1836" n/t Nathan, Lyman G., Mabel G., Lyman E., Naomi L., Salome & Jefferson G. Wheeler; Lyman was born in Montague, Mass 6 Jan 1806, he was the first child of eight born to Nathan Wheeler and Sussanah Heard. The other children were probably all born in Vermont and they all either came to Wisconsin or Northern Illinois about 1836.[13] Lyman married 2nd Betsy Grover (Conover), the Grovers were from Elm Grove.[14]

SW WHEELER Salome d.15Jul1860, "w/o Lyman Wheeler; aged 54y 7m" n/t Nathan, Lyman G., Mabel G., Lyman E., Naomi L., Lyman & Jefferson G. Wheeler; Salome's maiden name was Roblee, she was born 18 Jan 1807 and married Lyman 16 Jan 1839 in Milwaukee, she died in Granville.[15]

SW FOSTER Gladys Wheeler b.17Apr1891-d.29Oct1988, n/t Nathan, Lyman G., Mabel G., Lyman E. Naomi L., Lyman, and Jefferson G. Wheeler & Earl W. Foster; Gladys was the eldest child of Lyman and Mabel Wheeler [16]

SW FOSTER Earl Ware b.17Apr1892-d.8Oct1950, "Kentucky Lt. (CHC) US Navy WWI" n/t Nathan, Lyman G., Mabel G., Lyman E. Naomi L.,Lyman, and Jefferson G. Wheeler & Gladys W Foster; Earl was a Congregational minister from Kentucky, he was a Navy Chaplin in the 1920s on the Battleship Minnesota and met Gladys while she was visiting Panama.[17]

SW ROBLEE Mary d.15Mar1862, "Our Mother, aged 94y 11m 27d?" old stone, hard to read (could this be the mother of Solome Wheeler?)

SW WESSON Albert N. b.15Nov1836-d.17Oct1838, w/ George A., Francis, & Nathan Wesson

11 courtesy of Lyman E. Wheeler
12 courtesy of Lyman E. Wheeler
13 courtesy of Lyman E. Wheeler
14 The Wheeler Family in America
15 courtesy of Lyman E. Wheeler
16 courtesy of Lyman E. Wheeler
17 courtesy of Lyman E. Wheeler

SW WESSON George Alfred b.21Apr1845-d.30Jul1846, w/ Albert N.,
   Francis, & Nathan Wesson George has two stones
SW WESSON Francis d.5Nov1873, "aged 56y" w/ George A., Albert N.,
   & Nathan Wesson; Francis enlisted in the army 14 Sep 1861, he was an
   Artifficer in the 7th Batty., discharged 20 Nov 1862, disability[18]
SW WESSON Nathan b.5Aug1809-d.10Aug1875, w/ George A., Albert N.
   & Francis Wesson
SW STEVENSON Cleo B. b.1906-d.1988, w/ Robert S. Stevenson
SW STEVENSON Robert S. b.1908-d.1983, w/ Cleo B. Stevenson
SW HARWOOD Oliver H. b.15Apr1804-d.27Feb1867, w/ Clarissa W. &
   Oliver Harwood & Henry, Mary E., Helen A. & Clara J. Strong,
   Harwood Ave. was named for Oliver, he initiated a fund to build a
   public library, which was named in his honor, and the Lecture Associa-
   tion was established in his memory.[19]
SW HARWOOD Clarissa Wichtman b.18Oct1802-d.14Jun1880, w/
   Oliver H. & Oliver Harwood & Henry, Mary E., Helen A. & Clara J.
   Strong
SW HARWOOD Oliver, Jr. b.21Aug1832-d.17Mar1854, w/ Oliver H. &
   Clarissa Harwood & Henry, Mary E., Helen A. & Clara J. Strong
SW STRONG Henry b.6Feb1835-d.27Nov1881, w/ Mary E., Helen A. &
   Clara J. Strong & Clarissa, Oliver & Oliver H. Harwood
SW STRONG Mary Eliza b.19Aug1825-d.4Oct1849, w/ Henry, Helen A.
   & Clara J. Strong & Oliver, Clarissa & Oliver H. Harwood
SW STRONG Helen Adele b.29Oct1827-d.12Sep1853, w/ Mary E.,
   Henry & Clara J. Strong & Oliver, Clarissa & Oliver H. Harwood
SW STRONG Clara Jane b.6Jun1830-d.31May1849, w/ Mary E., Henry &
   Helen A. Strong & Oliver, Clarissa & Oliver H. Harwood
SW CAIN Cornelia b.1866-d.1957, "Mother" w/ George F. Cain
SW CAIN George F. b.1864-d.1951, "Father" w/ Cornelia Cain
SW DE CAMP Lizzie Diedrick b.1860-d.1929, "Mother"
SW WITTE Richard b.29Jan1830 Prenzlau, Prussia-d.21May1886, n/t
   Frances, Richard S. & Mabel W. Witte
SW WITTE Frances b.5Mar1842 Fayetteville, NY-d.14Aug1920, n/t
   Richard, Richard S. & Mabel W. Witte
SW KRAHN William b.12Jan1863-d.23Oct1892, "s/o Herman & Louise
   Krahn" n/t Louise & Herman Krahn & Walter, Herman E., Ella, Fred &
   Amelia Giencke
SW KRAHN Louise b.22Apr1832-d.18Apr1907, "Mutter" n/t William &
   Herman Krahn & Walter, Herman E., Ella, Fred & Amelia Giencke

18 *Roster of Wisconsin Volunteers, War Of The Rebellion, 1861-1865*
19 The Heritage of a Community, page 7

SW KRAHN Herman b.29Dez1829-d.22Mai1898, "Father" n/t William &
Louise Krahn & Walter, Herman E., Ella, Fred & Amelia Giencke
SW GIENCKE Walter b.28Nov1895-d.6Apr1896, n/t William & Louise
Krahn, Mabel Dege & Herman E., Ella, Fred & Amelia Giencke
SW GIENCKE Infant d.1925, "s/o Herman & Ella Giencke" w/ William &
Louise Krahn, Mabel Dege & Herman E., Ella, Fred & Amelia Giencke
SW GIENCKE Infant d.1923, "d/o Herman & Ella Giencke" w/ William &
Louise Krahn, Mabel Dege & Herman E., Ella, Fred & Amelia Giencke
SW GIENCKE Herman E. b.26Jan1901-d.12Oct1978, w/ Ella A. n/t Fred
& Walter Giencke & Louise & Herman Krahn & Mabel Dege
SW GIENCKE Ella A. b.27Nov1895-d.23Mar1985, w/Herman E., n/t
Fred & Walter Giencke & Louise & Herman Krahn & Mabel Dege
SW GIENCKE Fred b.1867-d.1953, "Father" w/Amelia, n/t Ella A.,
Herman E. & Walter Giencke, Louise & Herman Krahn & Mabel Dege
SW GIENCKE Amelia b.1865-d.1943, "Mother" w/ Fred, n/t Ella A.,
Herman E. & Walter Giencke, Louise & Herman Krahn & Mabel Dege
SW DEGE Mabel (GIENCKE) b.1897-d.1944, n/t Fred, Amelia, Ella A.
Herman E. & Walter Giencke & Louise & Herman Krahn
SW GERHART Elizabeth b.1823-d.1899, "Mother" w/ Henry, Katherine
& George Gerhart, no first name on stone, only Mother, given name is
from cemetery records
SW GERHART Henry b.1822-d.1921, "Father" w/ Elizabeth, Katherine &
George Gerhart, no first name on stone, only Father, given name is
from cemetery records
SW GERHART Katherine b.1848-d.1918, w/ Mother, Father & George
Gerhart
SW GERHART George b.1858-d.1894, w/ Mother, Father & Katherine
Gerhart
SW GARVENS Edwin A. b.3Mar1867-d.5Dec1934, n/t Clara S., Lamira,
Esther, Mother & Father Garvins, there is also a Liberty Garvens buried
here according to cemetery records
SW GARVENS Clara S. b.29Apr1875-d.19Jan1962, n/t Edwin A., Lamira,
Esther, Mother & Father Garvins
SW GARVENS Lamira b.21Jan1875-d.6Dec1897, n/t Edwin A., Clara S.,
Esther, Mother & Father Garvens
SW GARVENS Esther b.30Oct1883-d.7Feb1894, n/t Edwin A., Clara S.,
Lamira, Mother & Father Garvens, death year on stone is 1884
SW GARVENS Mother b.3Feb1843-d.17Mar1923, n/t Edwin A., Clara S.,
Lamira, Esther & Father Garvens
SW GARVENS Father b.24Jan1837-d.22Jul1904, n/t Edwin A., Clara S.,
Lamira, Esther & Mother Garvens

SW CLAPP Annie I. b.1858-d.1940, w/ Wardlaw A., n/t Carol A. Clapp
SW CLAPP Wardlaw A. b.1853-d.1938, w/ Annie I., n/t Carol A. Clapp
SW CLAPP Carol A. b.1893-d.1976, "Daughter" n/t Wardlaw A. & Annie I. Clapp
SW PLEHN Robert Edwin b.12May1921-d.4Mar1967, "Wis. 1st Lt. US Army WWII"
SW BAILEY Rebecca B. b.1813-d.1887, w/ James Bailey
SW BAILEY James b.1825-d.1888, w/ Rebecca B. Bailey
SW BROWN Emma b.1879-d.1956, w/ Theodore, William, Helen, Elizabeth, Theodore, Melvin E. & other Browns
SW BROWN Theodore b.1879-d.1943, w/ Emma, William, Helen, Elizabeth, Theodore, Melvin E. & other Browns
SW BROWN Theodore b.1833-d.1880, w/ Emma, William, Helen, Elizabeth, Theodore, Melvin E. & other Browns
SW BROWN Elizabeth b.1844-d.1929, w/ Emma, William, Helen, Theodore, Theodore, Melvin E. & other Browns
SW BROWN William b.3Jun1876, Wisconsin,d.9 Jun 1965, Milwaukee, Co. Wis., w/ Emma, Elizabeth, Helen, Theodore, Theodore, Melvin E. & other Browns; William was a retired physcian, his parents were Theodore De Witt Brown and Elizabeth Kuhlman, he died of Bronchopneumonia at Milwaukee County General Hospital in Wauwatosa.[20]
SW BROWN Helen b.1873-d.1961, w/ Emma, Elizabeth, William, Theodore, Theodore, Melvin E. & other Browns
SW BROWN Melvin E. d.Mar1925, w/ Emma, Elizabeth, William, Theodore, Helen & other Browns; only one date
SW BROWN Sarah b.1813-d.1878, w/ Emma, Elizabeth, William, Theodore, Harris, Oscar, O.A.,Helen & other Browns
SW BROWN Harris b.1801-d.1864, w/ Emma, Elizabeth, William, Theodore, Sarah, Oscar, O.A.,Helen & other Browns
SW BROWN Oscar b.1842-d.1906, w/ Emma, Elizabeth, William, Theodore, Sarah, Harris, O.A.,Helen & other Browns
SW BROWN O. A., no dates, "Co. B 21 Wisconsin Inf" w/ Emma, Elizabeth, William, Theodore, & other Browns, could this be Oscar? Oscar was residing in Winneconne when he enlisted, 15 Aug 1862, in the army, he was Mustered Out, 8 Jun 1865[21]
SW OBERNDORFER Arthur H. b.1885-d.1949, w/ Elsie Obendorfer Kohlmeyer
SW KOHLMEYER Elsie Obendorfer b.1889-d.1983, w/ Arthur H. Oberndorfer

---

20 Death Doc. no.5076-1965, Milwaukee Co. Courthouse, Register of Deeds Office
21 *Roster of Wisconsin Volunteers, War Of The Rebellion, 1861-1865*

SW FOOTE Carrie J. b.1861-d.1932, w/ Herbert A. Foote

SW FOOTE Herbert A. b.1859-d.1940, w/ Carrie J. Foote

SW WESSON Rebecca L. b.20Apr1807-d.24Mar1899, n/t Nathan, Albert N., George A., & Francis Wesson, Nathan has two stones

SW MOWER Harry T. b.1855-d.1915, n/t Lydia C., Mary A., Timothy B. Mower; one other stone illegible

SW MOWER Lydia C. b.1858-d.1950, n/t Harry T., Mary A., Timothy B. Mower; one other stone illegible

SW MOWER Mary A. b.1882-d.1903, n/t Harry T.,Lydia C., Timothy B. Mower; one other stone illegible

SW MOWER Timothy B. b.18Jun1811-d.1May1861, n/t Harry T., Lydia C., Mary A. Mower; one other stone illegible; Timothy Mower was an early settler of Wauwatosa, cemetery records show a Maria buried here too.

SW MOORE William H. b.1842-d.1936, "Co. E 24 Wis. Vol. Inf." n/t Julia B. & Elsie M. Moore; GAR mkr; he enlisted in the army in Milwaukee on 20 Aug 1862, he was wounded at Mission Ridge on 1 Dec 1862, released because of disability[22]

SW MOORE Julia B. b.1838-d.1923, n/t William H. & Elsie M. Moore

SW MOORE Elsie M. b.1875-d.1945, n/t William H. & Julia B. Moore

SW UNDERWOOD William Owens b.1790 Berkeley Co., Virginia-d.1864 Wauwatosa, "Came to Wisconsin Territory 1836" w/ Catherine H., Abram, Jarret, Enoch, Margaret M., Eliza M. & other Underwoods ; William O. Underwood was an early settler of Wauwatosa*

SW UNDERWOOD Catherine Hill b.1794 Marion Co., Virginia-d.1820, "His Wife (William O.)" w/ William O., Abram, Jarret, Enoch, Margaret M., Eliza M. & other Underwoods *

SW UNDERWOOD Abram b.1813-d.1830, "Their Children (William O. & Catherine)" w/ William O.,Catherine, Jarret, Enoch, Margaret M., Eliza M. & other Underwoods

SW UNDERWOOD Jarret b.1815-d.1820, "Their Children (William O. & Catherine)" w/ William O.,Catherine, Abram, Enoch, Margaret M., Eliza M. & other Underwoods

SW UNDERWOOD Enoch b.1817-d.1888, "Their Children (William O. & Catherine)" w/ William O.,Catherine, Abram, Jarret, Margaret M., Eliza M. & other Underwoods; E. D. Underwood was an early settler of Wauwatosa, his birthplace on the 1860 U.S. Census is shown as Virginia. In 1866 land for a new cemetery about 1 mile north of the original cemetery was donated to the cemtery association by Enoch Underwood. Local oral histories indicate that Enoch Underwood and his family were active participants in the Underground Railroad. He was the original pastor of the First Baptist Church of Wauwatosa and was noted for his abolitionist views on slavery during the pre-Civil War era."[23]

SW UNDERWOOD Margaret Morgan b.1800 Morgantown, VA-d.1897, "His Wife (William O.)" w/ William O.,Catherine, Abram, Jarret, Enoch, Jane, Eliza M. & other Underwoods *

SW UNDERWOOD Eliza Morgan b.1822-d.1879, "Their Children (William & Margaret)" w/ William O.,Catherine, Abram, Jarret, Enoch, Jane, Adeline & other Underwoods

SW UNDERWOOD Jane b.1825-d.1851, "Their Children (William & Margaret)" w/ William O.,Catherine, Abram, Jarret, Enoch, Eliza, Adeline & other Underwoods

SW UNDERWOOD Adeline Willard b.1827-d.1859, "Their Children (William & Margaret)" w/ William O.,Catherine, Abram, Jarret, Enoch, Eliza M., Jane & other Underwoods

SW UNDERWOOD Lucy b.1829-d.1903, "Their Children (William & Margaret)" w/ William O.,Catherine, Abram, Jarret, Enoch, Eliza M., Jane & other Underwoods

SW UNDERWOOD Jackson b.1832-d.1846, "Their Children (William & Margaret)" w/ William O.,Catherine, Abram, Jarret, Enoch, Eliza M., Jane & other Underwoods

SW UNDERWOOD Lucretia Martin b.1835-d.1858, "Their Children (William & Margaret)" w/ William O.,Catherine, Abram, Jarret, Enoch, Eliza M., Jane & other Underwoods

SW UNDERWOOD Hannah Shafer b.1838-d.1917, "Their Children (William & Margaret)" w/ William O.,Catherine, Abram, Jarret, Enoch, Eliza M., Jane & other Underwoods

SW UNDERWOOD Mahala Rood b.1842-d.1881, "Their Children (William & Margaret)" w/ William O.,Catherine, Abram, Jarret, Enoch, Eliza M., Jane & other Underwoods

SW CURTIS Frederick William b.1871-d.1936, w/ Maude S. Curtis

SW CURTIS Maude Stedman b.1876-d.1956, "His Wife (Frederick W.)" w/ Frederick W. Curtis

SW VAN DUSEN Marnie C. b.1909-d.no date, may be in Underwood or Wesson plot

SW UNDERWOOD Enoch D. b.1817 Virginia-d.1888 Wauwatosa, "For Forty Years minister of the Gosple in this town" w/Harriet D.,Sarah K. & other Underwoods; This must be the Elder Underwood mentioned in the vinyets of Lyman Wheeler, written in 1923. Mr. Lyman wrote:

23 The Heritage of a Community, page 5

"Elder Underwood was a farmer from Maryland (this could be wrong or he could have been born in Virginia and lived in Maryland later), he worked his farm like his neighbors did and was called on often in the absence of a minister to read the sermons at the Old Baptist Church. His voice was strong and clear and he was finally ordained as Clergyman, but he continued farming and said he made up his sermons as he followed his plow. He had two sons: Fred, who became president of the Erie Railroad and Will, who was general Superintendent of the Chicago Milwaukee, St. Paul and Pacific Railroad. His daughters were Sarah (Underwood) Curtis of Minneapolis and Emma (Underwood) Gray, who married a prominent hotel man of Minneapolis 'West Hotel' and Hattie Bell Underwood, who died young."*[24]

SW UNDERWOOD Harriet Denny b.1818 Massachusetts-d.1904, "His Wife (Enoch D.)" w/ Enoch D., Sarah K., Emma W., Hattie B., Frederick D. & William J. Underwood, her birthplace on the 1860 U.S. Census is shown as Mass. *

SW UNDERWOOD Sarah Katherine b.no date-d.no date, "Their Children (Enoch & Harriet)" w/ Enoch D., Harriet D., Emma W., Hattie B., Frederick D. & William J. Underwood; not in cemetery records

SW UNDERWOOD Emma Whittier b.no date-d.no date, "Their Children (Enoch & Harriet)" w/ Enoch D., Harriet D.,Sarah K., Hattie B., Frederick D. & William J. Underwood; not in cemetery records

SW UNDERWOOD Frederick Douglass b.no date-d.no date, "Their Children (Enoch & Harriet)" w/ Enoch D., Harriet D.,Sarah K., Hattie B., Emma W. & William J. Underwood; not in cemetery records *

SW UNDERWOOD William Jackson b.1832-d.1846, "Their Children (Enoch & Harriet)" w/ Enoch D., Harriet D.,Sarah K., Hattie B., Emma W. & Frederick D. Underwood; dates from cemetery records *

SW UNDERWOOD Hattie Bell b.1863-d.Oct 1888, "Their Children (Enoch & Harriet)" w/ Enoch D., Harriet D.,Sarah K.,William J., Emma W. & Frederick D. Underwood; dates from cemetery records *

SW CURTIS Sarah Katherine Underwood b.1843-d.1928, "w/o Charles E. Curtis"

SW CAIN Elmer Ellsworth b.1881-d.1940, n/t Eva C. & Frederick G. Cain & Almira C. Bevier

SW CAIN Eva Cleveland b.1856-d.1947, n/t ELmer E. & Frederick G. Cain & Almira C. Bevier

SW CAIN Frederick G. b.8Feb1847-d.29Dec1892, n/t ELmer E. & Eva C. Cain & Almira C. Bevier

24 The Wheeler Family in America

SW BEVIER Almira Cleveland b.1826-d.1916, "Mother" n/t ELmer E. & Eva C. & Frederick G. Cain

SW JOHNSON Vivian R. b.13Mar1898-d.22Mar1983

SW LUNDGREN Lydia b.1874-d.1954, w/ Gustaf Lundgren

SW LUNDGREN Gustaf b.1876-d.1954, w/ Lydia Lundgren

SW TISCHER Martha Emma b.1900-d.1991, "Mother" n/t William Tischer

SW TISCHER William b.1906-d.1955, "Father" n/t Martha E. Tischer

SW HAY Isabel Clapp b.1891-d.1933, "w/o Glenn R. Hay"

SW KNAUER George b.1890-d.1978, n/t Gertrude Knauer

SW KNAUER Gertrude b.1887-d.1964, n/t George Knauer

SW ENGELHART Clara b.1885-d.1960,

SW HINTERTHUER William b.1835-d.1910

SW ENGELHARDT Sophia b.1863-d.1909, n/t Henry Engelhardt

SW ENGELHARDT Henry b.1862-d.1930, n/t Sophia Engelhardt

SW MUNDT Gretchen b.1925-d.no date, w/ Edgar Mundt

SW MUNDT Edgar b.1912-d.1995, w/ Gretchen Mundt; southside of retaining wall

SW MOORE Lorenzo W. b.1804-d.1886, w/ Miranda I., Nellie C., Harvel L., Lamara Moore & Ester Fisher

SW MOORE Miranda I. b.1810-d.1882, "w/o L. W. Moore" w/ Lorenzo W., Nellie C., Harvel L., Lamara Moore & Ester Fisher

SW MOORE Nellie C. b.1849-d.1868, "d/o L. W. & M. I. Moore" w/ Lorenzo W., Miranda I., Harvel L., Lamara Moore & Ester Fisher

SW MOORE Harvel L. b.1850-d.1936, w/ Lorenzo W., Miranda I., Nellie C., Lamara Moore & Ester Fisher

SW MOORE Lamara b.1848-d.1930, "w/o H. L. Moore" w/ Lorenzo W., Miranda I., Nellie C., Harvel L. Moore & Ester Fisher

SW FISHER Ester b.1778-d.1863, w/ Lorenzo W., Miranda I., Nellie C., Harvel L. & Lamara Moore

SW MUNDSTOCK Emily b.1899-d.1973, w/ Frank Mundstock

SW MUNDSTOCK Frank b.1899-d.1975, w/ Emily Mundstock

SW MOWER Margaret West b.1876-d.1918, w/ Caroline, Thomas, Esther A. Mower & Thomas J., Cynthia Ann & other Rices

SW MOWER Caroline Rice b.1874-d.1967, w/ Margaret, Thomas, Esther A. Mower & Thomas J., Cynthia Ann & other Rices

SW THOMAS Esther Ann b.1841-d.1863, w/ Margaret & Caroline Mower & Ann F., Thomas J., Cynthia Ann & other Rices

SW RICE Thomas J. b.1807-d.1867, w/ Margaret & Caroline Mower & Ann F., Talitha, Cynthia Ann & other Rices; Thomas J. Rice was an early settler of Wauwatosa

SW RICE Cynthia Ann b.1814-d.1859, w/ Margaret & Caroline Mower & Ann F., Talitha, Thomas J. & other Rices

SW RICE Ann Fisher b.1821-d.1871, w/ Margaret & Caroline Mower & Harriet Talitha, Thomas J. & other Rices

SW RICE Harriet b.no date-d.no date, "Infant child of Thomas J. & Cynthia Rice" w/ Margaret & Caroline Mower & Cynthia A., Talitha, Thomas J. & other Rices; not in cemetery records

SW RICE Talitha b.no date-d.no date, "Infant child of Thomas J. & Cynthia Rice" w/ Margaret & Caroline Mower & Cynthia A., Harriet, Thomas J. & other Rices; not in cemetery records

SW KINNEY Helen b.1887-d.1945, n/t Mabel, Vernon, Emma, George, & Clara Kinney

SW KINNEY Mabel b.1891-d.1937, n/t Helen, Vernon, Emma, George, & Clara Kinney

SW KINNEY Vernon b.1853-d.1936, n/t Helen, Mabel, Emma, George, & Clara Kinney

SW KINNEY Emma b.1864-d.1959, n/t Helen, Mabel, Vernon, George, & Clara Kinney

SW KINNEY George b.1884-d.1886, n/t Helen, Mabel, Vernon, Emma, & Clara Kinney

SW KINNEY Clara b.1858-d.1928, n/t Helen, Mabel, Vernon, Emma, & George Kinney

SW SHELDON David S. b.1907-d.1920, "Son" n/t Carrol C. Sheldon

SW SHELDON Carroll C. b.1866-d.1918, "Husband" n/t David S. Sheldon

SW HART Joseph b.1861-d.1926, n/t Clara S. Hart

SW HART Clara S. b.9Apr1860-d.26Jan1920, "Wife" n/t Joseph Hart

SW GEVAART Jacob b.25Jun1838-d.1May1899, "Father" n/t Clara S. Gevaart

SW GEVAART Clara S. b.28Dec1839-d.18Mar1918, n/t Jacob Gevaart

SW KREHL Fredrich b.17Jul1857-d.25Apr1910, "Papa" n/t Elisabeth, Carl, Sophia & Ida Krehl; large family monument in German, with statue of a woman. *

SW KREHL Elisabeth (STOLL) b.16Jan1861-d.12Feb1897, "Mamma" n/t Fredrich, Carl, Sophia & Ida Krehl; large family monument in German, with a statue of a woman.

SW KREHL Carl b.4Jan1829-d.14May1905, "Vater" n/t Fredrich, Elisabeth, Sophia & Ida Krehl; large family monument in German, with a statue of a woman.

SW KREHL Sophia (JACH) b.12Nov1831-d.2Dec1900, "Mutter" n/t Fredrich, Elisabeth, Carl & Ida Krehl; large family monument in German, with a statue of a woman.

SW KREHL Ida b.30Aug1862-d.2Sep1935, "Mama" n/t Fredrich,
Elisabeth, Carl & Sophia Krehl; large family monument in German,
with a statue of a woman.

SW KREHL August b.24Jul1881-d.18Feb1907, appears to be in Fredrich
& Carl Krehl plot

SW BRAUN Maria b.20Mar1865-d.6Dez1912, n/t Friedrich W. Braun,
appears to be in Fredrich & Carl Krehl plot

SW BRAUN Friedrich W. b.4Jun1860-d.4Jun1914, n/t Maria Braun,
appears to be in Fredrich & Carl Krehl plot

SW JOHNSON Clarence M. b.30Mar1897-d.15Sep1955, "Wis. SFC 107
FLD SIG BN 32 DIV WWI" n/t Archie C. & Vivian R. Johnson; same
type stone as Grace Spalding

SW JOHNSON Archie C. b.1887-d.1965, same type stone as Grace W.
Spalding.

SW SPALDING Grace Watner b.1888-d.1965, n/t Tillie & Roy S. Watner;
same type stone as Archie C. Johnson

SW WATNER Tillie b.1875-d.1938, n/t Roy S. Watner & Grace Watner
Spalding

SW WATNER Roy S. b.1876-d.1935, n/t Tillie Watner & Grace Watner
Spalding

SW FERGUSON Edna R. b.1889-d.1970, n/t Theodore J. & Emma N.
Ferguson

SW FERGUSON Theodore J. b.1850-d.1928, n/t Edna R. & Emma N.
Ferguson

SW FERGUSON Emma N. b.1860-d.1942, n/t Edna R. & Theodore J.
Ferguson

SW HARRIMAN Della b.1849-d.1895, w/ Frank Harriman

SW HARRIMAN Frank b.1837-d.1917, w/ Della Harriman

SW BOELTER Wilhelm F. b.1Aug1833-d.30Mai1913, "Vater" n/t
Wilhelmine, Louis J. & Matie V. V. Boelter

SW BOELTER Wilhelmine b.26Jun1831-d.1Jun1895, "Mutter" n/t
Wilhelm F., Louis J. & Matie V. V. Boelter

SW BOELTER Louis J. b.1875-d.1967, "Father; m. 18Dec1901" w/ Matie
V. V., n/t Wilhelm F. & Wilhelmine Boelter

SW BOELTER Matie V. V. b.1880-d.1968, "Mother, m. 18Dec 1901" w/
Louis J. n/t Wilhelm F. & Wilhelmine Boelter

SW DELPSCH Charles F. b.1874-d.1942, n/t B. Florence, Grace & A.
Robt. Delpsch

SW DELPSCH B. Florence b.1878-d.1904, n/t Charles F., Grace & A.
Robt. Delpsch *

SW DELPSCH Grace b.1840-d.1919, "Mother" n/t Charles F., B. Florence & A. Robt. Delpsch

SW DELPSCH A. Robt. b.1826-d.1893, n/t Charles F., B. Florence & Grace DelpschSW FRANZ Louise b.1832-d.1927, w/ Carl, n/t Elizabeth B. & Ida Franz

SW FRANZ Carl b.1816-d.1897, w/ Louise, n/t Elizabeth B. & Ida Franz

SW FRANZ Elizabeth B. b.1886-d.1942, n/t Louise, Carl & Ida Franz

SW FRANZ Ida b.1861-d.1929, "Mother" n/t Louise, Carl & Elizabeth B. Franz

SW SMITH Mary E. b.1863-d.1962, n/t Albert W., Helen M., Ralph A., Michael & Catherine Smith

SW SMITH Albert W. b.1852-d.1933, n/t Mary E., Helen M., Ralph A., Michael & Catherine Smith; Albert was the principal of Wauwatosa High School around 1880, he was also superintendant of the Sunday School at the Old Baptist Church. This church is now the mortuary in the Wauwatosa Cemetery.[25]

SW SMITH Helen M. b.1889-d.1960, n/t Mary E., Albert W., Ralph A., Michael & Catherine Smith

SW SMITH Ralph A. b.1904-d.1998, n/t Mary E., Albert W., Helen M. Michael E. & Catherine Smith

SW SMITH Michael Emery b.10Sep1960-d.3Apr1976, "Son" n/t Mary E., Albert W., Helen M., Ralph A. & Catherine Smith

SW SMITH Catherine Garrett b.22Jul1932-d.no date, "Mother" n/t Mary E., Albert W., Helen M., Ralph A. & Michael E. Smith

SW GILBERT Kate E. b.1862-d.1945, n/t Jesse D., Glen D., Ruth P. & Richard & Nancy G. Gilbert

SW GILBERT Jesse D. b.1858-d.1928, n/t Kate E., Glen D., Ruth P. & Richard & Nancy G. Gilbert

SW GILBERT Glen D. b.1886-d.1973, n/t Kate E., Jesse D., Ruth P. & Richard & Nancy G. Gilbert

SW GILBERT Ruth P. b.1887-d.1979, n/t Kate E., Jesse D., Glen D. & Richard & Nancy G. Gilbert

SW GILBERT Richard b.6Jun1794 Rushville, NY-d.2May1877 Wauwatosa, n/t Kate E., Jesse D., Glen D., Ruth P., w/ Nancy G. Gilbert; Richard Gilbert, Sr. was an early settler of Wauwatosa

SW GILBERT Nancy Green b.2May1794 Winchester, NH-d.8Mar1880, "w/o Richard Gilbert" n/t Kate E., Jesse D., Glen D., Ruth P., w/ Richard Gilbert

SW OTTO Max A. b.1883-d.1957

SW COOLEY Justina b.1884-d.1968

SW PURCELL Henry H. b.1857-d.1910

25 The Wheeler Family in America

SW McNAIR Charles b.1864-d.1895, "s/o H.W. & M.J. McNair" n/t H.
W. & Mary J. McNair

SW McNAIR H. W. b.1828-d.1895, n/t Charles & Mary J. McNair

SW McNAIR Mary J. b.1831-d.1912, n/t Charles & H. W. McNair

SW SCHILDT August b.16Apr1844-d.26Sep1933, "Father" n/t Dorathea
Schildt

SW SCHILDT Dorathea b.29Mar1847-d.19Nov1928, "Mother" n/t
August Schildt

SW HEIDEN Christine b.18Feb1812-d.2Jan1895, same type stone as
August & Dorathea Schildt

SW VOGEL Nicholas b.14Aug1858-d.17Jan1932, n/t John, Frank,
Catharine, Henry, Jennie & Jacob Vogel

SW VOGEL John b.1Mar1855-d.19Dec1902, n/t Nicholas, Frank,
Catharine, Henry, Jennie & Jacob Vogel

SW VOGEL Frank b.2Sep1856-d.17Oct1895, n/t Nicholas, John,
Catharine, Henry, Jennie & Jacob Vogel

SW VOGEL Catharine b.1May1824-d.23Aug1911, "Mother" n/t Nicholas, John, Frank, Henry, Jennie & Jacob Vogel

SW VOGEL Henry b.20Oct1831-d.24Apr1911, "Father" n/t Nicholas,
John, Frank, Catharine, Jennie & Jacob Vogel

SW VOGEL Jennie b.16Sep1899-d.12Nov1944, n/t Nicholas, John,
Frank, Catharine, Henry & Jacob Vogel

SW VOGEL Jacob b.7Sep1862-d.17Apr1934, n/t Nicholas, John, Frank,
Catharine, Henry & Jennie Vogel

SW LINDEMEYER Caroline b.1860-d.1919, "Mother" n/t Wallace &
Alice Lindemeyer

SW LINDEMEYER Wallace b.1885-d.1925, "Brother" n/t Caroline &
Alice Lindemeyer

SW LINDEMEYER Alice b.26May1884-d.11Aug1976, n/t Caroline &
Wallace Lindemeyer; dates from cemetery records

SW LEISTIKOW Bertha Luetzow b.1858-d.1925, "Mother, w/o Louis
Leistikow"

SW BELTON Harry b.1878-d.1951, w/ Neva Belton

SW BELTON Neva b.1889-d.1986, w/ Harry Belton

SW ZOPHY Adelaid b.1883-d.1920,

SW PERRY Ramona V. b.2Feb1929-d.6Nov1977, n/t Wilson B., Salome
W., & Eugene M. Perry, Sr.

SW PERRY Wilson B. b.21Sep1926-d.18Feb1955, "Wisconsin S1
USNR" n/t Ramona V., Salome W., & Eugene M. Perry, Sr.

SW PERRY Salome W. b.13Oct1895-d.28Mar1985, n/t Ramona V.,
Wilson B., & Eugene M. Perry, Sr.

SW PERRY Eugene M., Sr. b.17Sep1895-d.19Oct1967, "Wisconsin Sgt US Army WWI" n/t Ramona V., Wilson B., & Salome W. Perry

SW GEVAAT John b.1865-d.1934, w/ Lisette, Clara & Elizabeth Gevaat & Irene & Earl Gruber, John H. Gevaat Family plot

SW GEVAAT Lisette b.1865-d.1943, w/ John, Clara & Elizabeth Gevaat & Irene & Earl Gruber, John H. Gevaat Family plot

SW GEVAAT Elizabeth b.1884-d.1979, w/ John, Lisette & Clara Gevaat & Irene & Earl Gruber, John H. Gevaat Family Plot

SW GEVAAT Clara b.1886-d.1971, w/ John, Lisette & Elizabeth Gevaat & Irene & Earl Gruber, John H. Gevaat Family plot

SW GRUBER Irene b.1899-d.1979, w/ John, Lisette, Clara & Elizabeth Gevaat & Earl Gruber, John H. Gevaat Family plot

SW GRUBER Earl b.1900-d.1990, w/ John, Lisette, Clara & Elizabeth Gevaat & Irene Gruber,John H. Gevaat Family plot

SW PILGRIM Robert b.20Aug1887-d.6Dec1916, n/t Joseph & Julia Pilgrim, Pilgrim & Gilbert family plot

SW PILGRIM Joseph b.1859-d.1936, "Father" n/t Robert & Julia Pilgrim, Pilgrim & Gilbert family plot

SW PILGRIM Julia b.21Aug1859-d. 6Apr1902, "Beloved w/o J. H. Pilgrim" n/t Robert & Joseph Pilgrim; Pilgrim & Gilbert family plot

SW GILBERT Ephraim d.28Mar1898, "Father, 75y" n/t Sarah & W. A. Gilbert; Pilgrim & Gilbert family plot; Ephraim Gilbert was an early settler of Wauwatosa.

SW GILBERT Sarah d.27May1911, "86y" n/t Ephraim & W. A. Gilbert; Pilgrim & Gilbert family plot

SW GILBERT W. A. d.13Apr1905, "51y" n/t Ephraim & Sarah Gilbert; Pilgrim & Gilbert family plot

SW GILBERT Georgie b.7Sep1850-d.21Sep1850, "child of Ephaim & Sarah Gilbert" n/t Ephraim & Sarah Gilbert; Pilgrim & Gilbert fam; name and date from cemetery records

SW BARNES Willie d.18Mar1862, "Our Darling, DR & ES Barnes, 9 mo"

SW MUNGER Elverton b.no date-d.no date, "Our Elverton Lives; D.H. & A. B. Munger" n/t D. H. Munger, not in cemetery records

SW MUNGER D. H. d.22Apr1858, "Father; 40y 7m 5d" n/t Elverton Munger

SW ZILLMER Otto A. b.1880-d.1969, w/ Estelle M. & Eric W. Zillmer *

SW ZILLMER Estelle M. b.1872-d.1964, w/ Otto A. & Eric W. Zillmer *

SW ZILLMER Eric W. b.1907-d.1928, w/ Otto A. & Estelle M. Zillmer

SW GRIDLEY Leander Lot b.1817-d.1906, n/t Mary R., Mary E., Lysander R., Elizabeth J., Lysander E. & other Gridleys

SW GRIDLEY Mary Roberts b.1819-d.1899, n/t Leander L., Mary E., Lysander R., Elizabeth J., Lysander E. & others Gridleys

SW GRIDLEY Mary E. b.1877-d.1957, n/t Leander L., Mary R., Lysander R., Elizabeth J., Lysander E. & others Gridleys

SW GRIDLEY Lysander R. b.1850-d.1934, n/t Leander L., Mary R., Mary E., Elizabeth J., Lysander E. & others Gridleys

SW GRIDLEY Elizabeth J. b.1850-d.1920, n/t Leander L., Mary R., Mary E., Lysander R., Lysander E. & others Gridleys

SW GRIDLEY Lysander E. b.1812-d.1845, n/t Leander L., Mary R., Mary E., Lysander R., Elizabeth J. & others Gridleys

SW GRIDLEY Levancia G. b.no date-d.no date, "d/o L. & M. Gridley; 6m" n/t Leander L., Mary R., Mary E., Lysander R., Elizabeth J. & others Gridleys

SW REYNOLDS Benjamin R. d.29Mar1858, "20y" n/t Leander L., Mary R., Mary E., Lysander R., & Elizabeth J. Gridley & others Gridleys

SW GRIDLEY Julia A. d.14May1842, "26y; w/o L. Gridley" n/t Leander L., Mary R., Mary E., Lysander R., & Elizabeth J. Gridley & others Gridleys

SW TOUSSAINT Mary Jo Lefeber b.1907-d.1970, w/ Charles I. Toussaint

SW TOUSSAINT Charles I. b.1898-d.1972, w/ Mary Jo L. Toussaint

SW SMITH Coley d.6May1862 Keokuk, Iowa, "33y 3m 4d; 1st Lieut Co A 18 Reg Wis Vol" w/ O.J. & Amanda E. Smith & James, Harri Hariette M. & James C. Lefeber; Coley enlisted in Saxeville 9 Sep 1861, he was a 1st Sergt in the 15th Infantry Co. A, wounded at Shiloh, died 6 May 1862, Keokuk, IA of wounds[26]

SW SMITH O. J. b.10Aug1826-d.1May1883, w/ Coley & Amanda E. Smith & James, Hariette M. & James C. Lefeber

SW SMITH Amanda E. b.19Nov1830-d.20Feb1898, "w/o O. J. Smith" w/ Coley & O. J. Smith & James, Hariette M. & James C. Lefeber

SW LEFEBER James III b.1915-d.1949, w/ Coley, O. J. & Amanda E. Smith & Hariette M. & James C. Lefeber

SW LEFEBER Harriette Moan b.1880-d.1945, w/ Coley, O. J. & Amanda E. Smith & James, III & James C. Lefeber

SW LEFEBER James Courtney b.1883-d.1955, w/ Coley, O. J. & Amanda E. Smith & James, III & Harriette M. Lefeber

SW JACKS James M., Sr. b.15Oct1812-d.28Jan1882, w/ Henrietta & Henrietta C. B. Jacks & Jennie Gregory

SW JACKS Henrietta b.29May1816-d.30Sep1880, w/ James M., Sr. & Henrietta C. B. Jacks & Jennie Gregory

---

26 *Roster of Wisconsin Volunteers, War Of The Rebellion, 1861-1865*

SW JACKS Henrietta Christa Bell b.6Jan1860-d.30Jul1863, w/ James
M., Sr. & Henrietta Jacks & Jennie GregorySW GREGORY Jennie
b.10Jan1853-d.10Sep1853, w/ James M., Sr., Henrietta & Henrietta C.
B. Jacks

SW CASE Bigelow b.1811-d.1886, w/ Elvira H. & Leverette B. Case &
Alice M. C. Frisby; Bigelow Case was an early settler of Wauwatosa.

SW CASE Elvira H. b.1809-d.1887, "w/o Bigelow Case" w/ Bigelow &
Leverette B. Case & Alice M. C. Frisby

SW CASE Leverett B. b.12Sep1841-d.25Jan1863 Murfreesboro, Tenn.
"Co A 24 Wisconsin Infantry" w/ Bigelow & Elvira H. Case & Alice M.
C. Frisby; resided in Greenfield when he enlisted in the army on 31 Jul
1862; he died from disease at Stone River[27]

SW FRISBY Alice M. Case b.19Apr1846-d.28Mar1923, w/ Bigelow,
Elvira H. & Leverett B. Case

SW SWAN Julia A. b.1870-d.1898, w/ Emery, Caroline M., Marion P,
Alvin H., Frank E., & Lilly A. Swan

SW SWAN Emery b.1800-d.1889, w/ Julia A.,Caroline M., Marion P,
Alvin H., Frank E., & Lilly A. Swan; Emery Swan was an early settler of
Wauwatosa

SW SWAN Caroline M. b.1805-d.1845, w/ Julia A., Emery, Marion P,
Alvin H., Frank E., & Lilly A. Swan

SW SWAN Marion P. b.1835-d.1904, w/ Julia A., Emery, Caroline M.,
Alvin H., Frank E., & Lilly A. Swan

SW SWAN Alvin H. b.1833-d.1916, w/ Julia A., Emery, Caroline M.,
Marion P., Frank E., & Lilly A. Swan; Alvin Swan was an early settler of
Wauwatosa

SW SWAN Frank E. b.1867-d.1949, w/ Julia A., Emery, Caroline M.,
Marion P., Alvin H., & Lilly A. Swan

SW SWAN Lilly A. b.1884-d.1953, w/ Julia A., Emery, Caroline M.,
Marion P., Alvin H., & Frank E. SwanSW GILBERT Henry Payson
b.13Aug1834-d.13Sep1907, w/ Mary E. & Evelyn Gilbert & Stickney,
Fisher & Swan families, large monument; H. Payson Gilbert was an
early settler of Wauwatosa.

SW GILBERT Mary Esther b.3Apr1841-d.3Oct1929, w/ Henry P. &
Evelyn Gilbert & Stickney, Fisher & Swan families, large monument

SW GILBERT Evelyn b.16Dec1877-d.20Sep1956, w/ Henry P. & Mary E.
Gilbert & Stickney, Fisher & Swan families, large monument

SW STICKNEY James S. b.8Aug1825-d.10Sep1904, w/ Calista J, Charles
& Julia M Stickney, & Gilbert, Fisher & Swan family, large stone, his
birthplace on the 1860 U.S. Census is shown as N.H.

---

27 *Roster of Wisconsin Volunteers, War Of The Rebellion, 1861-1865*

SW STICKNEY Calista J. b.13Mar1829-d.16Apr1885, w/ James S., Charles & Julia M Stickney, & Gilbert, Fisher & Swan family, large stone, her birthplace on the 1860 U.S. Census is shown as N.H.

SW STICKNEY Charles b.15Mar1849-d.5Sep1906, w/James S.,Calista J & Julia M Stickney, & Gilbert, Fisher & Swan family, large stone *

SW STICKNEY Julia M. b.8Jul1850-d.4Oct1936, w/James S.,Calista J & Charles Stickney, & Gilbert, Fisher & Swan family, large stone

SW FISHER Frederick T. b.1912-d.1980, w/ Georgian N., Nancy M. & other Fishers & Gilbert, Stickney & Swan family, large stone

SW FISHER Georgian N. (LONGENECKER) b.1917-d.no date, w/ Frederick T, Nancy M. & other Fishers & Gilbert, Stickney & Swan family, large stone

SW LONGENECKER Ernst A. b.1896-d.1998, w/ Frederick T., Nancy M. & other Fishers & Gilbert, Stickney & Swan family, large stone

SW FISHER Nancy M. b.28Sep1849-d.7Oct1924, w/ Frederick T., Georgian & other Fisher & Gilbert, Stickney & Swan family, large stone

SW FISHER Charles Thompson b.11Aug1846-d.16Jun1930, w/ Frederick T., Georgian & other Fisher & Gilbert, Stickney & Swan family, large stone

SW FISHER Charles Swan, Dr. b.28Dec1883-d.17May1928, w/ Frederick T., Georgian & other Fisher & Gilbert, Stickney & Swan family, large stone

SW FISHER Nellie M., Dr. b.23Sep1874-d.15May1963, w/ Frederick T., Georgian & other Fisher & Gilbert, Stickney & Swan family, large stone

SW FISHER William E. b.21Mar1871-d.22Nov1941, w/ Frederick T., Georgian & other Fisher & Gilbert, Stickney & Swan family, large stone *

SW FISHER Myrta A. b.1874-d.1958, w/ Frederick T., Georgian & other Fisher & Gilbert, Stickney & Swan family, large stone

SW SWAN Nathaniel J. b.26Apr1827-d.11Apr1905, w/ Hannah G. David M. & other Swans & Fisher, Stickney & Gilbert family, large stone; Nathaniel Swan was an early settler of Wauwatosa

SW SWAN Hannah Gilbert b.19Dec1827-d.21Oct1917, w/ Nathaniel J.,David M. & other Swans & Fisher, Stickney & Gilbert family, large stone

SW SWAN David More b.30Nov1880-d.24Mar1962, w/ Nathaniel J., Hannah & other Swans & Fisher, Stickney & Gilbert family, large stone

SW SWAN Clara May b.5Jun1883-d.19Dec1978, w/ Nathaniel J., Hannah & other Swans & Fisher, Stickney & Gilbert family, large stone

SW SWAN Betty James b.6Mar1911-d.1Jan1963, w/ Nathaniel J., Hannah & other Swans & Fisher, Stickney & Gilbert family, large stone

SW SWAN Craydon McGill b.24Oct1909-d.6Nov1982, w/ Nathaniel J., Hannah & other Swans & Fisher, Stickney & Gilbert family, large stone

SW BUTTERFIELD Sally d.21Oct1881, "83y 5m" w/ Benjamin Butterfield

SW BUTTERFIELD Benjamin d.6Feb1875, "75y 11m 10d" w/ Sally Butterfield

SW PEARSON Louise C. b.1918-d.no date, w/ Arthur G. Pearson

SW PEARSON Arthur G. b.1926-d.1984, w/ Louise C. Pearson

SW SCHOLTKA Edna C. b.1893-d.1986, w/ Edward P. Scholtka

SW SCHOLTKA Edward P. b.1896-d.1986, w/ Edna C. Scholtka

SW SULLIVAN Lois J. b.8May1928-d.7Mar1988, "Beloved Daughter & Mother"

SW HANNEMAN Walter F. b.1902-d.1977, w/ Manila D. Hanneman

SW HANNEMAN Manila D. b.1899-d.1982, w/ Walter F. Hanneman

SW VOELKEL Joseph H. b.1858-d.1925, "Father" American Legion mkr

SW GRIDLEY Leander L. b.27Jul1883-d.4Apr1972, n/t Helen S. & Julia I. Gridley

SW GRIDLEY Helen S. b.7Sep1883-d.25Feb1967, n/t Leander L. & Julia I. Gridley

SW GRIDLEY Julia Isabella b.6Jan1920-d.8Jan1920, n/t Leander L. & Helen S. Gridley

SW BARNEKOW Walter F. b.22Nov1896-d.1Oct1921, flags and it looks like a doctor's symbol on the stone

SW WILKE Augusta b.1864-d.1943, "Mother" w/ Herman Wilke

SW WILKE Herman b.1860-d.1935, "Father" w/ Augusta Wilke

SW MUELLER Esther b.1891-d.1967, w/Otto, Ilma, Kurt E. & Pamela S. Rupnow

SW RUPNOW Otto b.1895-d.1979, "PFC US Army WWI" w/ Ilma, Kurt E. & Pamela S. Rupnow & Esther Mueller

SW RUPNOW Ilma b.1894-d.1991, w/ Otto, Kurt E. & Pamela S. Rupnow & Esther Mueller

SW RUPNOW Kurt E. b.1950-d.1972, w/ Otto, Ilma & Pamela S. Rupnow & Esther Mueller

SW RUPNOW Pamela Sue b.1954-d.1966, w/ Otto, Ilma & Kurt E. Rupnow & Esther Mueller

SW SWAN Seth B. b.1829-d.1909, w/ Maria M., Ida M., Walter C. & Edward U. Swan; Seth Swan was an early settler of Wauwatosa

SW SWAN Maria M. b.1832-d.1889, "w/o S. B. Swan" w/ Seth B., Ida M., Walter C. & Edward U. Swan

SW SWAN Ida M. b.1856-d.1865, w/ Seth B., Maria M., Walter C. & Edward U. Swan

SW SWAN Walter C. b.1858-d.1864, w/ Seth B., Maria M., Ida M. & Edward U. Swan

SW SWAN Edward U. b.1863-d.1864, w/ Seth B., Maria M., Ida M. & Walter C. Swan

SW ? Linda b.14Mar1894-d.22Apr1921, n/t Moritz & Eliza ?, no last name on stone

SW ? Moritz b.14Jun1856-d.28Jan1943, n/t Linda & Eliza ?, no last name on stone

SW ? Eliza b.20Jun1857-d.23Mar1936, "Mother" n/t Linda & Moritz ?, no last name on stone

SW TULLY Marion I. b.1900-d.1987, n/t Maud G. & Thomas Wm. Tully

SW TULLY Maud G. b.1866-d.1958, n/t Marion I. & Thomas Wm. Tully *

SW TULLY Thomas Wm. b.1862-d.1904, n/t Marion I. & Maud G. Tully *

SW GILBERT Richard b.1830-d.1913, n/t Mary Gilbert; Richard Gilbert was an early settler of Wauwatosa *

SW GILBERT Mary b.1834-d.1873, n/t Richard Gilbert

SW STEINERT Emil b.1886-d.1946, "Father" w/ Frieda & Emma Steinert

SW STEINERT Frieda b.1884-d.1971, "Mother" w/ Emil & Emma Steinert

SW STEINERT Emma b.1888-d.1921, "Mother" w/ Emil & Frieda Steinert

SW SCHMECHEL Irma M. b.1904-d.no date, "Sister" w/ George F., n/t Wilma Schmechel

SW SCHMECHEL George F. b.1900-d.1969, "Brother" w/ Irma M., n/t Wilma Schmechel

SW SCHMECHEL Wilma b.1908-d.1993, n/t Irma M. & George F. Schmechel; wooden cross

SW HAESE Auguste b.6Apr1864-d.3Jun1941, n/t Herman & Charles Haese

SW HAESE Herman b.21Mar1859-d.12Jan1938, n/t Auguste & Charles Haese

SW HAESE Charles b.24Oct1890-d.28Sep1912, n/t Auguste & Herman Haese

SW GROLL Adella b.1893-d.1968, "Mother" n/t Lester Groll

SW GROLL Lester b.1890-d.1924, "Father" n/t Adella Groll

SW LANG Christian b.1880-d.1922, "Brother" n/t Carl G. & Otillie Lang & Johanna Lang Murphy

SW LANG Carl G. b.1874-d.1920, n/t Christian & Otillie Lang & Johanna Lang Murphy

SW LANG Otillie b.1841-d.1923, n/t Christian & Carl G. Lang & Johanna Lang Murphy

SW MURPHY Johanna Lang b.1877-d.1923, n/t Christian, Otillie & Carl G. Lang

SW SILVERNESS Harold O. b.1895-d.1956, w/ Ruth W. Silverness & Jeannette, Charles L. & Florence Wadsworth

SW SILVERNESS Ruth Wadsworth b.1900-d.1980, "His Wife (Harold)" w/ Harold O. Silverness & Jeannette, Charles L. & Florence Wadsworth

SW WADSWORTH Jeannette b.1902-d.1920, w/ Harold O. & Ruth Silverness & Charles L. & Florence Wadsworth

SW WADSWORTH Charles Lee b.1868-d.1941, w/ Harold O. & Ruth Silverness & Jeannette & Florence Wadsworth

SW WADSWORTH Florence b.1874-d.1957, w/ Harold O. & Ruth Silverness & Jeannette & Charles L. Wadsworth

SW FROELICH Augusta b.1861-d.1915, w/ Charles, Alma & Otto Froelich

SW FROELICH Charles b.1851-d.1924, w/ Augusta, Alma & Otto Froelich

SW FROELICH Alma b.1883-d.1958, w/ Augusta, Charles & Otto Froelich

SW FROELICH Otto b.1894-d.1958, w/ Augusta, Charles & Alma Froelich

SW HEIMANN Arnold R. b.2Dec1907-d.7Jun1919, n/t Edgar H., Helen & Robert Heimann

SW HEIMANN Edgar H. b.6Jan1904-d.10May1917, n/t Arnold R., Helen & Robert Heimann

SW HEIMANN Helen b.1877-d.1954, "Mother" w/ Robert, n/t Arnold R. & Edgar H. Heimann

SW HEIMANN Robert b.1873-d.1951, "Father" w/ Helen, n/t Arnold R. & Edgar H. Heimann

SW AWE Clara b.1894-d.1917, n/t Luella I., Richard F. & Mathilda & William Awe

SW AWE Luella I. b.1898-d.1984, w/ Richard F., n/t Clara, Mathilda & & William Awe

SW AWE Richard F. b.1898-d.1980, w/ Luella, n/t Clara, Mathilda & & William Awe

SW AWE Mathilda b.1863-d.1942, w/ William, n/t Clara, Luella I. & Richard F. Awe

SW AWE William b.1859-d.1941, w/ Mathilda, n/t Clara, Luella I. & Richard F. Awe

SW SWAN Emery A. b.1855-d.1927, n/t Julia E. Swan
SW SWAN Julia E. b.1856-d.1911, n/t Emery A. Swan
Sec6 BUCHHOLTZ Amelia b.1871-d.1936, "Mother" w/ Henry
Buchholtz
Sec6 BUCHHOLTZ Henry b.1864-d.1924, "Father" w/ Amelia Buchholtz
Sec6 BRIL Clara A. b.1883-d.1976, "Mother" n/t Allan Bril
Sec6 BRIL Allan b.1881-d.1925, "Father" n/t Clara A. Bril
Sec6 JONES David P. b.1850-d.1925, n/t Margaret Jones *
Sec6 JONES Margaret b.1905-d.1928, n/t David P. Jones
Sec6 DALTON Nathan Ford b.1846-d.1924, n/t Mary Test Dalton
Sec6 DALTON Mary Test b.1850-d.1925, n/t Nathan Ford Dalton
Sec6 LYONS Mary b.1854-d.1925, "Mother" w/ George S. Lyons
Sec6 LYONS George S. b.1888-d.1925, "Son" w/ Mary Lyons
Sec6 HABERMAN Ferdinand b.1853-d.1925, "Father" n/t Henrietta
Haberman
Sec6 HABERMAN Henrietta b.1861-d.1933, "Mother" n/t Ferdinand
Haberman
Sec6 REIS Elizabeth b.1869-d.1959, "Mother" w/ Jacob Reis
Sec6 REIS Jacob b.1851-d.1926, "Father" w/ Elizabeth Reis
Sec6 JAUTZ Freida b.1879-d.1976, w/ Gotthard, n/t Walter G. Jautz
Sec6 JAUTZ Gotthard b.1870-d.1959, w/ Frieda, n/t Walter G. Jautz
Sec6 JAUTZ Walter G. b.11Jun1916-d.8Jan1997, "Tec 4 US Army
WWII" n/t Frieda & Gotthard Jautz
Sec6 TOMPKINS John A. B. b.1857-d.1926, n/t Therese L. & Miriam D.
Thompkins
Sec6 TOMPKINS Miriam Downing b.1892-d.1954, n/t Therese L. & John
A. B. Thompkins
Sec6 TOMPKINS Therese LaDue b.1860-d.1945, n/t John A. B. &
Miriam D. Thompkins
Sec6 KLOKNER Teresa b.1866-d.1948, "Mother" w/ Alexander Klokner
& Anna M., Robert J., Carrie L., Adela J. & Lulu M. Dysart
Sec6 KLOKNER Alexander b.1863-d.1925, "Father" w/ Teresa Klokner
& Anna M., Robert J., Carrie L., Adela J. & Lulu M. Dysart
Sec6 DYSART Anna M. b.1878-d.1968, w/ Robert J., Carrie L., Adela J.
& Lulu M. Dysart & Terese & Alex. Klokner
Sec6 DYSART Robert J. b.1872-d.1914, w/ Anna M., Carrie L., Adela J.
& Lulu M. Dysart & Terese & Alex. Klokner
Sec6 DYSART Carrie L. b.1875-d.1947, w/ Anna M., Robert J., Adela J.
& Lulu M. Dysart & Terese & Alex. Klokner
Sec6 DYSART Adela J. b.1849-d.1911, w/ Anna M., Robert J., Carrie L. &⁻
Lulu M. Dysart & Terese & Alex. Klokner

Sec6 DYSART Lulu M. b.1878-d.1962, w/ Anna M., Robert J., Carrie L. & Adela J. Dysart & Terese & Alex. Klokner

Sec6 CLARK Lucy J. b.1858-d.1932, w/ Charles S. Clark

Sec6 CLARK Charles S. b.1856-d.1925, w/ Lucy J. Clark

Sec6 GROTH Helena b.1877-d.1935, "Mother" w/ August Groth

Sec6 GROTH August b.1863-d.1926, "Father" w/ Helena Groth

Sec6 MASCHMEYER Frieda b.1876-d.1948, "Mother" w/ Herman Maschmeyer

Sec6 MASCHMEYER Herman b.1870-d.1948, "Father" w/ Frieda Maschmeyer

Sec6 KLEINESCHAY Marie A. b.1880-d.1926, w/ Friedrich Kleineschay

Sec6 KLEINESCHAY Friedrich b.1879-d.1953, w/ Marie A. Kleineschay

Sec6 BARG Fredricka b.7Oct1844-d.4Apr1920, "Mother" w/ Frederick Barg

Sec6 BARG Frederick b.13Feb1842-d.27Dec1928, "Father" w/ Fredricka Barg

Sec6 ENGEL Otto H. b.1886-d.1921,

Sec6 CERNAHAN Kathryn b.1914-d.1926, "Daughter" w/ Lulu E. & Malcolm Cernahan

Sec6 CERNAHAN Lulu E. b.1882-d.1939, "Mother" w/ Kathryn & Malcolm Cernahan

Sec6 CERNAHAN Malcolm b.1880-d.19—, "Father" w/ Kathryn & Lulu E. Cernahan not in cemetery records, possibly buried elsewhere

Sec6 ARENZ Syrena b.1860-d.1923, "Mother" w/ William Arenz

Sec6 ARENZ William b.1861-d.1929, "Father" w/ Syrena Arenz

Sec6 BELL Laura G. b.1886-d.1955

Sec6 FALK Fred C. b.1872-d.1948, "Father"

Sec6 DUNGEY Clifford b.1893-d.1903, w/ Annie & James Dungey

Sec6 DUNGEY Annie b.1854-d.1924, w/ Clifford & James Dungey

Sec6 DUNGEY James b.1844-d.1919, w/ Clifford & Annie Dungey

Sec6 WENZEL Emma b.26Mar1873-d.27Dec1921, "Mother"

Sec6 SENKEL Jeanette W. b.1912-d.1981, n/t Vernon H. Senkel

Sec6 SENKEL Vernon H. b.10Jul1912-d.25Jun1997, n/t Jeanette W. Senkel

Sec6 HENDERSON Luella M. b.1893-d.1948, n/t Stanley V., Edwin F. & Mabel E. Henderson

Sec6 HENDERSON Stanley V. b.1887-d.1946, n/t Luella M., Edwin F. & Mabel E. Henderson

Sec6 HENDERSON Edwin F. b.1849-d.1920, n/t Luella M., Stanley V. & Mabel E. Henderson

Sec6 HENDERSON Mabel E. b.1865-d.1940, n/t Luella M., Stanley V. & Edwin F. Henderson

Sec6 KEENA Maude Myrtle b.1876-d.1920

Sec6 STREHLOW Gusta b.1858-d.1923, "Mother" w/ Henry Strehlow

Sec6 STREHLOW Henry b.1854-d.1920, "Father" w/ Gusta Strehlow

Sec6 ? Martha d.1961, "Baby" nothing more

Sec6 TISCHER Johanna b.1857-d.1946, n/t Karl, Mathilde & Charles Tischer

Sec6 TISCHER Karl b.1853-d.1920, n/t Johanna, Mathilde & Charles Tischer

Sec6 TISCHER Mathilde b.1870-d.1923, "Mother" n/t Johanna, Karl & Charles Tischer

Sec6 TISCHER Charles b.1880-d.1956, "Father" n/t Johanna, Karl & Mathilde Tischer

Sec6 McCORMICK Irene Bertha b.3Dec1915-d.1Feb1920, "Betty" n/t Irene F. & James A. McCormick

Sec6 McCORMICK Irene F. b.1887-d.1968, "Mother" w/ James A., n/t Irene B. McCormick

Sec6 McCORMICK James A. b.1883-d.1948, "Father" w/ Irene F., n/t Irene B. McCormick

Sec6 SIGRIST Christine b.1870-d.5Jun1937, "Mother" w/ Bert, n/t Eleanor & Bert Sigrist, death date from cemetery records

Sec6 SIGRIST Bert b.1861-d.1920, "Father" w/ Christine, n/t Eleanor & Bert Sigrist

Sec6 AURIS Ida b.1908-d.1927, "Daughter" n/t Ida, William, Albert C., Fred, & Eric Auris

Sec6 AURIS Ida b.1870-d.1943, n/t Ida, William, Albert C., Fred, & Eric Auris

Sec6 AURIS William d.26Sep1938, "Pvt 161 Depot Brig." n/t Ida, Ida, Albert C., Fred, & Eric Auris

Sec6 AURIS Albert C. b.1904-d.1961, "Son" n/t Fred, Eric, Ida, Ida & William Auris

Sec6 AURIS Fred b.1865-d.1921, n/t Albert, Eric, Ida, Ida & William Auris

Sec6 AURIS Eric b.1894-d.1920, "Son" n/t Albert, Fred, Ida, Ida & William Auris

Sec6 SIGRIST Eleanor b.1909-d.1940, n/t Christine & Bert Sigrist

Sec6 SIGRIST Bert d.15May1920, "Wis. Pvt Hospital Corps" n/t Eleanor & Christine Sigrist this must be a second stone for Bert

Sec6 CLASEN Anna b.1894-d.1920, "Mother" n/t Charles A. & Sophia H. Clasen, same type stone as Auris

Sec6 CLASEN Charles A. b.1862-d.1944, "Father" w/ Sophia H., n/t Anna Clasen, same type stone as Auris

Sec6 CLASEN Sophia H. b.1869-d.1947, "Mother" w/ Charles A., n/t Anna Clasen, same type stone as Auris

Sec6 BAGEMIHL Lydia b.10Aug1862-d.23Nov1921, "Mother" n/t Frank Bagemihl

Sec6 BAGEMIHL Frank b.4Nov1860-d.7May1930, "Father" n/t Lydia Bagemihl

Sec6 FALK Minie b.1864-d.1948, "Mother" w/ John A., n/t Adolph H. Falk

Sec6 FALK John A. b.1866-d.1926, "Father" w/ Minie, n/t Adolph H. Falk

Sec6 FALK Adolph H. b.1891-d.1921, n/t Minie & John A. Falk

Sec6 HOMUTH Friederike Johanna b.3Mai1854-d.13Feb1925, w/ Friedrich W. Homuth

Sec6 HOMUTH Friedrich Wilhelm b.10Jan1845-d.22Oct1921, w/ Friederike J. Homuth

Sec6 SCHLICHTING C. J. b.1857-d.1912, "Father"

Sec6 WIMBLE James b.1835-d.1922, w/ Mary J. Wimble

Sec6 WIMBLE Mary Jane b.1837-d.1920, w/ James Wimble

Sec6 GRAHAM Claire C. b.1883-d.1967, w/ James W. Graham

Sec6 GRAHAM James W. b.1882-d.1939, w/ Claire C. Graham

Sec6 WENZEL John R. b.1897-d.1919, "Vet. of the WW Sgt. Battery D 121 F.A. 32 Div. A.E.F." (picture of arrow) This division was called the Red Arrow Division.

Sec6 STARK Frank b.13Jan1875-d.23Oct1919, "Father" w/ Augusta Stark

Sec6 STARK Augusta b.8Aug1883-d.29May1955, "Mother" w/ Frank Stark

Sec6 McCORMICK Darleen A. b.10Mar1911-d.4Nov1980, "Daughter" n/t Irene B., Irene F. & James A. McCormick

Sec6 ROEHL Ernstina b.1901-d.1919, w/ Bertha, Frank, William & Karl Roehl

Sec6 ROEHL Bertha b.1869-d.1950, "Mother" w/ Ernstina, Frank, William & Karl Roehl

Sec6 ROEHL Frank b.1863-d.1933, "Father" w/Ernstina, Bertha, William & Karl Roehl

Sec6 ROEHL William b.1896-d.1938, w/ Ernstina, Bertha, Frank & Karl Roehl

Sec6 ROEHL Karl b.1898-d.1946, w/ Ernstina, Bertha, Frank & William Roehl

Sec6 SIEBRECHT Minna b.1856-d.1933, "Mother" w/ Max C. & Max J. Siebrecht

Sec6 SIEBRECHT Max C. b.1866-d.1934, "Father" w/ Minna & Max J. Siebrecht

Sec6 SIEBRECHT Max J. b.1895-d.1918 France, "Corp. Co H 341 Inf., died in France" w/ Minna & Max C. Siebrecht; American Legion mkr.

Sec6 JAUTZ Carl b.1907-d.1931, "Son"

Sec6 STARK Mary b.1847-d.1931, "Mother" w/ Christ Stark

Sec6 STARK Christ b.1845-d.1931, "Father" w/ Mary Stark

NE SACKETT Squire d.22Sep1878,,, "70y?" w/ Anna M. & Sarah Sackett; Squire Sackett was an early settler of Wauwatosa

NE SACKETT Anna M. b.29Oct1843-d.29Oct1898, "d/o Squire & Sarah Sackett" w/ Squire & Sarah Sackett

NE SACKETT Sarah d.27Apr1886, "76y" w/ Squire & Anna M. Sackett

NE KOLLER Oscar b.1897-d.1984, w/ Stella Koller

NE KOLLER Stella b.1898-d.1987, w/ Oscar Koller

NE STANTON John J. b.1928-d.1996, w/ Dolores S. Stanton

NE STANTON Delores S. b.1928-d.no date, w/ John J. Stanton

NE JEFFERY George b.1827-d.1917, "Father" n/t Anne Jeffery

NE JEFFERY Anne b.1836-d.1916, "Mother" n/t George Jeffery

NE WITTE Ida M. b.29Apr1864-d.3Sep1913, n/t George R. Witte

NE WITTE George R. b.11Oct1888-d.10Mar1889, n/t Ida M. Witte

NE SACKETT Edwin H. d.22Nov1863, "23y 6m; Died in Hospital at Fort Halleck Columbus, KY"; stone worn, hard to read; I don't find Columbus, KY on the map. His first name is shown as Elwin and he died in Nashville on 22 Nov 1862, from disease. He was residing in Wauwatosa when he enlisted in the army on 9 Aug 1862. He was in the 24th Infantry Co. E [28], *this is a memorial stone, he is not buried here*

NE DEXTER David Hathaway b.1822-d.25Mar1863, "Died in Hospital at Fort Halleck, Columbus, KY, LEUT. 31 REG. WIS. MFT. DM", w/ Addie M. W. & Mary J. D. Dexter; David enlisted in the Army in Butler 1 Jan 1863,, he was in 34th Infantry Co. K, he enrolled 19 Nov 1862, he was a 2nd Lt., died of disease 25 Mar 1863 in Columbus, KY.[29]

NE DEXTER Mary J. Dana b.1827-d.17Feb1904, "77y 4m 3d; w/o D. H. Dexter" w/ Addie M. W. & David H. Dexter there are two stones for Mary & David *

NE DEXTER Addie M. Witte b.1857-d.1943, w/ Mary J. D. & David H. Dexter

NE DeCAMP Agnes Annette d.6Sep1882, "9y 8m 16d?" n/t Wm., Roxana L., Frances E. & Elizabeth DeCamp

NE DeCAMP Wm. d.1911, "Father" n/t Agnes A., Roxana L., Frances E. & Elizabeth DeCamp

NE DeCAMP Roxana L. d.29Mar1856, "5m 15d" n/t Agnes A., Wm., Frances E. & Elizabeth DeCamp

---

28 *Roster of Wisconsin Volunteers, War Of The Rebellion, 1861-1865*

29 *Roster of Wisconsin Volunteers, War Of The Rebellion, 1861-1865*

NE DeCAMP Frances E. d.31Mar1856, "8y 2m 5d?" n/t Agnes A., Wm., Roxana L. & Elizabeth DeCamp;stone worn,hard to read

NE DeCAMP Elizabeth d.8Oct1866, "41y 7m 12d; w/o Wm. DeCamp" n/t Agnes A., Wm., Roxana L. & Frances E. DeCamp

NE HARTUNG Theodore d.10Oct1877, "58y 1m 22d" w/ Cora, Ralph, Max, Clara, Mother, Father, Max Ralph & Siebick Hartung

NE HARTUNG Cora b.1823-d.31May1912, "88y 1m" w/ Theodore, Ralph, Max, Clara, Mother, Father, Max Ralph & Siebick Hartung

NE HARTUNG Ralph d.12Apr1871, "22y 1m 21d" w/ Theodore, Cora, Max, Clara, Mother, Father, Max, & Siebick Hartung

NE HARTUNG Max d.4Jan1890, "29y 3m 21d" w/ Theodore, Cora, Ralph, Clara, Mother, Father, Ralph, & Siebick Hartung

NE HARTUNG Clara b.25May1865-d.3Nov1944, flat stones w/ mother, father, Max, Ralph & Siebick; 2 stones for some?; dates from cemetery records

NE HARTUNG Siebick b.no date-d.no date, flat stones w/ mother, father, Max, Ralph & Clara; 2 stones for some?; no cemetery record

NE ELLIS Clarissa d.9Apr1865, "20y 8d"

NE PILGRIM Sarah Jeffery b.1825-d.1912, "Mother" n/t Daniel T. & Lucretia J. Pilgrim; could she be related to George Jeffery?

NE PILGRIM Daniel T. b.1832-d.1907, "Father" n/t Sarah J. & Lucretia J. Pilgrim *

NE PILGRIM Lucretia J. b.1865-d.1933, "Daughter" n/t Sarah J. & Daniel T. Pilgrim

NE DE GRAFF Emma M. d.17Dec1848, "16y 6m 9d" w/ Wm. H., Jacob & Harriet De Graff, Jane Goodrich & Frances I. Gilbert

NE DE GRAFF Wm. H. d.19Apr1867 Central City, Col., "31y" w/ Emma M., Jacob & Harriet De Graff, Jane Goodrich & Frances I. Gilbert

NE DE GRAFF Jacob b.6Jan1805 Amsterdam, NY-d.16Jan1887, w/ Emma M., Wm. H. & Harriet De Graff, Jane Goodrich & Frances I. Gilbert

NE DE GRAFF Harriet b.4Feb1809 Galway, NY-d.8Dec1879, w/ Emma M., Wm. H. & Jacob De Graff, Jane Goodrich & Frances I. Gilbert

NE GOODRICH Jane d.4Mar1880, "96y" w/ Emma M., Wm. H., Harriet & Jacob De Graff & Frances I. Gilbert

NE GILBERT Frances I. b.1838-d.1898, "d/o J & H De Graff; w/o Richard Gilbert" w/ Emma M., Wm. H., Harriet & Jacob De Graff & Jane Goodrich

NE LANGE Albert W., Dr. b.16Apr1891-d.4Mar1945

NE HEATH Dorothy P. b.3May1903-d.3Jul1970, n/t Carrie F., Carrie G., Frederic & Elizabeth Heath & Robert J. Faries

NE HEATH Carrie Faries b.2Oct1840-d.20Oct1885, n/t Dorothy P.,
Elizabeth & Frederic, w/ Carrie G. Heath & Robert J. Faries
NE HEATH Carrie Gertrude b.23Nov1861-d.25Feb1862, n/t Dorothy P.,
Elizabeth & Frederic, w/ Carrie F. Heath & Robert J. Faries
NE HEATH Frederic b.1864-d.1954, w/ Elizabeth, n/t Carrie F. & Carrie
G. Heath & Robert J. Faries
NE HEATH Elizabeth b.1876-d.1958, w/ Frederic, n/t Carrie F., Carrie G.
Heath & Robert J. Faries
NE FARIES Robert J. d.11May1878, "88y" w/ Carrie F. & Carrie G., n/t
Dorothy, Frederic & Elizabeth Heath, death date could be wrong
NE ROBERTS Jennie A. b.1898-d.1956, w/ Grace & Richard Roberts &
Ellen, Dorothy, Jennie F. & Richard Skepper
NE ROBERTS Richard b.1793-d.1875, w/ Grace & Jennie A. Roberts &
Ellen, Dorothy, Jennie F., Ellen A. & Richard Skepper
NE ROBERTS Grace b.1900-d.1989, w/ Richard & Jennie A. Roberts &
Ellen, Dorothy, Jennie F., Ellen A. & Richard Skepper
NE SKEPPER Ellen b.1858-d.22Feb1882, w/ Richard, Grace & Jennie A.
Roberts & Dorothy, Jennie F., Ellen A. & Richard Skepper, death date
from cemetery record, she was 23 years old.
NE SKEPPER Dorothy b.1890-d.1933, w/ Richard, Grace & Jennie A.
Roberts & Ellen, Jennie F., Ellen A. & Richard Skepper
NE SKEPPER Jennie F. b.1866-d.1943, w/ Richard, Grace & Jennie A.
Roberts & Ellen, Edward C., Ellen A. & Richard Skepper
NE SKEPPER Edward C. b.1860-d.1933, w/ Richard, Grace & Jennie A.
Roberts & Ellen, Jennie F. & Richard Skepper
NE SKEPPER Richard b.13Feb1793-d.17May1875, w/ Ellen A., n/t
Ellen, Dorothy, Jennie F., Edward C., & Ellen A. Skepper & Roberts
family
NE SKEPPER Ellen A. b.16Sep1858-d.20Feb1882, w/ Richard, n/t Ellen,
Dorothy, Jennie F., Edward C. Skepper; probably a 2nd stone for her?
NE FULLER Lydia b.7Mar1818-d.30Dec1876, "w/o David Fuller"
NE HOLSTON Edith M. b.1864-d.1917, "Faithful to the End"
NE BECKER Johanna (STEINGREBER) b.28Feb1849-d.11Aug1891
NE WHEELER John M. b.1831-d.1919, w/ Mary E., Susan C., Merton J.,
Arthur B., & Julia Wheeler
NE WHEELER Mary E. b.1836-d.1870, w/ John M., Susan C., Merton J.,
Arthur B., & Julia Wheeler
NE WHEELER Susan C. b.1835-d.1904, w/ John M., Mary E., Merton J.,
Arthur B., & Julia Wheeler
NE WHEELER Merton J. b.1867-d.1917, w/ John M., Mary E., Susan C.,
Arthur B., & Julia Wheeler

NE WHEELER Arthur Boyden b.1861-d.1902, w/ John M., Mary E., Susan C., Merton J., & Julia Wheeler

NE WHEELER Julia b.1868-d.1925, w/ John M., Mary E., Susan C., Merton J., & Arthur B. Wheeler

NE PIETZ John C. b.12Mar1853-d.20Aug1932, n/t Marie Pietz

NE PIETZ Marie b.15Mar1871-d.23Mar1857, n/t John C. Pietz

NE GENSKE Karl F. b.17Nov1843-d.21May1879

NE BRANDT John b.1826-d.1914, n/t Mary Brandt

NE BRANDT Mary b.1820-d.1911, n/t John Brandt

NE ROSNER John, Jr. b.1874-d.1948, n/t Clara, Ervin, John, Sophie, Clara & Emma Rosner

NE ROSNER Clara b.1878-d.1943, n/t John, Jr., Ervin, John, Sophie, Clara & Emma Rosner

NE ROSNER Ervin b.1902-d.1924, n/t John, Jr., Clara, John, Sophie, Clara & Emma Rosner

NE ROSNER John b.1846-d.1896, n/t John, Jr., Clara, Ervin, Sophie, Clara & Emma Rosner

NE ROSNER Sophie b.1856-d.1919, n/t John, Jr., Clara, Ervin, John, Clara & Emma Rosner

NE ROSNER Clara d.1879, n/t John, Jr., Clara, Ervin, John, Sophie & Emma Rosner; only one date

NE ROSNER Emma d.1873, n/t John, Jr., Clara, Ervin, John, Sophie & Clara Rosner; only one date

NE GOERLITZ Caroline A. b.1862-d.1946, "Wife" w/ William G. Goerlitz

NE GOERLITZ William G. b.1858-d.1941, "Husband" w/ Caroline A. Goerlitz

NE ZIMMERMANN Franz b.8Mar1820-d.5Oct1910, "Vater" n/t Friedericke W. Zimmermann

NE ZIMMERMANN Friedericke W. (SCHAPLOW) b.10Aug1822-d.22Jun1899, n/t Franz Zimmermann

NE ACKER Louisa b.10Jul1855-d.22Nov1878, "Tochter" n/t Louisa Acker

NE ACKER Louisa b.15Sep1832-d.17Mar1903, "Mutter" n/t Louisa Acker

NE JESSEN Kathryn M. b.1912-d.no date, w/ John W. Jessen

NE JESSEN John W. b.1909-d.1983, w/ Kathryn M. Jessen

NE SCARRITT Eliza S. d.16Sep1856, "In the 31st year of her age, d/o Augustus" & Lucy Blodgett; w/o George H. Scarritt"

NE DELPSCH Laura L. b.1873-d.1956, "Sister" n/t Ida A. Delpsch & Lucy A. M. Scholz *

NE DELPSCH Ida A. b.1880-d.1956, n/t Laura L. Delpsch & Lucy A. M. Scholz *

NE SCHOLZ Lucy A. M. (DELPSCH) b.1873-d.1928, n/t Laura L. & Ida A. Delpsch

NE SCHOONMAKER John N. b.1824-d.1897, "Father" n/t Hannah B., Sarah M., M. Elizabeth, Charlotte R. & other Schoonmakers, the Schoonmaker family owned and operated one of the many quaries in Wauwatosa.[30]

NE SCHOONMAKER Hannah B. b.1834-d.1908, n/t John N., Sarah M., M. Elizabeth, Charlotte R. & other Schoonmakers

NE SCHOONMAKER Sarah M. b.1865-d.1941, n/t John N., Hannah B., M. Elizabeth, Charlotte R. & other Schoonmakers

NE SCHOONMAKER M. Elizabeth b.1868-d.1944, n/t John N., Hannah B., Sarah M., Charlotte R. & other Schoonmakers

NE SCHOONMAKER Charlotte R. b.1872-d.1949, n/t John N., Hannah B., Sarah M., M. Elizabeth & other Schoonmakers

NE SCHOONMAKER Sarah b.1861-d.1862, w/ Eli, n/t John N., Hannah B., Sarah M., M. Elizabeth & other Schoonmakers

NE SCHOONMAKER Eli b.1868-d.1868, w/ Sarah, n/t John N., Hannah B., Sarah M., M. Elizabeth & other Schoonmakers

NE SCHOONMAKER Bessie b.1886-d.1887, n/t John N., Hannah B., Sarah M., Carrie, M. Elizabeth & other Schoonmakers

NE SCHOONMAKER Henry G. b.1863-d.1938, n/t John N., Hannah B., Sarah M., Carrie, M. Elizabeth & other Schoonmakers *

NE SCHOONMAKER Carrie b.1862-d.1922, "Mother" n/t John N., Hannah B., Sarah M., John R., M. Elizabeth & other Schoonmakers

NE SCHOONMAKER John Raymond d.3Aug1935, "WISCONSIN SGT. ICL EVAC HOSP 33" n/t John N., Hannah B., Sarah M., Carrie, M. Elizabeth & other Schoonmakers

NE HALL Emma M. b.1849-d.1880, "Mama" n/t May, Linus J. & Robert Hall

NE HALL May b.1872-d.1904, n/t Emma M., Linus J. & Robert Hall

NE HALL Linus J. b.1839-d.1908, "Papa" n/t Emma M., May & Robert Hall

NE HALL Robert b.1874-d.1911, n/t Emma M., May & Linus J. Hall

NE BARTH John F. b.no date-d.no date, "Baby" n/t C. W. Barth; same type stone as De Hond family

NE BARTH C. W. b.6May1878-d.24Apr1898, "Wesley" n/t John F. Barth; same type stone as De Hond family

---

30 The Heritage of a Community, page 6

NE THOMAS Nellie (DE HOND) b.9May1854-d.9Aug1894, n/t Peter,
A., Elizabeth & Isaac De Hond & Maggie Du Mez
NE DE HOND Peter b.6Jan1858-d.28Sep1885, "Rest is the Sleep of
Death and Short the Pilgrimage on Earth" n/t A., Elizabeth & Isaac De
Hond, Nellie Thomas & Maggie Du Mez
NE DE HOND A. b.18Feb1860-d.24Aug1880, n/t Peter, Elizabeth &
Isaac De Hond, Nellie Thomas & Maggie Du Mez
NE DE HOND Elizabeth b.13Jul1822-d.30Nov1902, "Mother" n/t Peter,
A. & Isaac De Hond, Nellie Thomas & Maggie Du Mez
NE DE HOND Isaac b.16Mar1823-d.26Oct1893, n/t Peter, A. & Eliza-
beth De Hond, Nellie Thomas & Maggie Du Mez
NE DU MEZ Maggie (DE HOND) b.18Sep1859-d.5Jan1905, n/t Isaac,
Peter, A. & Elizabeth De Hond & Nellie Thomas
NE MOLL Peter b.1825-d.1899, n/t Louise, Marie D. & Johanna Moll
NE MOLL Louise b.1830-d.1880, n/t Peter, Marie D. & Johanna Moll
NE MOLL Marie D. b.1862-d.1894, n/t Peter, Louise & Johanna Moll
NE MOLL Johanna b.1864-d.1938, n/t Peter, Louise & Marie D. Moll
NE ACKMANN Alma H. b.1884-d.1920, "Mother" n/t David C. Ackmann
NE ACKMANN David C. b.1919-d.1920, "Baby" n/t Alma H. Ackmann
NE ZINN Betty b.1930-d.1933
NE ACKMANN Elvin C. b.1885-d.1971, n/t Joachim A. & Marie C.
Ackmann; Masonic Symbol
NE ACKMANN Joachim A. b.19Jul1852-d.7Apr1897, "Papa" n/t Elvin C.
& Marie C. Ackmann
NE ACKMANN Marie C. b.9Feb1858-d.18Mai1944, "Mama" n/t Elvin C.
& Joachim A. Ackmann
NE KARNATZ Carl b.21Aug1822-d.5Nov1907, "Vater, RUHE SANFT" n/
t Elisabeth & Henriette Karnatz
NE KARNATZ Elisabeth b.14Mai1828-d.22Jul1910, "RUHE SANFT", n/t
Carl & Henriette Karnatz
NE KARNATZ Henriette b.12Sep1861-d.11Nov1883, "19y 2m" n/t Carl
& Elisabeth Karnatz
NE MERTEN Grace May b.1891-d.1937
NE SCHOLTKA Julius b.1870-d.1919, n/t Magdalena, William, Minnie,
Carl W., Christian & Elizabeth Scholtka
NE SCHOLTKA Magdalena b.1875-d.1946, n/t Julius, William, Minnie,
Carl W., Christian & Elizabeth Scholtka
NE SCHOLTKA William b.1865-d.1944, n/t Julius, Magdalena, Minnie,
Carl W., Christian & Elizabeth Scholtka
NE SCHOLTKA Minnie b.1868-d.1924, n/t Julius, Magdalena, William,
Carl W., Christian & Elizabeth Scholtka

NE SCHOLTKA Carl W. b.10May1895-d.10Dec1970, "Wisconsin PVT 14 CASUAL DET WW1" n/t Julius, Magdalena, William, Minnie, Christian & Elizabeth Scholtka

NE SCHOLTKA Christian b.1826-d.1903, n/t Julius, Magdalena, William, Minnie, Carl W. & Elizabeth Scholtka

NE SCHOLTKA Elizabeth b.1830-d.1907, n/t Julius, Magdalena, William, Minnie, Carl W. & Christian Scholtka

NE WORM Maria L. b.5Jan1880-d.7Sep1881,

NE FEERICK Herbert b.1897-d.1902, "s/o Thomas & Augusta Feerick" n/t Alvina, Clarence, Julia, Caroline, & other Feericks & Mary Hartung

NE FEERICK Alvina b.1871-d.1887, "d/o Michael & Catherine Feerick" n/t Herbert, Clarence, Julia, Caroline, & other Feericks & Mary Hartung

NE FEERICK Clarence b.1903-d.1925, "s/o Thomas & Augusta Feerick" n/t Herbert, Alvina, Julia, Caroline, & other Feericks & Mary Hartung

NE HARTUNG Mary b.1861-d.1884, "d/o Michael & Catherine Feerick" n/t Herbert, Alvina, Julia, Caroline, Catherine, Michael & other Feericks

NE FEERICK Julia b.1857-d.1880, "d/o Michael & Catherine Feerick" n/t Herbert, Alvina, Catherine, Michael & other Feericks & Mary Hartung

NE FEERICK Caroline b.1854-d.1939, "d/o Michael & Catherine Feerick" n/t Herbert, Alvina, Catherine, Michael & other Feericks & Mary Hartung

NE FEERICK Catherine b.1831-d.1888, "Mother" n/t Herbert, Alvina, Caroline, Michael & other Feericks & Mary Hartung

NE FEERICK Michael b.1825-d.1907, "Father" n/t Herbert, Alvina, Caroline, Catherine & other Feericks & Mary Hartung

NE FEERICK Thomas J. b.1862-d.1928, "s/o Michael & Catherine Feerick" n/t Herbert, Alvina, Caroline, Catherine Augusta & other Feericks & Mary Hartung

NE FEERICK Augusta (SCHEUNERT) b.1869-d.1948, "w/o Thomas Feerick" n/t Herbert, Alvina, Caroline, Catherine Thomas J.& other Feericks & Mary Hartung

NE BROWN Silas I. b.19Dec1847-d.5Feb1868, n/t S. M., E. H., Elizabeth & Rudolph M. Brown

NE BROWN S. M. b.1May1810-d.5Sep1850, n/t Silas I., E. H., Elizabeth & Rudolph M. Brown

NE BROWN E. H. b.23Oct1810-d.5May1894, n/t Silas I., S. M., Elizabeth & Rudolph M. Brown

NE BROWN Elizabeth b.1869-d.1951, "w/o Rodolph M. Brown" n/t Silas I., S. M., E. H. & Rudolph M. Brown

NE BROWN Rodolph M. b.25May1839-d.11Jul1903, n/t Silas I., S. M., E. H. & Elizabeth Brown *

NE VAN VECTEN E. Elizabeth b.17Aug1862-d.22May1946, n/t Jacob T., Esther E., Lydia J., Callie, Squire, Philip & Allen Van Vecten; no cemetery record

NE VAN VECTEN Jacob T. b.8May1823-d.15Feb1908, n/t E. Elizabeth, Esther E., Lydia J., Callie, Squire, Philip & Allen Van Vecten; no cemetery record

NE VAN VECTEN Esther E. b.14Apr1831-d.30Oct1895, "w/o Jacob T. Van Vecten" n/t E. Elizabeth, Jacob T., Lydia J., Callie,Squire, Philip & Allen Van Vecten; no cemetery record

NE VAN VECTEN Lydia Jane b.no date-d.no date, n/t E. Elizabeth, Jacob T., Esther E., Callie, Squire, Philip & Allen Van Vecten; no cemetery record

NE VAN VECTEN Callie b.no date-d.no date, n/t E. Elizabeth, Jacob T., Esther E., Lydia, Squire, Philip & Allen Van Vecten; no cemetery record

NE VAN VECTEN Squire b.no date-d.no date, n/t E. Elizabeth, Jacob T., Esther E., Lydia, Callie, Philip & Allen Van Vecten; no cemetery record

NE VAN VECTEN Philip b.no date-d.no date, n/t E. Elizabeth, Jacob T., Esther E., Lydia, Callie, Squire & Allen Van Vecten; no cemetery record

NE VAN VECTEN Allen b.no date-d.no date, n/t E. Elizabeth, Jacob T., Esther E., Lydia, Callie, Squire & Philip VanVecten; no cemetery record

NE THICKENS Mary d.7Oct1891, "Mother, w/o John Thickens; 69y" n/t John & Mary E. Thickens & Lavina B. T. Franklin; death month could be Dec

NE THICKENS John b.1824-d.1901, n/t Mary & Mary E. Thickens & Lavina B. T. Franklin; GAR mkr

NE THICKENS Mary Emily b.1853-d.1903, n/t Mary & John Thickens & Lavina B. T. Franklin

NE FRANKLIN Lavina Bruce Thickens b.1856-d.1904, n/t John, Mary & Mary E. Thickens

NE LOVELAND Lena C. b.1885-d.1976, n/t Fanny S., Frank E., Laura A. & Grace E. Loveland

NE LOVELAND Fanny S. b.1856-d.1947, n/t Lena C., Frank E., Laura A. & Grace E. Loveland

NE LOVELAND Frank E. b.1855-d.1920, n/t Lena C., Fanny S., Laura A. & Grace E. Loveland *

NE LOVELAND Laura A. b.1883-d.1943, n/t Lena C., Fanny S., Frank E. & Grace E. Loveland

NE LOVELAND Grace E. b.1884-d.1976, n/t Lena C., Fanny S., Frank E. & Laura A. Loveland

NE BRANDT Louisa b.7Nov1858-d.23Nov1894, "w/o W. C. Brandt" n/t Adele, Louisa & William C. Brandt & Clifford A. & Erna Schwulst

NE BRANDT Louisa b.1858-d.1894, n/t Adele, Louisa & William C. Brandt & Clifford A. & Erna Schwulst, possibly a 2nd stone for her

NE BRANDT Adele b.1882-d.1884, n/t Louisa, Louisa & William C. Brandt & Clifford A. & Erna Schwulst

NE BRANDT William C. b.1857-d.1936, n/t Louisa, Louisa & Adele Brandt & Clifford A. & Erna Schwulst

NE SCHWULST Clifford A. b.23Apr1897-d.9Jan1949, "Wisconsin PVT 6 CO COAST ARTY WWI" n/t Louisa, Louisa, Adele William C. Brandt & Erna Schwulst, American Legion mkr

NE SCHWULST Erna (BRANDT) b.8Jan1899-d.5Oct1978, n/t Louisa, Louisa, Adele William C. Brandt & Clifford A. Schwulst

NE BARK Wm. F. b.1886-d.1920, n/t Minnie & Ferdinand Bark, Fred E., Fred E., & Mary Eggert

NE BARK Minnie b.1867-d.1949, w/ Ferdinand, n/t Wm. F. Bark, Fred E., Fred E. & Mary Eggert

NE BARK Ferdinand b.1863-d.1933, w/ Minnie, n/t Wm. F. Bark, Fred E., Fred E. & Mary Eggert

NE EGGERT Fred b.13Jul1865-d.23Nov1886, n/t Minnie, Ferdinand, & Wm. F. Bark, Fred & Mary Eggert *

NE EGGERT Fred b.2Jan1836-d.10Jun1891, n/t Minnie, Ferdinand, & Wm. F. Bark, Fred & Mary Eggert

NE EGGERT Mary b.3Jun1838-d.28Jan1886, n/t Minnie, Ferdinand, & Wm. F. Bark, Fred & Fred Eggert

NE STALEY William b.1863-d.1926, "Brother" n/t Mary, Alick J., Frank, & John Staley

NE STALEY Mary b.1861-d.1924, "Sister" n/t William, Alick J., Frank, & John Staley

NE STALEY Alick J. d.1Aug1901, "Brother; Beloved h/o Minnie Staley; 44y" n/t William, Mary, Frank, & John Staley

NE STALEY Frank d.27Aug1879, "11y" n/t William, Mary, Alick J., & John Staley

NE STALEY John d.27May1882, "Father; 60y" n/t William, Mary, Alick J., & Frank Staley

NE KIRCHNER Alma b.5Feb1889-d.7Feb1939, "Beloved w/o Louis C. Kirchner" n/t Louis, Harriet E., Rose, Minnie, William H., Emilia & William Kirschner

NE KIRCHNER Harriet E. b.1Jul1874-d.25Feb1907, "Beloved w/o Louis

C. Kirchner" n/t Louis, Alma, Rose, Minnie, William H., Emilia &
William Kirschner

NE KIRCHNER Louis b.8Nov1877-d.11Nov1967, n/t Harriet E., Alma,
Rose, Minnie William H., Emilia & William Kirschner

NE LeFEBER William b.1886-d.1936, "Husband" n/t Elsie LeFeber

NE LeFEBER Elsie b.1886-d.1942, n/t William LeFeber

NE KIRCHNER Rose b.27Jun1870-d.27Aug1952, n/t Minnie, William
H., Emilia, Alma, William, Louis & Harriet E. Kirchner

NE KIRCHNER Minnie b.25Feb1868-d.20Jul1948, n/t Rose, William H.,
Emilia, Alma, William, Louis & Harriet E. Kirchner

NE KIRCHNER William H. b.15Apr1866-d.18Apr1897, n/t Rose,
William, Emilia, Alma, Minnie, Louis & Harriet E. Kirchner

NE KIRCHNER Emilia b.26Dec1845-d.30Apr1932, "Mother" n/t Rose,
William H., William, Alma, Minnie, Louis & Harriet E. Kirchner

NE KIRCHNER William b.24Mar1840-d.27Jan1891, "Father" n/t Rose,
William H., Emilia, Alma, Minnie, Louis & Harriet E. Kirchner

NE BARK Laura b.1888-d.1961

NE EICHLER Lillian b.20Feb1884-d.24Oct1971

NE LeFEBER John b.14Jul1851-d.1Jul1901, n/t Nellie S. & Baby
LeFeber

NE LeFEBER Nellie (SANDEE) b.4Mar1858-d.14Sep1887, n/t John &
Baby LeFeber

NE LeFEBER Baby d.19Sep1884, "s/o J. & N. LeFeber" n/t John &
Nellie LeFeber; only one date

NE ZOBEL Gustave b.1869-d.1932, "Dad" n/t Susan Zobel

NE ZOBEL Susan b.1876-d.1955, "Mother" n/t Gustave Zobel

NE HANKS Stanley M. b.1907-d.1974, n/t Mary B., Judson E., & Clara G.
Hanks & Clarissa & Alvin R. Boorse

NE HANKS Mary B. b.1904-d.1984, n/t Stanley M., Judson E., & Clara G.
Hanks & Clarissa & Alvin R. Boorse

NE HANKS Judson Edward b.1848-d.1889, n/t Stanley M., Mary B., &
Clara G. Hanks & Clarissa & Alvin R. Boorse

NE HANKS Clara Gregg b.1846-d.1912, n/t Stanley M., Mary B., &
Judson E. Hanks & Clarissa & Alvin R. Boorse

NE BOORSE Clarissa b.1882-d.1958, n/t Stanley M., Mary B., & Judson
E. & Clara G. Hanks & Alvin R. Boorse

NE BOORSE Alvin R. b.1880-d.1971, n/t Stanley M., Mary B., & Judson
E. & Clara G. Hanks & Clarissa Boorse

NE GREGG Jefferson b.15Aug1836 Milwaukee, Wis.-d.21Dec1913,
Wauwatosa, Wis., w/ Rhoda J., Lewis H., Harriett L., Marion F.,
Hendrick, & other Greggs; Jefferson was the father of Mabel Gregg,

who married Lyman G. Wheeler. Jefferson lived on the south side of Blue Mound Rd. in the Town of Brookfield, south of the Elm Grove Depot.[31]

NE GREGG Rhoda Jane b.24Oct1845 Meadville, PA-d.5Mar1920 Wauwatosa, Wis., w/ Jefferson, Lewis H., Harriett L., Marion F., Hendrick, & other Greggs

NE GREGG Lewis H. b.16Aug1848 Wauwatosa, Wis.-d.19Jan1927 Waunakee, Wis., w/ Rhoda J., Jefferson, Harriett L., Marion F., Hendrick, & other Greggs

NE GREGG Harriett L. b.16Jul1850 Granville, Wis.-d.7Jun1934 St. Paul, Minn., w/ Rhoda J., Jefferson, Lewis H., Marion F., Hendrick, & other Greggs

NE GREGG Marion F. b.11Jan1882-d.27Feb1968, w/ Rhoda J., Jefferson, Lewis H., Harriett L., Hendrick, & other Greggs

NE GREGG Hendrick b.21Dec1807 Augusta, NY-d.3Dec1881 Elm Grove, Wis., w/ Rhoda J., Jefferson, Lewis H., Harriett L., Marion F., & other Greggs

NE GREGG Clarrissa M. b.28Nov1810 Grafton, Mass.-d.11May1882 Wauwatosa, Wis., w/ Rhoda J., Jefferson, Lewis H., Harriett L., Marion F., & other Greggs

NE GREGG Austin W. b.7Mar1879-d.17Nov1968, w/ Rhoda J., Jefferson, Lewis H., Harriett L., Marion F., & other Greggs

NE HALL Mildred E. b.1904-d.1980, w/ Sidney S. Hall

NE HALL Sidney S. b.1904-d.1987, w/ Mildred E. Hall

NE JUNG Alvin G. b.1900-d.1978, w/ Dorothy G. Jung

NE JUNG Dorothy G. b.1908-d.1995, w/ Alvin G. Jung

NE BECK Anna b.18Aug1886-d.21Dec1982, w/ John Beck; dates from cemetery records

NE BECK John b.29Sep1886-d.17Mar1977, w/ Anna Beck; dates from cemetery records

NE MILBOW Louis b.1896-d.1978, "US Army"

NE GUETZKOW Jimmie Olive (COLLAR) b.8Jul1910-d.1Apr1982, w/ Gilbert Louis Guetzkow

NE GUETZKOW Gilbert Louis b.1Jul1903-d.28May1988, w/ Jimmie Olive C. Guetzkow

NE WALTER Rebekka (BACH) b.7Dec1810-d.19Mar1891, "Hier Ruht in Frieden; Mother" n/t August Walter; may be in Fingado plot

NE WALTER August b.27Dec1830-d.1Nov?1880, n/t Rebekka B. Walter; may be in Fingado plot

---

31 The Wheeler Family in America

FINGADO Charles b.1841-d.1901, "Father" n/t Amalie, Laura E. & 1862,
Laura B. Fingado; Charles enlisted in the army in Wauwatosa 15 Aug
NE he was in the 24th Infantry Co E, discharged 26 Mar 1862, disabil-
ity[32]

NE FINGADO Amalie b.1845-d.1925, "Mother" n/t Charles, Laura E. &
Laura B. Fingado

NE FINGADO Laura E. b.5Sep1881-d.17Sep1881, n/t Charles, Amalie &
Laura B. Fingado

NE FINGADO Laura B. b.27Dec1867-d.11Aug1868, n/t Charles, Amalie
& Laura E. Fingado old stone, worn, death date could be wrong.

NE LEHMANN Julie E. b.18Sep1877-d.18Jul1983, n/t Esther &
Katherine Lehmann

NE LEHMANN Esther b.6May1889-d.15May1971, n/t Julie E. &
Katherine Lehmann, twins?

NE LEHMANN Katherine b.6May1889-d.3Jan1973, n/t Julie E. & Esther
Lehmann, twins?

NE SCHMID Nathalie B. b.1884-d.1971

NE STOLTENBERG William P. b.9May1906-d.23Nov1989, w/ Vera P.
Stoltenberg

NE STOLTENBERG Vera P. b.3Mar1912-d.15May1992, w/ William P.
Stoltenberg

NE KUEHN Evelyn A. b.1890-d.1975, w/ Albert H. Kuehn

NE KUEHN Albert H. b.1897-d.1972, w/ Evelyn A. Kuehn

NE JABLONSKI Helen V. b.1917-d.1971, w/ Walter T. Jablonski

NE JABLONSKI Walter T. b.1913-d.1990, w/ Helen V. Jablonski

NE KIRCHER Margaret L. b.1925-d.1972, "Beloved Wife & Mother"

NE PULS H. b.1906-d.1972

NE GAHL Lois Jane b.1917-d.1996

NE KEGLER Margaret R. b.1894-d.1975, w/ Edwin R. Kegler

NE KEGLER Edwin R. b.1891-d.1974, w/ Margaret R. Kegler

NE BRINKMAN Katherine b.1894-d.1968, "Mother" w/ Paul W.
Brinkman

NE BRINKMAN Paul W. b.1880-d.1968, "Father" w/ Katherine Brinkman

NE RICHTER Paul b.1899-d.1972, w/ Paula Richter

NE RICHTER Paula b.1897-d.1991, w/ Paul Richter

NE ZEUNERT Ida M. b.1886-d.1982

NE SMITH Ethel H. b.1907-d.no date, w/ Weston R. Smith

NE SMITH Weston R. b.1908-d.1973, w/ Ethel H. Smith

NE KAISER Martha B. b.1911-d.1991, w/ Erwin W. Kaiser

NE KAISER Erwin W. b.1900-d.1979, w/ Martha B. Kaiser

NE REICH Frances M. b.1909-d.1995, w/ Eugene F. Reich
NE REICH Eugene F. b.1909-d.1988, w/ Frances M. Reich
NE BATISTE John b.1906-d.1996, w/ Marie Batiste
NE BATISTE Marie b.no date-d.no date, w/ John Batiste
NE INDVIK Catherine b.1911-d.1977
NE TELFER Adam Ferguson b.1893-d.1979, w/ Eva Oliver Telfer
NE TELFER Eva Oliver b.1901-d.1982, w/ Adam F. Telfer
NE DREWS Iva E. b.1910-d.1977, w/ Arthur H. Drews
NE DREWS Arthur H. b.1909-d.1996, w/ Iva E. Drews
NE TRUE Paul G. b.26Dec1908-d.3Mar1993, w/ Peggy True
NE TRUE Peggy b.19Dec1920-d.no date, w/ Paul G. True
NE NARWOLD T. Josephine b.1893-d.1979, w/ Margaret J. Narwold
NE NARWOLD Margaret J. b.1927-d.no date, w/ T. Josephine Narwold
NE FRANKLIN Irene L. b.1919-d.no date, w/ Robert W. & Douglas R.
   Franklin
NE FRANKLIN Robert W. b.1910-d.1992, w/ Irene L. & Douglas R.
   Franklin
NE FRANKLIN Douglas R. b.1945-d.1993, w/ Irene L. & Robert W.
   Franklin
NE SCHUBERT Emma M. b.1886-d.1974, w/ Charles A., n/t Jeannette K.
   Schubert
NE SCHUBERT Charles A. b.1873-d.1969, w/ Emma M., n/t Jeannette K.
   Schubert
NE SCHUBERT Jeannette K. b.1909-d.1980, n/t Emma M. & Charles A.
   Schubert
NE NEILS Florence J. b.1912-d.no date, w/ Walter L. Neils
NE NEILS Walter L. b.1908-d.1971, w/ Florence J. Neils
NE WEST Thomas Burton b.1909-d.1993, w/ Shirley F. C. West; Masonic
   symbol
NE WEST Shirley Frances Cooper b.1913-d.1994, w/ Thomas B. West
NE DALLMANN Otto A. b.1890-d.1973
NE ARNAUD Gertrude b.1906-d.1998, "Beloved Aunt"
NE STANDART Oliver d.31Aug1854, n/t Dolly Standart; old stone
   broken; 61y, age from cemetery records
NE STANDART Dolly d.31Aug1854, "65y" n/t Oliver Standart; old stone
   broken; death date and age from cemetery records
NE KARST Alice T. b.1903-d.1991, w/ Walter E. Karst
NE KARST Walter E. b.1900-d.1990, w/ Alice T. Karst
NE IRION Carolina b.29Mar1824-d.12Mar1889, n/t Friedric H. Irion; old
   stones, dates could be wrong
NE IRION Friedric H. b.1825-d.1891, n/t Carolina Irion; old stones, dates
   could be wrong

NE THOMAS Jos R. b.24Feb1837-d.10Feb1910, "1st Sgt. 77 Co. 2 Vet. Res. Corps"; Jos. enlisted in the army in Granville 21 Aug 1862, he was a sergt. in the 24 Infantry Co. K, accidentally wounded 4 Oct 1863, transfered to VRC 21 Mar 1864[33]

NE DAHLKE Minnie b.1897-d.1985

NE GREGG Ella P. b.30Jun1850-d.17Oct1850, n/t Mary F., George W., Hendrick & Clarissa Gregg

NE GREGG Mary F. b.26Aug1838-d.22Aug1847, n/t Ella P., George W., Hendrick & Clarissa Gregg

NE GREGG George W. b.22Feb1843-d.31Dec1862, "Killed at the Battle of Stone-River Tenn" n/t Ella P., Mary F., Hendrick & Clarissa Gregg, GAR George enlisted in the army in Milwaukee 13 Aug 1862, he was in the 24th Infantry Co. D[34]

NE GREGG Hendrick b.21Dec1807-d.3Dec1881, n/t Ella P., Mary F., George W. & Clarissa Gregg

NE GREGG Clarissa b.28 Nov 1810-d.11May1882, n/t Ella P., Mary F., George W. & Hendrick Gregg

NW BARBER Wm. Gilbert b.1842-d.1918, w/Martha E., Eddie G., Gertrude, Beulah, Edward R., Belle and other Barbers

NW BARBER Martha Earls b.1847-d.1928, w/ Wm. Gilbert, Eddie G., Gertrude, Edward R., Belle and other Barbers

NW BARBER Eddie G. b.1Oct1870-d.15Feb1881, w/ Wm. Gilbert, Martha E., Gertrude, Edward R., & other Barbers; hard to read

NW BARBER Gertrude d.26Dec1883, "8y 10m 8d" w/ Wm. Gilbert, Martha E., Eddie G., Edward R., & other Barbers; hard to read

NW BARBER Beulah b.1881?-d.1881?, w/ Wm. Gilbert, Martha E., Eddie G., Edward R., & other Barbers; hard to read

NW BARBER Olive B. b.21Jan1806-d.3Jan1881

NW BARBER Edward R. b.8Feb1840-d.7May1863, "Sergt Co E 24 Wis Inf; Died in Hospital" w/ Wm. Gilbert, Martha E., Eddie G., Edward R., & other Barbers; hard to read; Edward resided in Milwaukee when he enlisted in the army on 8 Aug 1862, he died of disease in New Albany, Ind.,[35] which is just across the river from Louisville, Ky

NW BARBER Belle b.1872-d.1961, n/t Wm. Gilbert, Martha E., Eddie G., Edward R., & other Barbers

NW BARBER Sara Olive b.1916-d.1920, "d/o B.F. & C.M. Barber" n/t Wm. Gilbert, Martha E., Eddie G., Edward R., & other Barbers

NW BARBER Ben F. b.1886-d.12Oct1970, w/ Lottie M. n/t Wm. Gilbert, Martha E., Edward R., & other Barbers

33 *Roster of Wisconsin Volunteers, War Of The Rebellion, 1861-1865*
34 *Roster of Wisconsin Volunteers, War Of The Rebellion, 1861-1865*
35 *Roster of Wisconsin Volunteers, War Of The Rebellion, 1861-1865*

NW BARBER Lottie M. b.1890-d.1962, w/ Ben F. n/t Wm. Gilbert, Martha E., Edward R., & other Barbers

NW GROVER Mary b.17Mar1777-d.12May1858, "m/o B. Barber" w/ Ben F. n/t Wm. Gilbert, Martha E., Edward R., & other Barbers

NW GROVER Leonora L. d.17Aug1845, "d/o M.L. & Harriet Grover, 13m 11d" n/t Mary Grover, old stone lying flat

NW ORR Edward Joseph b.1865-d.1895, w/ Emily E. & Joseph G. Orr & Edward S. & Hannah A. Earls

NW ORR Emily Earls b.1844-d.1920, w/ Edward J. & Joseph G. Orr & Edward S. & Hannah A. Earls

NW ORR Joseph G. b.1835-d.1925, w/ Edward J. & Emily E. Orr & Edward S. & Hannah A. Earls

NW EARLS Edward S. d.18Jul1879, "71y 4m 7d" w/ Edward J., Joseph G. & Emily E. Orr & Hannah A. Earls

NW EARLS Hannah A. d.24Apr1879, "68y 4m" w/ Edward J., Joseph G. & Emily E. Orr & Edward S. Earls

NW MAJERUS Christine b.1905-d.1975, "Mother"

NW RINGROSE George b.1810-d.1894, n/t Florence I., Sarah & Georgia B. Ringrose & Jessie R. Davis

NW RINGROSE Sarah b.1805-d.1883, n/t Florence I., George & Georgia B. Ringrose & Jessie R. Davis

NW RINGROSE Georgia Bell b.1883-d.1885, n/t Florence I., George & Sarah Ringrose & Jessie R. Davis

NW DAVIS Jessie Ringrose b.1867-d.1916, n/t Georgia B., Florence I., George & Sarah Ringrose

NW RINGROSE Florence I. b.1885-d.1957, n/t Georgia B., George & Sarah Ringrose & Jessie R. Davis

NW PACZESNY Michael b.1901-d.1979, w/ Marion & Patricia Paczesny

NW PACZESNY Marion b.1907-d.1997, w/ Michael & Patricia Paczesny

NW PACZESNY Patricia b.1930-d.1998, w/ Michael & Marion Paczesny

NW JUDS Frank R. b.13Sep1898-d.13Dec1971, "Tec 5 588 QM Laundry Co. WWII" n/t Herman W., Olive & Gerald H. Juds

NW JUDS Gerald H. b.10Dec1934-d.9Mar1963, "Wis. SP5 HQ & HQ Co. 19 Inf. Korea" n/t Herman W., Olive & Frank R. Juds

NW JUDS Herman W. b.1902-d.1980, w/ Olive n/t Gerald H. & Frank R. Juds

NW JUDS Olive b.1903-d.1980, w/ Herman W., n/t Gerald H. & Frank R. Juds

NW KRESANEK Myra b.1906-d.1943, "Mother"

NW JOHNSON John b.11Sep1885-d.24Feb1935, "Father" n/t Lena Johnson

NW JOHNSON Lena b.9Sep1864-d.19Dec1918, "Mother" n/t John
Johnson

NW RICKERT Henry J. b.2Jan1865-d.29Dec1888, "Father"

NW CUNDALL Helen Louise b.28Sep1904-d.6Mar1906

NW SEYBOLD Warren A. b.1921-d.1977

NW TREUTELAAR Nora b.6Feb1890-d.30Jul1916, n/t Mattie & Harry
Treutelaar

NW TREUTELAAR Mattie b.1899-d.1961, n/t Nora W/ Harry Treutelaar

NW TREUTELAAR Harry b.1899-d.1977, n/t Nora w/ Mattie Treutelaar;
WWI mkr.

NW LEWIS Mabel b.1876-d.1969, n/t Dwight B., Irma A., Robert G.,
Edward M., Helen A. & Sarah S. Lewis

NW LEWIS Dwight B. b.15Apr1875-d.7Feb1918, n/t Mabel, Irma A.,
Robert G., Edward M., Helen A. & Sarah S. Lewis

NW LEWIS Irma A. b.1884-d.1964, w/ Robert G., n/t Mabel, Dwight B.
Edward M., Helen A. & Sarah S. Lewis

NW LEWIS Robert G. b.1886-d.1961, w/ Irma A., n/t Mabel, Dwight B.
Edward M., Helen A. & Sarah S. Lewis

NW LEWIS Edward M. b.19Apr1871-d.12Feb1908, n/t Irma A., Robert
G., Mabel, Dwight B., Helen A. & Sarah S. Lewis

NW LEWIS Mother b.6Aug1842-d.1Apr1906, only Mother on stone; n/t
Irma A., Robert G., Mabel, Dwight B., Helen A. & Sarah S. Lewis,
possibly Sarah S. Lewis

NW LEWIS Helen A. b.30Mar1867-d.3Oct1899, n/t Irma A., Robert G.,
Mabel, Dwight B., Edward M. & Sarah S. Lewis

NW LEWIS William C. b.18Jul1833-d.25Aug1890, "Father" n/t Irma A.,
Robert G., Mabel, Dwight B., Edward M., Helen A. & Sarah S. Lewis;
William was a Civil War Veteran

NW LEWIS Sarah S. b.6Aug1842-d.1Apr1906, "w/o Wm. E. Lewis" n/t
Irma A., Robert G., Mabel, Dwight B., Edward M. & Helen A. Lewis

NW FALK Berga A. b.1902-d.1960, w/ Erich A., n/t Henrietta, Fred &
Arthur Falk

NW FALK Erich A. b.1899-d.1971, w/ Berga A., n/t Henrietta, Fred &
Arthur Falk

NW FALK Henrietta b.1871-d.1952, "Mother" w/ Fred, n/t Berga A.,
Erich A. & Arthur Falk

NW FALK Fred b.1870-d.1950, "Father" w/ Henrietta, n/t Berga A., Erich
A. & Arthur Falk

NW FALK Arthur b.1Dec1894-d.9Aug1895, n/t Henrietta, Fred, Berga A.,
& Erich A. Falk

NW PAGENKOP Bessie b.1895-d.1981, w/ William Pagenkop, Eastern
Star symbol

NW PAGENKOP William b.1896-d.1952, w/ Bessie Pagenkop, Masonic symbol

NW SETTE James A. b.1887-d.1934, w/ Isabel Sette

NW SETTE Isabel b.1888-d.1969, w/ James A. Sette

NW MEIER Laura b.1896-d.1975, w/ Arthur Meier

NW MEIER Arthur b.1893-d.1957, w/ Laura Meier

NW MARGGRAFF Louisa (RICKERT) b.17Dez1859-d.7Oct1900, "Mutter" n/t Edward & Herman R. Marggraff

NW MARGGRAFF Edward b.4Mar1884-d.7Jul1903, n/t Louisa & Herman R. Marggraff*

NW MARGGRAFF Herman R. b.19Sep1851-d.18Aug1887, "Vater" n/t Louisa & Edward Marggraff

NW HAKE Eda L. b.1899-d.1982, w/ Melvin D. Hake

NW HAKE Melvin D. b.1897-d.1955, w/ Eda L. Hake

NW OELSTROM Earl O. b.25Apr1923-d.28Jan1967, "Wis. CPL 472 AIR SVC GP AAF WWII"

NW HEMBROOK Alice S. d.25Jan1967, "Our Mother" only one date

NW FARMER Fred W. b.1930-d.1974, w/ Marie M. & Fred H. Farmer

NW FARMER Fred H. b.1901-d.1975, w/ Marie M. & Fred W. Farmer

NW FARMER Marie M. b.1905-d.1981, w/ Fred H. & Fred W. Farmer

NW CARPENTER John B. b.7Jan1924-d.6Aug1980, "CAPT. US ARMY"

NW ODEGAARD Esther M. b.1889-d.1958, w/ Harold T. Odegaard

NW ODEGAARD Harold T. b.1895-d.1986, w/ Esther M. Odegaard

NW HOADLEY Leonora A. b.1893-d.1978, w/ George L. Hoadley, Eastern Star symbol

NW HOADLEY George L. b.1884-d.1962, w/ Leonora S. Hoadley, Masonic symbol

NW PASHEK Betty b.1893-d.1958, w/ John Pashek

NW PASHEK John b.1891-d.1960, w/ Betty Pashek

NW HARDER Lynn M. b.1950-d.no date, w/ Marie A. & Harold J. Harden

NW HARDER Marie A. b.1912-d.1992, w/ Lynn M. & Harold J. Harden

NW HARDER Harold J. b.1913-d.1997, w/ Lynn M. & Marie A. Harden

NW ULNESS Lyman D. b.29Apr1930-d.21Oct1971, "Wis. PVT HQ CO 23 INF"

NW SMITH Marilyn L. b.7Jan1942-d.8Sep1966,

NW KRUEGER Murriel L. b.1904-d.1983, w/ Harvey C. Krueger

NW KRUEGER Harvey C. b.1903-d.1975, w/ Murriel L. Krueger

NW PATTERSON Edward b.1865-d.1941, w/ Lorena M. Patterson

NW PATTERSON Lorena M. b.1874-d.1947, w/ Edward Patterson

NW CHATFIELD Theo. E. b.13Dec1840-d.14Jul1911, "CO. 1. 4 U.S.C.1." dates from cemetery records, military stone; Theo enlisted in the army in Racine 1 Jan 1864, he was in the 1st Cavalry Co. K, deserted[36]

NW MAHONEY May b.1869-d.1931

NW RICKERT Edward J. b.6Aug1854-d.15Jan1892, "Father"

NW HAMME Annie b.1867-d.1922, "Mother"

NW RICKERT Mathilda b.24Apr1831-d.21Mar1912, n/t Christoph Rickert, old stone lying flat

NW RICKERT Christoph b.3Mai1832-d.17Mai1920, n/t Mathilda Rickert, old stone lying flat

NW SPRAGUE Valerie L. b.1958-d.1981, "Daughter"

NW YANG Chue Cha b.6May1955-d.7Aug1983

NW XIONG Lee Hang b.1949-d.1984

NW YANG Xia b.1973-d.1981

NW KOON Sam'l d.4Feb1881, 51y; "CO. K. 1st WIS. H? A?" no dates, military stone, GAR mkr; death date and age from cemetery records; Samuel was living in Wauwatosa when he enlisted in the army on 22 Sept 1864, he was Mustered Out 26 Jun 1865. There was also a Justus Koon with the identical enlistment information except he enlisted on 20 Sept 1864[37]

NW KUSWA Minnie b.1875-d.1949, w/ Max R. Kuswa

NW KUSWA Max R. b.1874-d.1947, w/ Minnie Kuswa

NW STANFORD Lester A. b.30Sep1874-d.10Jan1875, w/ George A., Edward, Baby & Barbara S. Stanford & James & Agnes Stewart

NW STANFORD George A. b.6Sep1859-d.28Sep1878, w/ Lester A., Edward, Baby & Barbara S. Stanford & James & Agnes Stewart

NW STANFORD Baby b.7Oct1878-d.7Oct1878, w/ Lester A., George A, Edward & Barbara S., Stanford & James & Agnes Stewart

NW STANFORD Edward b.7Mar1822-d.29Jan1902, w/ Lester A., George A, Baby & Barbara S. Stanford & James & Agnes Stewart

NW STANFORD Barbara S. b.11Aug1833-d.9May1902, w/ Lester A., George A, Baby & Edward Stanford & James & Agnes Stewart

NW STEWART James b.8Sep1808-d.27Sep1873, w/ Agness Stewart, George A., Baby, Lester A., Edward & Barbara S. Stanford

NW STEWART Agness b.22Sep1811-d.11Feb1873, w/ James Stewart, George A., Baby, Lester A., Edward & Barbara S. Stanford

NW HOWIE Kelsie C. b.7Mar1878-d.28Jul1878, n/t David W. & Adelaide Howie

NW HOWIE David W., Jr. b.1874-d.1954, "Beloved Husband of Adelaide Howie" n/t Kelsie C. & Adelaide Howie

---

36 *Roster of Wisconsin Volunteers, War Of The Rebellion, 1861-1865*

37 *Roster of Wisconsin Volunteers, War Of The Rebellion, 1861-1865*

NW HOWIE Adelaide b.1876-d.1945, "Beloved Wife of Will Howie" n/t Kelsie C. & David W. Howie

NW LUCAS Ruth (TANNER) b.1911-d.1978

NW KELLOGG Alonzo F. b.1840-d.1920, w/ Harriet N., Henry, Harry, Lewis, Lamira & Orlando F. Kellogg *

NW KELLOGG Harriet Newell b.1840-d.1925, "w/o A. F. Kellogg" w/ Alonzo F., Henry, Harry, Lewis, Lamira & Orlando F. Kellogg

NW KELLOGG Henry b.no date-d.no date, "s/o A. F. & H. N. Kellogg" w/ Alonzo F., Harriet N., Harry, Lewis, Lamira & Orlando F. Kellogg; no cemetery record

NW KELLOGG Harry b.no date-d.no date, "s/o A. F. & H. N. Kellogg" w/ Alonzo F., Harriet N., Henry, Lewis, Lamira & Orlando F. Kellogg; no cemetery record

NW KELLOGG Lewis b.1813-d.1889, w/ Alonzo F., Harriet N., Henry, Harry, Lamira & Orlando F. Kellogg

NW KELLOGG Lamira b.1819-d.1894, "w/o Lewis Kellogg" w/ Alonzo F., Harriet N., Henry, Harry, Lewis & Orlando F. Kellogg

NW KELLOGG Orlando F. b.1844-d.1864, "s/o Lewis & Lamira Kellogg; A Member of Co B First Wis. Heavy Arty" w/ Alonzo F., Harriet N., Henry, Harry, Lewis & Orlando F. Kellogg: Orlando ensisted 3 Aug 1863, he was a Corp., he died 12 Mar 1864 in Lexington, KY of disease[38]

NW STORMA Elizabeth b.1892-d.1995, "Mother" this would make her about 103 years old

NW LELAND Charles W. d.23Nov1843, "s/o C & M Leland; 39y" n/t Mary A. & Charles Leland & Harriet S. Collins

NW LELAND Mary A. d.15Sep1873, "87y 4m 11d" n/t Charles W. & Charles Leland & Harriet S. Collins

NW LELAND Charles d.4May1841, "61y 6m" n/t Charles W. & Mary A. Leland & Harriet S. Collins; broken, hard to read *

NW COLLINS Harriet S. d.26Aug1842, "20y 8m, w/o E. R. Collins, d/o Charles & Mary Leland", n/t Charles W., Charles & Mary A. Leland

NW HART Sarah Winchester b.1808-d.19Jul1841, "32y; 1st w/o Charles Hart, Founder of Wauwatosa, d/o Charles & Mary Leland"; n/t Charles W., Charles & Mary Leland; marker installed by Edward Wilkomen

NW SHUMWAY P. J. b.11Dec1810-d.3Mar1863, w/ Mary G., Margaret, Harriet E. & Alfred Shumway & Michael Gibson; stone badly worn

NW SHUMWAY Mary Gibson b.30Jan1812-d.25Mar1896, w/ P.J., Margaret, Harriet E. & Alfred Shumway & Michael Gibson; stone badly worn

38 Roster of Wisconsin Volunteers, War Of The Rebellion, 1861-1865

NW SHUMWAY Margaret b.7Dec1839-d.10Sep1941, w/ P.J., Mary G., Harriet E. & Alfred Shumway & Michael Gibson; stone badly worn

NW SHUMWAY Harriet E. b.11Aug1843-d.2Apr1846, w/ P.J., Mary G., Margaret & Alfred Shumway & Michael Gibson; stone badly worn

NW SHUMWAY Alfred b.5Apr1847-d.8Apr1857, w/ P.J., Mary G., Margaret & Harriet E. Shumway & Michael Gibson; stone badly worn

NW BEVIER Martha Jane b.1834-d.1871, "w/o W. D. Bevier"

NW TANNER Lilah F. b.1890-d.1942, "w/o Chas. Tanner" n/t Charles M. Tanner

NW TANNER Charles M. b.1883-d.1979, n/t Lilah F. Tanner

NW EGGERT Viola b.1899-d.1943

NW HARTWELL Ford P. b.1890-d.1944, w/ Helen M. Hartwell

NW HARTWELL Helen M. b.1892-d.1957, w/ Ford P. Hartwell

NW HOCK Edward b.1881-d.1915

NW DITTMAR Henrietta b.1856-d.1941, "Mother" n/t Christian & Oscar J. Dittmar

NW DITTMAR Christian b.1852-d.1924, "Father" n/t Henrietta & Oscar J. Dittmar

NW DITTMAR Oscar J. b.29Aug1879-d.29Sep1879, n/t Henrietta & Christian Dittmar

NW GILLIAN Thomas C. d.31Jan1947, "Son" n/t June A. & Walter H. Gillian; only one date

NW GILLIAN June A. b.6Jun1920-d.26Jan1993, "Mother" n/t Thomas C. & Walter H. Gillian

NW GILLIAN Walter H. b.30Sep1919-d.no date, "Father" n/t Thomas C. & June A. Gillian

NW BENNETT Harry G. b.1867-d.1937

NW ROE Charlotte B. b.1878-d.1899

NW BENNETT Babes d.5Jul1885, n/t Charlie, Catherine & Henry D. Bennett

NW BENNETT Charlie b.no date-d.no date, n/t Babes, Catherine & Henry D. Bennett; probably died about 1885

NW BENNETT Catherine b.1828-d.1917, n/t Henry D., Babes & Charlie Bennett

NW BENNETT Henry D. b.1824-d.1914, n/t Catherine, Babes & Charlie Bennett

NW KRUGER Emma b.25Feb1893-d.14Aug1893, in William Lehmann plot

NW LEHMANN William F. b.4Feb1871-d.6Mar1895, n/t W., August G., & Annie A. L. Lehmann & Emma Kruger

NW LEHMANN W. b.22Mar1881-d.21Jun1887, "Mother" n/t Wiliam F., August G., & Annie A. L. Lehmann & Emma Kruger

NW LEHMANN August G. b.22Sep1864-d.9Jun1886, n/t Wiliam F., W., & Annie A. L. Lehmann & Emma Kruger

NW LEHMANN Annie A. L. b.7Apr1867-d.11May1884, n/t Wiliam F., W., & August G. Lehmann & Emma Kruger

NW KOEPSEL Julius b.17Jul1830-d.29Sep1906, "Hier Ruht in Gott"

NW WEBER Isabel M. b.1908-d.1975, w/ Earl C. Weber

NW WEBER Earl C. b.1910-d.1990, w/ Isabel M. Weber

NW ROGERS Jeremiah b.1842-d.1932, w/ Harriet, n/t Mother, Earl F. & Minnie Rogers

NW ROGERS Mother b.no date-d.no date, n/t Jeremiah, Harriet, Earl F. & Minnie Rogers; possibly Harriet, 2nd stone?

NW ROGERS Earl F. b.1884-d.1929, "Father" n/t Jeremiah, Harriet, Mother & Minnie Rogers

NW ROGERS Minnie b.1884-d.1961, "Mother" n/t Jeremiah, Harriet, Mother & Earl F. Rogers

NW ROGERS Harriet b.1847-d.1913, w/ Jeremiah, n/t Minnie, Mother & Earl F. Rogers

NW DEARSLEY Eleanor K. b.1906-d.1992, w/ Edward L., n/t Anna J., Caroline, Walter, John W. and other Dearsleys

NW DEARSLEY Edward L. b.1901-d.1995, w/ Eleanor K., n/t Anna J., Caroline, Walter, John W. and other Dearsleys

NW DEARSLEY Anna J. b.1899-d.1930, n/t Eleanor K., Edward L., Caroline, Walter, John W. and other Dearsleys

NW DEARSLEY Caroline b.1873-d.1936, n/t Eleanor K., Edward L., Anna J., Walter, John W. and other Dearsleys

NW DEARSLEY Walter b.1865-d.1953, n/t Eleanor K., Edward L., Anna J., Caroline, John W. and other Dearsleys

NW DEARSLEY Robert b.23May1930-d.28May1930, "Baby" n/t Eleanor K., Edward L., Anna J., Caroline, John W. and other Dearsleys; dates from cemetery records

NW DEARSLEY John W. b.1817-d.1875, n/t Eleanor K., Edward L., Anna J., Janet C., Henry D. and other Dearsleys

NW DEARSLEY Janet Coulthard b.1842-d.1900, n/t Eleanor K., Edward L., John W., Jennie, Henry D. and other Dearsleys

NW DEARSLEY Henry D. b.1864-d.1926, n/t Eleanor K., Edward L., John W., Jennie, Janet C. and other Dearsleys

NW DEARSLEY Jennie b.1860-d.1938, n/t Eleanor K., Edward L., John W., Henry D., Janet C. and other Dearsleys

NW BRANT John F. b.5Jun1775-d.26Jan1861, "Father" n/t J. G. & Martha Brant & Estella M. & Edwin C. Watkins

NW BRANT J. G. b.3Nov1809-d.17Mar1875, n/t John F. w/ Martha Brant & Estella M. & Edwin C. Watkins

NW BRANT Martha b.16Sep1816-d.3Jan1896, n/t John F. w/ J. G. Brant & Estella M. & Edwin C. Watkins

NW WATKINS Estella M. b.1879-d.1900, w/ Edwin C. Watkins & J. G. & Martha Brant, n/t John F. Brant

NW WATKINS Edwin C. b.1874-d.1926, w/ Estella M. Watkins & J. G. & Martha Brant, n/t John F. Brant

NW HART Thomas W. b.1835-d.1904, n/t Thomas B., Nancy B., Florence B., Kate L. & Jesse Hart & others; Hart family plot *

NW HART Thomas Benjamin b.1800-d.1887, n/t Thomas W., Nancy B., Florence B., Kate L. & Jesse Hart & others; Hart family plot; Thomas B. Hart was an early settler of Wauwatosa, he was the brother of Charles Hart and an influential citizen of Wauwatosa.[39]

NW HART Nancy Boyden b.1805-d.1884, n/t Thomas W., Thomas B., Florence B., Kate L. & Jesse Hart & others; Hart family plot

NW HART Florence B. b.1884-d.1952, n/t Thomas W., Thomas B., Nancy B., Kate L. & Jesse Hart & others; Hart family plot

NW HART Kate L. b.1850-d.1936, n/t Thomas W., Thomas B., Nancy B., Florence B. & Jesse Hart & others; Hart family plot

NW HART Jesse b.1850-d.1913, n/t Thomas W., Thomas B., Nancy B., J. W. C., J. W. C., Florence B.& Kate L.Hart & others; Hart family plot

NW GODFREY Isabel Hart b.1833-d.1915, n/t Thomas W., Thomas B., Nancy B., Florence B.& Kate L.Hart & others; Hart family plot

NW BOYDEN Elizabeth b.1811-d.1899, n/t Thomas W., Thomas B., Nancy B., Florence B.& Kate L.Hart & others; Hart family plot *

NW HART William Beylor b.1844-d.1847, "stone has only W.B.H." n/t Thomas W., Thomas B., Nancy B., Florence B.& Kate L.Hart & others; Hart family plot

NW HART J. W. C. b.no date-d.no date, "stone has only J.W.C." n/t Thomas W., Thomas B., Nancy B., Florence B.& Kate L.Hart & others; Hart family plot; probably a baby

NW MILLER Marguerite H. b.1889-d.1965, n/t Thomas W., Thomas B., Nancy B., J. W. C., W. B. H., Florence B.& Kate L.Hart & others; Hart family plot

NW MULLER Louise M. b.25Oct1866-d.28Oct1927, n/t Emilie T., Herman A., Minna F., Albert, Bernhard & Ernst J. Muller

NW MULLER Emilie T. b.4Jun1862-d.11Nov1930, n/t Louise M., Herman A., Minna F., Albert, Bernhard & Ernst J. Muller

NW MULLER Herman A. b.24Aug1851-d.8Feb1917 Berkeley, Cal., n/t Louise M., Emilie T., Minna F., Albert, Bernhard & Ernst J. Muller

---

39 The Heritage of a Community, page 1

NW MULLER Minna F. b.15Apr1858-d.22Oct1917, n/t Louise M., Emilie T., Herman A., Albert, Bernhard & Ernst J. Muller

NW MULLER Albert d.1864, w/ Bernhard, n/t Louise M., Emilie T., Herman A., Minna F., & Ernst J. Muller; only one date

NW MULLER Bernhard d.1889, w/ Albert, n/t Louise M., Emilie T., Herman A., Minna F., & Ernst J. Muller; only one date

NW MULLER Ernst J. b.23Jan1853-d.22Apr1937, n/t Louise M., Emilie T., Herman A., Minna F., Albert & Bernhard Muller

NW WERNER Wilhelm b.17Jun1869-d.3Mar1890

NW JUNG Henrietta Laura b.10Sep1899-d.9Aug1900, n/t Louis & Sophia Jung, no last name on stone only Laura; name from cemetery records

NW JUNG Louis b.31Mar1836-d.4Jan1919, "In Memory of" w/ Sophia Jung, n/t Laura Jung

NW JUNG Sophia b.31Dec1839-d.18Oct1929, "In Memory of" w/ Louis Jung, n/t Laura Jung

NW WICHNER Charles A. b.12Oct1868-d.3Dec1893, "Father" w/ Ida B. Wichner

NW WICHNER Ida Bower b.21Jan1869-d.22Jun1926, "Mother" w/ Charles A. Wichner

NW MÜLLER Bernhard b.11Nov1822-d.9Apr1888, n/t Wilhelmine B. Müller, Louise M., Emilie T., Herman A., Bernhard & other Mullers & August & Magdalina Braune

NW MÜLLER Wilhelmine (BRAUNE) b.2Apr1828-d.28May1905, n/t Bernhard Müller, Louise M., Emilie T., Herman A., Bernhard & other Mullers & August & Magdalina Braune

NW BRAUNE August b.29Nov1799-d.15Nov1893, n/t Magdalina Braune & Bernhard & Wilhelmine B. Müller

NW BRAUNE Magdalina b.3Oct1801-d.28Sep1886, n/t August Braune & Bernhard & Wilhelmine B. Müller

NW DAVIS Dawson Alan b.16Feb1938-d.10Apr1986, n/t Anna A. Davis & Peter E. Zellmer

NW DAVIS Anna Arnold b.25Mar1939-d.no date, n/t Dawson A. Davis, w/ Peter E. Zellmer

NW ZELLMER Peter Ernest b.21Aug1941-d.23Oct1989, n/t Dawson A. w/ Anna A. Davis

NW WERNER Emilie b.1877-d.1946, "Mother" w/ Friedrich Werner

NW WERNER Friedrich b.1879-d.1951, "Father" w/ Emilie Werner

NW GOODALE John C. III b.14Mar1925-d.4Nov1948

NW HILL Annis Avery b.13Apr1796-d.25May1885, D.A.R. plaque placed by Maunesha Chapter, at the dedication of the plaque the following information was given "Annis Avery Hill, for whom this chapter is named, was born in Enfield, Conneticut on April 13, 1796. She was the oldest daughter of Jonathan Avery and Pamila Fox Avery. Her father was a Private in a Minute Man Company in 1775, and an Orderly Sergeant in the Infantry in 1776, of the Revolutionary War. At the age of 19 on Christmas Day, 1815 Annis married Caleb Hill and moved to Massachusetts. To this union were born eight children. The youngest daughter died as a young child. The oldest daughter married Thomas Riddle and they moved to Wauwatosa in 1835. Caleb Hill passed away in 1842, leaving Annis a widow at age 44. Two years later, with her six sons (the youngest age 7), she traveled by covered wagon to Wauwatosa, joining her daughter and son-in-law on July 3, 1844."

NW RIDDLE Thomas b.1816-d.1869 (see also Riddell), w/ Adaline, n/t Samuel Riddle; Thomas M. Riddle was an early settler of Wauwatosa, he came to Wauwatosa in 1835 where he operated a tavern in his log building. He later purchased the Little Red Store from Dr. Levi Halsted for a grocery store. The store became the village post office and in 1861 Thomas was appointed postmaster.[40]

NW RIDDLE Adaline b.1820-d.1909, w/ Thomas, n/t Samuel Riddle

NW RIDDLE Samuel d.8Aug1851, "82y" n/t Thomas & Adaline Riddle; Samuel was in the Revolutionary War, he is shown on a Revolutionary War Soldier burial chart at the Milwaukee County Historical Society. The 1850 US Census for Wauwatosa, Milwaukee Co., Wis. pg. 486, dwelling 64, family 64, line 4 shows Samuel Riddle age 81, farmer, born in Mass., other members of his household are Thomas M. Riddle, age 34, farmer b. Mass.; A. A., female age 30, born Mass.; E. H., female age 8, born Wis.; and T. M., male age 4, born Wis.

NW DARROW Alden Stephen b.1824-d.1889, w/ Caroline H. & Mabel H. Darrow

NW DARROW Caroline Hall b.1828-d.1915, w/ Alden S. & Mabel H. Darrow

NW DARROW Mabel H. b.1861-d.1952, w/ Alden S. & Caroline H. Darrow

NW LEES Ella A. b.1884-d.1974, w/ Clone E. Lees

NW LEES Clone E. b.1883-d.1947, w/ Ella A. Lees

NW TRAY Sarah P. b.1903-d.1985, "Mother" n/t Steuart E. Tray

NW TRAY Steuart E. b.1904-d.1948, "Father" n/t Sarah P. Tray

NW CRANDALL Louise F. b.29Jun1899-d.31Jan1990,

NW BECKER Lucille M. b.1921-d.no date, "married 7Apr1945" w/ Donald J. Becker

---

40 The Heritage of a Community, page 6

NW BECKER Donald J. b.1922-d.1996, "married 7Apr1945" w/ Lucille M. Becker

NW HILDEBRAND Therese (BRAUNE) b.10Oct1831-d.10Mar1886, n/t Louis Hildebrand

NW HILDEBRAND Louis b.17Nov1819-d.10Jul1902, n/t Therese Hildebrand

NW MUSKAT Carl b.11Nov1855-d.10Oct1942, "Husband" w/ Emma Muskat

NW MUSKAT Emma b.15Nov1861-d.2Sep1940, "Wife" w/ Carl Muskat

NW PIETSCH Ida J. b.1865-d.1958, w/ Ferd, n/t Edna F. Pietsch

NW PIETSCH Ferd b.1864-d.1948, w/ Ida J., n/t Edna F. Pietsch

NW PIETSCH Edna Frida b.1894-d.1982, n/t Ida J. & Ferd Pietsch

NW HINRICHSEN Henry b.10Feb1826-d.12Mar1914, "Husband" w/ Amelie Hinrichsen

NW HINRICHSEN Amelie b.28Oct1851-d.11Sep1935, w/ Henry Hinrichsen

NW HORLE Clara C. b.16Apr1892-d.26Oct1966, n/t Clara & W. Arthur Horle, poss a second stone

NW HORLE Clara b.1892-d.1966, "Wife" n/t Clara C., w/ W. Arthur Horle

NW HORLE W. Arthur b.1884-d.1950, "Husband" n/t Clara C., w/ Clara Horle

NW GLANERT Ulricka b.1864-d.1942, "Mother"

NW CLAPP Grace b.1859-d.1879, n/t Harriet P., Henry, & Emma C. Watner

NW WATNER Harriet P. b.1846-d.1883, n/t Henry & Emma C. Watner & Grace Clapp

NW WATNER Henry b.1844-d.1913, n/t Harriett P. & Emma C. Watner & Grace Clapp

NW WATNER Emma C. b.1848-d.1932, n/t Harriett P. & Henry Watner & Grace Clapp

NW KRIEG Barbara Jean b.12Mar1966-d.2Oct1971

NW TEMPLE Anna M. b.1865-d.1948, w/ Henry S. Temple may be in Clarissa & Samuel Riddell plot

NW TEMPLE Henry S. b.1857-d.1942, w/ Anna M. Temple may be in Clarissa & Samuel Riddell plot

NW TAYLOR Mary E. b.1859-d.1949, n/t William G. Taylor may be in Clarissa & Samuel Riddell plot

NW TAYLOR William G. b.1856-d.1915, n/t Mary E. Taylor may be in Clarissa & Samuel Riddell plot

NW SMITH Elisabeth S. d.27May1865, "w/o E. C. Smith; 44y" w/ Erastus C. & Louisa J. Smith

NW SMITH Erastus C. b.1May1817-d.15Oct1884, w/ Elisabeth S. &
Louisa J. Smith

NW SMITH Louisa J. d.28Aug1889, "51y 11m 12d" w/ Elisabeth S. &
Erastus C. Smith

NW BROWN Hiram M. d.17Feb1851, "s/o S & S L Brown; 5y 6m 5d" n/t
Sylvester, Susan M., David C., Charles C., & William M. Brown;
cemetery show his age as 54

NW BROWN Sylvester b.1814-d.1886, w/ Hiram M., Susan M., David C.,
Charles C., & William M. Brown

NW BROWN Susan M. b.1819-d.1884, w/ Hiram M., Sylvester, David C.,
Charles C., & William M. Brown

NW BROWN David C. b.1858-d.1912, w/ Hiram M., Sylvester, Susan M.,
Charles C., & William M. Brown

NW BROWN Charles C. b.1837-d.1865, w/ Hiram M., Sylvester, Susan
M., David C., & William M. Brown

NW BROWN William M. b.1839-d.1861, w/ Hiram M., Sylvester, Susan
M., David C., & Charles C. Brown

NW CLAPP Luther Rev. b.1819-d.1894, "Father; For Half a Century Rev.
and Mrs. Clapp Labored in This Vicinity", n/t Harriet P. Clapp

NW CLAPP Harriet P. b.1819-d.1895, "Mother" n/t Luther Clapp

NW KUTZNER Ethel b.1872-d.1922

NW STEDMAN Sally Boardman b.1782-d.1852, "w/o Simeon Stedman"

NW RIDDELL Clarissa b.1812-d.1890, n/t Samuel Riddell; see William
G. Taylor and Henry S. Temple

NW RIDDELL Samuel b.1812-d.1888, n/t Clarissa Riddell; see William
G. Taylor and Henry S. Temple

NW CHRISTMAN Holly R. b.8Nov1943-d.5Jul1985, "Beloved Wife &
Mother"

NW BUCK Elfrieda b.9Dec1885-d.11May1973,

NW NOWACKI Cynthia K. b.5May1966-d.23Jun1986, "Dear Daughter of
Dale & Shirley"

NW WINTERS William b.12Jun1834-d.8Oct1890, "Father"

NW GILLIGAN Linda F. b.1909-d.no date, w/ Earl P. Gilligan

NW GILLIGAN Earl P. b.1903-d.1966, w/ Linda F. Gilligan

NW SARGEANT Harry W. b.28Jan1887-d.9Nov1970, "Wis Captain
Medical Corps WWI" n/t Katherine M. Sargeant

NW SARGEANT Katherine M. b.18Aug1900-d.23Aug1983, n/t Harry W.
Sargeant

NW BOHLMAN Walter b.1899-d.1966

NW BLODGETT Mary L. b.1861-d.1942, n/t Frank S., Ella A., Lamira A.
& Elisha L. Blodgett; old stones lying flat

NW BLODGETT Frank S. b.22Apr1852-d.29Oct1879, "s/o Elisha & Lamira Blodgett" n/t Mary L., Ella A., Lamira A. & Elisha L. Blodgett; old stones lying flat

NW BLODGETT Ella A. b.13Mar1858-d.19Dec1872, "d/o Elisha & Lamira Blodgett" n/t Mary L., Frank S., Lamira A. & Elisha L. Blodgett; old stones lying flat

NW BLODGETT Lamira A. b.6Sep1831-d.30Jul1901, "w/o Elisha L. Blodgett" n/t Mary L., Frank S., Ella A. & Elisha L. Blodgett; old stones lying flat

NW BLODGETT Elisha L. d.12Dec1863, "In His 43 Year" n/t Mary L., Frank S., Ella A. & Lamira A. Blodgett; old stones lying flat

NW MOWER Edmund C. d.8Apr1877, "In His 29 year" w/ Harriet E., Arba B., Caroline B. & Augustus B. Mower & Agnes M. & Thos. J. Rice

NW MOWER Harriet E. b.1849-d.1928, w/ Edmund C., Arba B., Caroline B. & Augustus B. Mower & Agnes M. & Thos. J. Rice

NW MOWER Arba B. b.2Jun1811-d.30Oct1888, w/ Edmund C., Harriet E., Caroline B. & Augustus B. Mower & Agnes M. & Thos. J. Rice, his birthplace on the 1860 U.S. Census is shown as N.Y.

NW MOWER Caroline B. b.9Jun1815-d.13Mar1900, w/ Edmund C., Harriet E., Arba B. & Augustus B. Mower & Agnes M. & Thos. J. Rice, her birthplace on the 1860 U.S. Census is shown as N.Y.

NW MOWER Infant d.21Jul1845, "d/o Arba B & Caroline Mower, 6w" w/ Edmund C., Harriet E., Arba B. & Caroline B. & Augustus B. Mower & Agnes & Thomas Rice

NW MOWER Augustus B. d.21Aug1864, "Sergt. in the 7th Wis Bat. Killed in an Attack on Memphis Tenn. in the 22nd Year of His Life" w/ Edmund C., Harriet E., Arba B. & Caroline B. Mower & Agnes M. & Thos. J Rice; Augustus was living in Wauwatosa when he enlisted in the army on 12 Sep 1861[41]

NW RICE Thos. J. b.1868-d.1905, w/ Edmund C., Harriet E., Arba B., Augustus B. & Caroline Mower & Agnes M. Rice

NW RICE Agnes M. b.1842-d.1908, w/ Edmund C., Harriet E., Arba B., Augustus B. & Caroline Mower & Thos. J. Rice

NW BOHNERT Harriett Rice b.1875-d.1961, w/ Otto H. Bohnert, n/t Thos. J. & Agnes M. Rice & Mower Family

NW BOHNERT Otto H. b.1881-d.1957, w/ Harriett R. Bohnert, n/t Thos. J. & Agnes M. Rice & Mower family

NW BLODGETT Augustus b.25Mar1787-d.16May1861, n/t Lucy P. & Lucy M. Blodgett

---

41 Roster of Wisconsin Volunteers, War Of The Rebellion, 1861-1865

NW BLODGETT Lucy P. b.29Sep1791-d.19Jan1868, "w/o Augustus Blodgett" n/t Augustus & Lucy M. Blodgett, stone broken at death date, dates from cemetery records.

NW BLODGETT Lucy M. d.11May1843, "25y 3m 19d" n/t Augustus & Lucy P. Blodgett, stone chipped

NW WILTERDING Ethel C. b.1893-d.1984, n/t Forest Wilterding

NW WILTERDING Forest b.1891-d.1965, n/t Ethel C. Wilterding

NW SHULTIS Dorothy E. b.1914-d.1971, w/ Arthur H. Shultis

NW SHULTIS Arthur H. b.1907-d.1979, w/ Dorothy E. Shultis; Masonic symbol

NW MEYERS Joseph b.1894-d.1977, "Father"

NW SCHEINBEIN Elimor M. b.1911-d.1994

NW WOOD George L. b.17Aug1917-d.24Sep1996, n/t Dorothy A. Wood; Masonic symbol

NW WOOD Dorothy A. b.23Oct1919-d.7Feb1974, n/t George L. Wood

NW HAASCH Ruth E. b.1908-d.no date, w/ Clarence L. Haasch

NW HAASCH Clarence L. b.1899-d.1989, w/ Ruth E. Haasch

NW De SWARTE Florence b.1906-d.1999, w/ Keith B. De Swarte

NW De SWARTE Keith B. b.1904-d.1971, w/ Florence De Swarte

NW RUECKENWALD George b.1918-d.1985, "PFC US ARMY WWII"

NW HILTERBRICK Eva M. b.1900-d.1991, w/ Maurice I. Hilterbrick

NW HILTERBRICK Maurice I. b.1893-d.1980, w/ Eva M. Hilterbrick

NW GRABOWSKY Robert M. b.17May1937-d.16Apr1968

NW HARWOOD Forest H. b.5Jul1820-d.9Jun1876, w/ Eunice A. Harwood

NW HARWOOD Eunice A. b.6Jun1822-d.23Jul1879, "w/o F. H. Harwood" w/ Forest H. Harwood

NW BLODGETT Freddy d.25Feb1859, "c/o I. A. & Caroline Blodgett; 2y" w/ Caroline, Mary, Caroline, n/t Chester A. & Caroline Blodgett

NW BLODGETT Caroline d.10Sep1866, "c/o I. A. & Caroline Blodgett; 2y 7m" w/ Freddy, Mary, Caroline, n/t Chester A. & Caroline Blodgett

NW BLODGETT Mary d.19Feb1851, "w/o I. A. Blodgett; 22y 8m 15d" w/ Caroline, Freddy, Caroline, n/t Chester A. & Caroline Blodgett

NW BLODGETT Caroline b.1842-d.23May1867, "w/o I. A. & Caroline Blodgett; 26y" w/ Freddy, Mary, Caroline, n/t Chester A. & Caroline Blodgett

NW BLODGETT Caroline b.1852-d.1893, "Mother" n/t Freddy, Mary, Caroline, Chester A. & Caroline Blodgett

NW BLODGETT Chester A. b.1827-d.1906, "Father" n/t Freddy, Mary, Caroline, Caroline & Caroline Blodgett

NW CURTIS Dell b.1878-d.1971, n/t Clara C., Perley J., Leonard S., & Elisabeth Curtis

NW CURTIS Clara C. b.1869-d.1905, n/t Dell, w/ Perley J., Leonard S., & Elisabeth Curtis

NW CURTIS Perley J. b.1871-d.1903, n/t Dell, w/ Clara C., Leonard S., & Elisabeth Curtis

NW CURTIS Leonard S. b.27Jan1815-d.27Mar1881, n/t Dell, w/ Clara C., Perley J., & Elisabeth Curtis

NW CURTIS Elisabeth b.20Feb1833-d.18Mar1917, "w/o L.S. Curtis" n/t Dell, w/ Clara C., Perley J., & Leonard S. Curtis

SEOE KAMRATH Caroline b.14Aug1895-d.7Oct1929, "Daughter" n/t Emma, F., W., Frank A., Emma & Albert Kamrath

SEOE KAMRATH Emma b.9Jun1899-d.8Feb1982, "Daughter" n/t Caroline, F., W., Frank A., Emma & Albert Kamrath

SEOE KAMRATH F. b.27Jan1831-d.6Jan1909, "Father" n/t Caroline, Emma, W., Frank A., Emma & Albert Kamrath, cemetery records show his name as Gottlieb Kamrath

SEOE KAMRATH W. b.26Apr1838-d.25Apr1918, "Mother" n/t Caroline, Emma, F., Frank A., Emma & Albert Kamrath, cemetery records show her name as Wilhelmina Kamrath

SEOE KAMRATH Frank A. b.22Sep1862-d.11Feb1928, n/t Caroline, Emma, F., W., Emma & Albert Kamrath

SEOE KAMRATH Emma b.17Apr1866-d.6Oct1935, n/t Caroline, Emma, F., W., Frank A. & Albert Kamrath

SEOE KAMRATH Albert b.12Apr1897-d.1Mar1898, n/t Caroline, Emma, F., W., Frank A. & Emma Kamrath

SEOE LEE Ossian F. b.1846-d.1906, n/t Rollie R. Lee

SEOE LEE Rollie R. d.12May1901, "26y" n/t Ossian F. Lee

SEOE VANS Helen b.1920-d.no date, w/ Christ Vans

SEOE VANS Christ b.1904-d.1978, w/ Helen Vans

SEOE SEUBERTH Lydia b.7Jul1896-d.22May1904, n/t Lillian Seuberth; drowned in Quarry; obituary in Abstracts of Wauwatosa News *

SEOE SEUBERTH Lillian b.15Sep1890-d.22May1904, n/t Lydia Seuberth; drowned in Quarry; obituary in Abstracts of Wauwatosa News *

SEOE PAUL Wilhelmina (MINDEMANN) b.8Nov1877-d.3Sep1954, "Mama" n/t Valentine & Wilhelmine Paul

SEOE PAUL Wilhelmine (HINTZ) b.8Aug1859-d.16Feb1901, n/t Valentine & Wilhelmina Paul

SEOE PAUL Valentine b.8Feb1861-d.15Dec1916, "Papa" n/t Wilhelmine & Wilhelmina Paul

SEOE ZEMKE Carl b.24Jul1849-d.14Mar1897, "Vater" n/t Augusta, Flora, Susie & Hermann Zemke

SEOE ZEMKE Augusta b.4Dec1850-d.20Mar1931, "Mutter" n/t Carl, Flora, Susie & Hermann Zemke

SEOE ZEMKE Flora b.5Mai1823-d.7Dec1911, n/t Carl, Augusta, Susie & Hermann Zemke

SEOE ZEMKE Susie b.1878-d.1951, n/t Carl, Augusta, Flora, w/ Hermann Zemke

SEOE ZEMKE Hermann b.1874-d.1957, n/t Carl, Augusta, Flora, w/ Susie Zemke

SEOE ANVELINK Edward b.1876-d.1940

SEOE BOUCHA Joseph b.1873-d.1948, n/t Clara Boucha

SEOE BOUCHA Clara b.1893-d.1970, n/t Joseph Boucha

SEOE MEYER Peter Fred W. b.1863-d.1904, "Father" w/ Mary Meyer

SEOE MEYER Mary b.1868-d.1953, "Mother" w/ Peter Fred W. Meyer

SEOE WEBER Herman b.1865-d.1895, "Father" w/ Annie, n/t William H. & Olive F. Weber

SEOE WEBER Annie b.1865-d.1936, "Mother" w/ Herman, n/t William H. & Olive F. Weber

SEOE WEBER William H. b.1889-d.1965, n/t Herman & Annie w/ Olive F. Weber

SEOE WEBER Olive F. b.1893-d.1946, n/t Herman & Annie w/ William H. Weber

SEOE VOGEL Albert b.24May1863-d.24Mar1906, "Father" n/t Anna, Caroline & Christian Vogel

SEOE VOGEL Anna b.5Dec1873-d.21Jul1893, "w/o Otto Vogel" n/t Albert, Caroline & Christian Vogel

SEOE VOGEL Caroline b.2Feb1827-d.25Apr1916, "Mother" n/t Albert, Anna & Christian Vogel

SEOE VOGEL Christian b.25Apr1825-d.8Sep1909, "Father" n/t Albert, Anna & Caroline Vogel

SEOE HALBERT Edwin G. b.1872-d.1920, n/t Mary J. Halbert

SEOE HALBERT Mary J. b.1886-d.1970, n/t Edwin G. Halbert

SEOE JAMES George A., Jr. b.1879-d.1897, n/t Julia Y. & George A. James

SEOE JAMES Julia Y. b.1842-d.1916, n/t George A. & George A. James

SEOE JAMES George A. b.1839-d.1917, n/t Julia Y. & George A. James

SEOE BARFORTH Dorothy (KRULL) b.9Jun1832-d.20Nov1903, n/t Ernst Barforth *

SEOE BARFORTH Ernst b.22May1831-d.22Mar1907, n/t Dorothy Barforth; Ernst enlisted in the army in Milwaukee 5 Oct 1861, he transfered from Co. H to the 9th Infantry, he was mustered out 3 Dec 1864, his term expired[42]

SEOE BARNEKOW Frederick b.12Dec1826-d.16May1904, w/ Mary, n/t Ernst, Augusta, John & Hannah Barnekow; Frederick enlisted in the army in Wauwatosa 15 Aug 1862, he was in the 24th Infantry Co. E, taken prisoner at Stone River; discharged 12 May 1862, disability in 1863[43] *

SEOE BARNEKOW Mary (HOLZ) b.21Nov1823-d.20Feb1904, w/ Frederick, n/t Ernst, Augusta, John & Hannah Barnekow *

SEOE BARNEKOW Ernst b.17Nov1865-d.10Jan1906, "Papa" n/t Frederick, Mary, Augusta, John & Hannah Barnekow

SEOE BARNEKOW Augusta b.22Aug1866-d.29Nov1938, "w/o John Barnekow" n/t Frederick, Mary, Ernst, John & Hannah Barnekow

SEOE BARNEKOW John b.6Nov1855-d.13Dec1921, "Father" n/t Frederick, Mary, Ernst, Augusta & Hannah Barnekow

SEOE BARNEKOW Hannah (MILLER) b.5Dec1858-d.26Feb1914, "Mother" n/t Frederick, Mary, Ernst, Augusta & John Barnekow

SEOE ANDERSON Virginia Edna b.13Feb1920-d.14Jan1998

SEOE BECHTEL Hilda b.1896-d.1916, "Mother" w/ Edwin Bechtel; cemetery does not have a her listed in their records

SEOE BECHTEL Edwin b.1889-d.1942, w/ Hilda Bechtel

SEOE MEYERPETER Elizabeth b.27Mai1837-d.24Apr1932, "Mutter" n/t John Meyerpeter

SEOE MEYERPETER John b.26Mar1838-d.31Aug1912, "Vater" n/t Elizabeth Meyerpeter

SEOE ANVELINK Amelia (MEYERPETER) b.1880-d.1927, "Mother" n/t Elizabeth & John Meyerpeter

SEOE FORRER Rudolph b.11Dec1829-d.10Jan1902

SEOE HINTZ Arthur b.23Nov1898-d.23Nov1898, n/t Maria Hintz

SEOE HINTZ Maria b.5Feb1905-d.15Apr1906, n/t Arthur Hintz

SEOE ZIEMER Henry b.8Dec1843-d.2Nov1907, w/ Bertha & Clara Ziemer

SEOE ZIEMER Bertha b.26Aug1850-d.23Jul1941, w/ Henry & Clara Ziemer

SEOE ZIEMER Clara b.3Oct1890-d.18Nov1918, w/ Henry & Bertha Ziemer

SEOE SCHWESTER Johanna Hoffman b.2Oct1888-d.27Apr1915, n/t Julius & Emilie M. Hoffmann, Johann & Henritte Marquardt & Wilhelmine & Martha Redzinski; Marquardt plot

SEOE HOFFMANN Julius b.22Oct1849-d.11Jun1894, "Papa" n/t Emilie M. Hoffmann, Johann & Henritte Marquardt & Wilhelmine & Martha Redzinski & Johanna H. Schwester

---

SEOE HOFFMANN Emilie (MARQUARDT) b.4Apr1862-d.16Mar1912, "Mamma" n/t Julius Hoffmann, Johann & Henritte Marquardt & Wilhelmine & Martha Redzinski & Johanna H. Schwester

SEOE MARQUARDT Johann b.8Mar1833-d.10Mar1914, "Vater" n/t Julius & Emilie Hoffmann, & Henritte Marquardt & Wilhelmine & Martha Redzinski & Johanna H. Schwester

SEOE MARQUARDT Henritte (sic) b.21Jan1833-d.24Jan1929, "Mutter" n/t Julius & Emilie Hoffmann, Johann Marquardt, Johanna H. Schwester & Wilhelmine & Martha Redzinski

SEOE REDZINSKI Wilhelmine (MARQUARDT) b.8Mar1858-d.6Sep1886, "Mamma" n/t Julius & Emilie Hoffmann, Johann & Henritte Marquardt, Johanna H. Schwester & Martha Redzinski; Marquardt plot

SEOE REDZINSKI Martha b.27Jun1886-d.15Aug1887, n/t Julius & Emilie Hoffmann, Johann & Henritte Marquardt, Johanna H. Schwester & Wilhelmine Redzinski; Marquardt plot

SEOE SIEGERT Herman E. b.1871-d.1924, "Father" n/t Willie, Benjamin E. & Friedrike Siegert; Masonic symbol

SEOE SIEGERT Willie b.20Apr1875-d.14Jun1893, n/t Herman E., Benjamin E. & Friedrike Siegert

SEOE SIEGERT Benjamin E. b.15Jan1843-d.16Jul1911, "Vater" n/t Herman E., Willie & Friedrike Siegert; GAR mkr; Benjamin enlisted the army in Milwaukee, he was in the 45th Infantry, Mustered Out 17 Jul 1865 [44]

SEOE SIEGERT Friederike b.1840-d.1928, "Mother" n/t Herman E., Willie & Benjamin E. Siegert

SEOE BONDURANT Emma b.18Jan1870-d.31Jan1955, n/t George, Harry & Lois Bondurant

SEOE BONDURANT George b.1866-d.1926, "Father" n/t Emma, Harry & Lois Bondurant

SEOE BONDURANT Harry b.29Dec1905-d.21Aug1991, n/t Emma, George & Lois Bondurant

SEOE BONDURANT Lois b.18Aug1905-d.22Jul1947, n/t Emma, George & Harry Bondurant

SEOE BIEDENBENDER Alvina b.1903-d.1966, "Mother" w/ August H., George A., Emilie M. & Emilie Biedenbender

SEOE BIEDENBENDER August H. b.1899-d.1975, "Father" w/ Alvina, George A., Emilie M. & Emilie Biedenbender

SEOE BIEDENBENDER George A. b.1866-d.1957, "Father" w/ Alvina, August H., Emilie M. & Emilie Biedenbender

SEOE BIEDENBENDER Emilie M. b.1870-d.1958, "Mother" w/ Alvina, August H., George A. & Emilie Biedenbender

SEOE BIEDENBENDER Emilie b.1906-d.1927, "Daughter" w/ Alvina, August H., George A. & Emilie M. Biedenbender

SEOE BENEZIS John P. b.1910-d.1976

SEOE VOULGARES Maria b.1886-d.1976, n/t Louis Voulgares

SEOE VOULGARES Louis b.1892-d.1970, n/t Maria Voulgares

SEOE MAAS Florella M. b.1912-d.1969, w/ William C. Maas, Sr.

SEOE MAAS William C., Sr. b.1901-d.1976, w/ Florella M. Maas

SEOE HINTZ Johann F. b.3Feb1819-d.4Mai1891, n/t Friedericke Hintz

SEOE HINTZ Friedericke (BISCHOFF) b.10Mai1827-d.23Apr1902, n/t Johann F. Hintz

SEOE ANVELINK Elmer J. b.1890-d.1937, "Father" n/t Frieda, Henry J., Hattie E. & Addie Anvelink

SEOE ANVELINK Frieda b.1892-d.1985, "Mother" n/t Elmer J., Henry J., Hattie E. & Addie Anvelink

SEOE ANVELINK Henry J. b.17Apr1861-d.7Nov1902, "Papa" n/t Elmer J., Frieda, Hattie E. & Addie Anvelink

SEOE ANVELINK Hattie E. b.8Aug1865-d.3Aug1902, n/t Elmer J., Frieda, Henry J. & Addie Anvelink

SEOE ANVELINK Addie b.13Nov1887-d.19Jan1888, n/t Elmer J., Frieda, Henry J. & Hattie E. Anvelink

SEOE BECHTEL Alma b.1882-d.1966, n/t Frank, Erwin, Ella, Annie & Jacob, Jr. Bechtel

SEOE BECHTEL Frank d.3Jul1936, "Wisconsin SGT 210 Engrs." n/t Alma, Erwin, Ella, Annie & Jacob, Jr. Bechtel

SEOE BECHTEL Erwin b.3May1891-d.14Oct1891, n/t Alma, Frank, Ella, Annie & Jacob, Jr. Bechtel, stone very worn

SEOE BECHTEL Ella b.27Feb1888-d.?Sep1888, n/t Alma, Frank, Erwin, Annie & Jacob, Jr. Bechtel, stone very worn

SEOE BECHTEL Annie b.1868-d.1942, "Mother" n/t Alma, Frank, Erwin, Ella & Jacob, Jr. Bechtel

SEOE BECHTEL Jacob Jr. b.1856-d.1924, "Father" n/t Alma, Frank, Erwin, Ella & Annie, Bechtel

SEOE WAGNER Paul C. b.7Sep1921-d.11Apr1997, "SGT US ARMY WWII"

SEOE ZEMKE Lillian F. b.1908-d.no date, "Mother" w/ Herman G. Zemke

SEOE ZEMKE Herman G. b.1905-d.1997, "Father" w/ Lillian Zemke

SEOE KELLAWAY Eva M. b.1885-d.1974, w/ William E. Kellaway

SEOE KELLAWAY William E. b.1885-d.1969, w/ Eva M. Kellaway

SEOE APOSTOLOS John b.1893-d.1970, "Beloved Husband From Wife, Anna"

SEOE ANVELINK Orville E. b.1919-d.1998, "Father" w/ Mildred & Robert Anvelink

SEOE ANVELINK Mildred b.1913-d.1975, "Mother" w/ Orville E. & Robert Anvelink

SEOE ANVELINK Robert b.1946-d.1953, "Son" w/ Orville E. & Mildred Anvelink

SEOE MEYER Christian b.1865-d.1913, "Father" w/ Emma, n/t Henry, Anna, John, Lucinda & Rosa May Meyer

SEOE MEYER Emma b.1871-d.1961, "Mother" w/ Christian, n/t Henry, Anna, John, Lucinda & Rosa May Meyer

SEOE MEYER Henry b.16Feb1825-d.30Apr1887, "Father" n/t Christian, Emma, Anna, John, Lucinda & Rosa May Meyer

SEOE MEYER Anna b.1827-d.1896, "Mother" n/t Christian, Emma, Henry, John, Lucinda & Rosa May Meyer

SEOE MEYER John b.1858-d.1939, n/t Christian, Emma, Henry, Anna, Lucinda & Rosa May Meyer

SEOE MEYER Lucinda b.1861-d.1933, "w/o John Meyer" n/t Christian, Emma, Henry, Anna, John & Rosa May Meyer

SEOE MEYER Rosa May b.1887-d.1943, n/t Christian, Emma, Henry, Anna, John & Lucinda Meyer

SEOE SOUTHERN John b.1895-d.no date, "32 Degree" w/ Jessie Southern, Masonic symbol

SEOE SOUTHERN Jessie b.1895-d.1974, w/ John Southern, Eastern Star symbol

SEOE NASS Caroline b.11Mai1855-d.5Mar1929, n/t Katherine & Wm. Nass

SEOE NASS Katherine b.3Mar1826 Schweitz-d.8Jul1904, "Mutter" n/t Caroline & Wm. Nass

SEOE NASS Wm. b.20Jan1820 Nassau-d.27Oct1901, "Vater" n/t Caroline & Katherine Nass

SEOE FREDRICH Walter b.20Sep1897-d.5Oct1897, "s/o Otto & Caroline Fredrich" n/t Edwin J., Caroline, Otto, Minna, John & Therese Fredrich & Herman Fraedrich

SEOE FREDRICH Edwin J. b.1900-d.1972, n/t Walter, Caroline, Otto, Minna, John & Therese Fredrich & Herman Fraedrich

SEOE FREDRICH Caroline b.1871-d.1940, w/ Otto, n/t Walter, Edwin J., Minna, John & Therese Fredrich & Herman Fraedrich

SEOE FREDRICH Otto b.1869-d.1941, w/ Caroline,n/t Walter, Edwin J., Minna, John & Therese Fredrich & Herman Fraedrich

SEOE FREDRICH Minna b.26Apr1826-d.9Feb1897, "Mutter" n/t Otto, Caroline, Walter, Edwin J., John & Therese Fredrich & Herman Fraedrich

SEOE FREDRICH John b.7Oct1832-d.25Jul1915, "Vater" n/t Otto, Caroline, Walter, Edwin J., Minna & Therese Fredrich & Herman Fraedrich

SEOE FREDRICH Therese b.17Dez1860-d.1Jan1931, n/t Otto, Caroline, Walter, Edwin J., Minna & John Fredrich & Herman Fraedrich

SEOE FRAEDRICH Herman b.23Nov1863-d.11Nov1890, n/t Otto, Caroline, Walter, Edwin J., Minna, John & Therese Fredrich; Fraedrich is probably the original spelling of the name

SEOE GRAPENGIESER Martha V. b.3Feb1884-d.3Mar1974, w/ Henry F. Grapengieser

SEOE GRAPENGIESER Henry F. b.15Dec1871-d.17Sep1948, w/ Martha V. Grapengieser

SEOE VEIT Walter b.22Jan1892-d.7Feb1968

SEOE LAWRENCE Mary A. b.1874-d.1970

SEOE BARTELS Meta b.1896-d.1969, w/ Bernard Bartels

SEOE BARTELS Bernard b.1894-d.1969, w/ Meta Bartels

SEOE CHRISTENSEN Harold E. b.7Jun1926-d.9Feb1967, "Wis TEC 5 213 FIELD ARTY BN WWII"

SEOE GRAPENGIESER Charles b.1Nov1869-d.16Aug1948, n/t Mary & Fred Grapengieser & S. & H. Klamfoot

SEOE GRAPENGIESER Mary b.22Apr1848-d.19Sep1918, "Mother" n/t Charles & Fred Grapengieser & S. & H. Klamfoot; first name from cemetery records

SEOE GRAPENGIESER Fred b.17Mar1845-d.1Apr1915, "Father" n/t Charles & Mary Grapengieser & S. & H. Klamfoot; first name from cemetery records

SEOE KLAMFOOT S. b.1819-d.1894, n/t Charles, Fred & Mary Grapengieser, w/ H. Klamfoot

SEOE KLAMFOOT H. b.1821-d.1891, n/t Charles, Fred & Mary Grapengieser, w/ S. Klamfoot

SEOE TARASOFF Evelyn A. b.1910-d.1990, w/ Peter N. Tarasoff

SEOE TARASOFF Peter N. b.1911-d.1976, w/ Evelyn A. Tarasoff

SEOE SCHNEIDER John b.19Feb1836-d.19Aug1915, "Father; CORPL CO C 24 WISCONSIN INF"; John was living in Waukesha when he enlisted in the army 5 Aug 1862, he was Mustered Out 10 Jun 1865[45]

SEOE VOGEL Otto d.14Jan1867, "s/o F. C. & Caroline Vogel; 1y 10m" old stone, lying flat, next two stones illegible

---

SEOE LORENZ Annetta b.1883-d.1968, w/ Max Lorenz

SEOE LORENZ Max b.1882-d.1961, w/ Annetta Lorenz

SEOE HIBBARD Mary A. b.1832-d.1901, w/ Jared A. Hibbard; the stone is a rock that is carved

SEOE HIBBARD Jared A. b.1828-d.1903, w/ Mary A. Hibbard; the stone is a rock that is carved

SEOE HARTZ Sterling J. b.1897-d.1944, w/ Alice M. Hartz

SEOE HARTZ Alice M. b.1899-d.no date, w/ Sterling J. Hartz; cemetery has no record of her burial.

SEOE DRACH Adam b.24Apr1845-d.10Feb1891, "Vater" n/t Margaretha & Adam Drach

SEOE DRACH Margaretha b.17Dec1844-d.7Mai1900, "Mutter" n/t Adam & Adam Drach

SEOE DRACH Adam b.26Oct1870-d.3Sep1943, "Sohn" n/t Adam & Margaretha Drach

SEOE MURPHY Clara A. b.1896-d.1974, w/ John W. Murphy

SEOE MURPHY John W. b.1895-d.1963, w/ Clara A. Murphy

SEOE KOENIGKRAMER Ernest H. b.1892-d.1974, "US NAVY" n/t Viola Koenigkramer

SEOE KOENIGKRAMER Viola b.1895-d.1976, n/t Ernest H. Koenigkramer

SEOE HARDTKE Maria (BRAASCH) b.28Jan1820-d.8Feb1898, n/t Christian Hardtke & Wilhelmina & August Hartke

SEOE HARDTKE Christian b.9Nov1814-d.8Jun1894, n/t Maria B. Hardtke & Wilhelmina & August Hartke

SEOE HARTKE Wilhelmina b.1857-d.1922, "Mother" n/t Maria B. & Christian Hardtke & August Hartke

SEOE HARTKE August b.1856-d.1929, n/t Maria B. & Christian Hardtke & Wilhelmina Hartke

SEOE SCHEIBE Emma b.1877-d.1913, n/t Martha Grebel & Emilie A., Alfred, Gustav, Wilhelmina & Amelia Scheibe

SEOE GREBEL Martha (SCHEIBE) b.1875-d.1908, n/t Emma, Emilie A., Alfred, Gustav, Wilhelmina & Amelia Scheibe *

SEOE SCHEIBE Emilie A. b.17Dec1848-d.9Oct1891, n/t Emma, Alfred, Gustav, Wilhelmina & Amelia Scheibe & Martha S. Grebel

SEOE SCHEIBE Alfred b.1887-d.1888, n/t Emma, Emilie A., Gustav, Wilhelmina & Amelia Scheibe & Martha S. Grebel

SEOE SCHEIBE Gustav b.1839-d.1914, "Father" n/t Emma, Emilie A., Alfred, Wilhelmina & Amelia Scheibe & Martha S. Grebel *

SEOE SCHEIBE Wilhelmina b.1845-d.1926, "Mother" n/t Emma, Emilie A., Alfred, Gustav & Amelia Scheibe & Martha S. Grebel

SEOE SCHEIBE Amelia b.1868-d.1953, n/t Emma, Emilie A., Alfred, Gustav & Wilhelmina Scheibe & Martha S. Grebel

SEOE HARTUNG Martha b.1878-d.1937, w/ Oscar, Arthur & Helene Hartung

SEOE HARTUNG Oscar b.1883-d.1936, w/ Martha, Arthur & Helene Hartung; the number 32 in a triangle, probably 32nd degree mason

SEOE HARTUNG Arthur b.1854-d.1887, w/ Martha, Oscar & Helene Hartung

SEOE HARTUNG Helene b.1854-d.1931, w/ Martha, Oscar & Arthur Hartung

SEOE SCHNEIDER Catherine b.9Jul1945-d.11Jul1918

SEOE WHITE Walter d.12Apr1877, "Native of Connaght Parish of (rest illegible)" 61y

SEOE MARTIN James M. b.4Jan1810-d.23Nov1885, "Father" n/t Susan B. & James W. Martin & Julia M. Wheeler

SEOE MARTIN Susan B. b.30Sep1820-d.13Dec1904, "Mother" n/t James M. & James W. Martin & Julia M. Wheeler

SEOE MARTIN James W. b.6Nov1846-d.22Jul1899, n/t Susan B. & James W. Martin & Julia M. Wheeler; GAR mkr

SEOE WHEELER Julia Martin d.24Oct1941, n/t Susan B., James M. & James W. Martin

SEOE HAHN Gertrude Bunker d.1Aug1932, "w/o Walter G. Hahn"

SEOE KOEPP Harold G. H. b.22Sep1911-d.21Nov1983, "US ARMY" n/t Anna, August, Gerhard, Norman, & Arthur H. Koepp

SEOE KOEPP Norman b.1907-d.1976, "Son" n/t Anna, August, Gerhard, Harold G. H. & Arthur H. Koepp

SEOE KOEPP Arthur H. b.1917-d.1942, n/t Anna, August, Gerhard, Harold G. H. & Norman Koepp

SEOE KOEPP Anna b.1882-d.1961, "Mother" w/ August & Gerhard, n/t Harold G. H., Arthur H. & Norman Koepp

SEOE KOEPP August b.1882-d.1959, "Father" w/ Anna & Gerhard, n/t Harold G. H., Arthur H. & Norman Koepp

SEOE KOEPP Gerhard b.1908-d.1987, "Son" w/ Anna & August, n/t Harold G. H., Arthur H. & Norman Koepp

SEOE BRADEE Charles G. b.1885-d.1952, "Father" n/t Lillian H. Bradee

SEOE BRADEE Lillian H. b.1886-d.1975, "Mother" n/t Charles G. Bradee

SEOE BORTZ Friedrich Johann b.22Sep1822-d.24Apr1909, "Vater" n/t Dorothea L. M. Bortz

SEOE BORTZ Dorothea Louisa (MALLOW?) b.22Sep1825-d.15Jan1900, "Mutter" n/t Friedrich J. Bortz

SEOE GOERLITZ Otto b.1861-d.1945, "Dad" n/t Johanna & Arthur Goerlitz

SEOE GOERLITZ Johanna b.11Sep1861-d.10Jul1906, "w/o Otto Goerlitz" n/t Otto & Arthur Goerlitz; first name from cemetery records, not on stone

SEOE GOERLITZ Arthur b.4Apr1893-d.5Apr1900, n/t Otto & Johanna Goerlitz

SEOE BENDER Isabella M. b.1896-d.1975, w/ Otto J. Bender

SEOE BENDER Otto J. b.1891-d.1982, w/ Isabella M. Bender

SEOE ZILLMER Josephina b.1873-d.1894, n/t Louise Zillmer

SEOE ZILLMER Louise b.1898-d.1899, "Baby of Michael & Mary Zillmer" n/t Josephina Zillmer

SEOE GASTEL Walter b.1884-d.1928, n/t Carl & Cordelia Gastel

SEOE GASTEL Carl b.1854-d.1894, n/t Walter & Cordelia Gastel

SEOE GASTEL Cordelia b.1855-d.1936, n/t Walter & Carl Gastel

SEOE ZILLMER August b.1831-d.1916, w/ Magdalene, n/t Carl, Michael, Josephine & Michael Zillmer

SEOE ZILLMER Magdalene b.1834-d.1902, w/ August, n/t Carl, Michael, Josephine & Michael Zillmer

SEOE ZILLMER Carl b.1885-d.1892, "c/o Michael & Mary Zillmer" w/ Michael & Josephine, n/t August & Magdalene & Michael Zillmer

SEOE ZILLMER Michael b.1891-d.1892, "c/o Michael & Mary Zillmer" w/ Carl & Josephine, n/t August & Magdalene & Michael Zillmer

SEOE ZILLMER Josephine b.1890-d.1892, "c/o Michael & Mary Zillmer" w/ Carl & Michael, n/t August & Magdalene & Michael Zillmer

SEOE ZILLMER Michael b.1791-d.1884, n/t Carl, Michael, Josephine, August & Magdalene Zillmer

SEOE HELBING Amalia b.1832-d.1910

SEOE BOLDT Carolina b.15Sep1860-d.26Dec1890, "Mutter, DIE STUNDE SCHLAGT ES IST DER LAUF VOLLBRACHT LEBT WOHL, LEBT WOHL, IHR LIEBEN! GUTE NACHT." on other side of stone is Hedwig Boldt

SEOE BOLDT Hedwig b.5Sep1890-d.13Jan1891, on other side of stone is Carolina Boldt

SEOE ? Vater b.10Sep1827-d.23Aug1889, "Vater" n/t Mutter, Emma, Lisetta & Franz ? & Clarence Ladwig; no last name on stone

SEOE ? Mutter b.11Feb1833-d.28Mar1903, "Mutter" n/t Vater, Emma, Lisetta & Franz ? & Clarence Ladwig; no last name on stone

SEOE ? Emma b.no date-d.no date, "age 3m" n/t Vater, Mutter, Lisetta & Franz ? & Clarence Ladwig; no last name on stone

SEOE ? Lisetta b. no date-d. no date, "6m" n/t Vater, Mutter, Emma & Franz ? & Clarence Ladwig; no last name on stone

SEOE ? Franz b. no date-d. no date, "1y 4m 12d" n/t Vater, Mutter, Emma & Lisetta ? & Clarence Ladwig; no last name on stone

SEOE LADWIG Clarence b.26Oct1892-d.26Feb1898, n/t Vater, Mutter, Emma, Lisetta & Franz

SEOE HENDERSON Gladys b.1902-d.1970, w/ Richard D. Henderson

SEOE HENDERSON Richard D. b.1898-d.1971, w/ Gladys Henderson

SEOE WORCESTER Sarah W. b.1905-d.1976, w/ George E. Worcester

SEOE WORCESTER George E. b.1907-d.1971, w/ Sarah W. Worcester

SEOE GOERLITZ Paul b.1876-d.1945, n/t Emilie & Ludwig Goerlitz

SEOE GOERLITZ Emilie b.1Nov1833-d.17Jul1908, "Mutter" n/t Paul & Ludwig Goerlit

SEOE GOERLITZ Ludwig b.3Feb1833-d.23Feb1893, "Vater" n/t Paul & Emilie Goerlitz

SEOE JACOBS George J. b.1875-d.1961, w/ Emma A. Jacobs, 9 pointed star on stone

SEOE JACOBS Emma A. b.1895-d.1971, w/ George J. Jacobs, 9 pointed star on stone

SEOE DUNNING Ann Gildea b.1915-d.no date, "m/o Vivian, Joyce, Doug & Lloyd," Physical Therapist" n/t Lloyd C. Dunning

SEOE DUNNING Lloyd Clark b.7Sep1948-d.6Jul1973, "WIS. SP 4 US ARMY" n/t Ann G. Dunning

SEOE ENGEL Clara A. b.1888-d.1975, w/ August J. Engel

SEOE ENGEL August J. b.1885-d.1968, w/ Clara A. Engel

SEOE BLUM Frank M. b.1880-d.1906, "Father" n/t Louis, Augusta & Henrietta Blum

SEOE BLUM Louis b.1839-d.1892, "Father" n/t Frank M., Augusta & Henrietta Blum

SEOE BLUM Augusta b.1838-d.1925, n/t Frank M., Louis & Henrietta Blum

SEOE BLUM Henrietta b.17Dec1865-d.10Sep1895, n/t Frank M., Louis & Augusta Blum

SEOE WINZENRIED Sophia b.1852-d.1912, "Mother" w/ Samuel & John Winzenried

SEOE WINZENRIED Samuel b.1842-d.1889, "Father" w/ Sophia & John Winzenried

SEOE WINZENRIED John b.1876-d.1952, "Son" w/ Sophia & Samuel Winzenried

SEOE EBERHARDT Minnie C. (GARVENS) b.4Dec1866-d.19Dec1914, n/t Julius J. H., Mary, Otto W. & Carl O. Garvens

SEOE GARVENS Julius J. H. b.5Oct1865-d.25Jul1907, n/t Mary, Otto W. & Carl O. Garvens & Minnie C. Eberhardt

SEOE GARVENS Mary b.24Oct1847-d.10Sep1901, "w/o O. Garvens" w/ Otto W., n/t Julius J. H. & Carl O. Garvens & Minnie C. Eberhardt

SEOE GARVENS Otto W. b.19Mar1839-d.7Oct1895, w/ Mary, n/t Julius J. H. & Carl O. Garvens & Minnie C. Eberhardt

SEOE GARVENS Carl O. b.11Mar1800-d.12Nov1889, n/t Mary, Otto W. & Julius J. H. Garvens & Minnie C. Eberhardt

SEOE WOLLERS Louisa b.1865-d.1935, "Mother" n/t Arthur Wollers

SEOE WOLLERS Arthur b.1898-d.1915, n/t Louisa Wollers

SEOE PHILLIPS Esther E. b.1860-d.1955, "Wife" n/t Nelson J. Russel C., Russel E., Caroline A., John & Julia P. Phillips

SEOE PHILLIPS Nelson J. b.1865-d.1910, "Husband" n/t Esther E., Russel C., Russel E., Caroline A., John & Julia P. Phillips

SEOE PHILLIPS Russel C. Watt b.1861-d.1Mar1890, "29y" n/t Esther E., Nelson J., Russel E., Caroline A., John & Julia P. Phillips

SEOE WATT Russel C. Watt b.1861-d.1890, n/t Esther E., Nelson J., Russel E., Caroline A., John & Julia P. Phillips

SEOE PHILLIPS Russel E. b.1827-d.1909, "Father" n/t Esther E., Nelson J., Russel C., Caroline A., John & Julia P. Phillips

SEOE PHILLIPS Caroline A. b.1829-d.1911, n/t Esther E., Nelson J., Russel C., Russel E., John & Julia P. Phillips

SEOE PHILLIPS John b.1855-d.1933, n/t Esther E., Nelson J., Russel C., Russel E.,Caroline A.& Julia P. Phillips

SEOE PHILLIPS Julia Pelton b.20Jul1859-d.25Jan1913, "Mamma" n/t Esther E., Nelson J., Russel C., Russel E., Caroline A. & John Phillips

SEOE ZIMMERMAN George b.1856-d.1931, "Father" n/t Minnie Zimmerman & Stella L. H. Zimmermann

SEOE ZIMMERMAN Minnie b.1862-d.1932, "Mother" n/t George Zimmerman & Stella L. H. Zimmermann

SEOE ZIMMERMANN Stella L. H. b.2Jun1892-d.19Feb1893, n/t George & Minnie Zimmerman

SEOE VAN DE WOESTYNE Helen B. b.6Jun1896-d.6Jun1987, "Beloved Wife" n/t Royal S., Nellie & Herbert Van De Woestyne

SEOE VAN DE WOESTYNE Royal S. b.5Jan1892-d.4Aug1967, "WIS. CAPT SIGNAL CORPS WWI" n/t Helen B., Nellie & Herbert Van De Woestyne

SEOE VAN DE WOESTYNE Nellie b.1865-d.1942, "Mother" w/ Herbert, n/t Helen B. & Royal S. Van De Woestyne

SEOE VAN DE WOESTYNE Herbert b.1861-d.1952, "Father" w/ Nellie, n/t Helen B. & Royal S. Van De Woestyne

SEOE HORSCH Rosella M. b.1923-d.1998,

SEOE LENZ William A. b.1905-d.1990, "m. 1928" w/ Lillian E. Lenz

SEOE LENZ Lillian E. b.1907-d.no date, "m. 1928" w/ William A. Lenz

SEOE MANN Louise B. b.1910-d.1996, w/ Gilbert A. Mann

SEOE MANN Gilbert A. b.1908-d.1993, w/ Louise B. Mann

SEOE HEDTKE Alma b.16Aug1885-d.13May1912, n/t Augusta, Gustave, Martha M., Lena & William Hedtke

SEOE HEDTKE Augusta b.1859-d.1932, w/ Gustave, Martha M., Lena & William, n/t Alma Hedtke

SEOE HEDTKE Gustave b.1859-d.1903, w/ Augusta, Martha M., Lena & William, n/t Alma Hedtke *

SEOE HEDTKE Martha M. b.1896-d.1982, w/ Augusta, Gustave, Lena & William, n/t Alma Hedtke

SEOE HEDTKE Lena b.1896-d.1897, w/ Augusta, Gustave, Martha M. & William, n/t Alma Hedtke

SEOE HEDTKE William b.1893-d.1954, w/ Augusta, Gustave, Martha M. & Lena, n/t Alma Hedtke

SEOE McCORMICK Albert B. d.3Mar1855, "3y 3m 17d" n/t D. Arvilla & Arthur McCormick

SEOE McCORMICK D. Arvilla d.20Aug1848, "7m 23d" w/ Arthur, n/t Albert B. McCormick

SEOE McCORMICK Arthur d.3Mar1852, "2y 7m 18d" w/ D. Arvilla, n/t Albert B. McCormick

SEOE SCHMITT Matilde F. b.1908-d.1985, w/ Eugene W. Schmitt

SEOE SCHMITT Eugene W. b.1908-d.1988, w/ Matilde F. Schmitt

SEOE LEARY Nancy L. b.17Jan1941-d.20Feb1988, w/ James E. Leary; there is a nice poem on stone

SEOE LEARY James E. b.25Dec1935-d.no date, w/ Nancy L. Leary; there is a nice poem on stone

SEOE STEINER J. W. b.1866-d.1925, n/t Minnie Steiner

SEOE STEINER Minnie b.1866-d.1942, n/t J. W. Steiner

SEOE HART Mattie M. b.26Jul1859-d.4Feb1897, n/t Ann, Charles, Charles B., Anges C., Marjorie & Florence Hart

SEOE HART Ann b.1824-d.1909, "Mother, w/o Chas. Hart" n/t Mattie M., Charles, Charles B., Agnes C., Marjorie & Florence Hart *

SEOE HART Charles b.1820-d.1903, n/t Mattie M., Ann, Charles B., Agnes C., Marjorie & Florence Hart; Charles Hart was an early settler of Wauwatosa, Charles and his brother, Thomas Benjamin Hart, established a sawmill around 1838 and a grist mill around 1841, Charles established the first cemetery, his wife, Sarah was buried on a hill overlooking Wauwatosa Ave. The land was sold to Wauwatosa with the stipulation it could only be used for a "public burying ground.[46] Charles Hart and the Wheelers had a tractor company called, Hartparr Tractor Co. in Charles City, Iowa, it was the first gas tractor, ammunition was made in the factory during WWI. Charles aslo had a ranch in Montana where they were trying to find a way to increase wheat production. Lyman and Jefferson Wheeler worked on this ranch for awhile.[47]

SEOE HART Charles B. b.1857-d.1930, "Father" n/t Mattie M., Ann, Charles, Agnes C., Marjorie & Florence Hart

SEOE HART Agnes C. b.1864-d.1940, "Mother" n/t Mattie M., Ann, Charles, Charles B. Marjorie & Florence Hart *

SEOE HART Marjorie Claflin b.1893-d.1921, n/t Mattie M., Ann, Charles, Charles B. Agnes C. & Florence Hart; middle name from cemetery records

SEOE HART Florence d.3Jun1888, "2y" n/t Mattie M., Ann, Charles, Charles B. Agnes C. & Marjorie Hart, stone worn, date of death and age from cemetery records

SEOE WANDSNIDER Alvin L. d.1894, "Son" only one date

SEOE PELTON Joanna b.7Mar1831-d.5Apr1915, "Mother" n/t J. L. Pelton

SEOE PELTON J. I. d.20Apr1884, "Father; 7 WISCONSIN L.A.; 79y" n/t Joanna Pelton; J. I. was living in Wauwatosa when he enlisted in the army on 28 Aug 1862, he was a Vet. and was Mustered Out on 5 May 1865[48]

SEOE PINE Sam'l b.12Aug1793-d.4Mar1885, "4 VT. MIL. WAR 1812"

SEOE PHILLIPS Jeannie b.1887-d.1889, n/t Mary & George Phillips

SEOE PHILLIPS Mary b.1846-d.1922, n/t Jeannie & George Phillips

SEOE PHILLIPS George b.1846-d.1919, n/t Jeannie & Mary Phillips

SEOE HOPPIN Henry C. b.no date-d.no date, "1st MINN BATT'Y" n/t Lewis H. Hoppin; cemetery records do not have dates either

SEOE HOPPIN Lewis H. d.22May1846, "s/o Richard & Lydia Hoppin; 5y 11m 15d" n/t H. C. Hoppin

NEOE REDOEHL Christian b.20Aug1833-d.12Nov1904,

NEOE LUETZOW Charlotte b.1827-d.1912, w/ Henry, J. F. William, Minnie, Esther, & Louis Luetzow

NEOE LUETZOW Henry b.1815-d.1901, w/ Charlotte, J. F. William, Minnie, Esther & Louis Luetzow

NEOE LUETZOW J. F. William b.1866-d.1955, w/ Charlotte, Henry, Minnie, Esther & Louis Luetzow

---

46 The Heritage of a Community, page 1 & 6

47 courtesy of Lyman E. Wheeler

48 Roster of Wisconsin Volunteers, War Of The Rebellion, 1861-1865

NEOE LUETZOW Minnie b.1870-d.1960, w/ Charlotte, Henry, J. F.
William, Esther & Louis Luetzow
NEOE LUETZOW Esther b.1894-d.1897, w/ Charlotte, Henry, J. F.
William, Minnie & Louis Luetzow
NEOE LUETZOW Louis b.1892-d.1892, w/ Charlotte, Henry, J. F.
William, Minnie & Esther Luetzow
NEOE HINCKLEY Horace H. b.1830-d.1899, w/ Elgin F., Adelaide,
Laura A., Franklin H. & Henrieta Hinckley
NEOE HINCKLEY Elgin F. b.1887-d.1910, w/ Horace H., Adelaide,
Laura A., Franklin H. & Henrieta Hinckley
NEOE HINCKLEY Adelaid b.1865-d.1914, w/ Horace H., Elgin F., Laura
A., Franklin H. & Henrieta Hinckley
NEOE HINCKLEY Laura A. b.1833-d.1919, w/ Horace H., Elgin F.,
Adelaide, Franklin H. & Henrieta Hinckley
NEOE HINCKLEY Franklin H. b.1852-d.1923, w/ Horace H., Elgin F.,
Adelaide, Laura A. & Henrieta Hinckley
NEOE HINCKLEY Henrieta b.1867-d.1949, w/ Horace H., Elgin F.,
Adelaide, Laura A. & Franklin H. Hinckley
NEOE WILL Ida b.17Dez1875-d.19Jun1894, n/t Otto, Caroline &
Chrisreich Will; no first name on stone, name from cemetery records
NEOE WILL Otto b.6Jun1883-d.9Dez1894, n/t Ida, Caroline &
Chrisreich Will; no first name on stone, name from cemetery records
NEOE WILL Caroline b.10Mai1841-d.7Nov1924, "Mutter" n/t Ida, Otto,
& Chrisreich Will
NEOE WILL Christreich b.12Nov1833-d.9Jun1916, "Vater" n/t Ida, Otto,
& Caroline Will
NEOE BECKER Heinrich F. b.1Feb1906-d.24Mai1906, n/t Jennie, Erwin,
Anna F., Julius W., Wilhelm & Maria H. Becker
NEOE BECKER Jennie b.1896-d.1916, "Daughter" n/t Heinrich F., Erwin,
Anna F., Julius W., Wilhelm & Maria H. Becker
NEOE BECKER Erwin b.1908-d.1932, "Son" n/t Heinrich F., Jennie,
Anna F., Julius W., Wilhelm & Maria H. Becker
NEOE BECKER Anna F. (FRANZ) b.20Dec1873-d.26Dec1911, "Mutter"
n/t Heinrich F., Jennie, Erwin, Julius W., Wilhelm & Maria H. Becker
NEOE BECKER Julius W. b.27Jul1869-d.16Apr1927, "Vater" n/t
Heinrich F., Jennie, Erwin, Anna F., Wilhelm & Maria H. Becker
NEOE BECKER Wilhelm b.24Aug1838-d.11Apr1900, n/t Heinrich F.,
Jennie, Erwin, Anna F., Julius W. & Maria H. Becker
NEOE BECKER Maria (HEBEL) b.18Mai1844-d.23Sep1923, n/t
Heinrich F., Jennie, Erwin, Anna F., Julius W. & Wilhelm Becker
NEOE FOESCH Anna Hopp b.1868-d.1948, "Mother" n/t Bennett Hopp
NEOE HOPP Bennett b.1865-d.1916, "Father" n/t Anna Hopp Foesch

NEOE GENSKE Frank b.1870-d.1942, w/ Ida & Elsie Genske
NEOE GENSKE Ida b.1875-d.1953, w/ Frank & Elsie Genske
NEOE GENSKE Elsie b.1909-d.1997, w/ Frank & Ida Genske
NEOE DRESNER Louisa M. b.1878-d.1947, "Mother"
NEOE KRAUSKOPF Caroline b.1851-d.19—, w/ Henry Krauskopf; not
   in cemetery records
NEOE KRAUSKOPF Henry b.1850-d.1927, w/ Caroline Krauskopf; not
   in cemetery records
NEOE GLEICHMANN Lawrence b.26Jun1855-d.21Jul1928,
NEOE KITZROW Emelia b.1843-d.1927
NEOE SMITH John M. b.10Aug1912-d.17Aug1988, "US ARMY WWII"
NEOE ROESSL Louise E. b.1914-d.1987, n/t Emma Roessl & John M.
   and Ruth Smith
NEOE SMITH Ruth b.1924-d.no date, between Emma and Louise E.
   Roessl
NEOE ROESSL Emma b.1884-d.1949, n/t Louise E. Roessl & John M.
   and Ruth Smith
NEOE ROCHWITE Catherine b.1874-d.1941, w/ August Rochwite
NEOE ROCHWITE August b.1874-d.1956, w/ Catherine Rochwite
NEOE HENKE Carl b.18Feb1818-d.21Mar1899, "Vater" n/t Wilhelmina
   Henke
NEOE HENKE Wilhelmina b.15Aug1821-d.19Jul1904, n/t Carl Henke
NEOE DIETZ Friedaricka b.1872-d.1940, w/ Nickolaus Dietz
NEOE DIETZ Nickolaus b.1869-d.1950, w/ Friedaricka Dietz
NEOE MENGE son d.1924, "s/o Mr. & Mrs. E. Menge" only one date
NEOE FREDRICH Anna b.10Jan1894-d.30May1896, "d/o Ferdinand &
   Minnie Fredrich" n/t Arthur, Ferdinand, Wilhelmine & Elsie Fredrich
NEOE FREDRICH Arthur b.31Jul1887-d.27Apr1902, "A Little Time on
   Earth He Spent Till God For Him His Angel Sent" n/t Anna, Ferdinand,
   Wilhelmine & Elsie Fredrich
NEOE FREDRICH Ferdinand b.8Mar1855-d.2Dec1922, "Father" n/t
   Anna, Arthur, Wilhelmine & Elsie Fredrich; another stone here just
   says baby
NEOE FREDRICH Wilhelmine b.2Mar1861-d.20Aug1937, n/t Anna,
   Arthur, Ferdinand & Elsie Fredrich; another stone here just says baby
NEOE FREDRICH Elsie b.1Dec1895-d.3Dec1918, n/t Anna, Arthur,
   Ferdinand & Wilhelmine Fredrich
NEOE HAERTEL John H. b.15Mar1895-d.23Feb1967, "Son" n/t
   Catherine, Henry, Herbert M. & Minnie A. Haertel
NEOE HAERTEL Catherine b.9Nov1858-d.2Feb1930, "Mother" n/t John
   H., Henry, Herbert M. & Minnie A. Haertel

94

NEOE HAERTEL Henry b.15Jan1858-d.21Sep1902, "Father" n/t John H., Catherine, Herbert M. & Minnie A. Haertel

NEOE HAERTEL Herbert M. b.29Oct1900-d.14Sep1931, "Father" n/t John H., Catherine, Henry & Minnie A. Haertel

NEOE HAERTEL Minnie A. b.12Dec1898-d.20Nov1977, "Mother" n/t John H., Catherine, Henry & Herbert M. Haertel

NEOE WENTZEL Johann b.1817-d.Oct1881, w/ Maria, n/t Philip Wentzel

NEOE WENTZEL Maria (WENTZEL) b.7Jul1814-d.28Jun1883, w/ Johann, n/t Philip Wentzel

NEOE WENTZEL Philip b.19Sep1855-d.11Feb1879, n/t Johann & Maria Wentzel

NEOE MILLER Hannah b.1877-d.1963, w/ Paul Miller

NEOE MILLER Paul b.1876-d.1949, w/ Hannah Miller

NEOE HARTMANN Heinrich b.8Aug1811-d.11Jan1877, w/ Hanna M., n/t Marie & Carl Hartmann

NEOE HARTMANN Hanna M. b.24Jun1825-d.12Aug1854, w/ Heinrich, n/t Marie & Carl Hartmann

NEOE HARTMANN Marie b.1849-d.1934, "Mutter" n/t Heinrich, Hanna M. & Carl Hartmann

NEOE HARTMANN Carl b.1847-d.1912, "Vater" "EIN TREUES VATERHERZ HAT AUFOEHORT ZU SCHLAGEN GES TILL TIST ALL SEIN SCHMERZ VER STUMMT SIND SEINE KLAGEN DIE MUDE SEEL IST NUM DAHEIM IM VATERHAUS DIE FLEISIGEN HANDE RUHN IN STILLER KAMMER AUS." n/t Heinrich, Hanna M. & Marie Hartmann

NEOE BREDE Frederick b.24Oct1809-d.1878, n/t Wilhelmine Brede, broken at the death date

NEOE BREDE Wilhelmine b.31Dec1814-d.23Jan1891, n/t Frederich Brede

NEOE KERBER none b.1819-d.1879, "m/o J. Kerber" n/t Ida W., Emma, Lillie, Minnie, William F., Friedericke B., & Johann Kerber, not in cemetery records

NEOE KERBER Ida W. (HARTKE) b.1881-d.1962, w/ William F., n/t Emma, Lillie, no name Minnie, Friedericke B. & Johann Kerber *

NEOE KERBER William F. b.1878-d.1955, w/ Ida W., n/t Emma, Lillie, no name, Minnie, Friedericke B. & Johann Kerber *

NEOE KERBER Emma b.28Jun1871-d.15Apr1874, n/t Ida W., Lillie, Minnie, William F., Friedericke B., no name & Johann Kerber

NEOE KERBER Lillie b.12Feb1877-d.8Sep1877, n/t Ida W., Emma, Minnie, no name, William F., Friedericke B. & Johann Kerber

NEOE KERBER Minnie b.20May1874-d.10Oct1884, n/t Ida W., Emma, Lillie, no name, William F., Friedericke B. & Johann Kerber

NEOE KERBER Friedericke (BREDE) b.16Oct1849-d.25Dec1922, "Mutter" n/t Ida W., Emma, Lillie, Minnie, no name, William F., & Johann Kerber

NEOE KERBER Johann b.15Mai1844-d.28Apr1921, "Vater" n/t Ida W., Emma, Lillie, Minnie, no name, William F., & Friedericke B. Kerber

NEOE BREDE Theodore, Jr. b.30Jun1881-d.17Jan1914, "Brother" n/t Theodore & Minnie Brede

NEOE BREDE Theodore b.15Jul1852-d.21Apr1888, "Father" n/t Theodore, Jr. & Minnie Brede

NEOE BREDE Minnie b.24Sep1853-d.9Jan1885, "Mother" n/t Theodore, Jr. & Theodore Brede

NEOE SMITH Harriet B. W. b.1879-d.1978

NEOE JOHNSON Charles b.1852-d.1912

NEOE ROSE Henry b.1833 Grand Isle, VT-d.1913, "Father" n/t Howard S., Roy, Harvey E. & Clara B. Rose & Dorothy R. Taylor

NEOE TAYLOR Dorothy (ROSE) b.1897-d.1921, n/t Howard S., Roy, Harvey E., Clara B. & Henry Rose

NEOE ROSE Roy b.1903-d.1920, n/t Howard S., Harvey E., Clara B. & Henry Rose & Dorothy R. Taylor

NEOE ROSE Howard S. b.1890-d.1928, n/t Henry, Roy, Harvey E. & Clara B. Rose & Dorothy R. Taylor

NEOE ROSE Harvey E. b.1860-d.1942, n/t Henry, Roy, Howard S. & Clara B. Rose & Dorothy R. Taylor

NEOE ROSE Clara B. b.1863-d.1944, n/t Henry, Roy, Howard S. & Harvey E. Rose & Dorothy R. Taylor

NEOE BROWN Robert b.1892-d.1893, n/t Jennie, Janet & James Brown

NEOE BROWN Jennie b.1871-d.1897, n/t Robert, Janet & James Brown

NEOE BROWN Janet b.1846-d.1915, n/t Robert, Jennie & James Brown

NEOE BROWN James b.1841-d.1912, n/t Robert, Jennie & Janet Brown

NEOE BUCHOLTZ Anton E. b.9Jun1898-d.15Jan1965, w/ Roselle Bucholtz

NEOE BUCHOLTZ Roselle b.22Sep1911-d.20Jul1977, w/ Anton E. Bucholtz

NEOE MEISSNER Carl H. b.1899-d.1986, "PVT US ARMY WWI" w/ Madeline L. Meissner, 2 stones

NEOE MEISSNER Madeline L. b.1902-d.1983, w/ Carl F. Meissner

NEOE PETERSEN P. M. b.1849-d.1925

NEOE KUSSMANN Theodore b.9Nov1834-d.17Jan1926, from Alterheim Poor Home; name from cemetery records

NEOE LOHF Caroline b.1842-d.1925

NEOE FREITAG Julius b.19Jun1841-d.3Apr1922
NEOE WINKEL Fred b.1846-d.1922
NEOE CONTANT Jennie A. b.26Apr1827-d.13Jun1918
NEOE WALKER Charles A., Jr. b.2Oct1903-d.12Apr1940, n/t Norma I.
Walker
NEOE WALKER Norma I. b.15Nov1900-d.1Jun1985, n/t Charles A.
Walker, Jr.
NEOE LENTZ Emilie b.28Nov1868-d.12Oct1958, "Mutter" n/t Adolph,
Selma, Ilma & Erwin Lentz
NEOE LENTZ Adolph b.6Nov1857-d.7Apr1939, n/t Emilie, Selma, Ilma
& Erwin Lentz
NEOE LENTZ Selma b.19Jun1865-d.28Jul1895, "Mutter" n/t Emilie,
Adolph, Ilma & Erwin Lentz
NEOE LENTZ Ilma b.1903-d.1904, "Tochter" n/t Emilie, Adolph, Selma
& Erwin Lentz
NEOE LENTZ Erwin b.1899-d.1900, "Sohn" n/t Emilie, Adolph, Selma &
Ilma Lentz
NEOE SEIFERT Richard H. b.6Jun1922-d.1Nov1967, "WIS. SGT 47
BOMB GP AAF WWII"
NEOE KLEMSTEIN Jay A. b.8Sep1950-d.8Oct1967
NEOE WINIGER Frederick J. b.1906-d.1968
NEOE MARVIN Mary Matilda d.31Jan1887, "d/o J M & H E Marvin; 2y
3m"
NEOE KEEBLER Horace E. b.1883-d.1959, n/t Margaret M. Keebler;
same type stone and n/t Brown Family
NEOE KEEBLER Margaret May b.1877-d.1959, n/t Horace E. Keebler;
same type stone and n/t Brown Family
NEOE LYNDS Henry L. d.5Jan1865, "s/o H. & E. Lynds; 6y 6m 20d" "I
See a Kind Sheperd Jesus Stands With All Engaging Charm, Hark How
He Calls the Tender Lambs and Folds Them In His Arms"
NEOE GIENCKE Gottlieb b.2Oct1840-d.5Jan1920, "Vater; DER
GRUND DA ICH MICH GRÜNDE IST CHRISTUS UND SEIN BLUT",
n/t Maria, Louis & Herman Giencke
NEOE GIENCKE Maria b.24Mai1839-d.21Feb1912, "Mutter; ICH
HABE LUST ABZUSCHEI DEN UND BEI CHRISTO ZU SEIN", n/t
Gottlieb, Louis & Herman Giencke
NEOE GIENCKE Louis b.12Mar1881-d.22Jul1881, n/t Gottlieb, Maria
& Hermann Giencke
NEOE GIENCKE Hermann b.25Apr1875-d.18Aug1875, n/t Gottlieb,
Maria & Louis Giencke
NEOE TURNER Carolyn S. b.1871-d.1953, n/t Ella M., Eva & Florence
Turner

NEOE TURNER Ella M. b.1877-d.1878, n/t Carolyn S., Eva & Florence Turner

NEOE TURNER Eva b.1875-d.1876, n/t Carolyn S.,Ella M. & Florence Turner

NEOE TURNER Florence b.1880-d.1916, n/t Carolyn S., Ella M. & Eva Turner

NEOE BAHLER John b.1888-d.1895

NEOE SCHMIDT Carl b.1829-d.1914, w/ Augusta Schmidt

NEOE SCHMIDT Augusta b.1825-d.1894, "His Wife" w/ Carl Schmidt

NEOE SCHABLOW Wilhelmine F. A. (KREULL) b.broken-d.28Oct1878, n/t Wilhelm, Louisa, Louisa, August, & Louise Schablow

NEOE SCHABLOW Wilhelm b.25Oct1830-d.21Mar1901, n/t Wilhelmine, Louisa, Louisa, August & Louise Schablow

NEOE SCHABLOW Louisa (BARNDT) b.23Mar1826-d.6Jan1899, n/t Wilhelmine, Wilhelm, Louisa, August, & Louise Schablow

NEOE SCHABLOW Louisa b.5Mai1869-d.20Jun1876, n/t Wilhelmine, Wilhelm, Louisa, August, & Louise Schablow

NEOE SCHABLOW August b.29Jul1851-d.1Jul1873, n/t Wilhelmine, Wilhelm, Louisa, Louisa, & Louise Schablow

NEOE SCHABLOW Louise b.1900-d.1902, n/t Wilhelmine, Wilhelm, Louisa, Louisa, & August Schablow

NEOE DAILEY Henry d.10Jan1866, "21y" stone broken

NEOE CASSIDY Thomas Michael b.28Aug1964-d.4Apr1991, "Our Son, Our Brother"

NEOE DE BRUINE Peter b.1829-d.1893, w/ Maria, n/t Peter, Mary, Amanda & Peter A. De Bruine

NEOE DE BRUINE Maria b.1830-d.1890, w/ Peter, n/t Peter, Mary, Amanda & Peter A. De Bruine

NEOE DE BRUINE Peter b.1860-d.1935, w/ Mary, n/t Peter, Maria, Amanda & Peter A. De Bruine

NEOE DE BRUINE Mary b.1871-d.1937, w/ Peter, n/t Peter, Maria, Amanda & Peter A. De Bruine

NEOE FISCHER Ann J. b.1870-d.1955, w/ Herman J., n/t G. Fischer

NEOE FISCHER Herman J. b.1865-d.1932, w/ Ann J., n/t G. Fischer

NEOE FISCHER G. b.17Dez1892-d.12Jun1893, n/t Ann J. & Herman J. Fischer

NEOE HAND Pearl A. b.1909-d.1988,

NEOE DE BRUINE Amanda b.1883-d.1961, w/ Peter A., n/t Peter, Maria, Peter & Mary De Bruine

NEOE DE BRUINE Peter A. b.1887-d.1948, w/ Amanda, n/t Peter, Maria, Peter & Mary De Bruine

NEOE DELINGKOWSKI Maria b.7Feb1833-d.15Apr1916, w/ Friedrick
Delingkowski

NEOE DELINGKOWSKI Friedrich b.12Dec1840-d.14Jul1933, w/ Maria
Delingkowski; GAR mkr; death date from cemetery records, name in
cemetery records is Fritz

NEOE NAHS Carl b.9Nov1851-d.26Jul1916, "Uncle; WIR MUSSEN
OUR VIELE TRUBSAL INS REICH GOTTES EIGEHEN"

NEOE PETERS Helen b.1Mai1869-d.19Aug1916

NEOE PLATH Hanna b.24Apr1847-d.12Mai1920, "CHRISTUS DER IST
MEIN LEBEN STERBEN" w/ Fred Plath

NEOE PLATH Fred b.26Apr1843-d.1Mar1915, "IST MEIN GEWINN" w/
Hanna Plath

NEOE PETERSEN Ida b.26Feb1843-d.25Feb1915, "BEWEINT UNS
NICHT IHR LIEBE" w/ Peter Petersen

NEOE PETERSEN Peter b.26Aug1841-d.15Jul1919, "WIR SIERBEN
GOTT NICHT EUCH WAS WOLLTLH EUCH BETRÜBE WIR SIND
IN GOTTES REICH" w/ Ida Petersen

NEOE DORN August b.1836-d.1915, "Father"

NEOE RUEGE Wilhelm b.23Mar1830-d.5Aug1914, w/ Wilhelmine
Ruege

NEOE RUEGE Wilhelmine b.1830-d.1914, w/ Wilhelm Ruege

NEOE MARSHALL Colin K. b.1930-d.1987

NEOE LENTZ Mabel K. b.1908-d.1979, w/ Emil W. & Kenneth W. Lentz

NEOE LENTZ Emil W. b.1902-d.1981, w/ Mabel K. & Kenneth W. Lentz

NEOE LENTZ Kenneth W. b.1932-d.1993, w/ Mabel K. & Emil W. Lentz

NEOE YOB Natalie b.22Sep1902-d.9Mar1987, "Beloved Mother &
Grandmother"

NEOE SIEGEL Alma b.1887-d.1961, w/ Frank Siegel

NEOE SIEGEL Frank b.1888-d.1954, w/ Alma Siegel

NEOE WOLF Mary b.1883-d.1958, w/ Leonard Wolf

NEOE WOLF Leonard b.1882-d.1960, w/ Mary Wolf

NEOE BROWN Carl Martin b.1925-d.1984

NEOE RIECK Alfred W. b.1886-d.1951

NEOE SCHETTER Julia b.1881-d.1957

NEOE JUNG Henriette (KREILL) b.6Nov1821-d.13Mar1892, n/t
Heinrich Jung

NEOE JUNG Heinrich b.16Feb1812-d.17Oct1894, n/t Henriette Jung

NEOE SIMONS Elsie (ESCHENBURG) b.28Sep1894-d.7Sep1925, n/t
Caroline, John & William Eschenburg

NEOE ESCHENBURG Caroline b.22Aug1862-d.28Aug1918, "Mutter"
n/t John & William Eschenburg & Elsie E. Simons

NEOE ESCHENBURG John b.29Mar1858-d.29Oct1934, n/t Caroline & William Eschenburg & Elsie E. Simons

NEOE ESCHENBURG William b.25Aug1885-d.10Dec1946, n/t Caroline & John Eschenburg & Elsie E. Simons

NEOE SCHROEDER Johann b.19Feb1824-d.11Mar1883, "Vater" n/t Friedericka Schroeder

NEOE SCHROEDER Friedericka b.14Feb1826-d.18Mai1903, "Mutter" n/t Johann Schroeder

NEOE BUEGE Johann b.4Aug1844-d.18Nov1907

NEOE MOLLER Johanna b.28Feb1843-d.26Mai1908

NEOE GENZ Wilhelm b.13Sep1835-d.12Mar1909

NEOE SCHROEDER August b.25Aug1824-d.27Mar1909, "Vater"

NEOE KRIEHN Friedericka b.25Apr1831-d.8Apr1911

NEOE KAEDING Auguste b.19Sep1836-d.4Jan1912, w/ Heinrich Kaeding; inscription in ornate German script, I am not sure of the words

NEOE KAEDING Heinrich b.7Jan1842-d.2Mai1933, w/ Auguste Kaeding; inscription in ornate German script, I am not sure of the words

NEOE SCHLIESKE Maria b.14Feb1838-d.10Jan1911

NEOE STRIKOWSKY Carl b.13Jul1843-d.21Sep1912

NEOE LEFEBER Infant b.no date-d.no date, "Baby; Infant of A. & J. Lefeber" n/t Anna, Sarah & Abraham Lefeber

NEOE LEFEBER Anna b.13Mar1887-d.16Jul1887, n/t Baby, Sarah & Abraham Lefeber

NEOE LEFEBER Sarah b.14May1872-d.14Sep1872, n/t Baby, Anna & Abraham Lefeber

NEOE LEFEBER Abraham b.12Feb1869-d.6Aug1869, n/t Baby, Anna & Sarah Lefeber

NEOE NIEUWENHUYSE Susanna (LEFEBER) b.20Mar1845-d.28Jun1874, "Mamma" n/t Susanna Nieuwenhuyse & Uohanna, Abraham & other Lefebers

NEOE NIEUWENHUYSE Susanna b.4May1874-d.12Aug1874, n/t Susanna Nieuwenhuyse & Uohanna, Abraham & other Lefebers

NEOE LEFEBER Uohanna b.20Feb1849-d.10May1907, "Mother" n/t Abraham, Abraham, Maria, & Elizabeth Lefeber & Susanna Nieuwenhuyse

NEOE LEFEBER Abraham b.11Jan1844-d.9Jun1922, "Father" n/t Uohanna, Abraham, Maria, & Elizabeth Lefeber & Susanna Nieuwenhuyse; GAR mkr; Abraham enlisted in the army in Rhine 10 Nov 1864, he was a Cpl. in the 45th Infantry Co. H, he was Mustered

Out 17 Jul 1865[49]

NEOE LEFEBER Abraham b.23Oct1811-d.26Jul1902, "Father" n/t
Uohanna, Abraham, Maria, & Elizabeth Lefeber & Susanna
Nieuwenhuyse

NEOE LEFEBER Maria b.22Apr1810-d.4Sep1902, "Mother" n/t
Uohanna, Abraham, Abraham, & Elizabeth Lefeber & Susanna
Nieuwenhuyse

NEOE LEFEBER Elizabeth b.12Sep1875-d.1Sep1954, "Daughter" n/t
Uohanna, Abraham, Abraham & Maria Lefeber & Susanna
Nieuwenhuyse

NEOE TREUTELAAR Jozias b.1822-d.1899, w/ Pieternella, Johann &
Peter Treutelaar & John, Anna & other Baas

NEOE TREUTELAAR Pieternella b.1832-d.1891, w/ Jozias, Johann &
Peter Treutelaar & John, Anna & other Baas

NEOE TREUTELAAR Johann b.1863-d.1882, w/ Jozias, Pieternella &
Peter Treutelaar & John, Anna & other Baas

NEOE TREUTELAAR Peter b.1864-d.1872, w/ Jozias, Pieternella &
Johann Treutelaar & John, Anna & other Baas

NEOE BAAS John b.1848-d.1879, w/ Anna, John, Jr. & Julius Baas &
Jozias Treutelaar & Flora Herrmann

NEOE BAAS Anna b.1854-d.1924, w/ John, John, Jr. & Julius Baas &
Jozias Treutelaar & Flora Herrmann

NEOE BAAS John, Jr. b.1920-d.1925, w/ John, Anna & Julius Baas &
Jozias Treutelaar & Flora Herrmann

NEOE BAAS Julius b.1921-d.no date, "WWII" w/ John, Anna & John, Jr.
Baas & Jozias Treutelaar & Flora Herrmann

NEOE HERRMANN Flora b.1876-d.1922, w/ John, Anna & John, Jr.&
Julius Baas & Jozias & Pieternella Treutelaar

NEOE KRAUS George d.25Jul1863, "32y, In Memory of...Died at
Nashville, Tenn. From the Effects of a Wound Received at the Battle of
Murfreesboro"; w/ Margaret & Julia Kraus; George enlisted in the
army 15 Aug 1862, he was in the 24th Infantry Co. E, he was wounded
at Stone River and died 25 Jun 1863 in Nashville, Tenn. of wounds, his
name is spelled Krause[50]

NEOE KRAUS Margaret d.12Aug1860, "21y 10m, w/o George Kraus" w/
George & Julia Kraus

NEOE KRAUS Julia b.no date-d.no date, "7w, Their Infant Daughter" w/
George & Margaret Kraus

NEOE SERCOMBE Selma b.1889-d.1964, "Mother"

49 *Roster of Wisconsin Volunteers, War Of The Rebellion, 1861-1865*

50 *Roster of Wisconsin Volunteers, War Of The Rebellion, 1861-1865*

NEOE JOHST Arno E. b.1896-d.1964, w/ Marie Johst
NEOE JOHST Marie b.1897-d.1991, w/ Arno E. Johst
NEOE HOLMES Frederick b.1892-d.1974, n/t Ellen Holmes
NEOE HOLMES Ellen b.1891-d.1961, n/t Frederick Holmes
NEOE LEHMANN Gottfried b.1804-d.1893, w/ William, Bertha M., Fred
J., Helena, Herman, Gottfried & Laura Lehmann & Johanna Schreiber
NEOE LEHMANN Gottfried b.1836-d.1901, w/ William, Bertha M., Fred
J., Helena, Herman, Gottfried & Laura Lehmann & Johanna Schreiber
NEOE LEHMANN William b.1877-d.1906, w/ Gottfried, Bertha M., Fred
J., Helena Herman, Gottfried & Laura Lehmann & Johanna Schreiber
NEOE LEHMANN Bertha M. b.1876-d.1948, w/ Gottfried, William, Fred
J., Helena, Herman, Gottfried & Laura Lehmann & Johanna Schreiber
NEOE LEHMANN Fred J. b.1866-d.1953, w/ Gottfried, William, Bertha
M., Helena Herman, Gottfried & Laura Lehmann & Johanna Schreiber
NEOE LEHMANN Helena b.1892-d.1894, w/ Gottfried, William, Bertha
M., Fred J., Herman, Gottfried & Laura Lehmann & Johanna Schreiber
NEOE LEHMANN Herman b.1869-d.1893, w/ Gottfried, William, Bertha
M., Fred J., Helena, Gottfried & Laura Lehmann & Johanna Schreiber
NEOE LEHMANN Laura b.1842-d.1909, w/ Gottfried, William, Bertha
M., Fred J., Helena, Gottfried & Herman Lehmann & Johanna
Schreiber
NEOE SCHREIBER Johanna b.1868-d.1910, w/ Gottfried, William,
Bertha M., Fred J., Helena, Gottfried, Herman & Laura Lehmann
NEOE LUBENAU Bertha b.1888-d.1924, n/t Ernst, Wilhelmina, Rosa,
Albert & Minnie Lubenau
NEOE LUBENAU Ernst b.1860-d.1898, n/t Bertha, Wilhelmina, Rosa,
Albert & Minnie Lubenau
NEOE LUBENAU Wilhelmina b.1861-d.1912, n/t Bertha, Ernst, Rosa,
Albert & Minnie Lubenau
NEOE LUBENAU Rosa b.1890-d.1899, n/t Bertha, Ernst, Wilhelmina,
Albert & Minnie Lubenau
NEOE LUBENAU Albert b.no date-d.no date, w/ Minnie,n/t Bertha, Ernst,
& Wilhelmina Lubenau; not in cemetery records
NEOE LUBENAU Minnie b.no date-d.no date, w/ Albert, n/t Bertha,
Ernst, & Wilhelmina Lubenau; not in cemetery records
NEOE HOEFT Carl b.1841-d.1930, "Father" n/t Fredericka Hoeft
NEOE HOEFT Fredericka b.1845-d.1924, n/t Carl Hoeft
NEOE DOEBKE Florence b.1907-d.1970, "Daughter"
NEOE VAN BORTEL Susan b.1886-d.1943, "Mother"
NEOE HINTZ Anna M. b.1891-d.1968, n/t Emma Hintz
NEOE HINTZ Emma b.1872-d.1915, "Mother" n/t Anna M. Hintz

102

NEOE KOVALESKE William b.1888-d.1971, w/ Laura Kovaleske
NEOE KOVALESKE Laura b.1880-d.1970, w/ William Kovaleske
NEOE HINTZ William L. b.27Oct1882-d.19Oct1913, n/t Fredericka,
    Friedrich & Arthur Hintz
NEOE HINTZ Arthur b.1885-d.1961, n/t Fredericka, Friedrich & William
    L. Hintz
NEOE HINTZ Fredericka b.1846-d.1929, "Mutter" w/ Friedrich, n/t
    William L. & Arthur Hintz
NEOE HINTZ Friedrich b.1834-d.1915, "Vater" w/ Friedericka, n/t
    William L. & Arthur Hintz
NEOE VAN BORTEL Joanna b.28Sep1848-d.3May1928, "Mother" n/t
    Peter Van Bortel
NEOE VAN BORTEL Peter b.23Dec1846-d.13Nov1909, n/t Joanna Van
    Bortel
NEOE GENSKE Minnie b.22Feb1843-d.15Jan1919, "Mother" n/t John
    Genske
NEOE GENSKE John b.7Jun1838-d.3Jan1922, "Father" n/t Minnie
    Genske
NEOE PARNEMAN Paul b.1884-d.23Jul1908, n/t Helen, Augusta &
    William Fredric Parneman
NEOE PARNEMAN Helen b.1894-d.1939, n/t Paul, Augusta & William
    Fredric Parneman
NEOE PARNEMAN Augusta b.1862-d.1954, n/t Paul, Helen & William
    Fredric Parneman
NEOE PARNEMAN William Fredric b.16Dec1892-d.4Aug1988, n/t Paul,
    Helen & Augusta Parneman
NEOE NOYES Terence b.23Jun1930-d.24Jul1992, "In Memory of; US
    ARMY KOREA" n/t Harvey Wm., Wilma E., Josephine E., Jane L. & J.
    F. Noyes
NEOE NOYES Wilma E. d.31May1892, "22y" n/t Terence, Harvey Wm.,
    Josephine E., Jane L. & J. F. Noyes
NEOE NOYES Harvey Wm. b.20Apr1895-d.12Jul1967, "WIS. PVT
    INFANTRY WWI" n/t Terence, Wilma E., Josephine E., Jane L. & J. F.
    Noyes
NEOE Josephine E. b.9Oct1897-d.13Sep1971, n/t Terence, Wilma E.,
    Harvey Wm., Jane L. & J. F. Noyes
NEOE NOYES Jane L. b.10Jul1933-d.30Jan1996, n/t Terence, Wilma E.,
    Harvey Wm., Josephine E. & J. F. Noyes
NEOE NOYES J. F. b.no date-d.no date, "10th WIS. BATTY?" n/t Terence,
    Wilma E., Harvey Wm., Josephine E. & Jane L. Noyes, hard to read;
    GAR mkr, no cemetery record; James F. enlisted in the army 13 Sept

1862, no city of residence given, he was a prisoner, he was Mustered Out 7 Jan 1865[51]

NEOE BLAIR Emma I. Noles b.30Jul1854-d.8Dec1883, "w/o Horace Blair"

NEOE FREY Carolina (DOBBERPHUL) b.1828-d.1869, "Mother" n/t Conrad & Carolina D. Frey & Engel Dobberphul

NEOE DOBBERPHUL Engel b.3Apr1797-d.10Apr1888, Mutter; ICH WEISS DASE MEIN ER=LÖSER LEBT UND ER WIRD MICH HERNACH AUS DER ERDEN AUFERWECKEN.

NEOE FREY Carolina (KRUEGER) b.22Aug1836-d.8May1899, "Mother" n/t Conrad & Carolina D. Frey & Engel Dobberphul

NEOE FREY Conrad b.1825-d.1911, "Father" n/t Carolina & Carolina D. Frey & Engel Dobberphul

NEOE STUDEMANN Carl b.11Apr1861-d.31Jan1885, w/ Maria & Ludwig Studemann & Friederike J. Schroder

NEOE STUDEMANN Maria b.8Apr1858-d.23Mai1881, "VER HEIR ATHET MIR JOHANN WÜRCHING" w/ Carl & Ludwig Studemann & Friederike J. Schroder

NEOE STUDEMANN Ludwig b.1820-d.1866, w/ Carl & Maria Studemann & Friederike J. Schroder

NEOE SCHRODER Friederike (JACOBS) b.1Jan1823-d.5Jul1889, w/ Carl, Maria & Ludwig Studemann

NEOE RABE Johann b.1837-d.1896, w/ Fred A., n/t Friederich, Carolina, Carl C., Bernarth A., William F., Anna W. & John A. Rabe

NEOE RABE Fred A. b.1882-d.1909, w/ Johann, n/t Friederich, Carolina, Carl C., Bernarth A., William F., Anna W. & John A. Rabe

NEOE RABE Anna W. b.1872-d.1878, w/ John A., n/t Friederich, Carolina, Carl C., Bernarth A., William F., Johann & Fred A. Rabe

NEOE RABE John A. b.1877-d.1878, w/ Anna W., n/t Friederich, Carolina, Carl C., Bernarth A., William F., Johann & Fred A. Rabe

NEOE RABE Friederich b.1842-d.1924, "Father" n/t Anna W., John A., Carolina, Carl C., Bernarth A., William F., Johann & Fred A. Rabe

NEOE RABE Carolina b.1844-d.1896, "Mother" n/t Anna W., John A., Friederich, Carl C., Bernarth A., William F., Johann & Fred A. Rabe

NEOE RABE Carl C. b.1870-d.1878, n/t Anna W., John A., Friederich, Carolina, Bernarth A., William F., & Fred A. Rabe

NEOE RABE Bernarth A. b.1875-d.1879, n/t Anna W., John A., Friederich, Carolina, Carl C., William F., & Fred A. Rabe

NEOE RABE William F. b.1879-d.1891, n/t Anna W., John A., Friederich, Carolina, Carl C., Bernarth A. & Fred A. Rabe

51 *Roster of Wisconsin Volunteers, War Of The Rebellion, 1861-1865*

NEOE MECKLENBURG Emma S. b.8Apr1885-d.28Feb1977, "Mother" w/ Herman Mecklenburg

NEOE MECKLENBURG Herman b.1880-d.1959, "Father" w/ Emma Mecklenburg

NEOE GLAUS Louise E. b.1879-d.1968, n/t Arnold Glaus

NEOE GLAUS Arnold b.1873-d.1927, n/t Louise E. Glaus

NEOE BEHLING Roland b.24Jul1891-d.28Jan1893, n/t Herman, Augusta, Norma K. & Armand A. Behling

NEOE BEHLING Herman b.1845-d.1933, "Father" n/t Roland, Augusta, Norma K. & Armand A. Behling

NEOE BEHLING Augusta b.1849-d.1930, "Mother" n/t Roland, Herman, Norma K. & Armand A. Behling

NEOE BEHLING Norma K. b.1902-d.1984, "Wife" n/t Roland, Herman, Augusta & Armand A. Behling

NEOE BEHLING Armand A. b.1895-d.1968, "Husband" n/t Roland, Herman, Augusta & Norma K. Behling

NEOE HENKE Herman b.1860-d.1913, "Bruder"

NEOE SMITH Millard Beale, Jr. b.18Feb1935-d.24Jan1990, "Son" w/ Millard B., Alice F., Alson A., Alson I., Lottie M. & Margaret Smith

NEOE SMITH Millard Beale b.14Apr1903-d.3Oct1965, "Husband" w/ Millard B., Jr., Alice F., Alson A., Alson I., Lottie M. & Margaret Smith

NEOE SMITH Alice Field b.11Nov1907-d.no date, "Wife" w/ Millard B., Jr., Millard B., Alson A., Alson I., Lottie M. & Margaret Smith

NEOE SMITH Alson Arthur d.19Sep1932, "s/o Millard & Alice Smith" w/ Millard B., Jr., Millard B., Alice F., Alson I., Lottie M. & Margaret Smith; only one date

NEOE SMITH Alson I. b.9Oct1868-d.9Mar1918, "Father" w/ Millard B., Jr., Millard B., Alice F., Alson A., Lottie M. & Margaret Smith

NEOE SMITH Lottie M. b.23Jun1871-d.13Sep1949, "Mother" w/ Millard B., Jr., Millard B., Alice F., Alson A., Alson I. & Margaret Smith

NEOE SMITH Margaret b.15Sep1905-d.2Dec1906, "Daughter" w/ Millard B., Jr., Millard B., Alice F., Alson A., Alson I. & Lottie M. Smith

NEOE WENDT Florence b.1878-d.1947, w/ Albert Wendt

NEOE WENDT Albert b.1873-d.1947, w/ Florence Wendt

NEOE EHNERT Lucille b.1910-d.1983, w/ Harry & Lydia Ehnert

NEOE EHNERT Harry b.1906-d.1977, w/ Lucille & Lydia Ehnert

NEOE EHNERT Lydia b.1905-d.1945, w/ Lucille & Harry Ehnert

NEOE BAUER George b.1827-d.1910, "Father" w/ Wilhelmina Bauer, may have two stones

NEOE BAUER Wilhelmina b.1832-d.1921, "Mother" w/ George Bauer

NEOE BAUER Geo. b.no date-d.no date, "CO. D. 17 WIS. INF." probably 2nd stone (military) for George Bauer; Geo. enlisted in the army 16 Nov 1864, no place of residence was given, he had been drafted, he was Mustered Out 14 Jul 1865[52]

NEOE ZELLER Casper b.1866-d.1921, "Father" w/ Sophie Zeller & Alma Brooks, n/t Walter C. Zeller

NEOE ZELLER Sophie b.1864-d.1947, "Mother" w/ Casper Zeller & Alma Brooks, n/t Walter C. Zeller

NEOE BROOKS Alma b.1893-d.1965, w/ Casper & Sophie Zeller, n/t Walter C. Zeller

NEOE ZELLER Walter C. b.1900-d.1953, n/t Casper & Sophie Zeller & Alma Brooks

NEOE ROSS Janet d.12Aug1917, only one date

NEOE CLAUSEN Ottilie b.1867-d.1916, w/ Charles Clausen

NEOE CLAUSEN Charles b.1864-d.1947, w/ Ottilie Clausen

NEOE STARK Genevieve b.26Aug1900-d.7Dec1992, w/ Clarence A. Stark

NEOE STARK Clarence A. b.16Sep1896-d.22Jan1983, "USN WWI FRANCE 1918-1919" w/ Genevieve Stark

NEOE TREUTELAAR Jennie b.1867-d.1907, w/ Isaac & Helen Treutelaar

NEOE TREUTELAAR Isaac b.1866-d.1941, w/ Jennie & Helen Treutelaar

NEOE TREUTELAAR Helen b.1898-d.1977, w/ Jennie & Isaac Treutelaar

NEOE MANSKE Edward J. A. b.20Jun1877-d.13Apr1878, n/t Adolf W., Adelina A. B., Infant & Emilie Manske; stone broken; first name from cemetery records

NEOE MANSKE Adolf W. b.10Jun1870-d.1Mar1878, n/t Edward J. A., Adelina A. B., Infant & Emilie R. Manske

NEOE MANSKE Adelina A. B. b.28Aug1875-d.22Oct1875, n/t Edward J. A., Adolf W., Infant & Emilie Manske; stone broken; first name from cemetery records

NEOE MANSKE Infant b.24Jan1872-d.24Jan1872, "Hier Ruht Kind Von Christ & Rosalia Manske (here rests the child of Christ & Rosalia Manske)", n/t Adolf W., Edward J. A., Adelina A. B. & Emilie R. Manske

NEOE MANSKE Emilie R. b.20Mai1873-d.10Jun1873, n/t Edward J. A., Adelina A. B., Adolf W., & Infant Manske

NEOE ALEWYNSE Peter b.3Feb1853-d.8Jan1864, "s/o M. & G. Alewynse" w/ Willie, Marinus, J. G. L., & S. Eliab Alewynse

NEOE ALEWYNSE Willie b.26Jan1865-d.Jun1876, w/ Peter, Marinus, J. G. L., & S. Eliab Alewynse

---

52 *Roster of Wisconsin Volunteers, War Of The Rebellion, 1861-1865*

NEOE ALEWYNSE Marinus b.6May1830-d.17Oct1883, w/ Peter, Willie, J. G. L., & S. Eliab Alewynse

NEOE ALEWYNSE J. G. Londewer d.28Nov1864, "45y; w/o M. Alewynse" w/ Peter, Willie, Marinus, & S. Eliab Alewynse

NEOE ALEWYNSE S. Eliab b.3Feb1836-d.2Jul1882, "w/o M. Alewynse" w/ Peter, Willie, Marinus, & J. G. Londewer Alewynse

NEOE MATHISON Esther M. b.1907-d.no date, w/ Chester V. Mathison

NEOE MATHISON Chester V. b.1907-d.1987, w/ Esther M. Mathison

NEOE LUETZOW Walter R. b.23Sep1895-d.12Mar1958, "WIS. PVT CO F 2 ENGINEERS" n/t Alfred, Elisabeth, Arthur, Ernst W., & Alois W. Luetzow

NEOE LUETZOW Alfred b.1850-d.1926, "Father" n/t Walter R., Elisabeth, Arthur, Ernst W. & Alois W. Luetzow

NEOE LUETZOW Elisabeth b.20Mai1856-d.19Apr1899, "Mutter" n/t Walter R., Alfred, Arthur, Ernst W. & Alois W. Luetzow *

NEOE LUETZOW Arthur b.23Dec1876-d.21Apr1912, "Vater" n/t Walter R., Alfred, Elisabeth, Ernst W. & Alois W. Luetzow

NEOE LUETZOW Ernst W. b.1879-d.1952, n/t Walter R., Alfred, Elisabeth, Arthur & Alois W. Luetzow

NEOE LUETZOW Alois W. b.1886-d.1960, n/t Walter R., Alfred, Elisabeth, Arthur & Ernst W. Luetzow

NEOE RUSSELL Alice Wadsworth b.28Feb1876-d.16Dec1943

NEOE DUNKEL Henry H. b.1867-d.1917, n/t Henry C. F. & Sibila Duenkel & Hattie A. Dunkel

NEOE DUNKEL Hattie A. b.1871-d.1952, n/t Henry C. F. & Sibila Duenkel & Henry H. Dunkel

NEOE DUENKEL Henry C. F. b.1841-d.1906, w/ Sibila Duenkel, n/t Henry H. & Hattie A. Dunkel

NEOE DUENKEL Sibila b.1845-d.1921, w/ Henry C. F. Duenkel, n/t Henry H. & Hattie A. Dunkel

NEOE GASTEL Lucy b.1886-d.1959, w/ Charles Gastel

NEOE GASTEL Charles b.1882-d.1960, w/ Lucy Gastel

NEOE HARTFIELD Florence W. (BRUDER) b.1908-d.1930, "Wife" n/t Eliza, Herman, Augusta & William Bruder & Hattie, Kathleen A. Kurtz & Willie

NEOE BRUDER Eliza b.1885-d.1945, w/ Herman, n/t Augusta & William Bruder & Florence W. B. Hartfield & Kathleen A. Kurtz & Willie

NEOE BRUDER Herman b.1882-d.1959, w/ Eliza, n/t Augusta & William Bruder & Florence W. B. Hartfield & Kathleen A. Kurtz & Willie

NEOE BRUDER Augusta b.1858-d.1896, "Mother" w/ William, n/t Eliza & Herman Bruder & Florence W. B. Hartfield & Kathleen A. Kurtz & Willie

NEOE BRUDER William b.1854-d.1932, "Father" w/ Augusta, n/t Eliza & Herman Bruder & Florence W. B. Hartfield & Kathleen A. Kurtz & Willie

NEOE KURTZ Hattie (BRUDER) b.1884-d.1961, n/tAugusta, William, Eliza & Herman Bruder & Florence W. B. Hartfield & Kathleen A. Kurtz & Willie

NEOE KURTZ Kathleen Ann b.25Jan1985-d.17Sep1985, n/t Augusta, William, Eliza & Herman Bruder & Florence W. B. Hartfield & Hattie Kurtz & Willie

NEOE ? Willie b.1893-d.1896, "no last name on stone, poss Bruder" n/t Augusta, William, Eliza & Herman Bruder & Florence W. B. Hartfield & Kathleen Kurtz

NEOE ARNDT Clara b.17Sep1895-d.24Jun1907, n/t Emilie & Herman Arndt

NEOE ARNDT Emilie b.1861-d.1944, "Mutter" w/ Herman, n/t Clara Arndt

NEOE ARNDT Herman b.1858-d.1939, "Vater" w/ Emilie, n/t Clara Arndt

NEOE BREU Minnie b.1860-d.1936, n/t Heinrich & Marie Breu

NEOE BREU Heinrich b.9Mar1825 Wagenhausen, Thurgan Schuriz d.12Feb1907, "Vater" n/t Minnie & Marie Breu

NEOE BREU Marie b.20Sep1829 Wagenhausen, Ki-Thurgan Schuerz d.25Mar1912 "Mutter" n/t Minnie & Heinrich Breu

NEOE KOENITZER Louis b.1853-d.1930, n/t Julia Koenitzer

NEOE KOENITZER Julia b.1861-d.1906, n/t Louis Koenitzer

NEOE WITTE Hedwig b.1856-d.1922, "Mother"

NEOE ENGELHARDT Mary b.1847-d.1927, "Wife" n/t Ernst E. Engelhardt

NEOE ENGELHARDT Ernst E. b.31Dec1849-d.2Nov1906, n/t Mary Engelhardt

NEOE BAEHR Edward T. b.29May1895-d.19Jan1959, "WIS. CPL CO D 107 ENG. WWI"

NEOE BODDENHAGEN Emily b.1887-d.1931, w/ Ann Hartzeim

NEOE HARTZEIM Ann b.1892-d.1940, w/ Emily Boddenhagen

NEOE BAEHR William b.1884-d.1930, "Son" n/t Bertha & Theodore Baehr

NEOE BAEHR Bertha b.1862-d.1906, "Mother" n/t William & Theodore Baehr

NEOE BAEHR Theodore b.1856-d.1917, "Father" n/t William & Bertha Baehr

NEOE RADER Louis b.1860-d.1924, "Husband" n/t Emma Rader

NEOE RADER Emma b.1870-d.1944, "Wife" n/t Louis Rader

NEOE REICHE Minnie b.1848-d.18Jan1929, "Mother" n/t Carl H.
Reiche; name in cemetery records is Wilhelmine

NEOE REICHE Carl H. b.4Apr1843 Europe-d.29Jul1905, "Father" n/t
Minnie Reiche; name in cemetery records is Charles; reintered here
from Mayville, Wis.

NEOE ROBERTS Frederick A. b.no date-d.21Jan1902, "CO. L 6 U.S.
INFANTRY" n/t Caroline E. Roberts, GAR marker; cemetery records
show he was in the Spanish American War

NEOE ROBERTS Caroline E. b.21Jan1851-d.8Jan1905, "Mother" n/t F.
A. Roberts

NEOE MARKLEY Mary C. b.1913-d.1998

NEOE SHAW Luella J. b.1856-d.1929, n/t Charles Shaw

NEOE SHAW Charles b.1847-d.1901, n/t Luella J. Shaw

NEOE WENDT Rose b.1900-d.1988, "Mom" n/t Henry, Henry, Bertha,
Henry, & Elisabeth Wendt & Wilhelmine & Gottfried Lutz

NEOE WENDT Henry b.1933-d.1990, "Hank" n/t Rose, Henry, Bertha,
Henry, & Elisabeth Wendt & Wilhelmine & Gottfried Lutz

NEOE WENDT Henry b.1898-d.1957, "Dad" n/t Rose, Henry, Bertha,
Henry, & Elisabeth Wendt & Wilhelmine & Gottfried Lutz

NEOE WENDT Henry b.1867-d.1930, n/t Rose, Henry, Bertha, Henry, &
Elisabeth Wendt & Wilhelmine & Gottfried Lutz

NEOE WENDT Bertha b.1869-d.1945, "Wife" n/t Rose, Henry, Henry,
Henry, & Elisabeth Wendt & Wilhelmine & Gottfried Lutz

NEOE WENDT Elisabeth b.22Feb1866-d.17Sep1911, "Mother" n/t Rose,
Henry, Henry, Henry, & Bertha Wendt & Wilhelmine & Gottfried Lutz

NEOE WENDT Theophil C. F. b.13Feb1892-d.3Sep1892, "s/o H. & E.
Wendt" n/t Rose, Henry, Henry, Henry, Bertha & Elisabeth Wendt &
Wilhelmine & Gottfried Lutz

NEOE LUTZ Wilhelmine b.1843-d.1921, "Mama" n/t Rose, Henry,
Henry, Henry, Bertha, Elisabeth, Theophil C. F. & ? Wendt & Gottfried
Lutz

NEOE LUTZ Gottfried b.1842-d.1925, "Papa" n/t Rose, Henry, Henry,
Henry, Bertha, Elisabeth, Theophil C. F. & ? Wendt & Wilhelmine Lutz

NEOE FALK Anna b.25Mar1879-d.23Aug1960, "Daughter" n/t
Wilhelmine & Friedrich Falk & Emilie & Adeline Reinke

NEOE FALK Wilhelmine b.7Nov1846-d.3Aug1944, "Mutter" n/t Anna &
Friedrich Falk & Emilie & Adeline Reinke

NEOE FALK Friedrich b.22Nov1845-d.20Apr1919, "Vater" n/t Anna &
Wilhelmine Falk & Emilie & Adeline Reinke

NEOE REINKE Emilie (FALK) b.4Dec1878-d.27Mar1912, "Mother" n/t
Anna, Friedrich & Wilhelmine Falk & Adeline Reinke

NEOE REINKE Adeline b.31Aug1898-d.28Jan1912, "d/o Mr. & Mrs. J. Reinke" n/t Anna, Friedrich & Wilhelmine Falk & Emilie F. Reinke

NEOE CARPENTER Lilliam M. b.23Jul1890-d.8May1970, "Mother" n/t Frank Carpenter

NEOE CARPENTER Frank b.28Jul1914-d.28Jun1919, n/t Lillian M. Carpenter

NEOE REINKE Albert L. b.1865-d.1946, n/t Florence & Wilbert Reinke

NEOE REINKE Florence b.1903-d.1977, w/ Wilbert, n/t Albert L. Reinke

NEOE REINKE Wilbert b.1898-d.1942, w/ Florence, n/t Albert L. Reinke

NEOE HARTMAN Carl L. b.1901-d.1971

NEOE REINKE Carol b.1927-d.no date, w/ Russell Reinke

NEOE REINKE Russell b.1927-d.1990, w/ Carol Reinke; American Legion mkr

NEOE GOLLNICK Monica b.1912-d.1978

NEOE HILL Eileen K. b.1909-d.1977, w/ Archie S. Hill

NEOE HILL Archie S. b.1904-d.1979, w/ Eileen K. Hill

NEOE GOVAN Roland E. b.2Dec1909-d.25Sep1952, "WIS. CAPT. US ARMY WWII"

NEOE MURKETT Jessie Y. b.1872-d.1928

NEOE BELNAR Anna R. (TONN) b.9Apr1825-d.23Apr1881

NEOE VICK Friedrich b.1875-d.1962

NEOE TWINEM Mattie b.4Jun1872-d.7Sep1913, "Mother" n/t Chas. H., Frieda & William C. Twinem

NEOE TWINEM Chas. H. b.11Aug1867-d.8May1919, "Father" n/t Mattie, Frieda & William C. Twinem

NEOE TWINEM Frieda b.1890-d.1956, "Mother" w/ William C., n/t Mattie & Chas. S. Twinem

NEOE TWINEM William C. b.1892-d.1958, "Father" w/ Frieda, n/t Mattie & Chas. S. Twinem

NEOE BREEN Elizabeth b.1837-d.1923, "Mother" n/t William Breen

NEOE BREEN William b.1834-d.1892, "Father" n/t Elizabeth Breen

NEOE GARRISON Johanna b.1883-d.1950, w/ William Garrison

NEOE GARRISON William b.1877-d.1952, w/ Johanna Garrison

NEOE EGGERT John b.1864-d.1938, "Father" n/t Theresa, Johann & Dorothea M., John & Roland Eggert

NEOE EGGERT Theresa b.1866-d.1930, "Mother" n/t John, Johann & Dorothea M., John & Roland Eggert

NEOE EGGERT Johann b.16Dec1824-d.14Apr1915, "Vater" n/t John, Theresa & Dorothea M., John & Roland Eggert

NEOE EGGERT Dorothea M. (JACH) b.17Apr1830 Schmasow KR OST, Starb, d.10Mar1898, "War Verheirathet (married) Mit Johann Eggert

Seit 12Mai1856, Priegnitz Prov.", Brandenburg"; n/t John, Theresa, Johann, John & Roland Eggert

NEOE EGGERT John b.1886-d.1915, "Papa" n/t John, Theresa, Johann, Dorothea M., & Roland Eggert

NEOE EGGERT Roland b.1908-d.1927, "Left to the Judgement of God" n/t John, Theresa, Johann, Dorothea M., & John Eggert

NEOE JOERS Frederick b.1912-d.1973

NEOE VICK Arthur b.1915-d.1970, "Till The Master of all Good Craftsman Shall Set Us to Work Anew"

NEOE QUITZOW Eliza W. b.1870-d.1957, w/ Hedwig & Henry A. Quitzow & William & Dorothea Jach

NEOE QUITZOW Hedwig d.1894, w/ Eliza W. & Henry A. Quitzow & William & Dorothea Jach; only one date

NEOE QUITZOW Henry A. b.1862-d.1941, w/ Eliza W. & Hedwig Quitzow & William & Dorothea Jach

NEOE JACH William b.1838-d.1906, w/ Dorothea Jach & Eliza W., Hedwig & Henry A. Quitzow; see Dorothea M. Eggert

NEOE JACH Dorothea b.1836-d.1909, w/ William Jach & Eliza W., Hedwig & Henry A. Quitzow

NEOE PEASE Spencer A. b.1888-d.1956, w/ Isabel S. & Robert S. Pease

NEOE PEASE Isabel S. b.1890-d.1969, w/ Spencer A. & Robert S. Pease

NEOE PEASE Robert S. b.1923-d.1974, w/ Spencer A. & Isabel S. Pease

NEOE KEHOSS Joseph b.1908-d.1982

NEOE NICKEL Peter J. b.10Jul1875-d.11Jan1911, n/t Maria & Peter Nickel

NEOE NICKEL Maria b.14Mai1838-d.12Dec1909, w/ Peter n/t Peter J. Nickel

NEOE NICKEL Peter b.17Apr1828-d.27Feb1905, w/ Maria n/t Peter J. Nickel

NEOE ZEMKE Clara b.1883-d.1918, "Mother"

NEOE BROWN Anna S. b.10Sep1857-d.15Aug1905

NEOE HEMSING-BOYD Rachael Rosetta b.1855-d.1929 "Mother"

NEOE BOYD, HEMSING- Rachael Rosetta b.1855-d.1929 "Mother"

NEOE HEMSING B. F. b.22Oct1851-d.31May1916, "Father" n/t Franz J., Laura H. Louise & Anton Schmidt *

NEOE SCHMIDT Laura Hemsing b.1884-d.1956, w/ Franz J. n/t Louise & Anton Schmidt & B. F. Hemsing

NEOE SCHMIDT Franz Joseph b.1880-d.1951, w/ Laura H. n/t Louise & Anton Schmidt & B. F. Hemsing

NEOE SCHMIDT Louise b.1837-d.1916, "Mother" n/t Laura H., Franz J. & Anton Schmidt & B. F. Hemsing

NEOE SCHMIDT Anton b.1832-d.1911, n/t Laura H., Franz J. & Louise Schmidt & B. F. Hemsing

NEOE BOESEL Christina b.26Aug1849-d.24Nov1917, "Mutter" n/t G. Gottlieb Boesel

NEOE BOESEL G. Gottlieb b.10Jun1836-d.10Sep1905, n/t Christina Boesel

NEOE KRESSIN Eunice Kirchner b.1902-d.1996, "Mother" n/t Glenway A. Kirchner

NEOE KIRCHNER Glenway A. b.1902-d.1941, "Father" n/t Eunice K. Kressin

NEOE ROSENTHAL Elsie b.no date-d.19Jul1892, no last name on stone; 7y; last name, date & age from cemetery records

NEOE COMBERT Frieda b.1877-d.1904, "w/o Victor M. Combert"

NEOE ZINN Viola L. b.26Sep1895-d.8Jan1987, n/t Carl W. Zinn

NEOE ZINN Carl Walter b.2Jun1893-d.6Feb1973, "WIS. PVT US ARMY WWI" n/t Viola L. Zinn

NEOE KLEINMANN Norma b.1895-d.1972, w/ Peter, Mary, Irene & Elroy Kleinmann

NEOE KLEINMANN Peter b.1869-d.1942, w/ Norma, Mary, Irene & Elroy Kleinmann

NEOE KLEINMANN Mary b.1873-d.1955, w/ Norma, Peter, Irene & Elroy Kleinmann

NEOE KLEINMANN Irene b.1897-d.1927, w/ Norma, Peter, Mary & Elroy Kleinmann

NEOE KLEINMANN Elroy b.1893-d.1894, w/ Norma, Peter, Mary & Irene Kleinmann

NEOE WATSON Mary J. b.1844-d.1928, "Mother" n/t C. Dwight & Thomas C. Watson

NEOE WATSON C. Dwight b.1841-d.1904, "CO. E 24th REG. WIS. VOL. INFANTRY" n/t Mary J. & Thomas C. Watson; Charles D. resided in Granville when he enlisted in the army on 7 Aug 1862; he held ranks of Corpl., Sergt., and 1st Sergt, he was wounded at Chickamauga; he was made Brevet Capt. 31 Dec 1862, Mustered Out 10 Jun 1865[53]

NEOE WATSON Thomas Courtney b.1915-d.1918, n/t Mary J. & C. Dwight Watson

NEOE KLATT Emil b.24Sep1856-d.22Jun1899, "Papa" n/t Minnie A. Klatt

NEOE KLATT Minnie (ACKMANN) b.6May1856-d.7Apr1906, "Mama" n/t Emil Klatt

NEOE ROSENTHAL Louise b.1839-d.1922, n/t Max, Emily & Hilda Rosenthal

NEOE ROSENTHAL Hilda b.1881-d.1931, n/t Max, Emily & Louise
Rosenthal
NEOE ROSENTHAL Max b.1853-d.1926, w/ Emily n/t Hilda & Louise
Rosenthal *
NEOE ROSENTHAL Emily b.1855-d.1948, w/ Max n/t Hilda & Louise
Rosenthal
NEOE DORAU Dorothea b.28Sep1828-d.28Apr1897, n/t Charles Dorau
NEOE DORAU Charles b.1Jan1835-d.16Jun1897, n/t Dorothea Dorau;
GAR mkr
NEOE WRASSE Lulu F. b.1896-d.1958, w/ Harry H. Wrasse
NEOE WRASSE Harry H. b.1894-d.1963, w/ Lulu F. Wrasse
NEOE RAASCH Frieda B. b.1906-d.1952, w/ Harry O. Raasch
NEOE RAASCH Harry O. b.1901-d.1950, w/ Frieda B. Raasch
NEOE SPORLEDER Fr. b.1825-d.1901, "Vater" n/t Marie Sporleder *
NEOE SPORLEDER Marie b.1832-d.1903, "Mutter" n/t Fr. Sporleder *
NEOE WALTER Wilhelm b.1854-d.1927, "Vater" w/ Katharina Walter
NEOE WALTER Katharina b.1857-d.1910, "Mutter" w/ Wilhelm Walter
NEOE DAUBERT Katharina b.1834-d.1921, "Mutter" n/t Adam Daubert
NEOE DAUBERT Adam b.12Aug1834-d.15Jul1901, n/t Katharina
Daubert
NEOE DEBACK Abraham b.15Nov1851-d.22Mar1915, w/ Marie &
Abraham Deback
NEOE DEBACK Marie b.7Apr1852-d.2May1900, w/ Abraham &
Abraham Deback
NEOE DEBACK Abraham b.4Nov1821-d.10Sep1904, "Gr. Father" w/
Abraham & Marie Deback; first name from cemetery records
NEOE WRIGHT Tom G. b.1882-d.1899, w/ Irving F. n/t Baby, Ione T. &
Walter H. Wright *
NEOE WRIGHT Irving F. b.1887-d.1898, w/ Tom G., n/t Baby, Ione T. &
Walter H. Wright
NEOE WRIGHT? Baby d.1935, n/t Tom G., Irving F., Ione T. & Walter H.
Wright, there is no card for a Wright who died in 1935 in the cemetery
records
NEOE WRIGHT Ione Turner d.17Apr1918, "In Memory of Beloved w/o
Walter H. Wright" n/t Tom G., Irving F., Baby, w/ Walter H. Wright
NEOE WRIGHT Walter H. b.1850-d.1928, n/t Tom G., Irving F., Baby, w/
Ione T. Wright
NEOE FALBE Arrie B. b.1885-d.1972, w/ Eugene, n/t Latara, Anton T., W.
F. C. & Arthur Falbe
NEOE FALBE Eugene b.1875-d.1948, w/ Arrie B., n/t Latara, Anton T., W.
F. C. & Arthur Falbe

NEOE FALBE Latara b.1831-d.1917, "Mother" n/t Arrie B., Eugene,
    Anton T., W. F. C. & Arthur Falbe
NEOE FALBE Anton T. b.1815-d.1899, n/t Arrie B., Eugene, Latara, W. F.
    C. & Arthur Falbe *
NEOE FALBE W. F. C. b.1858-d.1902, n/t Arrie B., Eugene, Latara, Anton
    T. & Arthur Falbe
NEOE FALBE Arthur b.1862-d.1904, n/t Arrie B., Eugene, Latara, Anton
    T. & W. F. C. Falbe
NEOE WALTER Caroline b.1888-d.1978, "Sister" w/ Adolph, n/t Kathryn
    & Otto Walter
NEOE WALTER Adolph b.1890-d.1962, w/ Caroline, n/t Kathryn & Otto
    Walter
NEOE WALTER Kathryn b.1892-d.1973, "Wife" w/ Otto, n/t Caroline &
    Adolph Walter
NEOE WALTER Otto b.1881-d.1945, "Husband" w/ Kathryn, n/t Caroline
    & Adolph Walter
NEOE VAN PIETERSOM James W. b.1912-d.1977,
NEOE IVENS Elizabeth Johnson b.1859-d.1930, "Mother" n/t William
    H., Caroline L. & John Ivens & Emma Ivens Wood
NEOE IVENS William H. b.1860-d.1932, "Father" n/t Elizabeth J.,
    Caroline L. & John Ivens & Emma Ivens Wood
NSOE IVENS Caroline Law b.1831 Thenford, England-d.1913, "Mother"
    n/t Elizabeth J., John & William H. Ivens & Emma Ivens Wood
NSOE IVENS John b.1825 Morton Pinkney, England-d.1901, "Father" n/t
    Elizabeth J., Caroline L. & William H. Ivens & Emma Ivens Wood
NSOE WOOD Emma Ivens b.13Dec1870-d.3Jan1899, n/t Elizabeth J.,
    John, Caroline H. & William H. Ivens
NSOE UHL Leonhard b.1828-d.1917, "Father" n/t Kunigunda & Emma
    Uhl & Edwin Fingado *
NSOE UHL Kunigunda b.1838-d.1920, "Mother" n/t Leonhard & Emma
    Uhl & Edwin Fingado
NSOE UHL Emma b.1868-d.1899, "Daughter" n/t Leonhard & Kunigunda
    Uhl & Edwin Fingado *
NSOE FINGADO Edwin b.1865-d.1898, "Father" n/t Emma, Leonhard &
    Kunigunda Uhl
NSub MERRICK Lewis b.1817-d.1907, w/ Keziah B. P. & Ellen Merrick
NSub MERRICK Keziah B. P. b.1815-d.1897, w/ Lewis & Ellen Merrick
NSub MERRICK Ellen b.1844-d.1928, w/ Lewis & Keziah B. P. Merrick
NSub EASTLAKE Mary D. b.21Oct1867-d.5Aug1931
NSub PORTER Hazel b.3Jun1888-d.27Aug1897, n/t Chester G., Margaret
    D., Frank W. & Arthur M. Porter

NSub PORTER Chester G. b.20Apr1858-d.4Jan1928, n/t Hazel, Margaret D., Frank W. & Arthur M. Porter

NSub PORTER Margaret D. b.19Sep1864-d.20Nov1940, n/t Hazel, Chester G., Frank W. & Arthur M. Porter

NSub PORTER Frank Weeks b.1895-d.1987, "Mother" w/ Arthur M., n/t Hazel, Chester G. & Margaret D. Porter

NSub PORTER Arthur Morris b.1891-d.1937, "Father" w/ Frank W., n/t Hazel, Chester G. & Margaret D. Porter

NSub MANEGOLD Elfrieda b.1875-d.1877, n/t Charles D. & Louise Manegold

NSub MANEGOLD Charles D. b.1851-d.1897, "Father" n/t Elfrieda & Louise Manegold

NSub MANEGOLD Louise b.1855-d.1942, "Mother" n/t Elfrieda & Charles D. Manegold

NSub CURRIE Elfriede G. b.1887-d.1869, n/t Magdalena, Adam, Henry D., George & Elizabeth Gettelmann, cemetery records show she was the wife of Herbert E. Currie and her maiden name was Gettelmann

NSub GETTELMANN Magdalena b.1850-d.1932, n/t Adam, Henry D., George & Elizabeth Gettelmann & Elfriede G. Currie

NSub GETTELMANN Adam b.1847-d.1925, n/t Magdslena, Henry D., George & Elizab eth Gettelmann & Elfriede G. Currie

NSub GETTELMANN Henry D. d.1884, n/t Magdalena, Adam, George & Elizabeth Gettelmann & Elfriede G. Currie; only one date

NSub GETTELMANN George d.1879, n/t Magdalena, Adam, Henry D. & Elizabeth Gettelmann & Elfriede G. Currie; only one date

NSub GETTELMANN Elizabeth b.1873-d.1876, n/t Magdalena, Adam, Henry D. & George Gettelmann & Elfriede G. Currie

NSub WOLLAEGER Amanda G. b.1880-d.1960

NSub HAUBERT Ida M. J. b.1881-d.1938, w/ George Haubert

NSub HAUBERT George b.1864-d.1941, w/ Ida M. J. Haubert

NSub JAMAR Kathleen Anne b.1955-d.1984

NSub DITTMAR Edna I. b.1892-d.1939, n/t Audrey, Addie & John F. Dittmar

NSub DITTMAR Audrey b.15Mar1894-d.6May1895, n/t Edna I., Addie & John F. Dittmar; stone is a fallen dove by a tree trunk

NSub DITTMAR Addie b.1868-d.1954, n/t Edna I., Audrey & John F. Dittmar

NSub DITTMAR John F. b.1861-d.1911, n/t Edna I., Audrey & Addie Dittmar

NSub FRICKE Christian b.1821 Alm, Braunschweig-d.14Nov1898, n/t Auguste N. M. Fricke

NSub FRICKE Auguste N. (MOSES) b.9Jul1819 Brunswick-
d.14Sep1904, n/t Christian Fricke

NSub HANDLEY Leta B. b.1891-d.1974

NSub HANEY Jeannette b.1877-d.1898, n/t Robert, Mary H. & Chas A.
Haney

NSub HANEY Robert b.1879-d.1880, n/t Jeannette, Mary H. & Chas A.
Haney

NSub HANEY Mary H. b.1852-d.1926, n/t Jeannette, Robert & Chas A.
Haney

NSub HANEY Chas A. b.1852-d.1917, n/t Jeannette, Robert & Mary H.
Haney

NSub SIEBERT Arnold W. b.1907-d.1971, w/ Mary, n/t William & Mary
F. Siebert

NSub SIEBERT Mary b.1907-d.19—, w/ Arnold W., n/t William & Mary
F. Siebert

NSub SIEBERT William b.26Oct1867-d.28Nov1950, "WIS. 1st SGT 1
INFANTRY SP AM WAR" n/t Arnold W., Mary & Mary F. Siebert

NSub SIEBERT Mary F. b.1871-d.1956, n/t Arnold W., Mary & William
Siebert

NSub ? Mutter d., n/t Vater; nothing else

NSub ? Vater d., n/t Mutter; nothing else

NSub NELL Carl b.14Mar1833-d.18Feb1900, "Vater" n/t Wilhelmine
Nell

NSub NELL Wilhelmine b.15Oct1836-d.5Apr1906, "Mutter" n/t Carl
Nell

NSub BUNKE Matilda b.1871-d.1933, "Mother" n/t Paul F. Bunke

NSub BUNKE Paul F. b.1874-d.1934, "Father" n/t Matilda Bunke

NSub BLUM Agnes b.16Apr1898-d.15Aug1952, "Wife" w/ Fred J., n/t
Bertha, Marie & John Blum

NSub BLUM Fred J. b.22Jul1899-d.26May1979, w/ Agnes, n/t Bertha,
Marie & John Blum

NSub BLUM Bertha b.10Apr1898-d.20Aug1914, "Daughter" n/t Agnes &
Fred J., w/ Marie & John Blum

NSub BLUM Marie b.20Apr1868-d.18May1945, "Mother" n/t Agnes &
Fred J., w/ Bertha & John Blum

NSub BLUM John b.1Jan1866-d.5Feb1952, "Father" n/t Agnes & Fred J.,
w/ Bertha & Marie Blum

NSub LOGAN Arline M. b.1898-d.1954

NSub MULHOLLAND Thompson b.1871-d.1933, "Father" n/t Meta
Mulholland

NSub MULHOLLAND Meta b.1875-d.1959, n/t Thompson Mulholland

NSub TENNANT Richard b.1May1843-d.19Jun1909, "Father" n/t Cora L,
Harriet D., Agnes D., Agnes S. & Richard Tennant & Robert Thomp-
son*
NSub TENNANT Cora L. b.23Jan1860-d.12Jun1930, n/t Richard, Harriet
D, Agnes D., Agnes S. & Richard Tennant & Robert Thompson
NSub TENNANT Harriet D. b.24Oct1884-d.22Mar1975, "Daughter" n/t
Richard, Cora L., Agnes D., Agnes S. & Richard Tennant & Robert
Thompson
NSub TENNANT Agnes D. b.1810-d.1900, "Mother" w/ Richard, n/t Cora
L., Harriet D., Agnes S. & Richard Tennant & Robert Thompson*
NSub TENNANT Richard b.1815-d.1900, w/ Agnes D., n/t Cora L.,
Harriet D., Agnes S. & Richard Tennant & Robert Thompson*
NSub THOMPSON Robert b.2Mar1816-d.16Feb1904, "Uncle" n/t Agnes
D., Cora L., Harriet D., Agnes S., Richard & Richard Tennant *
NSub TENNANT Agnes S. b.17Jun1847-d.26Jun1917, "Auntie" n/t Agnes
D., Cora L., Harriet D., Richard & Richard Tennant & Robert Thomp-
son *
NSub LUBLOW Viola b.1914-d.no date, w/ Benjamin Lublow
NSub LUBLOW Benjamin b.1909-d.1987, w/ Viola Lublow
NSub MOORE Phyllis E. b.1921-d.1980, "Ever Remembered Ever
Loved"
NSub HUNT Thomas Frederick b.1956-d.1986, n/t Laurine F. B., George
B. Hunt, Lydia, Harold, Sophia, John, Dorothea, Addie N. & Frederich
H. Bark
NSub HUNT Laurine F. (BARK) b.1900-d.1999, w/ George B.,n/t Thomas
F. Hunt & Lydia, Harold, Sophia, John, Dorothea, Addie N. & Frederich
H. Bark
NSub HUNT George B. b.1901-d.1969, w/ Laurine F. B., n/t Thomas F.
Hunt & Harold, Sophia, John, Dorothea, Addie N. & Frederich H. &
Lydia Bark
NSub BARK Lydia b.26Sep1894-d.12Oct1894, n/t Laurine F. B., George
B. & Thomas F. Hunt & Harold, Sophia, John, Dorothea, & Frederich
H. & Addie N. Bark
NSub BARK Harold b.1902-d.1918, n/t Laurine F. B., George B. &
Thomas F. Hunt & Lydia, Sophia, John, Dorothea, & Frederich H. &
Addie N. Bark
NSub BARK Sophia b.1835-d.1910, n/t Laurine F. B., George B. &
Thomas F. Hunt & Lydia, Harold, John, Dorothea, & Frederich H. &
Addie N. Bark
NSub BARK John b.1834-d.1910, n/t Laurine F. B., George B. & Thomas
F. Hunt & Lydia, Harold, Sophia, Dorothea, & Frederich H. & Addie N.
Bark

NSub BARK Dorothea (SIGGLOW) b.1871-d.1918, n/t Laurine F. B., George B. & Thomas F. Hunt, w/ Frederick H., n/t Lydia, Harold, & Frederich H., Sophia, John & Addie N. Bark

NSub BARK Frederich H. b.1867-d.1952, n/t Laurine F. B., George B. & Thomas F. Hunt, w/ Dorothea S., n/t Lydia, Harold, , Sophia, Addie N. & John Bark*

NSub BARK Addie (NOLL) b.1886-d.1939, n/t Laurine F. B., George B. & Thomas F. Hunt & Dorothea S., Lydia, Harold, John, Sophia & Frederich H. Bark

NSub POELTZIG Max E. b.16Mar1889-d.28Mar1974, w/ Edith L., n/t Harold C. Poeltzig

NSub POELTZIG Edith L. b.21Jun1890-d.30Jan1959, w/ Max E., n/t Harold C. Poeltzig

NSub POELTZIG Harold C. b.13Jun1925-d.5Apr1945, "WIS. S SGT 397 INFANTRY 100 DIV WWII" n/t Max E. & Edith L. Poeltzig

NSub DREW Susan M. b.1872-d.1950

NSub SYLVESTER Infant b.15Jun1889-d.13Sep1889, n/t Pauline, Bertha & Gustav A. Sylvester; can't read first name, but it ends with an "A"; no card in cemetery records

NSub SYLVESTER Pauline b.1824-d.1901, "Mutter" n/t Infant, Bertha & Gustav A. Sylvester

NSub SYLVESTER Bertha b.1866-d.1910, "Mother" n/t Infant, Pauline & Gustav A. Sylvester

NSub SYLVESTER Gustav A. b.1861-d.1939, "Father" n/t Infant, Pauline & Bertha Sylvester

NSub KNISPEK Anton b.23Aug1912-d.18Dec1983

NSub HOMBSCH Hildegard b.1904-d.1990, "Mother" w/ Clarence E. Hombsch

NSub HOMBSCH Clarence E. b.1905-d.1988, "Father" w/ Hildegard Hombsch

NSub FARRIES Mary B. b.1871-d.1899

NSub SCHOTT Patricia M. b.18Jan1938-d.29Mar1987

NSub FALK Lillie b.9Jun1901-d.16Jun1901, "Unser Liebling" n/t Olga & Charles W. Falk

NSub FALK Olga b.1877-d.1959, "Mother" n/t Lillie, w/ Charles W. Falk

NSub FALK Charles W. b.1873-d.1957, "Father" n/t Lillie, w/ Olga Falk

NSub AMES John A. b.8Dec1871-d.16Apr1900

NSub ADAMS Norma Z. b.1891-d.1957, w/ George C. Adams

NSub ADAMS George C. b.1885-d.1968, w/ Norma Z. Adams

NSub HARTEL Fred W. b.29Mar1892-d.27Jan1954, "WIS. SGT BGLR 120 FLD ARTY 32 DIV WWI"

NSub WALTERS Vera R. b.1893-d.1967, "Wife" w/ Fred H. Walters

NSub WALTERS Fred H. b.1886-d.1952, "Husband" w/ Vera R. Walters
NSub STONECIPHER Mary Wright b.1854-d.1986, P.E.O. mkr
NSub FALK Ella L. b.8Dec1895-d.7Nov1973, "Wife" w/ Henry E. Falk;
    dates completed from cemetery records
NSub FALK Henry E. b.1879-d.1948, "Husband" w/ Ella L. Falk
NSub WALLMANN William b.1870-d.1945
NSub SCHULT Ernst Joachim b.1850-d.1907, w/ Marie Schult
NSub SCHULT Marie b.1856-d.1941, w/ Ernst J. Schult
NSub COUTURE Hazel b.1901-d.1966
NSub MORRIS Ann b.1828-d.1905, w/ David Morris
NSub MORRIS David b.1823-d.1902, w/ Ann Morris
NSub WOODMANSEE Leroy W. d.12Jul1942, "WIS. CAPTAIN ORD-
    NANCE" n/t William & Persis E. Woodmansee; only one date
NSub WOODMANSEE William b.1840-d.1898, "CO. C 7 OHIO INF" w/
    Persis E., n/t Leroy W. Woodmansee; 2 stones
NSub WOODMANSEE Persis E. b.1845-d.1919, w/ William, n/t Leroy
    W. Woodmansee
NSub COIT Clinton b.1822-d.1898
NSub POTTER Laura W. b.1857-d.1916
NSub KELSEY Charles b.1853-d.1910, "Father" n/t Frances E. Kelsey
NSub KELSEY Frances Eva b.1858-d.1927, "Mother" n/t Charles Kelsey
NSub BOUSHEK Joseph b.1882-d.1925, "Father" n/t Russell Boushek
NSub BOUSHEK Russell b.24Jun1916-d.20Sep1978, "PFC US ARMY
    WWII" n/t Joseph Boushek
NSub HAMMOND Hattie d.1935, w/ Martha Krueger, n/t Minna & Julius
    Krueger
NSub KRUEGER Martha b.1885-d.1961, w/ Hattie Hammond, n/t Minna
    & Julius Krueger
NSub KRUEGER Minna b.1853-d.1926, "Mother" n/t Hattie Hammond &
    Martha & Julius Krueger
NSub KRUEGER Julius b.1844-d.1910, "Father" n/t Hattie Hammond &
    Martha & Minna Krueger
NSub JONES William R. b.1889-d.1911, "s/o David & Eliza Jones"
NSub RUTZ Ella b.1884-d.1965, "Mother" w/ John Rutz
NSub RUTZ John b.1884-d.1940, "Father" w/ Ella Rutz
NSub WOLFGRAM Bertha b.1879-d.1948, w/ William, Carl, Minnie &
    Fred Wolfgram
NSub WOLFGRAM William b.1872-d.1946, w/ Bertha, Carl, Minnie &
    Fred Wolfgram
NSub WOLFGRAM Carl b.1874-d.1940, w/ Bertha, William, Minnie &
    Fred Wolfgram

NSub WOLFGRAM Minnie b.1841-d.1911, w/ Bertha, William, Carl &
Fred Wolfgram

NSub WOLFGRAM Fred b.1835-d.1926, w/ Bertha, William, Carl &
Minnie Wolfgram

NSub LULL Joseph b.1896-d.1961, w/ Emma Lull

NSub LULL Emma b.1891-d.1951, w/ Joseph Lull

NSub CANRIGHT Lillie b.1865-d.1910

NSub MAYES Robert b.1917-d.1918

NSub RUTZ Eleanor d.19Apr1919, "Beloved Sisters" w/ Alvina Rutz

NSub RUTZ Alvina d.6Jan1985, "Beloved Sisters" w/ Eleanor Rutz

NSub WOLF Clarence A. b.2May1885-d.27May1916, "Just As I Am" n/t
Augusta & John Wolf

NSub WOLF Augusta b.1859-d.1951, n/t Clarence A. & John Wolf

NSub WOLF John b.5Mar1859-d.1Oct1899, n/t Clarence A. & Augusta
Wolf

NSub MORSE Jessie E. Rhodes b.1862-d.1900, "Beloved w/o Henry P.
Morse" GAR mkr; there is no record of Henry in cemetery rec; n/t
Marion E. Morse Husman

NSub HUSMAN Marion E. Morse b.1890-d.1935, "Beloved w/o John L.
Husman" n/t Jesse E. R. Morse

NSub JAEGER Bertha b.1889-d.1973, "Mother" w/ Fred Jaeger

NSub JAEGER Fred b.1894-d.1957, "Father" w/ Bertha Jaeger

NSub NEHRING Anne b.1894-d.19Nov1979, n/t Emil, Emma M. H.,
Anna H., Emma, Emil, & Wilhelm G. Nehring; DOD from cemetery
records.

NSub MUSOLF Anna b.26Jul1842-d.21Oct1928

NSub NEHRING Emil b.1901-d.1980, n/t Emma M. H., Anna H., Emma,
Emil, Anne & Wilhelm G. Nehring

NSub NEHRING Emma M. H. b.6Dez1896-d.2Nov1906, n/t Emil, Anna
H., Emma, Emil, Anne & Wilhelm G. Nehring

NSub NEHRING Anna H. b.14Sep1893-d.6Dez1893, n/t Emil, Emma M.
H., Emma, Emil, Anne & Wilhelm G. Nehring

NSub NEHRING Emma b.1865-d.1943, "Mother" w/ Emil, n/t Emma M.
H., Anna H., Emil, Anne & Wilhelm G. Nehring

NSub NEHRING Emil b.1865-d.1950, "Father" w/ Emma, n/t Emma M.
H., Anna H., Emil, Anne & Wilhelm G. Nehring

NSub NEHRING Wilhelm G. b.27Jan1899-d.18Feb1918, n/t Emma,
Emil, Emma M. H., Anna H., Emil, & Anne Nehring

NSub CHALKER Harriet E. b.1879-d.1959, n/t R. I., Julius, Amelia A. &
Gladstone Chalker & Blanch Comstock & Lucy Farrar

NSub CHALKER R. I. b.7 Jan 1918-d.30 Oct 1951, "Father, Capt." n/t
Harriet E., Julius, Amelia A., & Gladstone Chalker & Blanch Comstock

& Lucy Farrar, cemetery records show his name as Capt. Rex I. Chalker

NSub CHALKER Julius b.18Mar1841-d.26Mar1904, "Father" n/t Harriet E., R. I., Amelia & Gladstone Chalker & Blanch Comstock & Lucy Farrar; first name from cemetery records

NSub CHALKER Amelia Ann b.29Oct1836-d.9Dec1919, n/t Harriet E., R. I., Julius, & Gladstone Chalker & Blanch Comstock & Lucy Farrar; first name from cemetery records

NSub COMSTOCK Blanch (CHALKER) b.17May1870-d.7Dec1911, "w/o J. H. Comstock" n/t Harriet E., R. I., Julius, Amelia A., & Gladstone Chalker & Lucy C. Farrar

NSub FARRAR Lucy (CHALKER) b.27Mar1873-d.27Aug1903, "w/o J. B. Farrer" n/t Harriet E., R. I., Julius, Amelia A., & Gladstone Chalker & Blanch Comstock

NSub CHALKER Gladstone b.21Aug1866-d.10Jan1903, n/t Harriet E., R. I., Julius, Amelia A. Chalker & Blanch Comstock & Lucy Farrar

NSub WEBB Jeanne b.10Apr1925-d.10Nov1925, "Infants" w/ Wm. Webb; dates from cemetery records

NSub WEBB Wm. b.13Sep1920-d.13Sep1920, "Infants" w/ Jeanne Webb; dates from cemetery records

NSub PEASE Richard L. b.1919-d.1975, n/t Gertrude B. & Frederick J. Pease

NSub PEASE Gertrude B. b.1898-d.1974, w/ Frederick J., n/t Richard L. Pease

NSub PEASE Frederick J. b.1893-d.1974, w/ Gertrude B., n/t Richard L. Pease

NSub MAEDER Otto b.1888-d.1895

NSub MEWS Helene (SIEBRECHT) b.1872-d.1896

NSub KOEPSEL E. b.20Okt1829-d.27Sep1896, "Mutter", cemeter records show her name as Frederike Wilhelmina Henrietta Koepsel as her name, they didn't know which was her first name, but perhaps she was called Etta or Erike, she is buried in the Krueger Plot.

NSub KIESLICH Fred A. b.30Apr1838-d.28Jun1911, "CO C 9 WIS INF""; the name on the stone is A.F. Kieslich; dates from cemetery records; Fred resided in Milwaukee when he enlisted in the army on 10 Sept 1861, he was transfered from Co. I, Mustered Out 30 Jan 1866[54]

NSub WILKE Frances b.1894-d.1895, "Daughter"

NSub ANDERSEN Irma b.1896-d.1930

NSub MANTY Ernstina b.12Dez1825-d.25Nov1895

NSub KLAWITTER Adam d.30Nov1899

NSub KINDT Carl b.6Nov1905-d.2Sep1911

NSub SIEBRECHT Emma b.1893-d.1894
NSub ARMSTRONG James b.no dates-d.no dates
NSub JOHNSON Charles b.17Dec1864-d.25May1894
NSub BAHR William H. b.1879-d.1970, "Father" n/t Mary Bahr
NSub BAHR Mary b.1878-d.1942, "Mother" n/t William H. Bahr
NSub BRIGGS Hosia F. b.no date-d.1Dec1892, "CO D 88 ILL. INFAN-
TRY" death date and first name from cemetery records
NSub PRIEBE John b.1844-d.1914, "Father" n/t Henrietta, Martha,
Richard, Herman & Augusta Priebe
NSub PRIEBE Henrietta b.1846-d.1937, "Mother" n/t John, Martha,
Richard, Herman & Augusta Priebe
NSub PRIEBE Martha b.1882-d.1930, "Daughter" n/t John, Henrietta,
Richard, Herman & Augusta Priebe
NSub PRIEBE Richard b.1901-d.1956, n/t John, Henrietta & Martha, w/
Herman & Augusta Priebe
NSub PRIEBE Herman b.1875-d.1906, n/t John, Henrietta & Martha, w/
Richard & Augusta Priebe
NSub PRIEBE Augusta b.1875-d.1963, n/t John, Henrietta & Martha, w/
Richard & Herman Priebe
NSub GUENTHER Marian d.1912, w/ Wilhelmine, George, Elizabeth,
Henrietta & Fred Guenther & Augusta H., Bernhard & Henry Hoffman
family; only one date
NSub GUENTHER Wilhelmine b.1847-d.1935, w/ Marian, George,
Elizabeth, Henrietta & Fred Guenther & Augusta H., Bernhard & Henry
Hoffman family
NSub GUENTHER George b.1841-d.1920, w/ Marian, Wilhelmine,
Elizabeth, Henrietta & Fred Guenther & Augusta H., Bernhard & Henry
Hoffman family
NSub GUENTHER Elizabeth b.1913-d.1914, w/ Marian, George,
Wilhelmine, Henrietta & Fred Guenther & Augusta H., Bernhard &
Henry Hoffman family
NSub GUENTHER Henrietta b.1890-d.1935, w/ Marian, George,
Wilhelmine, Elizabeth & Fred Guenther & Augusta H., Bernhard &
Henry Hoffman family
NSub GUENTHER Fred b.1890-d.1925, w/ Marian, George, Wilhelmine,
Elizabeth & Henrietta Guenther & Augusta H., Bernhard & Henry
Hoffman family
NSub HOFFMAN Augusta H. b.1902-d.1987, w/ Bernhard & Henry
Hoffmann; otherside of Guenther family stone
NSub HOFFMAN Bernhard b.1879-d.1980, w/ Augusta & Henry
Hoffmann; otherside of Guenther family stone

NSub HOFFMAN Henry b.1871-d.1905, w/ Augusta & Bernhard Hoffmann; otherside of Guenther family stone
NSub BUSSE Lydia L. b.Apr 1894-d.Dec 1982, w/ Walter A. Busse
NSub BUSSE Walter A. b.Sep 1891-d.May 1936, w/ Lydia L. Busse
NSub MEIER Florence E. b.1908-d.no date, w/ George W. Meier; picture of horse on stone
NSub MEIER George W. b.1906-d.1995, w/ Florence E. Meier; picture of horse on stone
NSub HAAS N. Gertrude b.1899-d.1983
NSub WILL Ida b.1872-d.1942, w/ Julius, n/t Herbert & Hugo Will
NSub WILL Julius b.1863-d.1939, w/ Ida, n/t Herbert & Hugo Will
NSub WILL Herbert b.11Sep1900-d.17Jun1902, n/t Ida, Julius & Hugo Will
NSub WILL Hugo b.25Nov1892-d.30Nov1892, n/t Ida, Julius & Herbert Will
NSub HENKE Martin b.18Jul1911-d.18Jul1911, "Baby"
NSub BLOEDORN Arthur b.7Jan1908-d.15Aug1908, "Unser Liebling; s/o Carl & Minnie" Bloedorn"
NSub MILLER George b.1908-d.1910
NSub LINDQUIST Alvin O. b.28May1913-d.17Mar1914, "Son"
NSub BLOEDORN Karl b.17Jun1907-d.18Jun1907, w/ Willie Bloedorn
NSub BLOEDORN Willie b.17Jun1907-d.28Jun1907, w/ Karl Bloedorn
NSub MILLER Martha b.1902-d.1906
NSub HURLBURT Isabell b.Feb 1905-d.Mar 1906, "Baby"
NSub JOHA Infant b.1Jan1910-d.1Jan1910, "Baby d/o O. F. & E. Joha"
NSub BEECK Edwin d.11Feb1912, "Baby" only one date
NSub FOSTER, nothing other than Foster on stone
NSub PHILLIPS Joseph b.1835-d.1891
NSub McCORDY John T. b.no date-d.23Aug1891, "CO. H 22nd IND. INF." 47y 4m 26d; date, age and first name from cemetery records
NSub MUENCHOW August/Augusta W. b.22Jun1892-d.1Sep1897, no card in cemetery records
NSub FALK Ernestina b.1860-d.1897, "Mutter"
NSub BRADSHAW Jacobena b.22Dec1842-d.15Apr1893, "Mother"
NSub BAUER Fred b.1827-d.1893
NSub ARMSTRONG Robert b.no date-d.no date
NSub BAETZ Anna B. b.20Mar1819-d.17Nov1891
NSub GRAMS Eduard b.9Apr1860-d.15Oct1897, Vater
NW2 RAASCH Arthur b.9Apr1900-d.12Apr1900
NW2 GUNDERMANN John b.7Mar1844-d.26Jul1892
NW2 PITZKE Karl b.12Mar1824-d.30Jun1899

NW2 RADKE Louise d.4Mar1898 "54y"
NW2 DALKE Walter b.11Sep1897-d.1Feb1898
NW2 OLDENBURG Alfred b.24Sep1897-d.11Jan1898
NW2 KUMM Infant b.1890-d.1890 w/ Elsie Kumm
NW2 KUMM Elsie b.1891-d.1891 w/ Infant Kumm
NW2 BAHR Emilie b.6Mai1877-d.10Dez1890
NW2 KORTH August b.12Oct1831-d.24Dec1889 "Vater"
NW2 PECHMANN Louise b.2Feb1830-d.22Dez1889
NW2 HANDLEY Royal L. b.1876-d.1941 "Father"
NW2 KEMENY Anna d. can't read; no cemetery record; could be an
    infant
NW2 SHAFER Clarence b.25Feb1912-d.25Mai1915, "Hier Ruht in
    Frieden Unser Engel" (Here Rests in Peace our Angel)
NW2 STORTS Edwin b.24Apr1916-d.27Apr1916
NW2 CONKLYN James Edwards b.2Apr1915-d.30Jun1916
NW2 SIEMAN Elmer b.2May1916-d.22Mar1917
NW2 ERDMANN Harry S. b.17Aug1919-d.28May1920, "Son"
NW2 STACK Baby b.1919-d.1920
NW2 STREHLOW Hattie b.1919-d.1919, "Daughter"
NW2 ESCH Delores M. L. b.1918-d.1919
NW2 ZOBEL Richard b.1915-d.1918
NW2 BARTELT Ernestine d.1918, "Baby" only one date
NW2 HARRISON Vera b.1908-d.1940
NW2 MUTH Adam H. b.24Aug1809-d.13Nov1889, "Grossvater"
NW2 KURTH Herman b.7Aug1853-d.24May1888
NW2 QUINN Nathan Patrick b.18Aug1983-d.11Jan1986, "Our Little
    Boy"
NW2 SIMON Isaac E. b.1983-d.1985, "Beloved Son"
NW2 HAYES Robert Alan b.30Aug1975-d.22Feb1976, "Our Beloved
    Son"
NW2 SEIDER Cassandra K. b.5Jul1974-d.12Nov1975, "I Am Jesus'
    Little Lamb"
NW2 PILON Jane Elizabeth b.24Nov1962-d.13Jun1966, "Our Little
    Angel"
NW2 KRAUSE Joshua L. b.26Mar1979-d.6Jun1981, there is a sculpture
    of a bird and rose on the stone
NW2 MARGGRAFF ? b.14Mai1883-d.23Sep1883, can't read first name;
    no cemetery record
NW2 SCHROEDER Louisa Wilhelmina Caroline b.10Sep1845-
    d.7Jun1889
NW2 GRAY Willard A. b.1866-d.1908

124

NW2 DODGE Nenemiah, M.D. b.1855-d.1908
NW2 STIMSON George R. b.25May1825-d.1Jan1909, "Father"
NW2 MEWS Julius b.19Dez1856-d.1Jun1909
NW2 COX Wm. S. b.17Nov1820-d.1Aug1903, "CORPL. CO. D. 1 WIS.
INF. SP.-AM. WAR" military stone
NW2 MASCH Friedrich b.28Jan1866-d.5Feb1907, "Papa"
NW2 McCUSH Reason b.no date-d.25Apr1906, "CO. H. 30 IND. INF."
    military stone; age 71; Civil War Veteran; date, age and military
    infomation from cemetery records
NW2 GROTH Caroline b.1866-d.1905, "Mother"
NW2 NORDSTROM Erik d.20Jul1905, "18y 4m"
NW2 McCANN Jno. b.no date-d.7Dec1905, "CO. C. 110 PA. INF."
    military stone; age 70; Civil War Vet., GAR Member; date, age and
    military information from cemetery records
NW2 SCHERREIKS George b.1900-d.1905
NW2 SCHROEDER Grace b.1870-d.1940, "Mother"
NW2 BAHR Martin b.12Nov1843-d.1Dez1887
NW2 REDZINSKE Paul b.22Feb1888-d.20Jul1893
NW2 GUNDERMAN Baby b.1887-d.1887
NW2 SCHNEBLADEN/SONNEBLADEN Christina (BECKER?)
    b.5Feb1805-d.11Mai1887, hard to read; can't find in cemetery records
    under either name
NW2 KORNBERGER Ella b.17Oct1883-d.29Oct1886, hard to read
NW2 PITSKE Henriette b.29Nov1830-d.9Apr1899
NW2 PIERCE Donald b.18Apr1950-d.21Apr1950
NW2 WERNER Friedrich E. b.18Feb1827-d.17Nov1885, "Vater"
NW2 SCHWARTZ Catherine b.17Jul1857-d.19Feb1885
NW2 HARVEY Baby d.24Jun1898, "Infant s/o Wm. & Florence Harvey"
NW2 SIEGER Ernest W. d., can't read; no cemetery record
NW2 HOFFMANN Martha L. b.1880-d.13Mar1881, w/ Marie E.
    Hoffmann, stone broken, probably both babies; one date for one and the
    other date for the other
NW2 HOFFMANN Marie E. b.7Oct1880-d.22Mai1881, w/ Martha L.
    Hoffmann, stone broken, probably both babies; one date for one and the
    other date for the other
NW2 BIELEFELD Dorathea b.30Mar1837-d.13Jun1881
NW2 MARQUARDT Carl b.7Mai1800-d.23Jun1882, stone worn, hard to
    read
NW2 ACKMANN Elisabeth M. b.14Apr1828-d.2Apr1904, "Mother"
NW2 MEWS Carl b.30Oct1883-d.19Mai1884
NW2 GRUNWALD William b.6Aug1855-d.27Oct1884

NW2 CLAPP Children b.no date-d.no date, "Our Two Little Darlings, Infant Children of W. H. & H. G. Clapp"; they are buried in the 1884 area; no cemetery record

NW2 ANDREAS Margaretha b.27Dez1821-d.1Nov1885

NW2 HELLER Henry b.1873-d.1940

NW2 RADTKE Carl b.1854-d.1904

NW2 KANE Theresa b.9Mar1884-d.20Apr1904, "Sister"

NW2 GALEN Ivan b.no date Te Bergeik, Nederland Rov. Noordbraband?-d.no date, West Allis, (I think this should be Noordbraland or in English North Braland); no cemetery record

NW2 FONSTIEL Wm. M. b.no date-d.4Aug1904, "CO. K 14 OHIO INF." Civil War stone; date of death from cemetery records

NW2 KROENING Friedricke b.25Dec1823-d.10Aug1903

NW2 DEWEY Arthur R. or B. d.9Jan1852, "s/o—r A. & Cynthia Dewey, 5y 2m 16d" hard to read, some of the letters chipped, could only read the last letter of father's name

NW2 HERBST Jakob d.25Aug1877, "50?y 7m 17d" hard to read

NW2 KUNY Concordia b.1Jul1821-d.13Sep1877

NW2 KORTH Karl F. b.23Aug1849-d.19Sep1871

NW2 PICKER Loisa b.13Mai1873-d.10Nov1878, n/t Ida, Sofia & Joachim Picker

NW2 PICKER Ida? b.7Mar1880-d.17Mar1892, n/t Loisa, Sofia & Joachim Picker

NW2 PICKER Sofia b.17Aug1839-d.10Sep1899, w/ Joachim, n/t Loisa & Sofia Picker

NW2 PICKER Joachim b.30Sep1830-d.11Jun1902, w/ Sofia, n/t Loisa & Sofia Picker; his name may be spelled Joochim

NW2 KUNEY/OKUNEY Fredrich d.21Aug1879, name hard to read; no cemetery record under either name

NW2 JONES Bertha b.1868-d.1939

NW2 FALK Martin b.23Nov1834-d.4Apr1902, w/ Pauline Falk

NW2 FALK Pauline b.11Jun1838-d.3Dez1922, w/ Martin Falk

NW2 WHALEY Jas. b.no date-d.20May1902, "8 OHIO L.A." Civil War Veteran; DOD from cemetery records

NW2 STEFFEN Minnie b.3Apr1841-d.14Jun1902

NW2 METZGER John C. b.no date-d.26Aug1902, "CO. I 27 N.Y. INF." Death date from cemetery records, Civil War Veteran

NW2 PRIEBE Wilhelm b.11Sep1870-d.20Sep1902

NW2 KALIES Ernstine (THUROW) b.3Jun1841-d.18Mar1902

NW2 SYLLM Ad. Oscar b.18Dec1858-d.25Feb1902

NW2 STEGNER Frederick b.17Aug1831 Coburg, Saxony-d.1Jul1901

NW2 NELDNER W. F. b.1847-d.1901

NW2 GRIGG Benton b.1884-d.1937 w/ Hazel Grigg

NW2 GRIGG Hazel b.1901-d.1999 w/ Benton Grigg

NW2 TILLMANO ? Belle d.30Apr1868, "Dr. I. I. Tillmano" stone worn, hard to read

NW2 BENDINGER Phillip d.15Nov1864, "Vater; 41y; CO. D. 35th WIS. INF." he has two stones; Phillip resided in Milwaukee when he enlisted in the army on 22 Sept 1863, he was a veteran, recruit and died in Wauwatosa 13 Nov 1864 of disease according to [55]

NW2 OLDHAM Scott S. b.8Feb1962-d.3Aug1978, "Beloved Son"

NW2 PHAN Gy Viet b.3-6-1926-d.11-8-1985 Milwaukee, "CU; LANG XUYEN GIA LOCHAI DUONG"

NW2 GRANSEE Jordan W. b.1931-d.1980

NW2 DANCKER Lois b.1900-d.1983

NW2 SEVEDGE Millie Loretta b.1930-d.no date, w/ James & Dorothy Carrigan & James L. Sevedge

NW2 CARRIGAN James b.1928-d.no date, w/ Dorothy Carrigan, James L. & Millie L. Sevedge

NW2 SEVEDGE Dorothy (CARRIGAN) b.1905-d.1999, w/ James Carrigan, James L. & Millie L. Sevedge

Sec7 SEVEDGE James Lewis b.12Dec1902-d.25Jan1998, w/ Dorothy & James Carrigan, & Millie L. Sevedge

NW2 HURLBUT Daisy b.1877-d.1946, "Mother"

NW2 ALBORN Ardis b.12Feb1915-d.3Sep1917, n/t George, Eleanore G., & Harold P. Alborn

NW2 ALBORN George b.1877-d.1956, n/t Ardis, Eleanore G., & Harold P. Alborn

NW2 ALBORN Eleanore G. b.11Nov1908-d.4Feb1988, "Beloved Wife & Mother" n/t Ardis, George, & Harold P. Alborn

NW2 ALBORN Harold P. d.4Apr1958, "WIS. PVT. S.A.T.C.; Milwaukee School of Engineers"; only one date

NW2 DOSENMAGEN Anna b.1861-d.1918

NW2 CONRAD Elsie b.1876-d.1930, w/ Ferdinand Conrad

NW2 CONRAD Ferdinand b.1874-d.1917, w/ Elsie Conrad *

NW2 KUMM Herman b.7Feb1863-d.19Jul1917, "Father" n/t Bertha & George H. Kumm

NW2 KUMM Bertha b.2Jan1866-d.8Dec1962, "Mother" n/t Herman & George H. Kumm

NW2 KUMM George H. b.2Dec1894-d.22Oct1961, n/t Herman & Bertha Kumm

---

55 *Roster of Wisconsin Volunteers, War Of The Rebellion, 1861-1865*

NW2 DEXHEIMER Irma b.1905-d.1979, "Mother"

NW2 SCHICK Emilie b.1852-d.1916

NW2 MOSS Lillian C. b.10Apr1883-d.13Apr1883, n/t Roy M., Cornelia S., Dorothy C., & John Moss & Kate M. & Edward Lawless

NW2 MOSS Roy M. b.19Apr1884-d.23Dec1970, n/t Lillian C., Cornelia S., Dorothy C., & John Moss & Kate M. & Edward Lawless

NW2 MOSS Cornelia S. b.27Mar1886-d.14Jun1968, n/t Lillian C., Roy M., Dorothy C., & John Moss & Kate M. & Edward Lawless

NW2 MOSS Dorothy C. b.4Dec1901-d.23Sep1996, n/t Lillian C., Roy M., Cornelia S., & John Moss & Kate M. & Edward Lawless

NW2 MOSS John b.9Dec1852-d.23Oct1916, "The Children's Friend" n/t Lillian C., Roy M., Cornelia S., & Dorothy Moss & Kate M. & Edward Lawless, John was the founder of the Standard Paper Company and superintendent of the Wauwatosa Methodist Church sunday School. Because of his teaching methods, Moss was loved by all the children in his classes.[56]

NW2 LAWLESS Kate Moss b.1859-d.1951, n/t Lillian C., Roy M., Cornelia S., & Dorothy C. Moss & Edward Lawless

NW2 LAWLESS Edward b.8Jul1870-d.3Aug1946, n/t Lillian C., Roy M., Cornelia S., & Dorothy C. Moss & Kate M. Lawless

NW2 FORESTER Ethel M. b.9Nov1885-d.10Mar1972, n/t John L. Forester; may be in Moss family plot

NW2 FORESTER John L. b.5Dec1884-d.22Jan1954, n/t Ethel M. Forester; may be in Moss family plot

NW2 GLEISNER Emilie (KRUEGER) b.27Jul1857-d.7Jul1915, "Mother"

NW2 GORDON Gustavus Ede. D.D. b.1834-d.1914, "Founder Wis. Humane Soc. Sometime Chaplain Milw. L. H. Squadron, In Loving Memory of Him, His Veteran Comrades Erect this Stone"

NW2 SEMROW Ferdenand b.1Oct1849-d.3Feb1913, "Father" n/t Louise Semrow

NW2 SEMROW Louise b.9Nov1859-d.22Oct1941, "Mother" n/t Ferdinand Semrow

NW2 RIEBE Augusta b.1866-d.1930, w/ Albert Riebe

NW2 RIEBE Albert b.1859-d.1935, w/ Augusta Riebe

NW2 PROPP Henry b.1866-d.1940, w/ Margaret Propp

NW2 PROPP Margaret b.1871-d.1914, w/ Henry Propp

NW2 KRUGER Louis b.10Jan1839-d.9Feb1920, "Vater" n/t Wilhelmine Kruger

NW2 KRUGER Wilhelmine b.6Nov1845-d.12Apr1914, "Mutter" n/t Louis Kruger

NW2 BLOEDORN Karl b.18Sep1844-d.2Jan1928, "Vater" n/t
Friedericka Bloedorn

NW2 BLOEDORN Friedericka b.14Feb1845-d.21Sep1913, "Mutter" n/t
Karl Bloedorn

NW2 JOHNSTONE Cody Cramer b.1906-d.1913, "Our Cody"

NW2 BACH Gerry H. b.1911-d.1966

NW2 JOHNSTONE Stanley b.1903-d.1925, "God is Love"

NW2 HOLLENBECK Alice E. b.1909-d.1913, w/ Norman W. & Lillian F.
Hollenbeck, n/t Hubert G. & Ruth N. Cloninger

NW2 HOLLENBECK Norman W. b.1873-d.1927, w/ Alice E. & Lillian F.
Hollenbeck, n/t Hubert G. & Ruth N. Cloninger

NW2 HOLLENBECK Lillian F. b.1887-d.1975, w/ Alice E. & Norman W.
Hollenbeck, n/t Hubert G. & Ruth N. Cloninger

NW2 CLONINGER Hubert G. b.21May1916-d.10Sep1983, w/ Ruth N.
Cloninger, n/t Alice E., Norman W. & Lillian F. Hollenbeck; they
appear to be in the same plot

NW2 CLONINGER Ruth N. b.28Mar1917-d., w/ Hubert G. Cloninger, n/t
Alice E., Norman W. & Lillian F. Hollenbeck; they appear to be in the
same plot

NW2 KOLB Elizabeth b.6Aug1849-d.8Feb1913, w/ Abraham & Elizabeth
Kolb

NW2 KOLB Elizabeth b.4Jan1882-d.28May1886, w/ Abraham & Elizabeth Kolb

NW2 KOLB Abraham b.3Mar1844-d.3Sep1919, w/ Elizabeth & Elizabeth
Kolb

NW2 JOLLIFFE Samuel Rev. b.24Jun1839-d.13Sep1929, w/ Jennie M.
Jolliffe

NW2 JOLLIFFE Jennie M. b.28Sep1849-d.9Feb1938, "w/o Rev. S.
Jolliffe" w/ Samuel Jolliffe

NW2 BIGSBY Katherine b.1845-d.1919, w/ Edgar, Charles & Marie A.
Bigsby *

NW2 BIGSBY Edgar b.1844-d.1913, "14th VT. VOL? (fancy carving, hard
to" read) w/ Katherine, Charles & Marie A. Bigsby

NW2 BIGSBY Charles b.1863-d.1937, w/ Katherine, Edgar & Marie A.
Bigsby

NW2 BIGSBY Marie A. b.1867-d.1938, w/ Katherine, Edgar & Charles
Bigsby

NW2 BELL Erwin J. b.1887-d.1956, n/t Althea B. Danielsen & Oscar &
Mary Helgesen; Bell/Helgesen plot

NW2 DANIELSEN Althea Bell b.1888-d.1979, n/t Erwin J. Bell & Oscar
& Mary Helgesen; Bell/Helgesen plot

NW2 HELGESEN Oscar b.1856-d.1913, n/t Erwin J. Bell & Althea B. Danielsen & Mary Helgesen; Bell/Helgesen plot *

NW2 HELGESEN Mary b.1863-d.1946, n/t Erwin J. Bell & Althea B. Danielsen & Oscar Helgesen; Bell/Helgesen plot

Sec7 PRATT Anna d.8Dec1941, "age 84" n/t Scott Pratt; may be in same plot with John & Sofia Schwenn

NW2 PRATT Scott b.1847-d.1912, n/t Anna Pratt; may be in same plot with John & Sofia Schwenn

NW2 SCHWENN John b.12Apr1834-d.1Mar1915, "Vater" w/ Sofia Schwenn; may be in same plot with Anna & Scott Pratt

NW2 SCHWENN Sofia b.24Feb1834-d.6Jan1914, "Mutter" w/ John Schwenn; may be in same plot with Anna & Scott Pratt

NW2 BENOY Ida L. b.12Nov1865-d.9Mar1913, n/t John R. Benoy

NW2 BENOY John R. b.24Dec1861-d.23Feb1936, n/t Ida L. Benoy; John purchased the Wauwatosa News in 1907 and took over management followed by his son, Cornelius Benoy.*

NW2 OLMSTED Sidney B. b.1898-d.1910, n/t William B., Henry F., & Cordelia P. Olmsted

NW2 OLMSTED William B. b.1865-d.1903, n/t Sidney B., Henry F., & Cordelia P. Olmsted

NW2 OLMSTED Henry F. b.1825-d.1895, "Father" n/t Sidney B., William B., & Cordelia P. Olmsted

NW2 OLMSTED Cordelia P. b.1834-d.1892, "Mother" n/t Sidney B., William B., & Henry F. Olmsted

NW2 FREY Edwin H. b.1909-d.1982, "Father" n/t Margaret L., Otilie H., Fred, & Lillie Frey

NW2 FREY Margaret L. b.1918-d.1981, "Mother" n/t Edwin H., Otilie H., Fred, & Lillie Frey

NW2 FREY Ottilie H. b.1880-d.1967, "Mother" n/t Edwin H., Margaret L., Fred, & Lillie Frey

NW2 FREY Fred b.1871-d.1936, "Father" n/t Edwin H., Margaret L., Ottilie H. & Lillie Frey

NW2 FREY Lillie b.1901-d.1920, "Daughter" n/t Edwin H., Margaret L., Ottilie H. & Fred Frey

NW2 SCHMAH Elsa I. b.1904-d.1998, w/ August F. Schmah; may be in Frey plot

NW2 SCHMAH August F. b.1900-d.1970, w/ Elsa I. Schmahl; may be in Frey plot

NW2 PEDRICK Mary A. (BROWN) b.1841-d.1920, n/t Cyrus Pedrick & Charles L. Brown family

NW2 PEDRICK Cyrus b.1830-d.1915, n/t Mary A. B. Pedrick & Charles L. Brown family

SEC7 BROWN C. Elmo b.1878-d.1916, n/t Lillian M. & Charles L. Brown & Mary A. & Cyrus Pedrick

SEC7 BROWN Lillian M. b.1855-d.1907, n/t C. Elmo & Charles L. Brown & Mary A. & Cyrus Pedrick

SEC7 BROWN Charles L. b.1847-d.1928, n/t C. Elmo & Lillian M. Brown & Mary A. & Cyrus Pedrick

SEC7 HOUGHTON Laura Madge b.1878-d.1973, n/t Mary J. B., Frank W., Albert B., Janet F., Albert F., Mary N., Frank W., & Harry A. Houghton

SEC7 HOUGHTON Mary J. Balch b.1855-d.1936, n/t Laura M., Frank W., Albert B., Janet F., Albert F., Mary N., Frank W., & Harry A. Houghton

SEC7 HOUGHTON Frank Wilbur b.1849-d.1932, n/t Mary J. B., Laura M., Albert B., Janet F., Albert F., Mary N., Frank W., & Harry A. Houghton

SEC7 HOUGHTON Albert Balch b.1882-d.1969, n/t Mary J. B., Laura M., Frank W., Janet F., Albert F., Mary N., Frank W., & Harry A. Houghton

SEC7 HOUGHTON Janet Fox b.1883-d.1957, n/t Mary J. B., Laura M., Frank W., Albert B., Albert F., Mary N., Frank W., & Harry A. Houghton

SEC7 HOUGHTON Albert Fox b.1920-d.1960, n/t Mary J. B., Laura M., Frank W., Albert B., Janet F., Mary N., Frank W., & Harry A. Houghton

SEC7 HOUGHTON Mary Narcissa b.1917-d.1917, n/t Mary J. B., Laura M., Frank W., Albert B., Janet F., Albert F., Frank W. & Harry A. Houghton

SEC7 HOUGHTON Frank Wilbur, Jr. b.1884-d.1897, n/t Mary J. B., Laura M., Frank W., Albert B., Janet F., Albert F., Mary N., & Harry A. Houghton

SEC7 HOUGHTON Harry Abner b.1886-d.1914, n/t Mary J. B., Laura M., Frank W., Albert B., Janet F., Albert F., Mary N., & Frank W. Houghton

SEC7 FOELSKE Mary b.1872-d.1913, w/ Charles Foelske

SEC7 FOELSKE Charles b.1878-d.1955, w/ Mary Foelske

SEC7 KUMM Fred b.1870-d.1940, w/ Wilhelmina Kumm, n/t Lillian K. Bastian

SEC7 KUMM Wilhelmina b.1875-d.1942, w/ Fred Kumm, n/t Lillian K. Bastian

SEC7 BASTIAN Lillian Kumm b.1900-d.1952, n/t Wilhelmina & Fred Kumm

SEC7 ENGEL Sophia b.13Oct1846-d.12Oct1912, "Mutter" n/t Johann Engel

SEC7 ENGEL Johann b.28Aug1844-d.17Aug1913, n/t Sophia Engel

SEC7 LANDOLT Alice b.1848-d.1936, w/ William Landolt *

SEC7 LANDOLT William H. b.1843-d.1911, "CO. A 5 WIS. INF. 1st SGT." w/ Alice Landolt; GAR mkr; two stones; W. H. Landolt was the Postmaster in Wauwatosa; William resided in Port Washington when he enlisted in the army on 21 Apr 1861, he was a Vet., held the ranks of Corpl. and Sergt., he was transfered to Co. A. Ind. Bat. 13 Jul 1864, he was made Brevet Capt. 6 Apr 1865 [57]*

SEC7 THOMAS Adeline Kissam b.17Dec1831-d.12Jan1913, "Beloved w/o William H. Thomas" n/t William H. & James Thomas

SEC7 THOMAS William H. b.1834-d.1921, n/t Adeline K. & James Thomas

SEC7 THOMAS Major James b.10Nov1859-d.9Jul1932, "Family Genealogist Kissam, Long & Thomas" n/t Adeline K. & William H. Thomas; Erected in Grateful Memory by Marion Thomas Kincaid.

SEC7 EGGERT Gertrude (HELLBERG) b.1859-d.1915, w/ William J. C. Eggert

SEC7 EGGERT William J. C. b.1858-d.1938, w/ Gertrude H. Eggert

SEC7 KOENITZER Carl W. b.1839-d.1914, w/ Marie D. Koenitzer

SEC7 KOENITZER Marie D. b.1851-d.1934, w/ Carl W. Koenitzer

SEC7 STREHLOW Wilhelmina b.16Feb1853-d.28Feb1915, "Mutter" n/t August Strehlow

SEC7 STREHLOW August b.17Feb1851-d.9Mai1931, "Vater" n/t Wilhelmina Strehlow

SEC7 PUEHLER Blanche b.1887-d.1955

SEC7 McGILL A. W. b.1871-d.1915

SEC7 LINDEMEYER Lucy (HENKEL) b.18Aug1885-d.16Dec1915, "Wife" inscription inside a heart

SEC7 MEYERS Emma b.1896-d.1972, "Mother"

SEC7 HOARE Hilda b.23Jul1915-d.21Nov1916

SEC7 SPAUDE Erma b.1895-d.1953, w/ Walter Spaude

SEC7 SPAUDE Walter b.1893-d.1927, w/ Erma Spaude

SEC7 PIPER Joachim b.1844-d.25Apr1921, w/ Carolina Piper; date of death from cemetery records

SEC7 PIPER Carolina b.1849-d.16Oct1919, w/ Joachim Piper; date of death from cemetery records

SEC7 KAPHINGST Daisy W. b.16Jan1916-d.17Apr1917, w/ Naomi L. Geiger, n/t Daisy A., William F. & Emma M. Kaphingst; on a curve facing north

SEC7 GEIGER Naomi Louise b.16Apr1944-d.11May1952, w/ Daisy W. Kaphinst, n/t Daisy A., William F. & Emma M. Kaphingst; on a curve facing north

---

57*Roster of Wisconsin Volunteers, War Of The Rebellion, 1861-1865*

SEC7 KAPHINGST Daisy A. b.1886-d.1918, n/t Daisy W., William F. &
Emma M. Kaphingst & Naomi L. Geiger; on a curve facing north
SEC7 KAPHINGST William F. b.1879-d.1953, n/t Daisy W., Daisy A. &
Emma M. Kaphingst & Naomi L. Geiger; on a curve facing north
SEC7 KAPHINGST Emma M. b.1881-d.1969, n/t Daisy W., Daisy A. &
William F. Kaphingst & Naomi L. Geiger; on a curve facing north
SEC7 WEHR Helen (PUETZ) b.21Dec1862-d.29Apr1943, "Mother" w/
John Wehr
SEC7 WEHR John b.12Aug1861-d.20Feb1918, "Father" w/ Helen P.
Wehr
SEC7 McINDOE Marilyn b.1930-d.1966
SEC7 PEABODY Albert C. Jr. b.13Sep1834-d.10Jan1919, "CAPT. CO. I
51 WIS. INF." GAR mkr; Albert G. lived in Hammond when he enlisted
in the army 11 Aug 1862, he was a transfer from Co. A, 30th Wiscon-
sin Infantry and held the rank of 2nd Lieut. in Co. B, 22 Feb 1865 and
was made Capt. 27 Apr 1865, Mustered Out 6 Aug 1865[58]; dates and
first name from cemetery records
SEC7 KRAUSE Emma b.3Dec1872-d.8Dec1918, "Mutter" n/t Walter
Krause
SEC7 KRAUSE Walter b.1899-d.1938, n/t Emma Krause
SEC7 ZIMMERMANN Theodore E. b.1861-d.1924, n/t Etta A. &
Winfield D. Zimmermann
SEC7 ZIMMERMANN Etta A. b.1866-d.1917, n/t Theodore E. &
Winfield D. Zimmermann
SEC7 ZIMMERMANN Winfield D. b.1899-d.1948, n/t Theodore E. &
Etta A. Zimmermann
SEC7 EGGERT Anna b.1878-d.1971, "Wife" n/t Ida & Fred Eggert
SEC7 EGGERT Ida b.1878-d.1917, "Mother" n/t Anna & Fred Eggert
SEC7 EGGERT Fred W. b.1874-d.1941, "Husband" n/t Anna & Ida Eggert
SEC7 DE BRUINE Dorothy M. b.1893-d.1966, n/t Harry A., Ervin,
George F. & Frances De Bruine
SEC7 DE BRUINE Harry A. b.1891-d.1921, "BATTY F 333rd F.A. 86th
DIV." n/t Dorothy M., Ervin, George F. & Frances De Bruine
SEC7 DE BRUINE Ervin b.1902-d.1980, n/t Dorothy M., Harry A.,
George F. & Frances De Bruine
SEC7 SCHUMACHER Arthur L. b.1916-d.1925
SEC7 ARMSTRONG Frederic J. b.1891-d.1959, n/t Alice & John
Armstrong
SEC7 ARMSTRONG Alice R. b.8Nov1858-d.26Sep1936, n/t Frederic J.
& John Armstrong; cemetery records show Alice buried in same plot

---

58 *Roster of Wisconsin Volunteers, War Of The Rebellion, 1861-1865*

with Edwin Armstrong; middle initial and dates completed from cemetery records

SEC7 ARMSTRONG John b.1850-d.1914, n/t Frederic J. & Alice Armstrong

SEC7 HIRSCH M. L. b.1852-d.1933, n/t J. F. Hirsch

SEC7 HIRSCH J. F. b.1851-d.1913, n/t M. L. Hirsch

SEC7 REDZINSKI Carl b.1852-d.1929, "Father" n/t Caroline, Arthur, Mathilda & Rosette Redzinski

SEC7 REDZINSKI Caroline b.1862-d.1943, "Mother" n/t Carl, Arthur, Mathilda & Rosette Redzinski

SEC7 REDZINSKI Arthur b.1893-d.1922, n/t Carl, Caroline, Mathilda & Rosette Redzinski

SEC7 REDZINSKI Mathilda b.1875-d.1912, n/t Carl, Caroline, Arthur & Rosette Redzinski

SEC7 REDZINSKI Rosette b.1912-d.1912, n/t Carl, Caroline, Arthur & Mathilda Redzinski

SEC7 JAUTZ Evelyn L. b.1911-d.no date, w/ Martin G. Jautz

SEC7 JAUTZ Martin G. b.1909-d.1988, w/ Evelyn L. Jautz

SEC7 RASMUSSEN Adler T. b.1898-d.1972

SEC7 TENNYSON Addie Erast b.1864-d.1912, n/t Esther A. Tennyson

SEC7 TENNYSON Esther A. b.1888-d.1978, n/t Addie E. Tennyson

SEC7 KURTZ G. A. b.1860-d.1911

SEC7 WARREN Joseph Dennis b.1853-d.1912, n/t Kate C. Warren

SEC7 WARREN Kate C. b.1855-d.1908, n/t Joseph Warren

SEC7 ZIVANOVIC Virginia b.1920-d.no date, w/ Bora Zivanovic

SEC7 ZIVANOVIC Bora b.1908-d.1969, w/ Virginia Zivanovic

SEC7 WARREN Delinda H. b.1890-d.1983, w/ Paul C., n/t Roxena B. & Albert D. Warren

SEC7 WARREN Paul C. b.1881-d.1967, w/ Delinda H., n/t Roxena B. & Albert D. Warren

SEC7 WARREN Roxena B. b.1888-d.1982, w/ Albert D., n/t Delinda H. & Paul C. Warren

SEC7 WARREN Albert D. b.1878-d.1934, w/ Roxena B., n/t Delinda H. & Paul C. Warren

SEC7 HANSON Alice Kershaw b.1879-d.1952, n/t Albert Christian Hanson *

SEC7 HANSON Albert Christian b.1879-d.1963, n/t Alice K. Hanson *

SEC7 MYERS Jacob Oliver b.1839-d.1922, w/ Laura C. Myers, n/t Marion & Helen M. Ellis

SEC7 MYERS Laura Chapman b.1850-d.1931, w/ Jacob O. Myers, n/t Marion & Helen M. Ellis

SEC7 ELLIS Marion Elizabeth b.24Apr1911-d.6May1912, n/t Jacob O. & Laura C. Myers & Helen M. Ellis

SEC7 ELLIS Helen Myers b.1886-d.1919, n/t Jacob O. & Laura C. Myers & Marion Ellis

SEC7 CUTLER John R. b.30Jan1918-d.13Jun1993

SEC7 LOFSTROM Edith b.1900-d.1921

SEC7 GREGG Luther B. b.16Apr1845-d.19Jun1913, "Father" w/ Eliza B. & Belle Gregg & Grace Steiner; Pvt Civil War; GAR member *

SEC7 GREGG Eliza B. b.1850-d.1937, "Mother" w/ Luther B. & Belle Gregg & Grace Steiner *

SEC7 GREGG Belle b.9Sep1878-d.8Mar1920, w/ Luther B. & Eliza B. Gregg & Grace Steiner; cemetery records show her name as Eliza Belle; dates from cemetery records

SEC7 STEINER Grace b.1884-d.1969, w/ Luther B., Belle & Eliza B. Gregg *

SEC7 REINKE Irene H. b.1881-d.1977

SEC7 HIRSCH Delia A. b.1877-d.1953

SEC7 WIBLE Lida A. b.1860-d.1924, w/ Walter B. Wible

SEC7 WIBLE Walter B. b.1858-d.1952, w/ Lida A. Wible

SEC7 DE BRUINE George F. b.1859-d.1914, "Father" n/t Frances, Dorothy M., Harry A., & Ervin De Bruine

SEC7 DE BRUINE Frances b.1865-d.1939, "Mother" n/t Harry A., Ervin, George F. & Dorothy M. De Bruine

SEC7 REICHOW Adeline b.1895-d.1915, w/ Minnie & Michael Reichow

SEC7 REICHOW Minnie b.1864-d.1944, w/ Adeline & Michael Reichow

SEC7 REICHOW Michael b.1856-d.1934, w/ Adeline & Minnie Reichow

SEC7 CURTIS Don B. b.1868-d.1916

SEC7 WUNSCH Maria b.8Sep1894-d.29May1990, "Oma"

SEC7 GEIGER Louise b.1912-d.1990

SEC7 SCHARMER Amanda b.1894-d.1918, n/t Emilie & August Scharmer; on curve facing road

SEC7 SCHARMER Emilie b.1866-d.1955, "Mother" n/t Amanda & August Scharmer; on curve facing road

SEC7 SCHARMER August b.1860-d.1930, "Father" n/t Amanda & Emilie Scharmer; on curve facing road

SEC7 BECKER John H. b.1892-d.1976, w/ Emma Becker

SEC7 BECKER Emma b.1894-d.1986, w/ John H. Becker

SEC7 RICHARDS Janet H. b.1922-d.1990, w/ Harry B. Richards

SEC7 RICHARDS Harry B. b.1927-d.no date, w/ Janet H. Richards

SEC7 KLAWITTER Edward T. d.4Jul1917, w/ Anna Klawitter

SEC7 KLAWITTER Anna d.30Aug1932, w/ Edward T. Klawitter

SEC7 JONES Francis b.24Sep1857-d.20Nov1916, "Daddy"

SEC7 ZEMKE Amelia b.1866-d.1940, w/ Frank, n/t Paul Zemke

SEC7 ZEMKE Frank b.1862-d.1915, w/ Amelia, n/t Paul Zemke

SEC7 ZEMKE Paul b.1890-d.1962, n/t Amelia & Frank Zemke

SEC7 HAASCH Bertha b.1880-d.1960, "Mother" w/ Edward C., n/t Helen L. & Isabel L. Haasch

SEC7 HAASCH Edward C. b.1874-d.1934, "Father" w/ Bertha, n/t Helen L. & Isabel L. Haasch

SEC7 HAASCH Helen L. b.1916-d.1973, n/t Bertha, Edward C. & Isabel L. Haasch

SEC7 HAASCH Isabel L. b.1902-d.1916, n/t Bertha, Edward C. & Helen L. Haasch

SEC7 CASE Mary E. b.1848-d.1929, n/t Spenger L., Florence D., Winifred C. K., Lucy A. G., Halbert C. & Myrtle E. Case

SEC7 CASE Spenger L. b.1844-d.1924, n/t Mary E., Florence D., Winifred C. K., Lucy A. G., Halbert C. & Myrtle E. Case

SEC7 CASE Florence D. b.1883-d.1951, n/t Mary E., Spenger L., Winifred C. K., Lucy A. G., Halbert C. & Myrtle E. Case

SEC7 CASE Winifred C. Knapp b.1871-d.1970, n/t Mary E., Spenger L., Florence D., Lucy A. G., Halbert C. & Myrtle E. Case

SEC7 CASE Lucy A. Greutzmacher b.1888-d.1966, n/t Mary E., Spenger L., Florence D., Winifred C. K., Halbert C. & Myrtle E. Case

SEC7 CASE Halbert C. b.1893-d.1915, n/t Mary E., Spenger L., Florence D., Winifred C. K., Lucy A. G. & Myrtle E. Case

SEC7 CASE Myrtle E. b.1873-d.1945, n/t Mary E., Spenger L., Florence D., Winifred C. K., Lucy A. G. & Halbert C. Case

SEC7 ARMSTRONG Edwin b.1893-d.1953, "Father" w/ Anna Armstrong

SEC7 ARMSTRONG Anna b.8Nov1858-d.26Sep1936, "Mother" w/ Edwin Armstrong, cemetery records show her with the name Alice R., who it appears has two stones

SEC7 REUL Alma b.1875-d.1959, n/t Emil Reul

SEC7 REUL Emil Rev. b.1869-d.1901, n/t Alma Reul

SEC7 ARNDT Martha K. b.1910-d.1982, w/ Harvey A. Arndt

SEC7 ARNDT Harvey A. b.1914-d.1965, w/ Martha K. Arndt

SEC7 BEUTLER Howard b.20Jan1900-d.17Jan1913, n/t Grace M. & William F. Beutler

SEC7 BEUTLER Grace Mary b.17May1867-d.22Feb1929, "Mother" n/t Howard & William F. Beutler

SEC7 HUMPHREY Jessie S. b.1863-d.1943, n/t Seymour B. Humphrey; Jessie and Seymour are in different rows, but next to each other

SEC7 HUMPHREY Seymour B. b.1849-d.1911, n/t Jesse M. Humphrey; Jessie and Seymour are in different rows, but next to each other

136

SEC7 SCOFIELD Mary b.1831-d.1918

SEC7 ADAMS Georgianna B. b.1855-d.1947, n/t George P. Adams

SEC7 ADAMS George P. b.1845-d.1911, n/t Georgianna B. Adams

SEC7 KERSHAW Joseph A. b.1847-d.1912, n/t Rosetta Kershaw *

SEC7 KERSHAW Rosetta b.1852-d.1916, n/t Joseph A. Kershaw

SEC7 McGILL Hiram G. b.1861-d.1912, n/t Jessie McGill

SEC7 McGILL Jessie b.1860-d.1934, n/t Hiram G. McGill

SEC7 GRAY Thomas Sewell b.1846-d.1906, "CO. D. 2nd. ILLS. CAV." w/ Emma W. U. Gray

SEC7 GRAY Emma W. Underwood b.1847-d.1935, "His Wife" w/ Thomas S. Gray

SEC7 SWAN Virginia R. b.1908-d.1989, "Daughter" n/t Orlin J., Clara E., Jeanette S. & Nathaniel J. Swan; DAR mkr; on south curve

SEC7 SWAN Orlin J. b.1851-d.1919, "Father" n/t Virginia R., Clara E., Jeanette S. & Nathaniel J. Swan; on south curve *

SEC7 SWAN Clara E. b.1854-d.1940, "Mother" n/t Virginia R., Orlin J., Jeanette S. & Nathaniel J. Swan; on south curve

SEC7 SWAN Jeanette S. b.1879-d.1974, "Mother" n/t Virginia R., Orlin J., Clara E. & Nathaniel J. Swan; on south curve

SEC7 SWAN Nathaniel J. b.1880-d.1963, "Father" n/t Virginia R., Orlin J., Clara E. & Jeanette S. Swan; on south curve *

SEC7 NOLTE Sedate M. b.1904-d.1982, n/t Frederick W., Ruth S. & August Nolte

SEC7 NOLTE Frederick W. b.1897-d.1958, n/t Sedate M., Ruth S. & August Nolte

SEC7 NOLTE Ruth S. b.1867-d.1955, n/t Sedate M., Frederick W. & August Nolte

SEC7 NOLTE August b.1857-d.1909, n/t Sedate M., Frederick W. & Ruth S. Nolte

SEC7 DAVIS Florence A. b.1884-d.1951, n/t Charles R. & Charles A. Davis, Georgianna B. & George P. Adams

SEC7 DAVIS Charles R. b.1868-d.1956, n/t Florence A. & Charles A. Davis; Georgianna B. & George P. Adams

SEC7 DAVIS Charles Adams b.1919-d.1986, "T SGT US ARMY WWII" n/t Florence A. & Charles R. Davis; Georgianna B. & George P. Adams

SEC7 BEUTLER William F., Dr. b.24Dec1865-d.9Mar1929, "Father" n/t Howard & Grace M. Beutler

SEC7 JESSEL Mary J. b.1915-d.1973, w/ Hardy J., n/t Henry R. & Josephine A. Jessel

SEC7 JESSEL Hardy J. b.1907-d.1976, w/ Mary J., n/t Henry R. & Josephine A. Jessel

SEC7 JESSEL Henry R., Dr. b.1867-d.1933, n/t Mary J., Hardy J. & Josephine A. Jessel

SEC7 JESSEL Josephine A. b.1872-d.1945, n/t Mary J., Hardy J. & Henry R. Jessel

SEC7 SCHICANTEK Frank b.1878-d.no date, w/ Mathilda Schicantek & Albert, Hattie & Helen Priebe; no cemetery record, possibly an infant, only one date

SEC7 SCHICANTEK Mathilda b.1872-d.1916, w/ Frank Schicantek & Albert, Hattie & Helen Priebe

SEC7 PRIEBE Albert b.1888-d.1968, w/ Frank & Mathilda Schicantek & Hattie & Helen Priebe

SEC7 PRIEBE Hattie b.1886-d.1963, w/ Frank & Mathilda Schicantek & Albert & Helen Priebe

SEC7 PRIEBE Helen b.23Apr1915-d.28Apr1915, "Daughter" w/ Frank & Mathilda Schicantek & Albert & Hattie Priebe

SEC7 KRIENITZ Henriette b.1850-d.1932, w/ Wilhelm & Martha Krienitz

SEC7 KRIENITZ Wilhelm b.1848-d.1927, w/ Henriette & Martha Krienitz

SEC7 KRIENITZ Martha b.24Nov1877-d.17Dec1971, w/ Henriette & Wilhelm Krienitz; dates completed from cemetery records

SEC7 ARMSTRONG Frieda b.1897-d.1924

SEC7 SCHUMACHER Florence b.1885-d.1961, w/ Arthur Schumacher

SEC7 SCHUMACHER Arthur b.1885-d.1976, w/ Florence Schumacher

SEC7 MILLER Anna (HARTMAN) b.1878-d.1961, w/ John & Eva M., n/t Gottliebe & Fred Miller

SEC7 MILLER John b.1877-d.1963, w/ Anna H. & Eva M., n/t Gottliebe & Fred Miller

SEC7 MILLER Eva M. b.1903-d.1980, w/ Anna H. & John, n/t Gottliebe & Fred Miller

SEC7 MILLER Gottliebe b.1849-d.1929, "Mother" w/ Fred, n/t Anna H., Eva M. & John Miller

SEC7 MILLER Fred b.1846-d.1916, "Father" w/ Gottliebe, n/t Anna H., Eva M. & John Miller

SEC7 UNDERWOOD Frederick Douglass b.1849-d.1942, w/ Sarah V. S., Enoch W., Russell S., William J., Evelyn B. & other Underwoods & Alice V. Nelson; Frederick was the president of the Erie Railroad Company, he lived in New York.

SEC7 UNDERWOOD Sarah Virginia Smith b.1852-d.1919, "His Wife (Frederick Douglass)" w/ Frederick D., Enoch W., Russell S., William J., Evelyn B. & other Underwoods

SEC7 UNDERWOOD Enoch William b.1878-d.19—, "Their Children" w/
Frederick D., Sarah V. S., Russell S. William J., Evelyn B. & other
Underwoods; no cemetery record
SEC7 UNDERWOOD Russell Sage b.1880-d.1934, "Their Children" w/
Frederick D., Sarah V. S., Enoch W., William J., Evelyn B. & other
Underwoods
SEC7 UNDERWOOD William Jackson b.1852-d.1917, w/ Frederick D.,
Sarah V. S., Enoch W., Russell S., Evelyn B. & other Underwoods
SEC7 UNDERWOOD Evelyn Browne b.1857-d.1947, w/ Frederick D.,
Sarah V. S., Enoch W., Russell S., William J. & other Underwoods
SEC7 UNDERWOOD Kathryn Hill b.1889-d.1890, w/ Frederick D.,
Sarah V. S., Enoch W., Russell S., William J. & other Underwoods
SEC7 UNDERWOOD Charles Browne b.1891-d.1909, w/ Frederick D.,
Sarah V. S., Enoch W., Russell S., William J. & other Underwoods
SEC7 UNDERWOOD Robert Browne b.1902-d.1903, w/ Frederick D.,
Sarah V. S., Enoch W., Russell S., William J. & other Underwoods
SEC7 NELSON Alice U. b.1886-d.1975, w/ Frederick D., Sarah V. S.,
Enoch W., Russell S., William J. & other Underwoods
SEC7 TAYLOR Mary R. b.1880-d.1944, "w/o Martin M. Taylor" n/t
Martin M., Catherine, Cornelius & Elouise Taylor
SEC7 TAYLOR Martin M. b.1873-d.1947, n/t Mary R., Catherine,
Cornelius & Elouise Taylor
SEC7 TAYLOR Catherine b.1832-d.1920, n/t Mary R., Martin M.,
Cornelius & Elouise Taylor
SEC7 TAYLOR Cornelius b.1827-d.1915, n/t Mary R., Martin M.,
Catherine & Elouise Taylor
SEC7 TAYLOR Elouise b.1861-d.1924, n/t Mary R., Martin M., Catherine
& Cornelius Taylor
SEC7 CORLETT Philip D. b.1902-d.1976, "Father" w/ Esther G. Corlett
SEC7 CORLETT Esther G. b.1905-d.1994, "Mother" w/ Philip D. Corlett
SEC7 DITTMAR Herbert b.no date-d.no date, w/ Mary, Elsa, Mary, Elly,
Augusta, Albin, n/t Herbert M. Dittmar, see below, cemetery records
show only one Herbert buried here
SEC7 DITTMAR Mary b.5Mar1888-d.30Jul1967, w/ Herbert, Mary, Elsa,
Elly, Augusta, Albin, n/t Herbert M. Dittmar; dates from cemetery
records
SEC7 DITTMAR Mary O. b.18Jul1886-d.25Aug1946, w/ Herbert, Mary,
Elly, Elsa, Augusta, Albin, n/t Herbert M. Dittmar; dates from cemetery
records
SEC7 DITTMAR Elsa b.5Mar1884-d.25Dec1977, w/ Herbert, Mary, Elly,
Mary O., Augusta, Albin, n/t Herbert M. Dittmar

SEC7 DITTMAR Augusta b.7Jul1861-d.4Jun1925, w/ Herbert, Mary, Elsa, Mary, Elly, Albin, n/t Herbert M. Dittmar; dates from cemetery records

SEC7 DITTMAR Albin b.24Jun1858-d.15Jun1916, w/ Herbert, Mary, Elsa, Mary, Elly, Augusta, n/t Herbert M. Dittmar; dates from cemetery records

SEC7 DITTMAR Herbert M. b.14Jun1889-d.25Jan1983, w/ Herbert, Mary, Elsa, Mary, Elly, Augusta & Albin Dittmar

SEC7 UPTON William Clark, Jr. b.22Aug1915-d.8Feb1917, n/t Myrtle Upton

SEC7 UPTON Myrtle b.1881-d.1920, n/t William C. Upton

SEC7 BAUMGARTNER Olga Belle b.1899-d.1964, w/ Chas. D. Baumgartner

SEC7 BAUMGARTNER Chas. D. b.1898-d.1968, w/ Olga B. Baumgartner

SEC7 YOUNG Lloyd E. b.11Sep1915-d.6Mar1917, "Son" n/t Robert & Anna M. Young

SEC7 YOUNG Robert b.15Sep1879-d.5Mar1952, "Father" n/t Lloyd E. & Anna M. Young

SEC7 YOUNG Anna M. b.14Jul1882-d.5Aug1941, "Mother" n/t Lloyd E. & Robert Young

SEC7 WEGNER Gladys B. b.1895-d.1917, w/ Carrie A. & Albert H. Wegner

SEC7 WEGNER Carrie A. b.1863-d.1944, w/ Gladys B. & Albert H. Wegner

SEC7 WEGNER Albert H. b.1862-d.1938, w/ Gladys B. & Carrie A. Wegner

SEC7 KEEBLER Clara b.1855-d.1917, n/t Glen Keebler

SEC7 KEEBLER Glen b.1885-d.1918, n/t Clara Keebler

SEC7 WEATHERLY Frances b.1888-d.1931

SEC7 KRAUSE Harry P. b.1895-d.1931, "Daddy"

SEC7 ST. GEORGE Catherine b.1861-d.1927, "Mother" w/ Henry B. St. George

SEC7 ST. GEORGE Henry B. b.1857-d.1942, "Father" w/ Catherine St. George

SEC7 BUTCHER Grace Esther b.1871-d.1958

SEC7 FALK Norman F. b.27Jan1916-d.29Aug1935, n/t Arthur W., Louise A., Otto A., Minnie A., Charles F., & Hulda Falk

SEC7 FALK Arthur W. b.15Jul1896-d.29Jul1917, n/t Norman F., Louise A., Otto A., Minnie A., Charles F., & Hulda Falk

SEC7 FALK Hulda b.5Sep1903-d.3Aug1929, n/t Norman F., Louise A., Otto A., Minnie A., Charles F., & Arthur W. Falk

SEC7 FALK Louise A. b.1873-d.1951, "Mother" w/ Otto A., n/t Norman F., Hulda, Minnie A., Charles F., & Arthur W. Falk

SEC7 FALK Otto A. b.1871-d.1954, "Father" w/ Louise A., n/t Norman F., Hulda, Minnie A., Charles F., & Arthur W. Falk

SEC7 FALK Minnie A. b.22Feb1872-d.5Jun1952, "Mother" w/ Charles F., n/t Norman F., Hulda, Louise A., Otto A., & Arthur W. Falk

SEC7 FALK Charles F. b.18Sep1872-d.15Jul1956, "Father" w/ Minnie A., n/t Norman F., Hulda, Louise A., Otto A., & Arthur W. Falk

SEC7 KIRCHHOFF Gilbert A. b.29Jul1916-d.2Oct1998, "SGT US ARMY WWII" n/t Gilbert & Dorothy D. Kirchhoff & Julia A. & Bernhard W. De Bruine

SEC7 KIRCHHOFF Gilbert b.1916-d.1998, n/t Gilbert A., w/ Dorothy D., n/t Gilbert A. Kirchhoff & Julia A. & Bernhard W. De Bruine

SEC7 KIRCHHOFF Dorothy (DE BRUIN) b.1918-d.no date, w/ Gilbert, n/t Gilbert A. Kirchhoff & Julia A. & Bernhard W. De Bruine

SEC7 DE BRUINE Julia A. b.1892-d.1965, w/ Bernhard W. De Bruine, n/t Gilbert A., Gilbert & Dorothy D. Kirchhoff

SEC7 DE BRUINE Bernhard W. b.1889-d.1955, w/ Julia A. De Bruine, n/t Gilbert A., Gilbert & Dorothy D. Kirchhoff

SEC7 CASE Spencer L. b.1885-d.1959, n/t Elizabeth & Frieda Case

SEC7 CASE Elizabeth b.1890-d.1917, n/t Spencer L. & Frieda Case

SEC7 CASE Frieda b.1895-d.1968, n/t Spencer L. & Elizabeth Case

SEC7 KIRCHHOFF Mabel b.1872-d.1939, n/t Roger C., Agnes D. & Charles Kirchhoff; American Legion marker between stones

SEC7 KIRCHHOFF Charles b.1856-d.1916, n/t Mabel, Roger C. & Agnes D. Kirchhoff; American Legion marker between stones

SEC7 KIRCHHOFF Roger C. b.1890-d.1976, w/ Agnes D., n/t Mabel & Charles Kirchhoff; American Legion marker between stones

SEC7 KIRCHHOFF Agnes D. b.1892-d.1980, w/ Roger C., n/t Mabel & Charles Kirchhoff; American Legion marker between stones

SEC7 ANDERSON Keith Lee d.1962, only one date

SEC7 GARVENS Roland W. b.1912-d.1916, n/t Martha M. & Otto L. Garvens

SEC7 GARVENS Martha M. b.1882-d.1969, "Mother" w/ Otto L., n/t Roland W. Garvens

SEC7 GARVENS Otto L. b.1873-d.1948, "Father" w/ Martha M., n/t Roland W. Garvens

SEC7 HOLDEN Anna M. b.1888-d.1959, w/ Clarence S. Holden

SEC7 HOLDEN Clarence S. b.1884-d.1964, w/ Anna M. Holden

SEC7 JOHNSON Kathleen Ann b.27Nov1945-d.22Dec1994, "Loving Mother"

SEC7 FREY John B. P. b.1866-d.1945, w/ Bertha, Florence & John C. Frey

SEC7 FREY Bertha b.1877-d.1915, w/ John B. P., Florence & John C. Frey

SEC7 FREY Florence b.1914-d.no date, w/ John B. P., Bertha & John C. Frey

SEC7 FREY John C. b.1903-d.1969, w/ John B. P., Bertha & Florence Frey

SEC7 JACOBUS Delia Viola b.1869-d.1916, w/ Charles C., William H. & Millie Jacobus & Jean Lowry

SEC7 JACOBUS Charles C. b.1864-d.1936, w/ Delia V., William H. & Millie Jacobus & Jean Lowry

SEC7 JACOBUS William H. b.1866-d.1934, w/ Delia V., Charles C. & Millie Jacobus & Jean Lowry

SEC7 JACOBUS Millie b.1871-d.1937, w/ Delia V., Charles C. & William H. Jacobus & Jean Lowry

SEC7 LOWRY Jean b.1880-d.1943, w/ Delia V., Charles C., William H. & Millie Jacobus

SEC7 KOEHN Margaret b.1869-d.1952, W/ Gustav Koehn

SEC7 KOEHN Gustav b.1864-d.1950, W/ Margaret Koehn

SEC7 HENKE Elizabeth d.15Oct1959, w/ Lillian, Lena & Charles Henke; only one date

SEC7 HENKE Lillian b.1894-d.1918, w/ Elizabeth, Lena & Charles Henke

SEC7 HENKE Lena d.17Feb1949, w/ Elizabeth, Lillian & Charles Henke; only one date

SEC7 HENKE Charles b.1855-d.1934, w/ Elizabeth, Lillian & Lena Henke

SEC7 BLODGETT Isabel C. b.1887-d.1918, n/t James E., Catherine & Elbert Blodgett

SEC7 BLODGETT James E. b.1891-d.1918, n/t Isabel C., Catherine & Elbert Blodgett

SEC7 BLODGETT Catherine b.1859-d.1933, n/t Isabel C., James E. & Elbert Blodgett

SEC7 BLODGETT Elbert b.1860-d.1935, n/t Isabel C., James E. & Catherine Blodgett

SEC7 ROSENTHAL Bertha b.1840-d.1921, "Mother" n/t John Rosenthal

SEC7 ROSENTHAL John b.1834-d.1918, "Father" n/t Bertha Rosenthal

SEC7 FEERICK Louisa b.1867-d.1923, w/ Henry W. Feerick

SEC7 FEERICK Henry W. b.1858-d.1917, w/ Louisa Feerick

SEC7 RADKE Elva b.1878-d.1916, n/t Rudolph Radke

SEC7 RADKE Rudolph b.1874-d.1942, n/t Elva Radke

SEC7 HOPKINS Laura b.1895-d.1953

SEC7 SIEGESMUND Albert b.1891-d.1936, w/ Bertha S. Tuttle, n/t Ida & John Siegesmund

SEC7 TUTTLE Bertha Siegesmund b.1892-d.1971, w/ Albert Siegesmund,n/t Ida & John Siegesmund

SEC7 SIEGESMUND Ida b.1862-d.1926, w/ John, n/t Albert Siegesmund & Bertha S. Tuttle

SEC7 SIEGESMUND John b.1857-d.1930, w/ Ida, n/t Albert Siegesmund & Bertha S. Tuttle

SEC7 TINHOLT John b.1863-d.1919, w/ Martha Tinholt

SEC7 TINHOLT Martha b.1882-d.1938, w/ John Tinholt

SEC7 RHODE Otto R. b.1874-d.1963, w/ Augusta H. Rhode

SEC7 RHODE Augusta H. b.1879-d.1964, w/ Otto R. Rhode

SEC7 HUEBNER Edwin b.1915-d.1916, w/ Lydia & Ida Huebner

SEC7 HUEBNER Lydia d.1917, w/ Edwin & Ida Huebner; only one date

SEC7 HUEBNER Ida b.1884-d.1954, "Mother" w/ Edwin & Lydia Huebner

SEC7 GRUNWALD Emilia b.7Jun1857-d.31Oct1937, "Mother" w/ August Grunwald

SEC7 GRUNWALD August b.11Jul1849-d.2Jun1938, "Father" w/ Emilia Grunwald

SEC7 KOPF Audrey B. b.1911-d.1968, n/t Howard L., Alfred L. H. & Florence M., August F., Jacob, Caroline & Carolyn J. Koff

SEC7 KOPF Howard L. b.1908-d.1994, n/t Audrey B., Alfred L. H. & Florence M., August F., Jacob, Caroline & Carolyn J. Koff

SEC7 KOPF Alfred L. H. b.1872-d.1948, n/t Audrey B., Howard L., Florence M., August F., Jacob, Caroline & Carolyn J. Koff

SEC7 KOPF Florence M. b.1876-d.1957, n/t Audrey B., Howard L., Alfred L. H., August F., Jacob, Caroline & Carolyn J. Koff

SEC7 BUCHMANN Fredericka Joers b.4Dec1836-d.30Dec1918, w/ Fred & Wilhelmine, n/t Otto E. & August H. Buchmann

SEC7 BUCHMANN Fred b.2Dec1861-d.15Dec1935, w/ Fredericka J. & Wilhelmine, n/t Otto E. & August H. Buchmann

SEC7 BUCHMANN Wilhelmine b.12Aug1868-d.6May1952, w/ Fredericka J. & Fred, n/t Otto E. & August H. Buchmann

SEC7 BUCHMANN Otto E. b.16Oct1900-d.24Sep1979, "PFC US ARMY WWII" n/t Fredericka J., Fred, Wilhelmine & August H. Buchmann

SEC7 BUCHMANN August H. b.28Mar1892-d.27May1981, "PFC US ARMY WWI" n/t Fredericka J., Fred, Wilhelmine & Otto E. Buchmann

SEC7 BOELTER Emma E. b.1894-d.1969, "Mother" w/ Frank W. & Viola Boelter

SEC7 BOELTER Frank W. b.1883-d.1961, "Father" w/ Emma E. & Viola Boelter

SEC7 BOELTER Viola b.1917-d.1923, "Daughter" w/ Emma E. & Frank W. Boelter

SEC7 VOGEL Emma b.1876-d.1919

SEC7 BEHLING Robert C. b.1896-d.1918 France, "Son; WWI" n/t Harold A., Mabel C., Robert C., John E. & Mabel I.Behling, American Legion mkr

SEC7 BEHLING Harold A. b.1900-d.1919, "Son, In His Arms" n/t Robert C., Mabel C., Robert C., John E. & Mabel I. Behling

SEC7 BEHLING Mabel C. b.1878-d.1964, "Mother" w/ Robert C., n/t Harold A., Robert C., John E. & Mabel I. Behling

SEC7 BEHLING Robert C. b.1870-d.1952, "Father" w/ Mabel C., n/t Harold A., Robert C., John E. & Mabel I. Behling

SEC7 BEHLING John E. b.1910-d.1986, "Husband, Son" n/t Mabel C., Harold A., Robert C., Robert C. & Mabel I. Behling

SEC7 BEHLING Mabel I. b.1910-d.1962, "Wife, Daughter-In-Law" n/t Mabel C., Harold A., Robert C., Robert C. & John E. Behling

SEC7 PERRENTEN Anna (WETZEL) b.1883-d.1919, "Mother" n/t Fred Perrenten, & Emma, Alvin H. & Arthur J. Wetzel

SEC7 PERRENTEN Fred b.1886-d.1951, "Father" n/t Anna Perrenten, & Emma, Alvin H. & Arthur J. Wetzel

SEC7 WETZEL Emma b.1861-d.1941, w/ Alvin H., n/t Arthur J. Wetzel & Anna W. & Fred Perrenten

SEC7 WETZEL Alvin H. b.1856-d.1926, w/ Emma, n/t Arthur J. Wetzel & Anna W. & Fred Perrenten

SEC7 WETZEL Arthur J. b.1898-d.1940, n/t Emma & Alvin H. Wetzel & Anna W. & Fred Perrenten

SEC7 KOPF August F. b.1876-d.1960, n/t Jacob, Caroline, Carolyn J., Audrey B., Howard L., Alfred L. H. & Florence M. Kopf

SEC7 KOPF Jacob b.1844-d.1911, "Father" n/t August F., Caroline, Carolyn J., Audrey B., Howard L., Alfred L. H. & Florence M. Kopf

SEC7 KOPF Caroline b.1844-d.1935, "Mother" n/t August F., Jacob, Carolyn J., Audrey B., Howard L., Alfred L. H. & Florence M. Kopf

SEC7 KOPF Carolyn J. b.1885-d.1968, n/t August F., Jacob, Caroline, Audrey B., Howard L., Alfred L. H. & Florence M. Kopf

SEC7 GISSINGER Emily b.1886-d.1983, w/ Eugene Gissinger

SEC7 GISSINGER Eugene b.1881-d.1968, w/ Emily Gissinger

SEC7 ALCALA Emanuel b.1905-d.1982, w/ Ruth Alcala

SEC7 ALCALA Ruth b.1914-d.no date, w/ Emanuel Alcala
SEC7 SCHUETT Elizabeth b.1884-d.1934, n/t Wm. J., & Alwina Schuett
SEC7 SCHUETT Wm. J. b.23Aug6
1839-d.27Oct1918, w/ Alwina, n/t Elizabeth Schuett
SEC7 SCHUETT Alwina b.5Nov1843-d.12Dec1923, w/ Wm. J., n/t
Elizabeth Schuett
SEC7 HARTWIG Alvina b.1888-d.1942, "Mother" w/ Otto F. & Willis
Hartwig
SEC7 HARTWIG Otto F. b.1886-d.1919, "Father" w/ Alvina & Willis
Hartwig
SEC7 HARTWIG Willis b.1909-d.1918, "Brother" w/ Alvina & Otto F.
Hartwig
SEC7 TADDEY Ferdinand b.1858-d.1924, "Father" n/t Anna & Edward W.
Taddey
SEC7 TADDEY Edward Walter d.27Aug1941, "WIS. PVT. 1 CL. 55 INF. 7
DIV." n/t Anna & Ferdinand Taddey; only one date
SEC7 TADDEY Anna b.1861-d.1918, "Mother" n/t Ferdinand & Edward
W. Taddey
SEC7 LOCKER Arthur b.1890-d.1971, "Son" w/ Hugo, Ida, Alfred &
Laura C. Locker
SEC7 LOCKER Hugo b.1863-d.1940, "Father" w/ Arthur, Ida, Alfred &
Laura C. Locker
SEC7 LOCKER Ida b.1867-d.1917, "Mother" w/ Arthur,Hugo, Alfred &
Laura C. Locker
SEC7 LOCKER Alfred b.1892-d.1933, "Son" w/ Arthur, Hugo, Ida &
Laura C. Locker
SEC7 LOCKER Laura C. b.1894-d.1979, w/ Arthur, Hugo, Ida & Alfred
Locker
SEC7 OHM Amelia b.1874-d.1965, "Mother" w/ Charles, n/t Rose Ohm
SEC7 OHM Charles b.1875-d.1957, "Father" w/ Amelia, n/t Rose Ohm
SEC7 OHM Rose b.6Dec1898-d.4Jan1918, "Daughter" n/t Amelia &
Charles Ohm
SEC7 KRONSHAGE John b.1907-d.1968, w/ Ella Kronshage
SEC7 KRONSHAGE Ella b.1909-d.19—, w/ John Kronshage
SEC7 FALK Raymond b.11Jan1913-d.11Apr1986, w/ Hazel E., n/t
Frederick L., Thomas R. & Sandra E. Falk
SEC7 FALK Hazel E. b.15Feb1916-d.15May1987, w/ Raymond, n/t
Frederick L., Thomas R. & Sandra E. Falk
SEC7 FALK Frederick Lee b.9Nov1954-d.29Dec1974, n/t Raymond,
Hazel E., Thomas R. & Sandra E. Falk
SEC7 FALK Thomas R. b.22Feb1943-d.27Feb1943, "Babes" w/ Sandra
E., n/t Raymond, Hazel E., & Frederick L. Falk

SEC7 FALK Sandra E. b.22Feb1943-d.27Feb1943, "Babes" w/ Thomas
R., n/t Raymond, Hazel E., & Frederick L. Falk
SEC7 DOUGHERTY Earl L. b.1885-d.1969, n/t Margaret & Mary
Dougherty & George G. Lund
SEC7 DOUGHERTY Margaret b.1885-d.1938, n/t Earl L. & Mary
Dougherty & George G. Lund
SEC7 LUND George G. b.1873-d.1918, n/t Earl L., Margaret & Mary
Dougherty *
SEC7 DOUGHERTY Mary b.1911-d.1974, n/t Earl L. & Margaret
Dougherty & George G. Lund
NSUB CARY Baby b.28Feb1957-d.6May1957
NSUB GOODMAN Duane d.Nov1958, "s/o Tom & Carol Goodman" only
one date
NSUB DALLAS Robert b.1939-d.1947
NSUB HABERNICHT Johanna b.4Dec1877-d.no date, w/ Anna Gertz &
Herman & Amelia Ziemer; no cemetery record
NSUB GERTZ Anna b.22Feb1840-d.18Aug1911, w/ Johanna Habernicht
& Herman & Amelia Ziemer
NSUB ZIEMER Herman b.16Aug1871-d.5Oct1947, w/ Johanna
Habernicht, Anna Gertz & Amelia Ziemer
NSUB ZIEMER Amelia b.30Aug1875-d.1Jan1959, w/ Johanna
Habernicht, Anna Gertz & Herman Ziemer
NSUB MOULTON Elsie b.1894-d.1979, "Mother"
NSUB SEMROW Ferdinand b.1891-d.1919, "Father"
NSUB SEEMANN Harry b.1903-d.1946, "Son"
NSUB GAETH Hattie M. b.1896-d.1991, "Wife" n/t Walter F. Gaeth
NSUB GAETH Walter F. b.1898-d.1975, "Father" n/t Hattie M. Gaeth
NSUB BERGMANN Gertrude b.15Jan1908-d.26Apr1937, "Mother"
NSUB SEEMANN Wilhelmina b.22Jul1869-d.17Oct1945, "Mother" n/t
William & Arthur Seemann
NSUB SEEMANN William b.17Oct1865-d.20May1928, "Father" n/t
Wilhelmina & Arthur Seemann
NSUB SEEMANN Arthur b.4Apr1888-d.1Feb1913, "Son" n/t Wilhelmina
& William Seemann
NSUB PRIEBE Emma b.1880-d.1944, "Mother" n/t Gustav H. Priebe
NSUB PRIEBE Gustav H. b.1877-d.1950, "Father" n/t Emma Priebe
NSUB LOHSE Minnie M. (HABERMANN) b.1887-d.1981, n/t Theodore
& Albertine Habermann
NSUB HABERMANN Theodore b.1849-d.1922, w/ Albertine
Habermann, n/t Minnie M. H. Lohse
NSUB HABERMANN Albertine b.1852-d.1915, w/ Theodore
Habermann, n/t Minnie M. H. Lohse

NSUB BAHLER Albertina (SCHMIDT) b.1Aug1853-d.1Nov1924, "Mother" n/t Ferdinand F. Bahler

NSUB BAHLER Ferdinand F. b.8Nov1849-d.7Apr1911, n/t Albertina S. Bahler

NSUB WAGNER Wm. b.26Feb1890-d.20Jan1920, "Daddy" n/t Herman Wagner

NSUB WAGNER Herman b.30Jul1844-d.10Aug1919, "Father" n/t Wm. Wagner

NSUB SCHMIDT Ernestine b.21Oct1847-d.7Apr1918

NSUB GUNDEMAN William G. b.1871-d.1949, "Father" n/t Anna M., Clarence R. & Raymond W. Gundeman

NSUB GUNDEMAN Anna M. b.1873-d.1946, "Mother" n/t William G., Clarence R. & Raymond W. Gundeman

NSUB GUNDEMAN Clarence R. b.6Aug1896-d.31Jan1974, "WIS. CPL US ARMY WWI" n/t William G., Anna M. & Raymond W. Gundeman; American Legion mkr.

NSUB GUNDEMAN Raymond W. b.3Jan1901-d.7Jan1901, "Baby" n/t William G., Anna M. & Clarence R. Gundeman

NSUB ERIKSEN Martin b.1856-d.1911, n/t Elisabeth Eriksen

NSUB ERIKSEN Elisabeth b.1858-d.1949, n/t Martin Eriksen

NSUB LUBENAU Edward b.1889-d.1952

NSUB GUNDEMAN Cora b.1885-d.1915, n/t Matilda P., Edward P., Mary & Jacob Gundeman

NSUB GUNDEMAN Mary b.1849-d.1911, "Mother" n/t Matilda P., Edward P., Cora & Jacob Gundeman

NSUB GUNDEMAN Jacob b.1842-d.1914, "Father" n/t Matilda P., Edward P., Cora & Mary Gundeman; GAR mkr

NSUB GUNDEMAN Matilda P. b.1875-d.1956, w/ Edward P., n/t Cora, Jacob & Mary Gundeman

NSUB GUNDEMAN Edward P. b.1875-d.1911, w/ Matilda P., n/t Cora, Jacob & Mary Gundeman

NSUB FESSENBECKER Erwin b.1899-d.1948, "Son" n/t Bertha & William Fessenbecker

NSUB FESSENBECKER Bertha b.1877-d.1950, "Mother" w/ William, n/t Erwin Fessenbecker

NSUB FESSENBECKER William b.1868-d.1935, "Father" w/ Bertha, n/t Erwin Fessenbecker

NSUB PICKER Friedrich b.3Mai1861-d.3Okt1910, w/ Emelia Picker *

NSUB PICKER Emelia b.2Jul1863-d.25Sep1913, w/ Friedrich Picker

NSUB CHAPIN Mary b.1888-d.1971, w/ Emily, Oliver T., Gloria M., Frida A., Oliver C., Oliver H. & Alice C. Chapin

NSUB CHAPIN Emily b.1895-d.no date, w/ Mary, Oliver T., Gloria M., Frida A., Oliver C., Oliver H. & Alice C. Chapin

NSUB CHAPIN Oliver T. b.1927-d.no date, w/ Mary, Emily, Gloria M., Frida A., Oliver C., Oliver H. & Alice C. Chapin

NSUB CHAPIN Gloria M. b.1931-d.no date, w/ Mary, Emily, Oliver T., Frida A., Oliver C., Oliver H. & Alice C. Chapin

NSUB CHAPIN Frida A. b.1897-d.no date, w/ Mary, Emily, Oliver T., Gloria M., Alice C., Oliver C., & Oliver H., & Alice C. Chapin; no cemetery record

NSUB CHAPIN Oliver C. b.1885-d.1968, w/ Mary, Emily, Oliver T., Gloria M., Frida A., Oliver H. & Alice C. Chapin

NSUB CHAPIN Oliver H. b.1852-d.1910, w/ Mary, Emily, Oliver T., Gloria M., Frida A., Oliver C. & Alice C. Chapin

NSUB CHAPIN Alice C. b.1857-d.1947, w/ Mary, Emily, Oliver T., Gloria M., Frida A., Oliver C. & Oliver H. Chapin

NSUB NOBLES Frederick A. b.1823-d.1910, n/t Louisa M. Nobles

NSUB NOBLES Louisa M. b.1840-d.1917, n/t Frederick A. Nobles

NSUB LEONARD Dennis J. b.1865-d.1920, w/ Nellie M. Leonard

NSUB LEONARD Nellie M. b.1871-d.1921, w/ Dennis J. Leonard

NSUB KEATING Emma b.18Oct1880-d.11Aug1929, "w/o John Keating"

NSUB BARNEKOW Charlotte b.1860-d.1936, "Mother" w/ Frank Barnekow

NSUB BARNEKOW Frank b.1858-d.1913, "Father" w/ Charlotte Barnekow *

NSUB MAEHL Alice b.1885-d.1911, "w/o Fred Maehl" *

NSUB BARNEKOW Harrison b.18Jan1889-d.29Apr1910

NSUB PICKER Arthur L. b.20Sep1897-d.10Sep1975, "PVT US ARMY WWI & II"

NSUB RYAN George b.10Sep1861-d.15Jun1926, w/ Ida & Elmer Ryan

NSUB RYAN Ida b.22Jul1860-d.27Nov1949, w/ George & Elmer Ryan

NSUB RYAN Elmer b.9Oct1884-d.24Apr1910, "s/o G. & I. Ryan"

NSUB REIMER Christian b.9Mar1833-d.30Mar1927, w/ Louisa, n/t Lillian A., August F. Reimer & Emil E. & Myrtle Krnez

NSUB REIMER Louisa b.10Jan1834-d.20Dec1918, "His wife" w/ Christian, n/t Lillian A., August F. Reimer & Emil E. & Myrtle Krnez

NSUB REIMER Lillian A. b.1884-d.1922, "Mother" n/t Christian, Louisa, August F. Reimer & Emil E. & Myrtle Krnez

NSUB REIMER August F. b.1880-d.1933, n/t Christian, Louisa, Lillian A. Reimer & Emil E. & Myrtle Krnez

NSUB KRENZ Emil E. b.1890-d.1960, "Husband" n/t Christian, Louisa, Lillian A. & August F. Reimer & Myrtle Krnez

NSUB KRENZ Myrtle H. b.1910-d.1996, "Wife" n/t Christian, Louisa, Lillian A., August F. Reimer & Emil E. Krenz
NSUB LEISTIKOW Sophia b.1861-d.1936, "Mother" n/t Herman Leistikow
NSUB LEISTIKOW Herman b.1867-d.1931, "Father" n/t Sophia Leistikow
NSUB MATTHIESON Alvin b.1893-d.1909
NSUB BARTH Alma b.1901-d.1957, "Faithful Friend"
NSUB BROWN Mettra H. b.1898-d.1979, "Gone But Not Forgotten"
NSUB BACKUS Gertrude b.1904-d.1984
NSUB DUENKEL Barbara b.1845-d.1927, "Mother" n/t Charles Duenkel
NSUB DUENKEL Charles b.16Nov1843-d.4Feb1909, "Father" n/t Barbara Duenkel
NSUB DANCE Gladys Lefeber b.1893-d.1920, n/t May A. & Cornelius G. and other Lefebers; first letter in last name chipped
NSUB LEFEBER May A. b.l884-d.1957, "Mother" w/ Cornelius G., n/t Mary C., James, Mabel G., Hattie and other Lefebers & Gladys L. Dance
NSUB LEFEBER Cornelius G. b.1886-d.1968, "Father" w/ May A., n/t Mary C., James, Abraham, Mabel G., Hattie and other Lefebers & Gladys L. Dance
NSUB LEFEBER Mary C. b.1852-d.1938, w/ James, n/t May A., Joseph, Abraham, Mabel G., Hattie and other Lefebers & Gladys L. Dance
NSUB LEFEBER James b.1854-d.1935, w/ Mary C., n/t May A., Joseph, Abraham, Mabel G., Hattie and other Lefebers & Gladys L. Dance
NSUB LEFEBER Mabel G. b.1881-d.1984, n/t Mary C., May A., Joseph, Abraham, James, Hattie and other Lefebers & Gladys L. Dance
NSUB LEFEBER Hattie b.1852-d.1941, w/ Abraham, n/t May A., Mary C., Joseph, James and other Lefebers & Gladys L. Dance
NSUB LEFEBER Abraham b.1852-d.1944, w/ Hattie, n/t May A., Mary C., Joseph, James, Cornelius G. and other Lefebers & Gladys L. Dance
NSUB LEFEBER Cornelius b.1817-d.1906, n/t Hattie, May A., Mary C., Joseph, James, Cornelius G. and other Lefebers & Gladys L. Dance
NSUB LEFEBER Joseph b.1856-d.1940, w/ Harriett L., n/t May A., Mary C., James, Cornelius G. and other Lefebers & Gladys L. Dance
NSUB LEFEBER Harriett L. b.1864-d.1936, w/ Joseph, n/t May A., Mary C., Hattie, James, Cornelius G. and other Lefebers & Gladys L. Dance
NSUB LEFEBER Edwin S. b.1886-d.1924, n/t Joseph, May A., Mary C., Hattie, James, Cornelius G. and other Lefebers & Gladys L. Dance
NSUB LEFEBER Florence E. b.1883-d.1914, n/t Joseph, May A., Mary C., Hattie, James, Cornelius G. and other Lefebers & Gladys L. Dance

NSUB LEFEBER Clarence b.1885-d.1909, n/t Joseph, May A., Mary C., Hattie, James, Cornelius G. and other Lefebers & Gladys L. Dance

NSUB NORWOOD Sarah L. b.1859-d.1944, n/t James W. Norwood

NSUB NORWOOD James W. b.1862-d.1939, n/t Sarah L. Norwood

NSUB JOHNSON Grace L. b.1896-d.1962, "MIZPAH" w/ Archie E., n/t Louie D., Archie E., Jennie & Albert Johnson

NSUB JOHNSON Archie E. b.1894-d.1972, "MIZPAH" w/ Grace L., n/t Louie D., Archie E., Jennie & Albert Johnson

NSUB JOHNSON Louie D. b.1865-d.1931, "Mother" n/t Archie E., Grace L., Archie E., Jennie & Albert Johnson

NSUB JOHNSON Archie E. b.1863-d.1936, "Father" n/t Archie E., Grace L., Louie D., Jennie & Albert Johnson

NSUB JOHNSON Jennie b.1868-d.1952, n/t Archie E., Grace L., Louie D., Archie E. & Albert Johnson

NSUB JOHNSON Albert b.1855-d.1908, n/t Archie E., Grace L., Louie D., Archie E. & Jennie Johnson

NSUB PILGRIM Grace M. b.1886-d.1935, n/t Elmer C., Estelle M., Elizabeth, & Daniel T. Pilgrim

NSUB PILGRIM Elmer C. b.1885-d.1952, n/t Grace M., Estelle M., Elizabeth, & Daniel T. Pilgrim

NSUB PILGRIM Estelle M. b.1890-d.1962, n/t Grace M., ELmer C., Elizabeth, & Daniel T. Pilgrim; American Legion mkr

NSUB PILGRIM Elizabeth b.1858-d.1947, n/t Grace M., ELmer C., Estelle M., & Daniel T. Pilgrim

NSUB PILGRIM Daniel T. b.1861-d.1934, n/t Grace M., ELmer C., Estelle M., & Elizabeth Pilgrim

NSUB STEVENS Hazel L. b.1893-d.1975, n/t Wayne H. Stevens

NSUB STEVENS Wayne H. b.1894-d.1961, n/t Hazel L. Stevens

NSUB DE BRUINE Erma b.1892-d.1915

NSUB WEHR Gustav b.1873-d.1912, w/ Georgia, n/t Mary & John Wehr & Emma W. Ellis & Minnie W. Hope

NSUB WEHR Georgia b.1872-d.1912, w/ Gustav, n/t Mary & John Wehr & Emma W. Ellis & Minnie W. Hope

NSUB WEHR Mary b.1832-d.1908, "Mother" w/ John, n/t Gustav & Georgia Wehr & Emma W. Ellis & Minnie W. Hope

NSUB WEHR John b.1827-d.1917, "Father" w/ Mary, n/t Gustav & Georgia Wehr & Emma W. Ellis & Minnie W. Hope

NSUB HOPE Minnie Wehr b.1862-d.1930, n/t Gustav, Georgia, Mary & John Wehr & Emma W. Ellis

NSUB ELLIS Emma Wehr b.1879-d.1959, n/t Gustav, Georgia, Mary & John Wehr & Minnie W. Hope

NSUB TWINEM Clara T. b.1876-d.1922, "Mother" n/t Cross, Jane,
Chester E., Martha, James, James & Annie Twinem

NSUB TWINEM Cross b.1830-d.1908, "Father" n/t CLara T., Jane,
Chester E., Martha, James, James & Annie Twinem

NSUB TWINEM Jane b.1842-d.1925, "Mother" n/t CLara T., Cross,
Chester E., Martha, James, James & Annie Twinem

NSUB TWINEM Chester E. b.1903-d.1947, n/t CLara T., Cross, Jane,
Martha, James, James & Annie Twinem

NSUB TWINEM James b.1838-d.1910, "Husband" n/t CLara T., Cross,
Jane, Martha, Chester E., James & Annie Twinem

NSUB TWINEM Annie b.1842-d.1930, "Wife" n/t CLara T., Cross, Jane,
Martha, Chester E., James & James Twinem

NSUB TWINEM Martha b.1872-d.1938, "Mother" w/ James, n/t CLara T.,
Cross, Jane, Chester E., Annie & James Twinem

NSUB TWINEM James b.1870-d.1942, "Father" w/ Martha, n/t CLara T.,
Cross, Jane, Chester E., Annie & James Twinem

NSUB CORDIE Peter b.1868-d.1951, "Father" w/ Minnie Cordie

NSUB CORDIE Minnie b.1881-d.1964, "Mother" w/ Peter Cordie

NSUB FISK M. H., Dr. b.1843-d.1906, "CO. E 40 WIS. INF." Masonic
Symbol; Melancton H. was living in Appleton when he enlisted in the
army 13 May 1864, he was Mustered Out 16 Sept 1864, when his term
expired[59]

NSUB DUNCEY Nellie b.1865-d.1955, n/t Archie Duncey

NSUB DUNCEY Archie b.1885-d.1967, n/t Nellie Duncey

NSUB QUAST Florence P. b.1911-d.1995, w/ John A. Quast

NSUB QUAST John A. b.1900-d.1958, w/ Florence P. Quast

NSUB PRUDISCH Emily b.1881-d.1935, w/ Fred, n/t Metha J. & Walter
H. Prudisch

NSUB PRUDISCH Fred b.1875-d.1945, w/ Emily, n/t Metha J. & Walter
H. Prudisch *

NSUB PRUDISCH Metha J. b.1902-d.1971, w/ Walter H., n/t Emily &
Fred Prudisch; Eastern Star symbol

NSUB PRUDISCH Walter H. b.1903-d.1981, w/ Metha J., n/t Emily &
Fred Prudisch; Masonic symbol

NSUB GRAY Frank E. b.1904-d.1970, w/ Lois B. Gray & Fay A., G.
Mortimer, Jessie, Mary J. & Adolph G. Becker

NSUB GRAY Lois B. b.1906-d.1976, w/ Frank E. Gray & Fay A., G.
Mortimer, Jessie, Mary J. & Adolph G. Becker

NSUB BECKER Fay A. b.1901-d.1981, w/ Frank E. & Lois B Gray & G.
Mortimer Jessie, Mary J. & Adolph G. Becker

NSUB BECKER G. Mortimer b.1898-d.1978, w/ Frank E. & Lois B. Gray & Fay A., Jessie, Mary J. & Adolph G. Becker

NSUB BECKER Jessie b.1900-d.1904, w/ Frank E. & Lois B. Gray & Fay A., G. Mortimer, Mary J. & Adolph G. Becker

NSUB BECKER Mary Jane b.1868-d.1936, w/ Frank E. & Lois B. Gray & Fay A., G. Mortimer, Jessie & Adolph G. Becker

NSUB BECKER Adolph G. b.1867-d.1938, w/ Frank E. & Lois B. Gray & Fay A., G. Mortimer, Jessie & Mary J. Becker

NSUB KLUMB Elizabeth b.17May1868-d.22Oct1918, "Mother" w/ William Klumb

NSUB KLUMB William b.25Sep1867-d.8Aug1916, "Father" w/ Elizabeth Klumb

NSUB DUNKEL Louis W. b.1867-d.1922, n/t Kate Dunkel

NSUB DUNKEL Kate b.1866-d.1939, n/t Louis W. Dunkel

NSUB ALLEN Alice b.1849-d.1905, "Mother"

NSUB RANK Jeanie b.7Dec1920-d.no date, w/ Robert Rank

NSUB RANK Robert b.17Feb1920-d.17Mar1992, w/ Jeanie Rank

NSUB CORNWALL Anna b.20Mar1830-d.15May1904, "d/o Eber & Cynthia Cornwall" w/ Newbury, Ruth & Bashua Cornwall & Daisy W. Ellis & Eliza S. Baker

NSUB CORNWALL Newbury b.2May1823-d.2Jan1911, "s/o Eber & Cynthia Cornwall" w/ Anna, Ruth & Bashua Cornwall & Daisy W. Ellis & Eliza S. Baker,2 stones, dates on other stone 1822-1919

NSUB CORNWALL Ruth b.1827-d.1919, "d/o Eber & Cynthia Cornwall" w/ Anna, Newbury & Bashua Cornwall & Daisy W. Ellis & Eliza S. Baker

NSUB CORNWALL Bashua b.1820-d.1923, "d/o Eber & Cynthia Cornwall" w/ Anna, Newbury & Ruth Cornwall & Daisy W. Ellis & Eliza S. Baker

NSUB ELLIS Daisy Wilson b.7Apr1869-d.24Feb1903, "w/o Geo A Ellis" w/ Anna, Newbury, Bashua & Ruth Cornwall & Eliza S. Baker

NSUB BAKER Eliza S. b.1848-d.1920, w/ Anna, Newbury, Bashua & Ruth Cornwall & Daisy W. Ellis

NSUB SHELDON Roscoe b.1845-d.1917,

NSUB BARK William W. b.21Sep1865-d.10Oct1910

NSUB HEIDEN Fredericka (EGGERT) b.3Mar1839-d.31Aug1903, "Mother" n/t John Heiden *

NSUB HEIDEN John b.3Mar1833-d.31Jan1907, "Father" n/t Fredericka Heiden *

NSUB LYMAN Tom P. b.1931-d.1993, "Beloved Son" n/t Nanci A., Estelle M. & Philip M. Lyman

NSUB LYMAN Nanci A. b.3Oct1928-d.16Apr1983, "US NAVY KOREA" n/t Tom P., Estelle M. & Philip M. Lyman

NSUB LYMAN Estelle M. b.1907-d.1988, "Wife" w/ Philip M., n/t Tom P. & Estelle M. Lyman

NSUB LYMAN Philip M. b.1903-d.1978, "Husband" w/ Estelle M., n/t Tom P. & Estelle M. Lyman

NSUB BRENDEMUEHL Elmer A. b.14Sep1910-d.19May1973, "WIS. T SGT US ARMY WWII"

NSUB BARTHOLOMEW Henry b.11Sep1895-d.11Feb1945, "INDIANA 1 LIEUT. INFANTRY" n/t Dorothy B. Bartholomew & Abe & Nellie J. Brown

NSUB BARTHOLOMEW Dorothy Brown b.31Oct1897-d.10Sep1992, n/t Henry Bartholomew & Abe & Nellie J. Brown

NSUB BROWN Abe b.1863-d.1955, "Father" w/ Nellie J. Brown, n/t Henry & Dorothy B. Bartholomew; Masonic Sym

NSUB BROWN Nellie Johnson b.1868-d.1945, "Mother" w/ Abe Brown, n/t Henry & Dorothy B. Bartholomew

NSUB GALLOWAY Sarah A. b.5Jan1846-d.8Feb1903 *

NSUB JOHNSON Edward Benjamin b.1861-d.1903, w/ Jane C. Johnson, n/t Ray C. Edwards & Alfred C. & Merle R. Johnson

NSUB JOHNSON Jane Campbell b.1868-d.1964, w/ Edward B. Johnson, n/t Ray C. Edwards & Alfred C. & Merle R. Johnson

NSUB EDWARDS Ray Campbell b.7Sep1954-d.6Feb1983, n/t Alfred C., Merle R., Edward B. & Jane C. Johnson

NSUB JOHNSON Alfred Campbell b.1897-d.1995, w/ Merle R. Johnson, n/t Ray C. Edwards & Edward B. & Jane C. Johnson; Masonic sym.

NSUB JOHNSON Merle Robertson b.1898-d.1997, w/ Alfred C. Johnson, n/t Ray C. Edwards & Edward B. & Jane C. Johnson

NSUB BROWN Grace May b.17Sep1888-d.13Apr1903, n/t Theodore E. & Bessie B. Lusk

NSUB LUSK Theodore E. b.1892-d.1983, w/ Bessie B. Lusk, n/t Grace M. Brown

NSUB LUSK Bessie Brown b.1892-d.1931, w/ Theodore E. Lusk, n/t Grace M. Brown

NSUB MEDICK Dorothy F. b.17Apr1919-d.17Mar1998, w/ Theodore E., n/t Robert W. & Helen E. B. Lusk, Grace M. Brown

NSUB LUSK Robert W. b.1922-d.1979, "CAPT. US ARMY WWII" n/t Helen E., Bessie B., & Theodore E. Lusk, & Grace M. Brown

NSUB LUSK Helen E. (BRENDEMUEHL) b.24Feb1924-d.16Dec1984, n/t Robert W., Bessie B., & Theodore E. Lusk, & Grace M. Brown

NSUB MADSEN Christian d.5Dec1906, "24y" n/t Tina Madsen

NSUB MADSEN Tina d.13Dec1903, "27y" n/t Christian Madsen *

NSUB SWAN James b.11Jan1868-d.29Jul1906, "Papa"
NSUB KUTSCHENREUTER Wilhelmine b.1828-d.1903, "Grandmother"
n/t Wilhelmine S. & William Kutschenreuter
NSUB KUTSCHENREUTER Wilhelmine (STERNKE) 3Jan1856-
d.13Jul1920, n/t Wilhelmine & William Kutschenreuter
NSUB KUTSCHENREUTER William b.1857-d.1936, "Father" n/t
Wilhelmine & Wilhelmine S. Kutschenreuter
NSUB SCHMUTZLER August d.25Apr1907, w/ Christine Schmutzler
NSUB SCHMUTZLER Christine b.22Mar1836-d.19Mar1906, w/ August
Schmutzler
NSUB BILTY Charles H. b.1877-d.1952, n/t Catherine E. & James C.
Bilty; Spanish American War mkr
NSUB BILTY Catherine E. b.1877-d.1950, n/t Charles H. & James C.
Bilty
NSUB BILTY James C. b.1927-d.1951, "KOREA 38 INF. 2 DIV. KILLED
IN ACTION" n/t Charles H. & Catherine E. Bilty; American Legion
mkr
NSUB DE BACK Johanna (ISRAEL) b.27Feb1870 GROE OF?
NETHERLAND-d.19Feb1904, "Mrs. Peter, Married 20Apr1893,
Landed in United States 20May1893" n/t Susana De Back
NSUB DE BACK Susanna b.1870-d.1924, "Mother" n/t Johanna I. De
Back
NSUB RESEBURG Laura S. b.1884-d.1962, w/ Arwin Reseburg
NSUB RESEBURG Arwin b.1887-d.1961, w/ Laura S. Reseburg
NSUB FISHER Ennis E. b.1862-d.1929, n/t Theadosia M. & Erskine
Fisher
NSUB FISHER Theadosia M. b.1861-d.1907, n/t Ennis E. & Erskine
Fisher
NSUB FISHER Erskine b.1900-d.1901, n/t Ennis E. & Theadosia M.
Fisher
NSUB BECHERER Franz b.1847-d.1913, "Father" w/ Amelia Becherer
NSUB BECHERER Amelia b.1857-d.1944, "Mother" w/ Franz Becherer
NSUB RESEBURG Ruth L. b.4Aug1915-d.7Jul1917, w/ Arwin O.
Reseburg
NSUB RESEBURG Arwin O. b.16Oct1918-d.19Jan1919, w/ Ruth L.
Reseburg
NSUB RAACK Johanna b.16Mai1830-d.5Jul1911
NSUB NAAB Adam b.1862-d.1948, "Father" n/t Amelia K. & Georgiana
K. Naab
NSUB NAAB Amelia Keeler b.1867-d.1934, "Mother" n/t Adam &
Georgiana K. Naab

NSUB NAAB Georgiana K. b.1902-d.1948, "Sister" n/t Adam & Amelia
K. Naab
NSUB WELTON Carrie E. b.1861-d.1916, "Sister"
NSUB KEELER Harriet b.1840-d.1904, "Mother"
NSUB BECHERER Frank b.15Mar1877-d.15Sep1913, n/t Lulu W.
Becherer
NSUB BECHERER Lulu (WHEELER) b.13Mai1833-d.30Jun1907, n/t
Frank Becherer
NSUB RUEHMER Emma b.1881-d.1891, n/t Ida, Wilhelm & Mathilda
Ruehmer
NSUB RUEHMER Ida b.1889-d.1908, n/t Emma, Wilhelm & Mathilda
Ruehmer
NSUB RUEHMER Wilhelm b.1852-d.1925, "Father" n/t Emma, Ida &
Mathilda Ruehmer
NSUB RUEHMER Mathilda b.1851-d.1926, "Mother" n/t Emma, Ida &
Wilhelm Ruehmer
NSUB ANDERSON George b.1854-d.1937, n/t Mary J. Anderson;
Masonic symbol
NSUB ANDERSON Mary J. b.1864-d.1953, n/t George Anderson
NSUB WILLIAMS Ellen b.1839-d.1909
NSUB BOLTE Alice b.1870-d.1952, n/t August H. Bolte
NSUB BOLTE August H. b.1870-d.1905, n/t Alice Bolte
NSUB GILBERT Julia Maria b.1854-d.1907, "Mother"
NSUB POST George W. b.27Jul1885-d.7Aug1907
NSUB LANDOLT Minnie M. b.10Oct1854-d.11Mar1907, w/ Albert
Landolt
NSUB LANDOLT Albert b.25Jan1848-d.11Aug1927, w/ Minnie M.
Landolt
NSUB GILSON John b.11Jun1850-d.23Mar1919, n/t Elizabeth Gilson &
Frances G. & Alvin G. Drahos; American Legion mkr
NSUB GILSON Elizabeth b.5Oct1853-d.15Mar1914, n/t John Gilson &
Frances G. & Alvin G. Drahos
NSUB DRAHOS Frances Gilson b.1886-d.1917, w/ Alvin G. Drahos, n/t
John & Elizabeth Gilson
NSUB DRAHOS Alvin Gilson b.18Apr1917-d.12May1917, w/ Frances G.
Drahos, n/t John & Elizabeth Gilson
NSUB FLEMING Madeline b.1888-d.1977, w/ Herbert Shubert, Otillie &
Sophia Falbe, Lucille Funke, Maria & Fred Schoen, A. A. & Louise
Schaper
NSUB SHUBERT Herbert b.1911-d.1991, w/ Madeline Fleming, Otillie
& Sophia Falbe, Lucille Funke, Maria & Fred Schoen, A. A. & Louise
Schaper

155

NSUB FALBE Otillie b.1877-d.1960, w/ Madeline Fleming, Herbert Shubert & Sophia Falbe, Lucille Funke, Maria & Fred Schoen, A. A. & Louise Schaper

NSUB FALBE Sophia b.1853-d.1933, w/ Madeline Fleming, Herbert Shubert & Otillie Falbe, Lucille Funke,Maria & Fred Schoen, A. A. & Louise Schaper

NSUB FUNKE Lucille b.1905-d.1934, w/ Madeline Fleming, Herbert Shubert & Otillie & Sophia Falbe,Maria & Fred Schoen, A. A. & Louise Schaper

NSUB SCHAPER Louise b.1881-d.1927, w/ Madeline Fleming, Herbert Shubert & Otillie & Sophia Falbe, Maria & Fred Schoen, A. A. & Louise Schaper

NSUB SCHAPER A. A. b.1881-d.1936, w/ Madeline Fleming, Herbert Shubert & Otillie & Sophia Falbe, Maria & Fred Schoen, A. A. & Louise Schaper

NSUB SHOEN Maria b.1827-d.1925, w/ Madeline Fleming, Herbert Shubert & Otillie & Sophia Falbe, Fred Schoen, A. A. & Louise Schaper

NSUB SHOEN Fred b.1823-d.1911, w/ Madeline Fleming, Herbert Shubert & Otillie & Sophia Falbe, Maria Schoen, A. A. & Louise Schaper

NSUB FALK Annie b.1878-d.1916, "Mother"

NSUB WILKE Fritz O. P. b.4Jan1900-d.26Okt1916, "Sohn"

NSUB SCHERNECK Rudolph b.26Aug1872-d.27Nov1916

NSUB RANWICK Herdrikke b.1877-d.1966, "Mother"

NSUB HAGEMAN Walter O. b.10Sep1903-d.30Apr1916

NSUB SCHELLIN Karl b.20Jun1830-d.13Nov1915, "Vater"

NSUB ZAHN Andrew b.no date-d.no date, no cemetery record, possibly an infant

NSUB SCHRUM Rosa A. b.1895-d.1956

NSUB RANWICK Alfred b.1900-d.1959, American Legion mkr

NSUB MICHEL Wilhelmina b.31Jan1836-d.29Apr1915, "Mutter"

NSUB SEMROW Wilhelm b.6Jan1836-d.22Mai1915, "Vater"

NSUB MILLER John b.1860-d.1915

NSUB RADTKE Marie b.1908-d.1915, "Daughter"

NSUB RAWSON Elizabeth b.1910-d.1962

NSUB TROST John b.22Sep1846-d.12Apr1915, "Father"

NSUB JAEGER Anna b.8Jun1881-d.2Mar1915, "Mamma"

NSUB KLUG Wilhelmina Miller b.1875-d.1953

NSUB HAACK William b.15Oct1862-d.27Jan1915, "Father"; dates from cemetery records

NSUB BEHLING Emilie b.1848-d.1914, "Mother"

NSUB CSELETZ Katharina b.2Sep1878-d.24Jul1914

NSUB HAACK Anna b.5Oct1868-d.1Feb1914; dates from cemetery
records

NSUB HALE Ben b.1887-d.1955, "Grandpa"

NSUB HARRISON Frank W. b.1869-d.1955

NSUB YORK Orpha b.31Aug1894-d.29Apr1913

NSUB MASTERBROOK Ray M. b.17Jul1892-d.29Jun1913

NSUB GÜCKSTOCK Auguste b.1849-d.1913

NSUB SCHREIBER Rose b.1890-d.1931, "Mother"

NSUB CRAVEN John W. b.1869-d.1953

NSUB JAHNKE Carl b.1890-d.1953

NSUB PECK Newton S. b.19Sep1836-d.19Jan1912, "9 WIS. L. A." aka
Logan S. Peck according to the cemetery records; Newton lived in
Burlington when he enlisted in the army on 9 Jan 1864, he was disch.
11 Aug 1865;[60] dates from cemetery records.

NSUB RIEMER-EGGERT Clara b.1887-d.1911, NSUB ALBEDYLL
Minnie b.1870-d.1911

NSUB EGGERT-RIEMER Clara b.1887-d.1911, NSUB ALBEDYLL
Minnie b.1870-d.1911

NSUB SCHUETZ Robert b.22Sep1973-d.14Jan1912, "Bruder" n/t Franz
Schuetz

NSUB SCHUETZ Franz b.10Oct1866-d.1Mar1912, "Vater" n/t Robert
Schuetz

NSUB STRENG Mayme b.22May1888-d.9Sep1912, "Mother"

NSUB FARRAR James Harvey b.1834 Richford, VT-d.1909 Milwaukee,
WI

NSUB SANBORN Upham T. b.1855-d.1911

NSUB KARNATZ Johann b.7Feb1827-d.28Jun1910

NSUB KALIES Carl b.6Nov1843-d.10Feb1810

NSUB ROEMER Howard H. b.1891-d.1953, "Father"

NSUB LUNDQUIST Arthur C. b.20Oct1881-d.26Jun1950, "Dad" n/t
Gladys Lundquist

NSUB LUNDQUIST Gladys b.3Jun1909-d.3Dec1963, "Daughter" n/t
Arthur C. Lundquist

NSUB NOEL Jesse M. b.1870-d.1917

NSUB MAHNKE Albert b.1866-d.1917

NSUB HEIMANN Herman b.1869-d.1917

NSUB HOGE Harold C. b.25May1915-d.12Dec1966, "WIS. T SGT 3508
BASE UNIT AAF WWII AM &" OLC" I believe AM is the Air Medal and
OLC Oak Leaf Cluster

NSUB LUNDQUIST Anna L. (GUSTAFSON) b.8Feb1882-d.1Aug1930, "Mother" n/t Roy C. Lundquist

NSUB LUNDQUIST Roy C. b.24Jul1904-d.3Mar1918, "Son"

NSUB HARTWIG Ida T. b.1882-d.1917, "Mother"

NSUB KOCH George b.28Apr1882-d.30Oct1918, w/ Lillie Koch

NSUB KOCH Lillie b.23Nov1887-d.26Oct1918, w/ George Koch; they died so close together, could it have been the flue epidemic?

NSUB HAACKER Minnie b.1888-d.1925, "Mother"

NSUB KAGEL Harold A. b.1906-d.1960

S-11 MARQUARDT C. b.1856-d.1921

S-11 LEMMON Cassendana b.Nov1859-d.Aug1920, "Mother"

S-11 ADAMSON Estelle H. b.1858-d.1920

S-11 WARNECKE Henry b.1845-d.1919

S-11 WILKE Frank H. b.19May1893-d.4Jan1960, "Husband"

S-11 SEVERIN Gustav b.1852-d.1925

S-11 LEEHOUTS Isaac b.1880-d.1921, "Brother"

S-11 DRESNER Albert J. b.1874-d.1921, "Father"

S-11 BOSCH Richard L. b.1923-d.1925

S-11 PORTER June b.1920-d.1923

S-11 POENITZSCH Harry b.18Nov1913-d.17Nov1922

S-11 HARTEL June Marie b.1917-d.1922

S-11 GREENMAN Wm. G., Jr. b.18Jul1922-d.11Mar1923

S-11 STREHLOW William b.1917-d.1926, "Son"

S-11 HILDEBRANDT Alfred b.1914-d.1926

S-11 ARMSTRONG Judith Ann b.1945-d.1947, "Baby"

S-11 HOVDE John Robert b.Mar1933-d.Jul1936

S-11 SCHEMBERGER Harold b.1923-d.1931, "Son"

S-11 RUFFLE Erna (WEBER) b.1891-d.1921, "Mother"

S-11 BARTELT Tillie b.1872-d.1921, "Mother"

S-11 KOVATSH Katherine b.1877-d.1921, "Mother"

S-11 BULTING Jacob b.1849-d.1924

S-11 POENITZSCH Fred b.28Nov1879-d.25Mar1924, "Father"

S-11 GRUBER Emilie b.1882-d.1924, "Mother"

S-11 RICKE Otto b.no date-d.no date, possibly an infant; no cemetery record

S-11 ERDMANN Ella b.1893-d.1944, "Mother"

S-11 FRANZ Magdeline b.1886-d.1924

S-11 QUADE Lorraine b.1906-d.1925

S-11 PEARSON John d.1925, only one date

S-11 MILLS John b.1853-d.1921

S-11 WICHMANN Anna Neldner b.27Apr1859-d.29Oct1929, "Mother"

S-11 RILEY Jane (STIMSON) b.1860-d.1922
S-11 ERDMAN Fred E. b.28Jun1891-d.19Nov1955, "Father"
S-11 WAGNER Anna d.25Aug1922, only one date
S-11 BAHR Amelia b.1843-d.1922
S-11 ROEMER W. F. b.1867-d.1923
S-11 ELLIS John A. b.1845-d.1925, "Father"
S-11 CRAVEN Priscilla C. b.1858-d.1925, "Mother"
S-11 STOUT Ora Fay b.1885-d.1946, w/ Levi Stout
S-11 STOUT Levi b.1869-d.1940, w/ Ora Fay Stout
S-11 MITCHELL Anna M. b.1879-d.1925
S-11 WEHE Edward C. b.1862-d.1926, "Father"
S-11 ? Elsie b.no date-d.no date, nothing other than first name, buried in
    the 1926 area
S-11 TOOMBS Clifford R. b.1896-d.1926
S-11 BERNDT Fred b.1864-d.1926, "Father"
S-11 HARTMANN Margaret b.1854-d.1923, "Mother"
S-11 WANGELIN Anna b.1874-d.1938, "Wife"
S-11 ZIMDARS William b.1847-d.1924
S-11 TOOMBS Flora J. b.1889-d.1958
S-11 WHITE Baby d.2Jan1926, "d/o Frank & Mabel White" only one date
S-11 KOMOR Arthur Curt b.15May1926-d.29Aug1926, w/ Edward
    Komor; there appears to be two children, but would the dates be the
    same for both of them?
S-11 KOMOR Edward b.15May1926-d.29Aug1926, w/ Arthur C. Komor;
    there appears to be two children, but would the dates be the same for
    both of them?
S-11 WELCH Oscar b.1925-d.1926
S-11 DALLMAN Wm. b.1873-d.1926, "Father"
S-11 DRESSLER Douglas H. d.4Aug1925, "WIS. CORP. 161 DEPOT
    BRIG." only one date
S-11 ADAMSON William H. b.1858-d.1942
S-11 STREHLOW Walter A. b.15Jan1894-d.29Oct1943, "Father"
S-11 WILKE Frank b.1866-d.1943, "Husband"
S-11 KNELLWOLF Johannes b.1855-d.1926
S-11 POENITZSCH Anna b.1881-d.1966, "Mother"
S-11 HABERMAN Henry b.1888-d.1927, "Father"
S-11 KRENZ August b.1845-d.1928
S-11 SPLIES Laura b.1897-d.1927, "Wife"
S-11 HALL John Davis b.6Sep1938-d.19Sep1938
S-11 BUEGE Robert d.8Oct1927, only one date
S-11 ELHART Infant d.31Aug1928, "s/o Bernard & Clara Elhart" only one
    date

S-11 GARON Raymond G. b.1914-d.1958
S-11 WINTERS Caroline E. b.1891-d.1927
S-11 HOPP Mabel b.1876-d.1958, w/ Matt Hopp
S-11 HOPP Matt b.1875-d.1958
S-11 OLNEY Minnie b.1895-d.1928
S-11 TILLOTSON C. Eugene b.1891-d.1928
S-11 BUEGE Mary b.16Jul1873-d.27May1928, "Mother" n/t Charles
Buege
S-11 BUEGE Charles b.19May1864-d.8Feb1941, "Father" n/t Mary
Buege
S-11 KING Josephine b.1855-d.1931, "Mother" n/t Joseph King
S-11 KING Joseph b.1847-d.1929, "Daddy" n/t Josephine King
S-11 SCHUELER Henry J. b.1859-d.1929
S-11 BUCHHOLTZ Joseph b.1911-d.1931, "Son"
S-11 KUNDE Cora B. b.1905-d.1931
S-11 KRUEGER Ottile b.1875-d.1947, n/t Gustav Krueger
S-11 KRUEGER Gustav b.1871-d.1946, n/t Ottile Krueger
S-11 THOMPSON Charles b.1850-d.1928,
S-11 RADTKE Christ b.1852-d.1928
S-11 SCHMELING Anna b.1872-d.1958, "Mother" w/ Albert, n/t Walter
Schmeling
S-11 SCHMELING Albert b.1863-d.1943, "Father" w/ Anna, n/t Walter
Schmeling
S-11 SCHMELING Walter b.1886-d.1931, "Daddy" n/t Anna & Albert
Schmeling
S-11 SCHAUER Alfred Fred b.23May1893-d.4Aug1932, "WIS. CORP.
161 DEPOT BRIG." w/ Catherine B. Schauer
S-11 SCHAUER Catherine B. b.24Jul1895-d.4Aug1932, "His Wife" w/
Alfred F. Schauer
S-11 DRESSLER Ella b.1899-d.1934, "Mother"
S-11 CRAVEN Tom b.1860-d.1934, "Father"
S-11 BUEGE Walter F. b.14Feb1895-d.11Apr1934, "WIS. PVT 161
DEPOT BRIG"
S-11 SCHUELER Katherine b.1860-d.1931,
S-11 NAESER Arthur b.1888-d.1934
S-11 ROSENTHAL Isadore b.1845-d.1938
S-11 LEE Charles b.1853-d.1935
S-11 STEPHENSON William H. b.1877-d.1944
S-11 LANGE Herman F. b.1857-d.1944
S-11 HEIM Rose E. b.23Sep1890-d.21Mar1936, "Mother"
S-11 CSELETZ Carl A. b.1873-d.1936
S-11 STEPHENSON Bessie b.1880-d.1936, "Mother"

S-11 TIMM Fred F. b.1872-d.1937
S-11 BAHR Tilly b.1886-d.1936
S-11 PRIOR Barbara b.1870-d.1936, "Mother" n/t Henry Prior
S-11 PRIOR Henry b.1871-d.1948, "Father" n/t Barbara Prior
S-11 LENTZ Richard d.3Mar1937, "WIS. PVT 44 INF. 15 DIV." only one date
S-11 HARRISON Elizabeth b.1880-d.1937
S-11 JUSTIN Richard A. b.1892-d.1936, w/ Ida S. Justin
S-11 JUSTIN Ida S. b.1891-d.1966, w/ Richard A. Justin
S-11 MASTENBROOK Josephine K. b.1903-d.1946, "Sister"
S-11 SZUPPA Marie Fellows b.1901-d.1960, "Wife"
S-11 HARRISON George E. b.1903-d.1948
S-11 SCHMELING Arthur H. b.1899-d.1959, n/t Alvera Schmeling
S-11 SCHMELING Alvera b.1906-d.1948, n/t Arthur H. Schmeling
S-11 KRUEGER Clara b.1911-d.no date, w/ George O. Krueger
S-11 KRUEGER George O. b.1897-d.1952, w/ Clara Krueger
S-11 RANWICK Oswald b.1899-d.1980
S-11 LEMKE Oscar Ralph b.18Jul1896-d.20Dec1984, "PVT US ARMY WWI"
S-11 SCHMELING Charles b.30Aug1896-d.5Apr1967, w/ Florence Schmeling
S-11 SCHMELING Florence b.15Mar1897-d.15May1957, w/ Charles Schmeling
S-11 SCHEMBERGER Gladys b.1899-d.1958, "Mama" w/ Micheal Schemberger
S-11 SCHEMBERGER Micheal (sic) b.1898-d.1965, "Daddy" w/ Gladys Schemberger
S-11 BONDS Bette J. b.1925-d.no date, "Mom" w/ John M. Bonds
S-11 BONDS John M. b.1925-d.1993, w/ Bette J. Bonds
S-11 RITCHIE Shirley b.1936-d.no date, "Mickey" w/ Claude Ritchie
S-11 RITCHIE Claude b.1932-d.1998, "Jr." w/ Shirley Ritchie
S-11 CURTISS Virginia M. b.1921-d.no date, "Mama" w/ Floyd L. Curtiss
S-11 CURTISS Floyd L. b.1921-d.1973, "Daddy" w/ Virginia M. Curtiss; American Legion mkr
S-11 DAMITZ Marion J. b.1917-d.1993, w/ Leo H. Damitz
S-11 DAMITZ Leo H. b.1910-d.1981, w/ Marion J. Damitz
S-11 HAYWARD June Amanda b.27Aug1924-d.no date, "Daughter" w/ Amanda J. & William C. Hayward
S-11 HAYWARD Amanda J. b.24Dec1891-d.15Jul1967, "Mother" w/ June A. & William C. Hayward
S-11 HAYWARD William Clark b.29Jun1892-d.4Dec1984, "Dad" w/ June A. & Amanda J. Hayward

S-11 ELHART Clara E. b.1893-d.1971, "Mother"

S-11 KOPPELMAN Jessie b.4Mar1903-d.11May1963, w/ Andrew Koppelman

S-11 KOPPELMAN Andrew b.23Apr1896-d.7Apr1972, w/ Jessie Koppelman

S-11 SZUPPA Henry b.1893-d.1978, "Husband"

S-11 ZIERHUT Joseph B. b.27Jan1917-d.18Mar1999, "PFC US ARMY WWII"

S-11 SIMMONS Jerold G. b.1929-d.1983, "Beloved Father" n/t Dorothy M. Simmons

S-11 SIMMONS Dorothy Mae b.3Dec1932-d.19Jan1998, n/t Jerold G. Simmons

S-11 ARMSTRONG Elsa G. b.19Feb1912-d.28Dec1989, "Mother"

S-11 HOVDE Kenneth b.1932-d.1996

S-11 JASIN Mary Jane b.1934-d.no date, w/ Katherine M. & Walter F. Jasin

S-11 JASIN Katherine M. b.1910-d.1993, w/ Mary J. & Walter F. Jasin

S-11 JASIN Walter F. b.1910-d.no date, w/ Mary J. & Katherine M. Jasin

S-11 DOOLITTLE Carolyn b.1914-d.1997, "Married 3 June 1933" w/ Jay A. Doolittle

S-11 DOOLITTLE Jay A. b.1908-d.1997, "Married 3 June 1933" w/ Carolyn Doolittle

S-11 BARZDUKAS Vivian A. b.1923-d.no date, w/ Albert C. Barzdukas

S-11 BARZDUKAS Albert C. b.1915-d.1985, w/ Vivian A. Barzdukas

S-11 HAAS Dorothy O. b.1898-d.1995, w/ Oscar A. Haas

S-11 HAAS Oscar A. b.1899-d.1984, w/ Dorothy O. Haas

S-11 BAHR Elmer R. b.1912-d.1986, "Father"

SEC8 SPORLEDER Ida b.1874-d.1922, w/ H. C. & Marie Sproleder, Robert Menzies, Baby ? & Herlene S. Huntley

SEC8 SPORLEDER Baby b.no date-d.no date, w/ Ida, H. C. & Marie Sproleder, Robert Menzies, Baby ? & Herlene S. Huntley

SEC8 SPORLEDER H. C. b.1872-d.1942, w/ Ida & Marie Sproleder & Robert Menzies, Baby ? & Herlene S. Huntley

SEC8 SPORLEDER Marie b.1906-d.1929, w/ Ida & H. C. Sproleder & Robert Menzies, Baby ? & Herlene S. Huntley

SEC8 MENZIES Robert b.1931-d.1937, w/ Ida, H. C. & Marie Sproleder & Baby ? & Herlene S. Huntley

SEC8 HUNTLEY Herlene S. b.1901-d.1960, w/ Ida, H. C. & Marie Sproleder & Baby ? & Robert Menzies

SEC8 COBABE Frances F. b.1869-d.1922, "Father" w/ Fred E. & Cecelia C. Kohloff

SEC8 KOHLOFF Fred E. b.1900-d.1969, w/ Cecelia C. Kohloff &
Frances F. Cobabe

SEC8 KOHLOFF Cecelia C. b.1904-d.1976, w/ Fred E. Kohloff &
Frances F. Cobabe

SEC8 ASBACH Betty J. b.1925-d.no date, w/ Donald L. Asbach

SEC8 ASBACH Donald L. b.1920-d.1996, w/ Betty J. Asbach

SEC8 MANDT Faith Leola b.1902-d.1979, w/ Paul H. Mandt

SEC8 MANDT Paul Harold b.1906-d.1983, w/ Faith L. Mandt

SEC8 PEASE Ruth Marie b.1898-d.1978, w/ Harlow H. Pease

SEC8 PEASE Harlow Heath b.1897-d.1982, w/ Ruth M. Pease

SEC8 URBAN Gertrude b.1879-d.1970, n/t Frederick Urban

SEC8 URBAN Frederick b.1879-d.1937, n/t Gertrude Urban

SEC8 WELLS George E. b.1856-d.1921, w/ Florence E., Florence A.,
Miriam, Margarette A., Carrie B. & Howard A. Wells

SEC8 WELLS Florence E. b.1858-d.1929, w/ George E., Florence A.,
Miriam, Margarette A., Carrie B. & Howard A. Wells

SEC8 WELLS Florence A. b.1886-d.1964, w/ George E., Florence E.,
Miriam, Margarette A., Carrie B. & Howard A. Wells

SEC8 WELLS Miriam b.1889-d.1964, w/ George E., Florence E.,
Florence A., Margarette A., Carrie B. & Howard A. Wells

SEC8 WELLS Margarette A. b.1891-d.1991, w/ George E., Florence E.,
Florence A., Meriam, Carrie B. & Howard A. Wells

SEC8 WELLS Carrie B. b.1890-d.1980, w/ George E., Florence E.,
Florence A., Meriam, Margarette A. & Howard A. Wells

SEC8 WELLS Howard A. b.1893-d.1974, w/ George E., Florence E.,
Florence A., Meriam, Margarette A. & Carrie B. Wells

SEC8 SCHMIDT Edwin b.1916-d.1933, "Son" n/t Alma & Orlo Schmidt

SEC8 SCHMIDT Alma b.1897-d.1974, w/ Orlo n/t Edwin Schmidt

SEC8 SCHMIDT Orlo b.1893-d.1967, w/ Alma n/t Edwin Schmidt

SEC8 FROEMMING Gustave b.1869-d.1946, "Father" n/t Theresa
Froemming

SEC8 FROEMMING Theresa b.1875-d.1930, "Mother" n/t Gustave
Froemming

SEC8 RAMSTACK George b.24Jul1842-d.12Aug1902, w/ Amelia
Ramstack

SEC8 RAMSTACK Amelia b.20Jun1852-d.26Mar1924, w/ George
Ramstack

SEC8 SHIELLS Alexander E. b.1888-d.1918, "Father, 1st LIEUT. CO. E.
107th ENG."

SEC8 JAHNKE Roy Emil b.1907-d.1974, "Son" n/t Minnie M., Emil F.,
Wilhelmina & Herman Jahnke

SEC8 JAHNKE Minnie M. b.1885-d.1965, "Mother" n/t Roy E., Emil F., Wilhelmina & Herman Jahnke

SEC8 JAHNKE Emil F. b.1879-d.1951, "Father" n/t Roy E., Minnie M., Wilhelmina & Herman Jahnke

SEC8 JAHNKE Wilhelmina b.1852-d.1924, "Mother" n/t Roy E., Minnie M., Emil F. & Herman Jahnke

SEC8 JAHNKE Herman b.1847-d.1921, "Father" n/t Roy E., Minnie M., Emil F. & Wilhelmina Jahnke

SEC8 CURTIS Dwight C. b.1878-d.1953, n/t Ella Curtis

SEC8 CURTIS Ella b.1878-d.1922, n/t Dwight C. Curtis

SEC8 STRONG Madelaine Freeman b.5Aug1911-d.10Feb1988, n/t Gordon M., Signe F., Jessie E., Henry F., Myron W., Mary A., Reuben M. & Mary E. F. Strong

SEC8 STRONG Gordon M. b.1911-d.1989, w/ Signe F., Jessie E., Henry F., Myron Myron W., Mary A., n/t Madelaine, Reuben & Mary E. F. Strong

SEC8 STRONG Signe (FELLAND) b.1916-d.1972, w/ Gordon M., Jessie E., Henry F., Myron W., Mary A., n/t Madelaine, Reuben & Mary E. F. Strong

SEC8 STRONG Jessie E. b.1886-d.1956, w/ Gordon M., Signe F., Henry F., Myron W., Mary A., n/t Madelaine, Reuben & Mary E. F. Strong

SEC8 STRONG Henry F. b.1874-d.1967, w/ Gordon M., Signe F., Jessie E., Myron W., Mary A., n/t Madelaine, Reuben & Mary E. F. Strong

SEC8 STRONG Myron W. b.1845-d.1938, w/ Gordon M., Signe F., Jessie E., Henry F., Mary A., n/t Madelaine, Reuben & Mary E. F. Strong

SEC8 STRONG Mary A. b.1851-d.1922, w/ Gordon M., Signe F., Jessie E., Henry F., Myron W., n/t Madelaine, Reuben & Mary E. F. Strong

SEC8 STRONG Reuben Myron b.8Oct1872-d.11Aug1964, w/ Mary E. F., n/t Signe F., Jessie E., Henry F., Myron W., Madelaine, & Mary A., Strong

SEC8 STRONG Mary Ethel Freeman b.11Nov1876-d.6Dec1962, "His Beloved Wife" w/ Reuben M., n/t Signe F., Jessie E., Henry F., Myron W., Madelaine, Mary A. Strong

SEC8 TENGES Anna b.1876-d.1947, "Daughter" n/t Sophie, Gottfried & Louisa Tenges

SEC8 TENGES Sophie b.1853-d.1933, "Mother" n/t Anna, Gottfried & Louisa Tenges

SEC8 TENGES Gottfried b.1851-d.1922, "Father" n/t Anna, Sophie & Louisa Tenges

SEC8 TENGES Louisa b.1881-d.1964, "Daughter" n/t Anna, Sophie & Gottfried Tenges

SEC8 MARVIN Josephine V. b.1867-d.1956, w/ Fred H., George E &
Agnes P. Marvin
SEC8 MARVIN Fred H. b.1867-d.1923, w/ Josephine V., George E &
Agnes P. Marvin
SEC8 MARVIN George E. b.1898-d.1948, w/ Josephine V., Fred H. &
Agnes P. Marvin
SEC8 MARVIN Agnes P. b.1890-d.1972, w/ Josephine V., Fred H. &
George E. Marvin
SEC8 RAASCH Otto b.1869-d.1923, "Father" n/t Pauline Raasch
SEC8 RAASCH Pauline b.1873-d.1938, "Mother" n/t Otto Raasch
SEC8 SCHMIDT Bernice b.1921-d.1924, "Daughter" n/t Lloyd, Michael
& Theresa Schmidt
SEC8 SCHMIDT Lloyd b.1917-d.1941, "Husband" n/t Bernice, Michael
& Theresa Schmidt
SEC8 SCHMIDT Michael b.1885-d.1971, "Father" w/ Theresa, Bernice &
Lloyd Schmidt
SEC8 SCHMIDT Theresa b.1886-d.1949, "Mother" w/ Michael, Bernice
& Lloyd Schmidt
SEC8 SEHLER Walter G. b.1895-d.1974, w/ Hazel Sehler
SEC8 SEHLER Hazel b.1897-d.1986, w/ Walter G. Sehler
SEC8 GREENE David Benjamin b.1862-d.1929 w/ Ella M. D. Greene
SEC8 GREENE Ella May Davis b.1860-d.1924, "His Wife" w/ David B.
Greene
SEC8 STRENG Caroline b.1857-d.1924, "Mother" w/ Adam Streng
SEC8 STRENG Adam b.1837-d.1930, "Father" w/ Caroline Streng
SEC8 AEPLER Herman b.1856-d.1923
SEC8 SCHMIDT-DELON Emilie b.1866-d.1923, "Mother" n/t Ferdinand
Schmidt
SEC8 DELON-SCHMIDT Emilie b.1866-d.1923, "Mother" n/t Ferdinand
Schmidt
SEC8 SCHMIDT Ferdinand b.1854-d.1910, "Father" n/t Emilie Schmidt-
Delon
SEC8 PAULSON Grete Johnson b.1861-d.1929, n/t Irving Johnson
SEC8 JOHNSON Irving b.1909-d.1923, n/t Grete J. Paulson
SEC8 KRAUSE Anna E. b.1895-d.1968, w/ Rine C., Mamie, George &
Minnie Krause
SEC8 KRAUSE Rine C. b.1886-d.1952, w/ Anna E., Mamie, George &
Minnie Krause; Masonic symbol
SEC8 KRAUSE Mamie b.1875-d.1935, w/ Anna E., Rine C., George &
Minnie Krause; Eastern Star symbol
SEC8 KRAUSE George b.1882-d.1921, w/ Anna E., Rine C., Mamie &
Minnie Krause; Masonic symbol

SEC8 KRAUSE Minnie b.1859-d.1935, w/ Anna E., Rine C., Mamie & George Krause

SEC8 WEGNER Alvina b.1887-d.1981, w/ Howard Wegner

SEC8 WEGNER Howard b.1888-d.1958, w/ Alvina Wegner

SEC8 FEERICK Adie H. b.10May1893-d.22Feb1923

SEC8 KLENCK Mary b.20Apr1868-d.3Dec1922, w/ Emil Klenck

SEC8 KLENCK Emil b.25May1856-d.4Dec1931, w/ Mary Klenck

SEC8 JOHST Otto b.1862-d.1919, n/t Klara Johst

SEC8 JOHST Klara b.1864-d.1943, n/t Otto Johst

SEC8 HERTHEL Alice Breen Tifft b.1893-d.1985, w/ Eugene C., Henry D., Infant, Edith C. & Nancy Herthel

SEC8 HERTHEL Eugene Coerper b.1894-d.1974, w/ Alice B. T., Henry D., Infant, Edith C. & Nancy Herthel

SEC8 HERTHEL Henry D. b.1863-d.1919, w/ Alice B. T., Eugene C., Infant, Edith C. & Nancy Herthel

SEC8 HERTHEL Edith C. b.1870-d.1920, w/ Alice B. T., Eugene C., Infant, Henry D. & Nancy Herthel

SEC8 HERTHEL Nancy b.1928-d.1928, w/ Alice B. T., Eugene C., Infant, Henry D. & Edith C. Herthel

SEC8 HERTHEL Infant d.1923, "Daughter" w/ Alice B. T., Eugene C., Nancy, Henry D. & Edith C. Herthel; only one date

SEC8 HEINRICHS Joseph b.8Oct1924-d.11Feb1970, "Father, Married 27 Apr 1946" w/ Shirley Heinrichs, Catholic symbol on stone

SEC8 HEINRICHS Shirley b.6Nov1924-d.no date, "Married 27 Apr 1946" w/ Joseph Heinrichs, Catholic symbol on stone

SEC8 WILL Ruth N. b.1897-d.1922

SEC8 PRUST Elise b.1884-d.1951, w/ Charles Prust

SEC8 PRUST Charles b.1882-d.1961, w/ Elise Prust

SEC8 HEINRICHS Raymond E. b.17Jul1958-d.24Apr1984, "Beloved Son"

SEC8 JOERS Ruth F. b.1899-d.1995, w/ Walter E., n/t Jerome G. Joers

SEC8 JOERS Walter E. b.1895-d.1978, w/ Ruth F., n/t Jerome G. Joers

SEC8 JOERS Jerome G. b.8Dec1923-d.28Jul1957, "WIS. CPL 1001 ENGR FORS BN WWII" n/t Ruth F. & Walter E. Joers

SEC8 SMITH Henry H. b.6Feb1894-d.23Nov1948

SEC8 URBAN John b.1841-d.1925, n/t Marie, Edward G., Ruth A., Leopold C., Frederick & Gertrude Urban

SEC8 URBAN Marie b.1839-d.1923, n/t John, Edward G., Ruth A., Leopold C., Frederick & Gertrude Urban

SEC8 URBAN Edward G. b.1876-d.1925, n/t John, Marie, Ruth A., Leopold C., Frederick & Gertrude Urban

SEC8 URBAN Ruth A. b.1874-d.1936, n/t John, Marie, Edward G.,
Leopold C., Frederick & Gertrude Urban
SEC8 URBAN Leopold C. b.1869-d.1937, n/t John, Marie, Edward G.,
Ruth A., Frederick & Gertrude Urban
SEC8 HAMMOND Frances M. b.1863-d.1947, "Mother" n/t Theodore M.
Hammond
SEC8 HAMMOND Theodore M. b.1864-d.1923, "Father" n/t Frances M.
Hammond *
SEC8 ARDERN William F. b.1864-d.1959, w/ Ethel M. Ardern
SEC8 ARDERN Ethel M. b.1874-d.1963, w/ William F. Ardern
SEC8 WOOD Dorothy A. b.1867-d.1929, n/t Ben Wood
SEC8 WOOD Ben b.1862-d.1941, n/t Dorothy A. Wood
SEC8 THOMAS Dorothy M. b.1892-d.1924, in Dorothy A. & Ben
Wood's plot
SEC8 LAMB Marjorie b.1932-d.1975
SEC8 SCHULTZ Anna L. b.1901-d.1994, w/ Harry W., Caroline & Robert
Schultz
SEC8 SCHULTZ Harry W. b.1896-d.1977, w/ Anna L., Caroline & Robert
Schultz
SEC8 SCHULTZ Caroline b.1852-d.1926, w/ Anna L., Harry W. & Robert
Schultz
SEC8 SCHULTZ Robert b.1852-d.1934, w/ Anna L., Harry W. & Caroline
Schultz
SEC8 RUCK Lena b.1869-d.1923, w/ Herman Ruck
SEC8 RUCK Herman b.1866-d.1937, w/ Lena Ruck
SEC8 DAHNKE Elina b.1864-d.1926, "Mother" w/ John & John, Jr.
Dahnke
SEC8 DAHNKE John b.1864-d.1958, "Father" w/ Elina & John, Jr.
Dahnke
SEC8 DAHNKE John Jr. b.1901-d.1924, w/ Elina & John Dahnke
SEC8 BREU Anna b.1879-d.1922, w/ August Breu
SEC8 BREU August b.1868-d.1930, w/ Anna Breu
SEC8 FIDO Fred G., Jr. b.1916-d.1938, "Son" n/t Fred, Bertha & Ottery J.
W. Fido
SEC8 FIDO Fred b.1877-d.1928, "F. W. Fido" w/ Bertha, n/t Fred G., Jr. &
Ottery J. W. Fido
SEC8 FIDO Bertha b.1879-d.1948, w/ Fred, n/t Fred G., Jr. & Ottery J. W.
Fido
SEC8 FIDO Ottery J. W. b.1908-d.1973, "In Memory of Son," n/t Fred,
Fred G., Jr. & Bertha Fido
SEC8 WHITE Donald G. b.1928-d.1944

SEC8 WILL Frederick b.31Jan1862-d.23Mar1939, "Father" n/t Ulricka Will

SEC8 WILL Ulricka b.9Sep1866-d.20Apr1922, "Mother" n/t Frederick Will

SEC8 WILKINSON Charles E. b.1860-d.1928, n/t Louisa M. Wilkinson

SEC8 WILKINSON Louisa M. b.1834-d.1922, n/t Charles E. Wilkinson

SEC8 ANDERSON Hazel b.1890-d.1972, n/t Erick J. & Frances C. Anderson

SEC8 ANDERSON Erick John b.1860-d.1922, n/t Hazel & Frances C. Anderson

SEC8 ANDERSON Frances Cowin b.1863-d.1938, n/t Hazel & Erick J. Anderson

SEC8 SECORD William L. b.1919-d.1971, n/t W. Lloyd, Ethelnore R. & Courtland F. Secord

SEC8 SECORD W. Lloyd b.1889-d.1963, n/t William L., Ethelnore R. & Courtland F. Secord

SEC8 SECORD Ethelnore R. b.1890-d.1978, n/t William L., W. Lloyd & Courtland F. Secord

SEC8 SECORD Courtland Frank b.1915-d.1922, n/t William L., W. Lloyd & Ethelnore R. Secord

SEC8 KIRBY Thomas F. b.12Oct1927-d.20Nov1994, "US NAVY WWII KOREA" n/t Patricia C. Kirby; 2 stones

SEC8 KIRBY Patricia C. b.1926-d.no date, n/t Thomas F. Kirby

SEC8 RASEY Mabel U. b.1891-d.1981, w/ Lee C. Rasey

SEC8 RASEY Lee C. b.1890-d.1979, w/ Mabel U. Rasey

SEC8 GLAMM Mary Louise C. b.1922-d.1985, "Pearl Harbor Association Survirors emb." w/ Robert A. & Ryan T. Glamm

SEC8 GLAMM Robert A. b.1918-d.no date, "Pearl Harbor Association Survirors emb." w/ Mary L. C. & Ryan T. Glamm

SEC8 GLAMM Ryan T. d.8Jan1994, w/ Mary L. C. & Robert A. Glamm; only one date

SEC8 SIEGEL Roland J. b.1Jan1894-d.16Aug1980, "PFC US ARMY WWI" w/ Caroline F. Siegel, Frances, August B., Louise, Frances G. & August F. Vogel; 2 stones

SEC8 SIEGEL Caroline F. b.1892-d.1982, w/ Roland J. Siegel, Frances, August B., Louise, Frances G. & August F. Vogel

SEC8 VOGEL Frances L. b.1901-d.no date, w/ Caroline F. & Roland J Siegel, August B., Louise, Frances G. & August F. Vogel

SEC8 VOGEL August B. b.1900-d.1979, w/ Caroline F. & Roland J Siegel, Frances L., Louise, Frances G. & August F. Vogel

SEC8 VOGEL Louise d.1898, w/ Caroline F. & Roland J Siegel, Frances L., August B., Frances G. & August F. Vogel; only one date

168

SEC8 VOGEL Frances G. b.1858-d.1950, w/ Caroline F. & Roland J Siegel,Frances L., August B., Louise & August F. Vogel

SEC8 VOGEL August F. b.1855-d.1924, w/ Caroline F. & Roland J Siegel,Frances L., August B., Louise & Frances G. Vogel

SEC8 PARSLOE Mary b.1865-d.1939, w/ Frederick, Irving, Wanda, Harold & Charles Parsloe

SEC8 PARSLOE Frederick b.1864-d.1926, w/ Mary, Irving, Wanda, Harold & Charles Parsloe

SEC8 PARSLOE Irving b.1899-d.1924, w/ Mary, Frederick, Wanda, Harold & Charles Parsloe

SEC8 PARSLOE Wanda b.1900-d.1990, w/ Mary, Frederick, Irving, Harold & Charles Parsloe

SEC8 PARSLOE Harold b.1903-d.1991, w/ Mary, Frederick, Irving, Wanda & Charles Parsloe

SEC8 PARSLOE Charles b.1905-d.1975, w/ Mary, Frederick, Irving, Wanda & Harold Parsloe

SEC8 MUENCHOW Henry b.1894-d.1924, "Father" n/t Henry Muenchow

SEC8 MUENCHOW Henry b.1923-d.1941, "Son" n/t Henry Muenchow

SEC8 YUNGKANS Bertha b.1875-d.1956, w/ Fred Yungkans

SEC8 YUNGKANS Fred b.1867-d.1929, w/ Bertha Yungkans

SEC8 TIMESON George F. b.1874-d.1930, "Father" w/ Grace E. & Gay B. Timeson

SEC8 TIMESON Grace E. b.1908-d.1925, "Daughter" w/ George F. & Gay B. Timeson

SEC8 TIMESON Gay B. b.1877-d.1961, "Mother" w/ George F. & Grace E. Timeson

SEC8 STERNKE Wilhelmina b.1869-d.1923, "Mother" w/ Ernst, Ella, Robert, Arthur, Herman F. & Gertrude Sternke

SEC8 STERNKE Ernst b.1869-d.1940, "Father" w/ Wilhelmina, Ella, Robert, Arthur, Herman F. & Gertrude Sternke

SEC8 STERNKE Ella b.1894-d.1973, w/ Wilhelmina, Ernst, Robert, Arthur, Herman F. & Gertrude Sternke

SEC8 STERNKE Robert b.1897-d.1987, w/ Wilhelmina, Ernst, Ella, Arthur, Herman F. & Gertrude Sternke

SEC8 STERNKE Arthur b.1893-d.1972, w/ Wilhelmina, Ernst, Ella, Robert, Herman F. & Gertrude Sternke

SEC8 STERNKE Herman F. b.1899-d.1977, w/ Wilhelmina, Ernst, Ella, Robert, Arthur & Gertrude Sternke

SEC8 STERNKE Gertrude b.1900-d.1962, w/ Wilhelmina, Ernst, Ella, Robert, Arthur & Herman F. Sternke

SEC8 WARNECKE Ruth d.18Jun1926, "Baby" w/ Olga M. & Herman K. Warnecke; only one date

SEC8 WARNECKE Olga M. b.1892-d.1961, "Mother" w/ Ruth & Herman K. Warnecke

SEC8 WARNECKE Herman K. b.1882-d.1965, "Father" w/ Ruth & Olga M. Warnecke

SEC8 HART Everett C. b.10Jan1885-d.6Nov1956, "WIS. MAJOR US ARMY WWI" n/t William A. & Ruby D. Hart

SEC8 HART William A. b.1842-d.1926, w/ Ruby D., n/t Everett C. Hart

SEC8 HART Ruby D. b.1849-d.1934, w/ William A., n/t Everett C. Hart

SEC8 NELSON Bruce George b.4Nov1927-d.19Jan1958, "WIS. SI US COAST GUARD RES WWII" n/t Andrew, Cicilie, Jessie L. & George A. Nelson

SEC8 NELSON Andrew b.12Sep1857-d.30Apr1940, "Father" n/t Bruce G., Cicilie, Jessie L. & George A. Nelson

SEC8 NELSON Cicilie b.9May1853-d.25Dec1927, "Mother" n/t Bruce G., Andrew, Jessie L. & George A. Nelson

SEC8 NELSON Jessie L. b.1892-d.1984, "Wife, Excellent-Honest-Faithful" n/t Bruce G., Andrew & Cicilie, w/ George A. Nelson

SEC8 NELSON George A. b.1886-d.1976, "Husband, COOK WWI" n/t Bruce G., Andrew & Cicilie, w/ Jessie L. Nelson

SEC8 PETERSON Christine b.2Sep1881-d.14Dec1983, "Wife" w/ Laurence Peterson; dates completed from cemetery records

SEC8 PETERSON Laurence b.1878-d.1948, "Husband" w/ Christine Peterson

SEC8 HOPE Samuel N., Jr. b.1924-d.1991, w/ Beverly D., Samuel, Agnes M. & David C. Hope

SEC8 HOPE Beverly D. b.1923-d.1989, w/ Samuel N., Jr., Samuel N., Agnes M. & David C. Hope

SEC8 HOPE Samuel N. b.1887-d.1969, w/ Samuel N., Jr., Beverly D., Agnes M. & David C. Hope

SEC8 HOPE Agnes M. b.1891-d.1984, w/ Samuel N., Jr., Beverly D., Samuel N. & David C. Hope

SEC8 HOPE David C. b.1922-d.1972, "In Memory of" w/ Samuel N., Jr., Beverly D., Samuel N. & Agnes M. Hope

SEC8 MARONEK George W. b.2Mar1894-d.24Apr1922, n/t Clara & William C. Maronek

SEC8 MARONEK Clara b.5Jun1877-d.1May1919, n/t George W. & William C. Maronek

SEC8 MARONEK William C. b.29Oct1870-d.18Apr1942, n/t George W. & Clara Maronek

170

SEC8 SKINNER Isabel Elder b.1880-d.1971, n/t James M. & Mary L. Skinner

SEC8 SKINNER James Martin b.1852-d.1926, w/ Mary L. n/t Isabel E. Skinner

SEC8 SKINNER Mary Low b.1854-d.1932, w/ James M. n/t Isabel E. Skinner

SEC8 SHAPE Minnie b.1869-d.1947, same type stone as Hedtke

SEC8 HEDTKE Elizabeth M. b.1896-d.1950, n/t Adolph C. Hedtke; same type stone as Shape

SEC8 HEDTKE Adolph C. b.1890-d.1959, n/t Elizabeth M. Hedtke; same type stone as Shape

SEC8 HAGIE Marvin b.26Jun1930-d.26Jun1930, "Baby" n/t Cora R. Hagie, Ernstine & Adolph Radtke; fancy carving, hard to read; dates completed from cemetery records

SEC8 HAGIE Cora Radtke b.25May1911-d.16Mar1944, n/t Marvin Hagie, Ernstine & Adolph Radtke; dates completed from cemetery records

SEC8 RADTKE Ernstine b.1889-d.1937, "Mother" n/t Adolph Radtke & Marvin & Cora R. Hagie

SEC8 RADTKE Adolph b.1889-d.1932, "Father" n/t Ernstine Radtke & Marvin & Cora R. Hagie

SEC8 LEENHOUTS Johanna b.1881-d.1978, w/ Johanna & Peter Leenhouts

SEC8 LEENHOUTS Johanna b.1902-d.1928, w/ Johanna & Peter Leenhouts

SEC8 LEENHOUTS Peter b.1874-d.1959, w/ Johanna & Johanna Leenhouts

SEC8 LAYBOURN Minnie K. b.1873-d.1924, n/t John H. Laybourn

SEC8 LAYBOURN John H. b.1865-d.1948, n/t Minnie K. Laybourn

SEC8 LOCKER Marie E. b.27May1928-d.15Apr1948

SEC8 PICKER Lena b.1870-d.1945, w/ William Picker & James F., Janet I., A. F. & Hilda P. Schnell

SEC8 PICKER William b.1867-d.1959, w/ Lena Picker & James F., Janet I., A. F. & Hilda P. Schnell

SEC8 SCHNELL James F. b.1924-d.no date, w/ Lena & William Picker & Janet I., A. F. & Hilda P. Schnell

SEC8 SCHNELL Janet I. b.1924-d.1984, w/ Lena & William Picker & James F., A. F. & Hilda P. Schnell

SEC8 SCHNELL A. F. b.1900-d.19—, w/ Lena & William Picker & James F., Janet I. & Hilda P. Schnell

SEC8 SCHNELL Hilda (PICKER) b.1905-d.1924, w/ Lena & William Picker & James F., Janet I. & A. F. Schnell

SEC8 VAN VECHTEN Edwin F. b.7Sep1869-d.1Jul1940, w/ Sarah V. Douglass, no cemetery record; there was a Sheriff Van Vechten in Milwaukee County around 1880[61.] I found Peter Van Vechten, Jr., under-sheriff living at 532 Jefferson in the Milwaukee City Directory in 1881 and 1886.

SEC8 DOUGLASS Sarah Van Vechten b.1854-d.1923, "w/o J. K. Douglass" w/ Edwin F. Van Vechten

SEC8 HAYWARD William A. b.1853-d.1923, "Father" n/t Adaline F. & Joseph L. Hayward

SEC8 HAYWARD Adaline F. b.1857-d.1944, n/t William A. & Joseph L. Hayward

SEC8 HAYWARD Joseph Lowe b.8Jan1897-d.23Mar1959, "WIS. PVT SIGNAL CORPS WWI" n/t William A. & Adaline F. Hayward

SEC8 TOUSSAINT Isaac b.1869-d.1960, "Father" n/t Lauretta A. Toussaint

SEC8 TOUSSAINT Lauretta A. b.1871-d.1923, "Mother" n/t Isaac Toussaint

SEC8 GREGERSEN Dorothy Buchholz b.1898-d.1923, n/t Gasten A., Jennie & Robert W. Buchholz

SEC8 BUCHHOLZ Gasten A. b.27May1902-d.18Sep1996, n/t Jennie & Robert W. Buchholz & Dorothy B. Gregersen

SEC8 BUCHHOLZ Jennie b.13Dec1871-d.6Sep1939, n/t Gasten A. & Robert W. Buchholz & Dorothy B. Gregersen

SEC8 BUCHHOLZ Robert William b.1865-d.1958, n/t Gasten A. & Jennie Buchholz & Dorothy B. Gregersen

SEC8 SCHNELL Sophie J. b.1889-d.1964, "Wife" w/ August F. Schnell

SEC8 SCHNELL August F. b.1900-d.1979, "Husband" w/ Sophie J. Schnell

SEC8 KUTSCH Martha b.1897-d.1983, w/ Gustave & Minnie n/t Amalia & August Kutsch & Martha M. & Walter G. Buege

SEC8 KUTSCH Gustave b.1898-d.1988, w/ Martha & Minnie n/t Amalia & August Kutsch & Martha M. & Walter G. Buege

SEC8 KUTSCH Minnie b.1901-d.1924, w/ Martha & Gustave, n/t Amalia & August Kutsch & Martha M. & Walter G. Buege

SEC8 KUTSCH Amalia b.1872-d.1940, w/ August, n/t Gustave, Martha & Minnie Kutsch & Martha M. & Walter G. Buege

SEC8 KUTSCH August b.1868-d.1940, w/ Amalia, n/t Gustave, Martha & Minnie Kutsch & Martha M. & Walter G. Buege

SEC8 BUEGE Martha M. b.1899-d.1977, w/ Walter G. Buege, n/t Gustave, Martha, Minnie, Amalia & August Kutsch

---

61 The Wheeler Family in America original text by by Lyman Grover Wheeler in 1923 assembled and edited by Lt. Col. Lyman Edward Wheeler IV, 2000, unpublished

SEC8 BUEGE Walter G. b.1896-d.1965, w/ Martha M. Buege, n/t Gustave, Martha, Minnie, Amalia & August Kutsch

SEC8 GRUENWALD Frieda b.1911-d.1914, w/ Elmer, n/t Charles Gruenwald

SEC8 GRUENWALD Elmer b.1914-d.1914, w/ Frieda, n/t Charles Gruenwald

SEC8 GRUENWALD Charles b.1909-d.1926, "Son", n/t Frieda & Elmer Gruenwald

SEC8 WESTLEY Helen b.1919-d.1944, "Daughter"

SEC8 GRUENWALD Kate b.1886-d.1953, "Daughter" n/t August Gruenwald

SEC8 GRUENWALD August b.1883-d.1948, "Father" n/t Kate Gruenwald

SEC8 OLDENBURG Frieda b.1862-d.1937, w/ Fred, n/t Charley & Fred J. Oldenburg

SEC8 OLDENBURG Fred b.1861-d.1939, w/ Frieda, n/t Charley & Fred J. Oldenburg

SEC8 OLDENBURG Charley d.8Dec1937, "WIS. CK. 22 US INF." n/t Frieda, Fred & Fred J. Oldenburg

SEC8 OLDENBURG Fred J. b.1891-d.1963, n/t Frieda, Fred & Charley Oldenburg

SEC8 KURTH William H. b.8Oct1888-d.1Jun1961, "WIS. PVT US ARMY WWI"

SEC8 HANSON Rosemary H. b.22Sep1939-d.30Nov1991

SEC8 PARKINSON Roberta S. b.1930-d.no date, w/ Rev. Donald M. Parkinson

SEC8 PARKINSON Donald M., Rev. b.1929-d.1995, w/ Roberta S. Parkinson

SEC8 KRESSIN Frank A. b.1880-d.1962, w/ Elisabeth Kressin

SEC8 KRESSIN Elisabeth b.1883-d.1945, w/ Frank A. Kressin

SEC8 KEMPF Cora Trunde b.1899-d.1973, w/ Fred, Auguste & Julius Kempf, Emil, Minnie, Eleanore, Lorraine & Raymond A. Pagel

SEC8 KEMPF Fred b.1897-d.1979, w/ Cora T, Auguste & Julius Kempf, Emil, Minnie, Eleanore, Lorraine & Raymond A. Pagel

SEC8 KEMPF Auguste b.1865-d.1938, w/ Cora T., Fred & Julius Kempf, Emil, Minnie, Eleanore, Lorraine & Raymond A. Pagel

SEC8 KEMPF Julius b.1862-d.1946, w/ Cora T., Fred & Auguste Kempf, Emil, Minnie, Eleanore, Lorraine & Raymond A. Pagel

SEC8 PAGEL Emil b.1893-d.1956, w/ Cora T., Julius,Fred & Auguste Kempf, Minnie, Eleanore, Lorraine & Raymond A. Pagel

SEC8 PAGEL Minnie b.1892-d.1986, w/ Cora T., Julius,Fred & Auguste Kempf, Emil, Eleanore, Lorraine & Raymond A. Pagel

SEC8 PAGEL Eleanor d.1915, w/ Cora T., Julius,Fred & Auguste Kempf, Emil, Minnie, Lorraine & Raymond A. Pagel; only one date

SEC8 PAGEL Lorraine d.1916, w/ Cora T., Julius,Fred & Auguste Kempf, Emil, Minnie, Eleanor & Raymond A. Pagel; only one date

SEC8 PAGEL Raymond A. b.1919-d.1945, "Son; In Memory Of" w/ Cora T., Julius,Fred & Auguste Kempf, Emil, Minnie, Eleanor & Lorraine Pagel

SEC8 LEFEBER Janet M. (SMITH) b.1872-d.1933

SEC8 PAUL Eunice S. b.1867-d.1935, "Mother" n/t Harvey S. Paul

SEC8 PAUL Harvey S. b.1866-d.1959, n/t Eunice S. Paul

SEC8 FERGUSON Gladys P. b.1889-d.1985, w/ Frank N., n/t Ellen E. & Donald S. Ferguson

SEC8 FERGUSON Frank N. b.1891-d.1961, w/ Gladys P., n/t Ellen E. & Donald S. Ferguson

SEC8 FERGUSON Ellen E. b.20Feb1922-d., w/ Donald S., n/t Gladys P. & Frank N. Ferguson

SEC8 FERGUSON Donald Sheldon b.6Jun1918-d.1Dec1988, w/ Ellen E., n/t Gladys P. & Frank N. Ferguson

SEC8 WANDSNIDER Thressa H. b.1861-d.1925, "Mother"

SEC8 HERMANN Katie b.1848-d.1925, "Mother" w/ Fred Hermann; Hermann/Bruins plot

SEC8 HERMANN Fred b.1855-d.1929, "Father" w/ Katie Hermann; Hermann/Bruins plot

SEC8 BRUINS Flora Belle b.10Apr1881-d.30Dec1962 Ft. Myers, Florida, "Mother", n/t Dirk Bruins; Hermann/Bruins plot; dates from cemetery records; w/o Dr. Dirk Bruins

SEC8 BRUINS Dirk b.21Aug1878-d.12Sep1968, "LT COL MC-RES SPAN WAR WWI PH DOCTOR OF MEDICINE"; n/t Flora B. & Mother Bruins; Hermann/Bruins plot; h/o Flora Belle Bruins

SEC8 BURLINGAME Elizabeth M. b.1919-d.1957

SEC8 CHURCH Frederick E. b.1921-d.1990, n/t Frederick E. & Lillie M. Church

SEC8 CHURCH Frederick E. b.1887-d.1950, w/ Lillie M. n/t Frederick E. Church

SEC8 CHURCH Lillie M. b.1888-d.1946, w/ Frederick E., n/t Frederick E. Church

SEC8 MERTZ Caroline b.1857-d.1934

SEC8 STOLZ Elizabeth b.1852-d.1934, "Mother"

SEC8 BANSEMER Adelheid b.1861-d.1933, w/ Johann Bansemer

SEC8 BANSEMER Johann b.1857-d.1941, w/ Adelheid Bansemer

SEC8 BAST Helene b.2Jul1857-d.25Sep1933; dates completed from cemetery records

SEC8 BOW Orrin Wright b.1865-d.1927, w/ Nellie G. Bow & Loring T. & Marion B. Hammond

SEC8 BOW Nellie Garner b.1872-d.1963, w/ Orrin W. Bow & Loring T. & Marion B. Hammond

SEC8 HAMMOND Loring Theodore b.1899-d.1970, w/ Orrin W. & Nellie G. Bow & Marion B. Hammond

SEC8 HAMMOND Marion Bow b.1903-d.1999, w/ Orrin W. & Nellie G. Bow & Loring T. Hammond

SEC8 BROUWER Stephen John b.28Dec1876-d.5Apr1946, n/t Elizabeth E. & Roy Brouwer

SEC8 BROUWER Elizabeth Ellis b.24Jul1875-d.30Oct1936, n/t Stephen J. & Roy Brouwer

SEC8 BROUWER Roy b.25May1918-d.28Feb1927, n/t Stephen J. & Elizabeth E. Brouwer

SEC8 CLASEN David R. b.1889-d.1946, w/ Natalie Clasen

SEC8 CLASEN Natalie b.1886-d.1982, w/ David R. Clasen

SEC8 WEST Hattie b.1879-d.1966, w/ John West

SEC8 WEST John b.1875-d.1944, w/ Hattie West

SEC8 KINDT Margaret (MARX) b.1880-d.1952, "Wife" w/ Paul Kindt

SEC8 KINDT Paul b.1859-d.1928, "Husband" w/ Margaret M. Kindt

SEC8 OWEN William D. b.1911-d.1990, n/t Margaret W. Owen & Norman A., Caroline B., Helen E., Edwin J. & Ralph Wigdale; Wigdale plot

SEC8 OWEN Margaret W. b.1911-d.1987, n/t William D. Owen & Norman A., Caroline B., Helen E., Edwin J. & Ralph Wigdale; Wigdale plot

SEC8 WIGDALE Norman A. b.1873-d.1927, n/t William D. & Margaret W. Owen & Caroline B., Helen E., Edwin J. & Ralph Wigdale; Wigdale plot

SEC8 WIGDALE Caroline B. b.1871-d.1945, n/t William D. & Margaret W. Owen & Norman A., Helen E., Edwin J. & Ralph Wigdale; Wigdale plot

SEC8 WIGDALE Helen Echols b.1909-d.1979, n/t William D. & Margaret W. Owen & Norman A., Caroline B., Edwin J. & Ralph Wigdale; Wigdale plot

SEC8 WIGDALE Edwin James b.1907-d.1998, n/t William D. & Margaret W. Owen & Norman A., Caroline B., Helen E. & Ralph Wigdale; Wigdale plot

SEC8 WIGDALE Ralph S. b.1939-d.1986, n/t William D. & Margaret W. Owen & Norman A., Caroline B., Helen E. & Edwin Wigdale; Wigdale plot

SEC8 HOOK Asa C. b.1887-d.1962, n/t Clara L. Hook
SEC8 HOOK Clara L. b.1886-d.1946, n/t Asa C. Hook
SEC8 BAHR Frederick b.25Dec1893-d.24Jan1949, "WIS. PVT 161 DEPOT BRIG WWI"
SEC8 KAUTH Dorothy b.1901-d.19—, "Wife" w/ Mathew Kauth
SEC8 KAUTH Mathew b.1891-d.1930, "Husband" w/ Dorothy Kauth
SEC8 HAGMANN Christian G. b.1889-d.1944
SEC8 BRUSS Mary Thiel b.1844-d.1931, "Mother"
SEC8 ADRIANSEN John A. b.1851-d.1931
SEC8 SIECKE A. P. b.1863-d.1931
SEC8 MIERSWA Joseph b.1863-d.1937
SEC8 FINK Marie b.1857-d.1937
SEC8 SCHOEPP Emma b.1862-d.15Jul1943; date of death from cemetery records
SEC8 SCHOLL Katie b.1859-d.1931
SEC8 HESSLER Emilie b.1858-d.1942, w/ Ernst Hessler
SEC8 HESSLER Ernst b.1858-d.1930, w/ Emilie Hessler
SEC8 NAGEL Margaret b.1854-d.1926, w/ William Nagel
SEC8 NAGEL William b.1853-d.1932, w/ Margaret Nagel
SEC8 BESECKE Gustav b.1852-d.1932, "Father"
SEC8 CARON Minnie L. b.1897-d.1969
SEC8 SCHABLOW Henrietta M. b.1874-d.1954, "Mother" n/t Louis H. Schablow
SEC8 SCHABLOW Louis H. b.1864-d.1928, "Father" n/t Henrietta M. Schablow
SEC8 GARVENS Minnie C. b.1884-d.1945, w/ Albert B., n/t Charles O. Garvens
SEC8 GARVENS Albert B. b.1882-d.21Nov1977, w/ Minnie C., n/t Charles O. Garvens; date of death from cemetery records
SEC8 GARVENS Charles O. b.1868-d.1928, "Brother" n/t Minnie C. & Albert B. Garvens
SEC8 BOELTER Ida L. b.16Dec1862-d.8May1928, "Wife" n/t Herman J. Boelter
SEC8 BOELTER Herman J. b.26Feb1860-d.9Aug1934, "Husband" n/t Ida L. Boelter
SEC8 BOEHM Laura b.1901-d.1946, "Daughter" n/t Bertha & Herman Boehm
SEC8 BOEHM Bertha b.1870-d.1970, "Mother" n/t Laura & Herman Boehm
SEC8 BOEHM Herman b.1872-d.1926, "Father" n/t Laura & Bertha Boehm

176

SEC8 BARTELT Augusta A. b.1877-d.1940, "Mother" w/ Charles T. Bartelt

SEC8 BARTELT Charles T. b.1877-d.1929, "Father" w/ Augusta A. Bartelt

SEC8 HIDDE William b.1875-d.1953, w/ Hannah Hidde

SEC8 HIDDE Hannah b.1874-d.1946, w/ William Hidde

SEC8 STEGE Minnie b.1858-d.1941, w/ Gust Stege

SEC8 STEGE Gust b.1858-d.1945, w/ Minnie Stege

SEC8 BAUKAT John b.28May1863-d.3Aug1937; dates completed from cemetery records

SEC8 BORNMANN Anna b.10Mar1857-d.11Jan1937

SEC8 FREI Seraphina b.1865-d.1949, w/ Joseph Frei

SEC8 FREI Joseph b.1865-d.1937, w/ Seraphina Frei

SEC8 BOESEL Herman b.1849-d.1938, "Father"

SEC8 MILL Rebecca b.1853-d.1944, "Mother"

SEC8 MASTERS James C. b.27Sep1907-d.18Jan1991, w/ Erna M. Masters

SEC8 MASTERS Erna M. b.28May1911-d.28Oct1992, w/ James C. Masters

SEC8 KLAUSCH Paul B. b.1847-d.1939

SEC8 EINFALT Maria b.1849-d.1939, w/ John Einfalt; she resided at Altenheim Lutheran Home, now Lutheran Manor

SEC8 EINFALT John b.1852-d.2Nov1943, w/ Maria Einfalt; he resided at Altenheim Lutheran Home, now Lutheran Manor; date of death completed from cemetery records

SEC8 WESENBERG Louise W. b.1858-d.1939, "Mother"

SEC8 BECKER Ida J. b.1872-d.1965, w/ Otto H. Becker

SEC8 BECKER Otto H. b.1871-d.1957, w/ Ida J. Becker

SEC8 HAWTREY M. Christopher b.1904-d.1935

SEC8 BARTEL Clair b.1902-d.1935

SEC8 MEDWAY Caroline Ivens b.1868 Milwaukee, Wis.-d.1947, n/t Francis W., Reginald V., Helen S., Langdon P. & Willard F. Medway

SEC8 MEDWAY Francis Wm. b.1867 St. Briavels, England-d.1932, n/t Caroline I., Reginald V., Helen S., Langdon P. & Willard F. Medway

SEC8 MEDWAY Reginald V. b.1903-d.1994, w/ Helen S., n/t Caroline I., Francis W., Langdon P. & Willard F. Medway

SEC8 MEDWAY Helen S. b.1904-d.1995, w/ Reginald V., n/t Caroline I., Francis W., Langdon P. & Willard F. Medway

SEC8 MEDWAY Langdon P. b.1900-d.1999, w/ Willard F., n/t Caroline I., Francis W., Reginald V. & Helen S. Medway

SEC8 MEDWAY Willard F. b.1901-d.1989, w/ Langdon P., n/t Caroline I., Francis W., Reginald V. & Helen S. Medway

SEC8 TIFFT Verna B. b.1921-d.1971, n/t J. Ringland, Edna N., George L. & Jennie R. Tifft

SEC8 TIFFT George L. b.1865-d.1934, n/t J. Ringland, Edna N., Verna B. & Jennie R. Tifft

SEC8 TIFFT Jennie R. b.1865-d.1929, n/t J. Ringland, Edna N., Verna B. & George L. Tifft

SEC8 TIFFT J. Ringland b.1889-d.1949, w/ Edna N., n/t Verna B. & George L. Tifft

SEC8 TIFFT Edna N. b.1887-d.1972, w/ J. Ringland, n/t Verna B. & George L. Tifft

SEC8 ROEPKE Clara T. b.27Dec1888-d.3Jul1951, "Mother" w/ Emil & Harold Roepke

SEC8 ROEPKE Emil b.19May1886-d.15May1955, "Father" w/ Clara T. & Harold Roepke

SEC8 ROEPKE Harold b.7Jan1910-d.27Nov1928, "Son" w/ Clara T. & Emil Roepke

SEC8 GRUPE Minnie b.30Jan1860-d.13Aug1942

SEC8 SCHWARTZ Martha b.1885-d.1954, w/ Louis Schwartz

SEC8 SCHWARTZ Louis b.1880-d.1967, w/ Minnie Schwartz

SEC8 BEHNKE William b.1857-d.1944

SEC8 BELL August L. b.1872-d.1944

SEC8 FLEISCHAUER Tina b.1852-d.1943

SEC8 FISCHER Gustav b.1868-d.1948, "Father"

SEC8 KRECKLOW Bertha b.1871-d.1951, "Mother"

SEC8 ALLWARDT Mary b.1868-d.1953

SEC8 DEBLER Lina b.1Mar1872-d.9Sep1953

SEC8 KRENKE Minnie b.1872-d.1964

SEC8 SHERKUS Blanche b.1885-d.1962

SEC8 SADEWASSER Herman b.1886-d.1961

SEC8 BAUER Marie b.1866-d.1956

SEC8 CHRISTIANSEN Selma b.1881-d.1970, "Mother"

SEC8 UNGER Edward b.1885-d.1982, w/ Louise Unger

SEC8 UNGER Louise b.1892-d.1978, w/ Edward Unger

SEC8 RENNER Marjorie Sullivan b.1909-d.no date, w/ Joseph J. Renner

SEC8 RENNER Joseph J. b.1908-d.1982, w/ Marjorie S. Renner

SEC8 HOCHSCHILD Oliver C. b.1905-d.1948, w/ Elsie I. Hochschild

SEC8 HOCHSCHILD Elsie I. b.1903-d.1994, w/ Oliver C. Hochschild

SEC8 BESECKE Selma b.1894-d.1979, w/ Gustav Besecke

SEC8 BESECKE Gustav b.1894-d.1970, w/ Selma Besecke

SEC8 ARNDT Anna b.1884-d.1951, "Mother" w/ Alvin Arndt

SEC8 ARNDT Alvin b.1885-d.1971, "Father" w/ Anna Arndt

SEC8 KOEPP Evelyn I. b.18Nov1918-d.8May1935, "Daughter" n/t Elmer W., Olga M. & Charles H. Koepp

SEC8 KOEPP Elmer W. b.16Apr1922-d.24Jun1944, "WIS. PFC 106 INF 27 INF DIV WWII" n/t Evelyn I., Olga M. & Charles H. Koepp

SEC8 KOEPP Olga M. b.1897-d.1961, "Mother" w/ Charles H., n/t Elmer W. & Evelyn I. Koepp

SEC8 KOEPP Charles H. b.1889-d.1951, "Father" w/ Olga M., n/t Elmer W. & Evelyn I. Koepp

SEC8 SHAW Sandra Lee d.1946, "Baby" n/t Enid C. & Eugene M. Shaw; only one date

SEC8 SHAW Enid C. b.8Mar1920-d.24Mar1962, "Beloved Mother" n/t Sandra L. & Eugene M. Shaw

SEC8 SHAW Eugene M. b.25Mar1920-d.27Mar1995, "Beloved Father; Forever in Our Hearts" n/t Sandra L. & Enid C. Shaw; his picture is on stone

SEC8 STATZ Daniel b.1887-d.1943, w/ Martha Statz

SEC8 STATZ Martha b.1894-d.1945, w/ Daniel Statz

SEC8 CARRICK James b.1864-d.1945, "Father" w/ Christina Carrick

SEC8 CARRICK Christina b.1867-d.1943, "Mother" w/ James Carrick

SEC8 WEGNER Marie R. b.1905-d.1991, "Together 56 Years" w/ Herman J. Wegner

SEC8 WEGNER Herman J. b.1907-d.1991, "Together 56 Years" w/ Marie R. Wegner

SEC8 VOLZ Fred b.1897-d.1946

SEC8 SCHOENWETTER Marie b.1876-d.1945, w/ Victor & Elsie Schoenwetter

SEC8 SCHOENWETTER Victor b.1899-d.1969, w/ Marie & Elsie Schoenwetter

SEC8 SCHOENWETTER Elsie b.1903-d.1957, w/ Marie & Victor Schoenwetter

SEC8 SULLIVAN Bertha Kimball b.1879-d.1961, w/ Edward C. Sullivan, n/t Marjorie Sullivan & Joseph J. Renner

SEC8 SULLIVAN Edward C. b.1868-d.1940, w/ Bertha K. Sullivan, n/t Marjorie Sullivan & Joseph J. Renner

SEC8 ROBINSON Harrison Page b.4Jan1870 Venice, Ohio-d.7Jan1932, Wauwatosa, Wis., w/ Elizabeth B. Robinson

SEC8 ROBINSON Elizabeth Balsley b.8Jun1872 N. Amherst, Ohio, d.27Feb1943 Wauwatosa, Wis., w/ Harrison P. Robinson

SEC8 SPORLEDER Ralph De Hond b.4Oct1888-d.22Oct1951, n/t Suzanne D., Frederick H. L. & Ruth E. & Edna H. Sporleder

SEC8 SPORLEDER Edna H. b.15Feb1890-d.18Apr1982, n/t Suzanne D., Frederick H. L. & Ruth E. & Ralph D. Sporleder

SEC8 SPORLEDER Suzanne De Hond b.16Dec1855-d.1Jan1950, w/
Frederick H. L. & Ruth E., n/t Ralph D. & Edna H. Sporleder
SEC8 SPORLEDER Frederick H. L. b.4Sep1853-d.13Dec1933, w/
Suzanne D. & Ruth E., n/t Ralph D. & Edna H. Sporleder
SEC8 SPORLEDER Ruth Elizabeth b.1882-d.1962, w/ Suzanne D. &
Frederick H. L., n/t Ralph D. & Edna H. Sporleder
SEC8 ROBERTSON Lydia Fournes b.1893-d.1968, w/ Raymond K.,
Richard K. & Thomas C. Robertson
SEC8 ROBERTSON Raymond Karn b.1895-d.1966, w/ Lydia F., Richard
K. & Thomas C. Robertson
SEC8 ROBERTSON Richard Karn b.1927-d.no date, w/ Lydia F.,
Raymond K. & Thomas C. Robertson
SEC8 ROBERTSON Thomas Charles b.1923-d.1939, w/ Lydia F.,
Raymond K. & Richard K. Robertson
SEC8 HERTTING Gertrude C. b.1918-d.1940, "Daughter" n/t Alta G. &
Hugo V. Hertting
SEC8 HERTTING Alta G. b.1895-d.1987, "Mother" w/ Hugo V., n/t
Gertrude C. Hertting
SEC8 HERTTING Hugo V. b.1892-d.1972, "Father" w/ Alta G., n/t
Gertrude C. Hertting
SEC8 KAAD Edna b.1911-d.no date, w/ John J. Kaad
SEC8 KAAD John J. b.1906-d.1980, w/ Edna Kaad
SEC8 KRUEGER Bertha b.1886-d.1958, w/ Joseph Krueger
SEC8 KRUEGER Joseph b.1893-d.no date, w/ Bertha Krueger; no
cemetery record
SEC8 KEALTY Beatrice b.1917-d.1926, w/ Harold Kealty
SEC8 KEALTY Harold b.1907-d.1954, w/ Beatrice Kealty
SEC8 DIERKING Elizabeth b.1892-d.1945, "Mother"
SEC8 SWEET Charlotte M. b.1847-d.1937, w/ Lucien S. & Blanche
Sweet
SEC8 SWEET Lucien S. b.1877-d.1947, w/ Charlotte M. & Blanche
Sweet
SEC8 SWEET Blanche b.1872-d.1956, w/ Charlotte M. & Lucien S.
Sweet
SEC8 WEGNER Johanna b.1877-d.1955, w/ William, n/t Helen J., Earl
A., Roger W., William, Mary, Charles, Margaret M., Mary A., Emma
M., Charles F. Emma M., Charles F. & Frank P. Wegner
SEC8 WEGNER William b.1882-d.1966, w/ Johanna, n/t Helen J., Earl
A., Roger W., William, Mary, Charles, Margaret M., Mary A., Emma
M., Charles F. & Frank P. Wegner
SEC8 RIETZKE Anna W. b.16Oct1888-d.10Mar1967, "Mother"

SEC8 WEGNER Helen J. b.1908-d.no date, w/ Earl A., n/t Roger W.,
William, Mary, Charles, Margaret M., Mary A., Frank P., Johanna,
Emma M., Charles F., & William Wegner & Anna W. Befi
SEC8 WEGNER Earl A. b.1905-d.1982, w/Helen J., n/t Roger W.,
William, Mary, Charles, Margaret M., Mary A., Frank P., Johanna,
Emma M., Charles F., & William Wegner & Anna W. Befi
SEC8 WEGNER Roger W. b.1936-d.1939, n/t Helen J., Earl A., William,
Mary, Charles, Margaret M., Mary A., Frank P., Johanna, Emma M.,
Charles F., & William Wegner & Anna W. Befi
SEC8 WEGNER Margaret M. b.1908-d.1939, n/t Helen J., Earl A.,
William, Mary, Charles, Roger W., Mary A., Frank P., Johanna, Emma
M., Charles F., & William Wegner & Anna W. Befi
SEC8 WEGNER Mary A. b.1906-d.1970, n/t Helen J., Earl A., William,
Mary, Charles, Roger W., Margaret M., Frank P., Johanna, Emma M.,
Charles F., & William Wegner & Anna W. Befi
SEC8 WEGNER Frank P. b.1901-d.1993, n/t Helen J., Earl A., William,
Mary, Charles, Roger W., Margaret M., Mary A., Johanna, Emma M.,
Charles F., & William Wegner & Anna W. Befi
SEC8 WEGNER William b.1912-d.1982, w/ Mary & Charles, n/t Helen
J., Earl A., Frank P, Roger W., Margaret M., Mary A., Johanna, Emma
M., Charles F., & William Wegner & Anna W. Befi
SEC8 WEGNER Mary b.1880-d.1952, w/ William & Charles, n/t Helen
J., Earl A Frank P, Roger W., Margaret M., Mary A., Johanna, Emma M.,
Charles F., & William Wegner & Anna W. Befi
SEC8 WEGNER Charles b.1880-d.1932, w/ William & Mary, n/t Helen
J., Earl A., Frank P, Roger W., Margaret M., Mary A., Johanna, Emma
M., Charles F., & William Wegner & Anna W. Befi
SEC8 WEGNER Emma M. b.1Apr1905-d.19Sep1955, "Mom" w/ Charles
F. ,n/t Helen J., Earl A., Frank P, Roger W., Margaret M., Mary A.,
Johanna, Charles F., & William Wegner & Anna W. Befi
SEC8 WEGNER Charles F. b.25Oct1900-d.26Mar1980, w/ Emma M. ,n/t
Helen J., Earl A., Frank P, Roger W., Margaret M., Mary A., Johanna,
Emma M., Charles & William Wegner & Anna W. Befi
SEC8 BEFI Anna (WEGNER) b.31Aug1908-d.7Sep1933, n/t Emma M.,
Helen J., Earl A., Frank P, Roger W., Margaret M., Mary A., Johanna,
Emma M., Charles F., & William Wegner
SEC8 FITZGERALD J. Arthur b.1888-d.1947
SEC8 MEYER Frank b.1866-d.1935
SEC8 WILSON Charles E. b.1869-d.1934, w/ Mary A. Wilson
SEC8 WILSON Mary A. b.1871-d.1966, w/ Charles E. Wilson
SEC8 WALKER Constance M. b.12Aug1905 Coleman, Wis.-d.7Aug1985
Milwaukee, Wis., "w/o E. L. Walker 1949-1967" n/t Ella M., Jesse M.,

Mabelle S. & Emery L. Walker

SEC8 WALKER Ella Mays b.9Oct1858 McMinnville, OR.-d.25May1942 Tacoma, WN., "w/o J. M. Walker" n/t Constance M., Jesse M., Mabelle S. & Emery L. Walker

SEC8 WALKER Jesse M. b.29Oct1847 Morristown, Tenn.-d.27Nov1933 Wauwatosa, Wis., "Oregon Pioneer" n/t Constance M., Ella M., Mabelle S. & Emery L. Walker

SEC8 WALKER Mabelle Scott b.16Aug1874 Bareilly, India-d.7Oct1945 Wauwatosa, Wis., "w/o E. L. Walker" n/t Constance M., Ella M., Jesse M., & Emery L. Walker

SEC8 WALKER Emery L. b.12Nov1878 Weston, Oregon-d.23Aug1967, Milwaukee, Wis., "Dearly Beloved Husband & Father" n/t Constance M., Ella M., Jesse M., & Mabelle S. Walker

SEC8 TOBEY M. Leroy b.1898-d.1928

SEC8 TOBEY Marshall b.1871-d.1946 "Father"

SEC8 TOBEY Lucy E. b.1877-d.1944 "Mother, She Hath Done What She Could"

SEC8 GRIDLEY Orin L. b.1858-d.1940, "Father", n/t Loura E. & Margaret E. Gridley

SEC8 GRIDLEY Loura E. b.1862-d.1932 "Mother", n/t Orin L. & Margaret E. Gridley

SEC8 GRIDLEY Margaret E. b.1892-d.1982 "Daughter", n/t Loura E. & Orin L. Gridley

SEC8 HARTZ Josephine b.1866-d.1946, w/ Ernst Hartz

SEC8 HARTZ Ernst b.1867-d.1934, w/ Josephine Hartz

SEC8 THIEL Amelia b.1876-d.1971, w/ William F. Thiel

SEC8 THIEL William F. b.1869-d.1960, w/ Amelia Thiel

SEC8 GAUGER Irene W. b.1905-d.1968, w/ Reuben W. Gauger

SEC8 GAUGER Reuben W. b.1906-d.1994, w/ Irene W. Gauger

SEC8 KARCH Ida b.1875-d.1959, w/ John Karch

SEC8 KARCH John b.1884-d.1969, w/ Ida Karch

SEC8 WIDERBORG Jessie M. b.1906-d.1970, w/ Elmer Widerborg

SEC8 WIDERBORG Elmer b.1897-d.1966, w/ Jessie M. Widerborg

SEC8 EGGERT Almond H. b.22Jun1897-d.3Aug1944, "WIS. PVT. O. M. CORPS"

SEC8 HADRIAN Augusta b.1876-d.1943, "Mother" w/ Julius Hadrian

SEC8 HADRIAN Julius b.1871-d.1954, "Father" w/ Augusta Hadrian

SEC8 WIENKE Ella b.25Oct1914-d.19Oct1961, "Mother" w/ Theodore R., n/t Theodore Wienke

SEC8 WIENKE Theodore R. b.12Jan1913-d.12Oct1987, "Father" w/ Ella, n/t Theodore Wienke

SEC8 WIENKE Theodore b.1937-d.1942, "Son" n/t Ella & Theodore R. Wienke

SEC8 GARVENS Bertha b.1880-d.1937, w/ Henry Garvens

SEC8 GARVENS Henry b.1871-d.1960, w/ Bertha Garvens

SEC8 BROWN Elizabeth b.1872-d.1941, w/ Albert Brown

SEC8 BROWN Albert b.1867-d.1936, w/ Elizabeth Brown

SEC8 VANDEN BREUL Frieda b.1894-d.1938, "Mother" w/ William Vanden Breul

SEC8 VANDEN BREUL William b.1881-d.1943, "Father" w/ Frieda Vanden Breul

SEC8 FEZER Harold b.1901-d.1935

SEC8 BLOEDORN Anna b.1880-d.1931, w/ Reinhard Bloedorn

SEC8 BLOEDORN Reinhard b.1876-d.1930, w/ Anna Bloedorn

SEC8 BALL Henrietta E. b.1860-d.1933, "Mother" w/ George W., n/t Emma & Lester R. Ball

SEC8 BALL George W. b.1852-d.1929, "Father" w/ Henrietta E., n/t Emma & Lester R. Ball; WWI mkr

SEC8 BALL Emma N. b.1884-d.1968, "Wife" w/ Lester R. n/t Henrietta E. & George W. Ball

SEC8 BALL Lester R. b.1889-d.1968, "Husband; M/SGT. W.W.I" w/ Emma N. n/t Henrietta E. & George W. Ball

SEC8 BUSZ August L. b.15Apr1891-d.11May1968, "WIS. CPL 2 CO PROV GUARD WWI" n/t Emelia H. & Charles F. Busz

SEC8 BUSZ Emelia H. b.1859-d.1939, "Mother" n/t August L. & Charles F. Busz

SEC8 BUSZ Charles F. b.1859-d.1928, "Father" n/t August L. & Emelia H. Busz

SEC8 KAMRATH Elmer F. b.1916-d.1938, n/t Louise & Edward Kamrath

SEC8 KAMRATH Louise b.1894-d.1928, n/t Elmer F. & Edward Kamrath

SEC8 KAMRATH Edward b.1892-d.1975, n/t Elmer F. & Louise Kamrath

SEC8 BOESEL Josephine b.1868-d.1930, "Mother" w/ Hermann Boesel

SEC8 BOESEL Hermann b.1866-d.1941, "Father" w/ Josephine Boesel

SEC8 SCHANING Melitta Raschig b.1897-d.1936, "Mother"

SEC8 HOMBSCH Caroline b.1870-d.1935, "Mother" w/ Bernhard Hombsch

SEC8 HOMBSCH Bernhard b.1866-d.1941, "Father" w/ Caroline Hombsch

SEC8 MUELLNER Clara b.1883-d.1964, w/ Adolph Muellner

SEC8 MUELLNER Adolph b.1880-d.1942, w/ Clara Muellner

SEC8 FRASER George H. b.1861-d.1945, w/ Clara M., H. Morley & Fanny F. Fraser

SEC8 FRASER Clara M. b.1870-d.1941, w/ George H., H. Morley &
Fanny F. Fraser
SEC8 FRASER H. Morley b.1894-d.1966, w/ George H., Clara M. &
Fanny F. Fraser
SEC8 FRASER Fanny F. b.1893-d.1966, w/ George H., Clara M. & H.
Morley Fraser
SEC8 SWEET Ross b.1873-d.1964, w/ Hattie Sweet
SEC8 SWEET Hattie b.1882-d.1943, w/ Ross Sweet
SEC8 AURIS Walter H. b.1899-d.1976, w/ Anna M. Auris
SEC8 AURIS Anna M. b.1900-d.1988, w/ Walter H. Auris
SEC8 PRITCHARD Emily May b.19May1908-d.no date, w/ W. Howell &
Howell W. Pritchard
SEC8 PRITCHARD W. Howell b.2Sep1910-d.28Oct1985, w/ Emily M. &
Howell W. Pritchard
SEC8 PRITCHARD Howell W. d.21Oct1938, w/ Emily M. & W. Howell
Pritchard; only one date
SEC8 CLAUSEN William J. b.1924-d.1941
SEC8 SCHAFFER Frank J. b.1903-d.1988, w/ Alice M. Schaffer
SEC8 SCHAFFER Alice M. b.1907-d.1993, w/ Frank J. Schaffer
SEC8 ROTH Lena S. b.28Mar1902-d.3Jun1997, "Mother" w/ Daniel F.
Roth
SEC8 ROTH Daniel F. b.6Jan1895-d.26Dec1967, "Father" w/ Lena S.
Roth
SEC8 SCHWARTZBURG Robert A. b.1877-d.1940, n/t Alvena M.
Schwartzburg
SEC8 SCHWARTZBURG Alvena M. b.1877-d.1958, n/t Robert A.
Schwartzburg
SEC8 ZAHRTE Lenore H. b.1906-d.1978, w/ Kenneth H. Zahrte
SEC8 ZAHRTE Kenneth H. b.1903-d.1966, w/ Lenore H. Zahrte
SEC8 SEIBERLICH Roy J. b.1899-d.1983, w/ Anita Seiberlich; Masonic
symbol
SEC8 SEIBERLICH Anita b.1895-d.24Apr1990, w/ Roy J. Seiberlich;
date of death from cemetery records
SEC8 STRENG Anna b.1892-d.1983, w/ Adam Streng, Jr.
SEC8 STRENG Adam, Jr. b.1886-d.1942, w/ Anna Streng
SEC8 ELIAS John b.1859-d.1930, n/t Rachel Elias
SEC8 ELIAS Rachel b.1857-d.1929, n/t John Elias
SEC8 LEISTIKOW Louise b.1886-d.1975, w/ Alfred, George &
Geraldine Leistikow
SEC8 LEISTIKOW Alfred b.1880-d.1928, w/ Louise, George &
Geraldine Leistikow

SEC8 LEISTIKOW George b.1911-d.1976, w/ Louise, Alfred &
Geraldine Leistikow

SEC8 LEISTIKOW Geraldine b.1913-d.1989, w/ Louise, Alfred &
George Leistikow

SEC8 BOELTER Emma b.1891-d.1974, w/ Alvina L. & William Boelter

SEC8 BOELTER Alvina L. b.1890-d.1928, w/ Emma & William Boelter

SEC8 BOELTER William b.1885-d.1962, w/ Emma & Alvina L. Boelter

SEC8 HASSMAN Andrew U. b.1860-d.1929, "Father" n/t Estelle
Hassman and Walter, Jr., Mary J. & Ethel M. & Walter G. Winding

SEC8 WINDING Walter G. b.1887-d.1940, "Dad" n/t Andrew U. &
Estelle Hassman & Walter Jr., Mary J. & Ethel M. Winding

SEC8 WINDING Walter Jr. b.1915-d.1992, w/ Estelle Hassman, Mary J.
& Ethel M., n/t Walter Winding & Andrew U. Hassman

SEC8 WINDING Mary Jane b.1913-d.1972, w/ Estelle Hassman, Walter
Jr. & Ethel M. Winding, n/t Walter Winding & Andrew U. Hassman

SEC8 WINDING Ethel M. b.1887-d.1957, w/ Estelle Hassman, Walter Jr.
& Mary J. Winding, n/t Walter Winding & Andrew U. Hassman

SEC8 GOULD Annette (ROSENTHAL) b.1873-d.1947, w/ Lucius T.
Gould

SEC8 GOULD Lucius T. b.1863-d.1935, w/ Annette R. Gould

SEC8 KEDING Louis b.1864-d.1939, "Father" w/ Emilie Keding

SEC8 KEDING Emilie b.1866-d.1939, "Mother" w/ Louis Keding

SEC8 VERFURTH Frieda b.1872-d.1939, "Mother" w/ Richard Verfurth

SEC8 VERFURTH Richard b.1872-d.1943, "Father" w/ Frieda Verfurth

SEC8 GALLETT Alfred J. b.1863-d.1917, "In Memory of Peace Perfect
Peace With Loved Ones Far Away"; erected by his wife and family; w/
Mary A., Mabel, Mildred A. & John F., n/t Francis S., Violet, Robert M.
& Alfred S. Gallett

SEC8 GALLETT Mary Ann b.1865-d.1944, w/ Alfred J., Mabel, Mildred
A. & John F., n/t Francis S., Violet, Robert M. & Alfred S. Gallett

SEC8 GALLETT Mabel b.1892-d.1979, w/ Alfred J., Mary A., Mildred A.
& John F., n/t Francis S., Violet, Robert M. & Alfred S. Gallett

SEC8 GALLETT Mildred A. b.1909-d.no date, w/ Alfred J., Mary A.,
Mabel & John F., n/t Francis S., Violet, Robert M. & Alfred S. Gallett

SEC8 GALLETT John F. b.1905-d.1965, w/ Alfred J., Mary A., Mabel &
Mildred A., n/t Francis S., Violet, Robert M. & Alfred S. Gallett

SEC8 GALLETT Francis S. b.1895-d.1973, "Father" n/t Alfred J., Mary
A., Mabel, Mildred A. & John F. w/ Violet, Robert M. & Alfred S.
Gallett

SEC8 GALLETT Violet b.1895-d.1991, "Mother" n/t Alfred J., Mary A.,
Mabel, Mildred A. & John F. w/ Francis S., Robert M. & Alfred S.
Gallett

SEC8 GALLETT Robert M. b.1920-d.1941, "Son" n/t Alfred J., Mary A., Mabel, Mildred A. & John F. w/ Francis S., Violet & Alfred S. Gallett

SEC8 GALLETT Alfred S. b.1920-d.1991, "Son" n/t Alfred J., Mary A., Mabel, Mildred A. & John F. w/ Francis S., Violet & Robert M. Gallett

SEC8 KINGSBURY Ethel A. b.1878-d.1941, w/ Howard B. Kingsbury

SEC8 KINGSBURY Howard B. b.1878-d.1941, w/ Ethel A. Kingsbury; WWI mkr

SEC8 CLAUSEN John C. b.1885-d.1970, n/t Anna Clausen

SEC8 CLAUSEN Anna b.1888-d.1940, n/t John C. Clausen

SEC8 JOHNSON Catherine A. b.1890-d.1941, n/t Marie H. & Harry S. Johnson

SEC8 JOHNSON Marie H. b.1902-d.1962, n/t Catherine A. & Harry S. Johnson

SEC8 JOHNSON Harry S. b.1901-d.1986, n/t Catherine A. & Marie H. Johnson

SEC8 ROSENSPIES Frank H. b.1911-d.1980, w/ Kathryn G. Rosenspies

SEC8 ROSENSPIES Kathryn G. b.1910-d.1997, w/ Frank H. Rosenspies

SEC8 STREHLOW Antoinette b.1879-d.1929, "Mother" w/ Robert Strehlow

SEC8 STREHLOW Robert b.1877-d.1948, "Father" w/ Antoinette Strehlow

SEC8 SCHMIDT Jessie R. b.1880-d.1962, w/ Dr. Hugo E., n/t Alfrieda A., Mathilda & Franz D. Schmidt & Edward A. & Elsie S. Ashdown

SEC8 SCHMIDT Hugo E., Dr. b.31 May 1879-d.21 Jan 1961, w/ Jessie R., n/t Alfrieda A., Mathilda & Franz D. Schmidt & Edward A. & Elsie S. Ashdown; birth and death dates from cemetery records

SEC8 SCHMIDT Alfrieda A. b.1883-d.1961, n/t Jessie R., Dr. Hugo E., Mathilda & Franz D. Schmidt & Edward A. & Elsie S. Ashdown

SEC8 SCHMIDT Mathilda b.1852-d.1933, n/t Jessie R., Dr. Hugo E., Alfrieda A., & Franz D. Schmidt & Edward A. & Elsie S. Ashdown

SEC8 SCHMIDT Franz D. b.1853-d.1928, n/t Jessie R., Dr. Hugo E., Alfrieda A., & Mathilda Schmidt & Edward A. & Elsie S. Ashdown

SEC8 ASHDOWN Edward Albert b.1875-d.1964, w/ Elsie S. Ashdown, n/t Jessie R., Dr. Hugo E., Alfrieda A., Franz D. & Mathilda Schmidt

SEC8 ASHDOWN Elsie Schmidt b.1890-d.27Sep1971, w/ Edward A., n/t Jessie R., Dr. Hugo E., Alfrieda A., Franz D. & Mathilda Schmidt & Edward A.; she was cremated in Winters Park, FL; dates are from cemetery records

SEC8 BARRY Sidney Ferris b.29Jun1911-d.30Dec1940, "Son" n/t Sarah M. & Arthur R. Barry; 2 stones

SEC8 BARRY Sarah M. b.1876-d.1928, "Mother" n/t Sidney F. & Arthur R. Barry

SEC8 BARRY Arthur R. b.1877-d.1931, "Father" n/t Sidney F. & Sarah M. Barry

SEC8 RUSSLEY Adelaide M. b.28Mar1902-d.3Dec1988, w/ John H. Russley

SEC8 RUSSLEY John H. b.7Feb1896-d.23Dec1979, w/ Adelaide M. Russley

SEC8 KOHLOFF Anna b.1870-d.1928, w/ Fred & Ella I., n/t Clara E. & Walter A. Kohloff

SEC8 KOHLOFF Fred b.1862-d.1950, w/ Anna & Ella I., n/t Clara E. & Walter A. Kohloff

SEC8 ILLGEN Ella b.1891-d.1959, w/ Anna & Fred, n/t Clara E. & Walter A. Kohloff

SEC8 KOHLOFF Clara E. b.12Aug1898-d.2Jul1968, n/t Anna, Fred, Ella I. & Walter A. Kohloff

SEC8 KOHLOFF Walter A. b.13Feb1895-d.1Oct1964, "WIS. SFC QUARTERMASTER CORPS WWI" n/t Anna, Fred, Ella I. & Clara E. Kohloff

SEC8 RUCK Anna b.26Jun1890-d.24Jul1979, "Mother" w/ Vernharet & Vernon, n/t Mathilda & Gustave Ruck

SEC8 RUCK Vernharet b.1898-d.1931, "Father" w/ Anna & Vernon, n/t Mathilda & Gustave Ruck

SEC8 RUCK Vernon b.1924-d.1945, "Son" w/ Anna & Vernharet, n/t Mathilda & Gustave Ruck

SEC8 RUCK Mathilda b.1876-d.1935, "Mother", w/ Gustave, n/t Anna, Vernon & Vernharet Ruck

SEC8 RUCK Gustave b.1868-d.1935, "Father" w/ Mathilda, n/t Anna, Vernon & Vernharet Ruck

SEC8 BROWN Polly b.1904-d.1929, n/t David, Daniel & Mary Brown

SEC8 BROWN David b.1909-d.1929, n/t Polly, Daniel & Mary Brown

SEC8 BROWN Daniel b.1907-d.1930, n/t Polly, David & Mary Brown

SEC8 BROWN Mary b.1876-d.1962, n/t Polly, David & Daniel Brown

SEC8 LUDINGTON Frederick b.1903-d.1936, n/t sundial on large urn w/ Ludington name on it

SEC8 JACOBUS Garrett C. b.1923-d.1948, w/ Garrett & Ruth M. Jacobus

SEC8 JACOBUS Garrett b.1896-d.1944, w/ Garrett C. & Ruth M. Jacobus

SEC8 JACOBUS Ruth Marie b.1900-d.1974, w/ Garrett C. & Garrett Jacobus

SEC8 JAECKEL Peggy b.1925-d.1989, "Sleep Well Mom" w/ John Jaeckel

SEC8 JAECKEL John b.1920-d.no date, w/ Peggy Jaeckel

SEC8 OWEN George b.1863-d.1937, n/t Mary A. Owen

SEC8 OWEN Mary A. b.1859-d.1934, n/t George Owen

SEC8 EGGERT Lillian b.1893-d.1933

SEC8 OLSON Herbert W. b.1902-d.1966

SEC8 DEJARLAIS Selma b.6Feb1897-d.22Aug1928, "Mother" her name also appears as Selma Des Jarlais with Ethel & Harriet Des Jarlais

SEC8 O'NEIL Dorothy b.1889-d.1941, w/ Charles O'Neil

SEC8 O'NEIL Charles d.1969, w/ Dorothy O'Neil; only one date

SEC8 DE SWARTE Thomas b.1867-d.1957, w/ Donie De Swarte

SEC8 DE SWARTE Donie b.1868-d.1943, w/ Thomas De Swarte

SEC8 BARK Bertha b.3Oct1870-d.10Aug1939, "Ruhe Staette" w/ Gustav Bark

SEC8 BARK Gustav b.1870-d.1952, "Ruhe Staette" w/ Bertha Bark

SEC8 HARTWIG Auguste b.6Apr1867-d.7Aug1960, w/ Albert Hartwig

SEC8 HARTWIG Albert b.7Mar1966-d.19Nov1935, w/ Auguste Hartwig

SEC8 GUENTHER Arthur b.1899-d.1922, w/ John, Anna & Frederick W. Guenther & Selma, Ethel & Harriet Des Jarlais

SEC8 GUENTHER John b.1917-d.1938, w/ Arthur, Anna & Frederick W. Guenther & Selma, Ethel & Harriet Des Jarlais

SEC8 GUENTHER Anna b.19876-d.1946, w/ Arthur, John & Frederick W. Guenther & Selma, Ethel & Harriet Des Jarlais

SEC8 GUENTHER Frederick Wm. b.1867-d.1943, w/ Arthur, John & Anna Guenther & Selma, Ethel & Harriet Des Jarlais

SEC8 DES JARLAIS Selma b.1897-d.1928, w/ Frederick Wm., Arthur, John & Anna Guenther & Ethel & Harriet Des Jarlais; she has two stones the other under the name Dejarlais

SEC8 DES JARLAIS Ethel b.no date-d.no date, w/ Frederick Wm., Arthur, John & Anna Guenther & Selma & Harriet Des Jarlais; no cemetery record

SEC8 DES JARLAIS Harriet b.no date-d.no date, w/ Frederick Wm., Arthur, John & Anna Guenther & Selma & Ethel Des Jarlais; no cemetery record

SEC8 DUCAT Caralin Day b.1873-d.1976, w/ Forest C. Gardinier

SEC8 GARDINIER Forest C. b.1897-d.1961, "Ashes of my son" w/ Caralin D. Ducat

SEC8 PECK Norman b.1879-d.1932

SEC8 THOMPSON Winnefrede b.27Jun1876-d.24Aug1932, w/ Irving P. Thompson

SEC8 THOMPSON Irving P. b.31May1880-d.15May1951, w/ Winnefrede Thompson; date of death from cemetery records

SEC8 FISCHER Grace Heineman b.1908-d.1934, n/t Emma Heineman
SEC8 HEINEMAN Emma b.1874-d.1947, "Mother" n/t Grace H. Fischer
SEC8 OLSON Mary A. b.1871-d.1958, "Mother" w/ Olof P. Olson
SEC8 OLSON Olof P. b.1857-d.1936, "Father" w/ Mary A. Olson
SEC8 McGOVERN James W. b.1887-d.1973, w/ Mary McGovern, Karen
    Schnell, Charles T. & Bertha Redzinske & Emilie, Emil & Douglas
    Hartzke
SEC8 McGOVERN Mary b.1895-d.1973, w/ James W., McGovern, Karen
    Schnell, Charles T. & Bertha Redzinske & Emilie, & Douglas Hartzke
SEC8 SCHNELL Karen b.1944-d.1945, w/ James W. & Mary McGovern,
    Charles T. & Bertha Redzinske & Emilie, & Douglas Hartzke
SEC8 REDZINSKE Charles J. b.1883-d.1963, w/ James W. & Mary
    McGovern, Karen Schnell, Bertha Redzinske & Emilie, & Douglas
    Hartzke
SEC8 REDZINSKE Bertha b.1891-d.1958, w/ James W. & Mary
    McGovern, Karen Schnell, Charles T. Redzinske & Emilie, & Douglas
    Hartzke
SEC8 HARTZKE Emilie b.1870-d.1950, "Mother" w/ James W. & Mary
    McGovern, Karen Schnell, Charles T. & Bertha Redzinske & Emil &
    Douglas Hartzke
SEC8 HARTZKE Emil b.1861-d.1941, "Father" w/ James W. & Mary
    McGovern, Karen Schnell, Charles T. & Bertha Redzinske & Emilie &
    Douglas Hartzke
SEC8 HARTZKE Douglas b.1939-d.1941, w/ James W. & Mary
    McGovern, Karen Schnell, Charles T. & Bertha Redzinske & Emil &
    Emilie Hartzke
SEC8 ERIKSEN Claire Guequierre b.1888-d.1980, w/ Fred E. Eriksen
SEC8 ERIKSEN Fred Esbern b.1885-d.1950, w/ Clair G. Eriksen
SEC8 READ Bessie Ferne b.20Feb1894-d.14May1942, n/t Victor A.
    Read
SEC8 READ Victor A. b.19Jun1892-d.11Sep1960, "WIS. BAND CPL HQ
    CO 326 INF" n/t Bessie F. Read
SEC8 VOSS Helen E. b.1912-d.1995, w/ George J. Voss
SEC8 VOSS George J. b.1900-d.1957, w/ Helen E. Voss
SEC8 BULGRIN Martha b.1877-d.1932, n/t Richard & Frank Bulgrin
SEC8 BULGRIN Frank b.1902-d.1936, "Daddy" n/t Richard & Martha
    Bulgrin
SEC8 BULGRIN Richard b.1876-d.1940, "Father" n/t Frank & Martha
    Bulgrin
SEC8 KARLL Walter R. b.1890-d.1967, "Father" n/t Marie K. Karll
SEC8 KARLL Marie K. b.1891-d.1945, "Mother" n/t Walter R. Karll

SEC8 BOYLE Evelyn G. b.1903-d.1976
SEC8 EVANS Lona M. b.1889-d.1944, w/ William A. Evans
SEC8 EVANS William A. b.1893-d.1953, w/ Lona M. Evans
SEC8 DANNIES May B. b.1885-d.1972, w/ Fred R. Dannies
SEC8 DANNIES Fred R. b.1885-d.1967, w/ May B. Dannies
SEC8 HAYWARD Mildred L. b.1904-d.1942, w/ Nina A. & Ralph L. Hayward
SEC8 HAYWARD Nina A. b.1882-d.1972, w/ Mildred L. & Ralph L. Hayward
SEC8 HAYWARD Ralph L. b.1881-d.1968, w/ Mildred L. & Nina A. Hayward
SEC8 DWYER Harold N. b.7Jun1911-d.no date, w/ Mary E. Dwyer
SEC8 DWYER Mary E. b.15Jun1912-d.27Nov1994, w/ Harold N. Dwyer
SEC8 ALTHEIMER Donald W. b.1921-d.1994, "S.A.R." w/ Corinne E. Altheimer
SEC8 ALTHEIMER Corinne E. b.1923-d.no date, "COCO" w/ Donald W. Altheimer
SEC8 WENDLAND Lester E. b.1902-d.1953, Masonic symbol
SEC8 AEPLER Jeanette b.1900-d.1Jul1978, w/ Herbert Aepler; cremated in Clearwater, FL
SEC8 AEPLER Herbert b.1893-d.1953, w/ Jeanette Aepler
SEC8 BAIER Jeanette b.1916-d.1993, w/ Robert E. Baier
SEC8 BAIER Robert E. b.1914-d.no date, w/ Jeanette Baier
SEC8 GALLETT Leonard C. b.1908-d.1979, w/ Alice C., n/t Mary, James A. & Catherine W. Gallett; crossed golf clubs on stone
SEC8 GALLETT Alice C. b.1907-d.no date, w/ Leonard C., n/t Mary, James A. & Catherine W. Gallett; crossed golf clubs on stone
SEC8 GALLETT Mary b.1887-d.1968, w/ James A., n/t Catherine W., Leonard C. & Alice C. Gallett
SEC8 GALLETT James A. b.1885-d.1959, w/ Mary, n/t Catherine W., Leonard C. & Alice C. Gallett
SEC8 GALLETT Catherine W. b.1918-d.1985, n/t Mary, James A., Leonard C. & Alice C. Gallett
SEC8 WALTERS William A. b.1912-d.1957
SEC8 HADRIAN Elizabeth b.26Oct1904-d.20Jul1994, "d/o Augusta & Julius Hadrian"
SEC8 ZOBEL Irene b.1903-d.18Oct1973, w/ Mary A. & Henry Zobel; date of death from cemetery records
SEC8 ZOBEL Mary Ann b.1942-d.1956, w/ Irene & Henry Zobel
SEC8 ZOBEL Henry b.1893-d.27Jan1981, w/ Irene & Mary A. Zobel; date of death from cemetery records

SEC8 BALISTRERI Stephen A. b.24Nov1931-d.29Feb1988, "CPL US ARMY KOREA"

SEC8 MELIN Donna L. b.1915-d.1991, w/ Robert J. Melin

SEC8 MELIN Robert J. b.1914-d.1999, w/ Donna L. Melin

SEC8 GRIFFIN Irma B. b.1884-d.1959, w/ Frank J. Griffin

SEC8 GRIFFIN Frank J. b.1876-d.1954, w/ Irma B. Griffin; Masonic symbol

SEC8 BELL Clara L. b.17Jan1892-d.no date, w/ Orbie R. Bell; not buried here according to cemetery records

SEC8 BELL Orbie R. b.3Jun1890-d.25Jun1955, w/ Clara L. Bell

SEC8 TREIBER Ruth L. b.5Sep1897-d.4Mar1980, n/t Arthur P. Treiber

SEC8 TREIBER Arthur P. b.22Feb1896-d.15Sep1947, n/t Ruth L. Treiber

SEC8 YONK Marietta E. b.1897-d.1953, w/ Ewold J. Yonk

SEC8 YONK Ewold J. b.1895-d.no date, w/ Marietta E. Yonk; no cemetery record

SEC8 ARNDT Gertrude E. b.1908-d.1997, w/ Allen L. Arndt

SEC8 ARNDT Allen L. b.1907-d.1991, w/ Gertrude E. Arndt

SEC8 KOHLER Rachel C. b.1901-d.1962, w/ Roy W. Kohler

SEC8 KOHLER Roy W. b.1901-d.1975, w/ Rachel C. Kohler

SEC8 BLOEDORN Edward J. b.1911-d.1957, "Father" w/ Esther Bloedorn

SEC8 BLOEDORN Esther b.1915-d.no date, "Mother" w/ Edward J. Bloedorn

SEC8 RUSH Grace R. b.1916-d.1950, "Mother"

SEC8 KINDER Bernice M. b.1918-d.1986, "Beloved Sister"

SEC8 BORWELL Ruth Lange b.1926-d.1963

SEC8 TETZLAFF Bill b.1957-d.1994, w/ Shirley M. & William J. Tetzlaff

SEC8 TETZLAFF Shirley M. b.1929-d.1995, w/ Bill & William J. Tetzlaff

SEC8 TETZLAFF William J. b.1931-d.no date, w/ Bill & Shirley M. Tetzlaff

SEC8 COLWELL Brendan b.20Mar1963-d.22Nov1988, "Born to Run" "by request of Brendan Colwell taken suddenly in a construction accident. Our beautiful and brave son, brother and friend. Your intense love, laughter and music is sealed in our hearts forever. Bren, we'll always love and miss you. Great memories, God Bless; The Family"

SEC8 CARTER Karen Seitz b.25Jul1956-d.10Apr1987

SEC8 SUTTON Jerry L. b.1935-d.1984

SEC8 LATORRACA Rocco b.10Apr1920-d.24Mar1999

SEC8 REIN Clarence E. b.10Oct1894-d.6Feb1958, "WIS. SGT AIR SERVICE WWI"

SEC8 SCHWARTZ Oscar C. b.1904-d.1967, n/t Dorothy E. Schwartz

SEC8 SCHWARTZ Dorothy E. b.1903-d.no date, n/t Oscar C. Schwartz

SEC8 REMICK Laura C. b.1861-d.1947, w/ Wilson H. Remick

SEC8 REMICK Wilson H. b.1862-d.1948, w/ Laura C. Remick

SEC8 LOOMIS Sarah Phillips b.1882-d.1963, "Mother" n/t Charles W. Loomis & Winifred E. Phillips; Eastern Star sym

SEC8 LOOMIS Charles Warren b.1882-d.1929, n/t Sarah P. Loomis & Winifred E. Phillips; Masonic sym

SEC8 PHILLIPS Winifred Estelle b.1880-d.1963, n/t Sarah P. & Charles W. Loomis

SEC8 MECKLENBURG Henry F. b.1886-d.1943, "Father"

SEC8 WEINZ Pauline b.1873-d.1955, w/ John Weinz

SEC8 WEINZ John b.1870-d.1958, w/ Pauline Weinz

SEC8 SCHWEITZER Minnie C. b.1881-d.1944, "In Memory of Our Beloved Parents" w/ Fred W. Schweitzer

SEC8 SCHWEITZER Fred W. b.1876-d.1966, "In Memory of Our Beloved Parents" w/ Minnie C. Schweitzer

SEC8 MUNNINGHOFF Louise b.1882-d.1949, "Mother" w/ August Munninghoff

SEC8 MUNNINGHOFF August b.1876-d.1944, "Father" w/ Louise Munninghoff

SEC8 GETTELMAN Kenneth W. b.1909-d.1989, n/t Jean, Helen & Jacob Gettelman

SEC8 GETTELMAN Jean b.1909-d.1961, n/t Kenneth W., Helen & Jacob Gettelman

SEC8 GETTELMAN Helen b.1883-d.1946, w/ Jacob, n/t Kenneth W. & Jean Gettelman

SEC8 GETTELMAN Jacob b.1882-d.1946, w/ Helen, n/t Kenneth W. & Jean Gettelman

SEC8 TETTING Elsie b.1905-d.no date, "Mother"

SEC8 VAN UXEN Thomas b.1928-d.no date, w/ Abraham, Mary & Virginia Van Uxen & Florence & George J. Duwe

SEC8 VAN UXEN Abraham b.1874-d.1951, w/ Thomas, Mary & Virginia Van Uxen & Florence & George J. Duwe

SEC8 VAN UXEN Mary b.1877-d.1950, w/ Thomas, Abraham & Virginia Van Uxen & Florence & George J. Duwe

SEC8 VAN UXEN Virginia b.1913-d.1930, w/ Thomas, Abraham & Mary Van Uxen & Florence & George J. Duwe

SEC8 DUWE Florence b.1896-d.19—, w/ Thomas, Abraham, Virginia & Mary Van Uxen & George J. Duwe; no cemetery record

SEC8 DUWE George J. b.1895-d.1957, w/ Thomas, Abraham, Virginia & Mary Van Uxen & Florence Duwe; American Legion mkr

SEC8 KUTSCHENREUTER Richard b.1925-d.1926, w/ Fred & Helen Kutschenreuter

SEC8 KUTSCHENREUTER Fred b.1897-d.1977, w/ Richard & Helen Kutschenreuter

SEC8 KUTSCHENREUTER Helen b.1902-d.1989, w/ Richard & Fred Kutschenreuter

SEC8 JOHA Emil b.1870-d.1951, "Father" n/t Jacob & Dora Fehl & Emma Joha

SEC8 FEHL Jacob b.1855-d.1925, "Father" n/t Dora Fehl & Emil & Emma Joha

SEC8 FEHL Dora b.1864-d.1925, "Mother" n/t Jacob Fehl & Emil & Emma Joha

SEC8 JOHA Emma b.1885-d.1959, "Mother" n/t Jacob & Dora Fehl & Emil Joha

SEC8 JOERS William b.1865-d.1952, "Father" n/t Anna Joers

SEC8 JOERS Anna b.1873-d.1932, "Mother" n/t William Joers

SEC8 NAGEL Irma b.1904-d.1976, n/t Paul Nagel

SEC8 NAGEL Paul b.1909-d.1945, "Father" n/t Irma Nagel

SEC8 MARIE? Ethel Ann b.28Jun1897-d.24Jun1971, no cemetery record under this name so it may be wrong

SEC8 BULGRIN Anton Fred b.5Apr1898-d.5Apr1962, "WIS. PFC US ARMY WWI"

SEC8 WHITE Minnie b.1885-d.1976, w/ John E. White

SEC8 WHITE John E. b.12Feb1871-d.9Mar1946, w/ Minnie White

SEC8 WEGNER Lottie L. b.1870-d.1937, w/ Fred Wm. Wegner

SEC8 WEGNER Fred Wm. b.1870-d.1935, w/ Lottie L. Wegner

SEC8 ESCHENBERG Minnie b.1869-d.1949, w/ Fred Eschenberg

SEC8 ESCHENBERG Fred b.1866-d.1933, w/ Minnie Eschenberg

SEC8 WATTERS Patrick J. b.17Nov1883-d.20Nov1937, "Father"

SEC8 DOFFER Joseph b.7Aug1927-d.26Sep1971, "WIS RD 3 US NAVY WWII"

SEC8 KOEPP George A. b.13Feb1901-d.18Oct1980, "Beloved Husband & Father" n/t Louise, Charles J., Frank & Anna Koepp

SEC8 KOEPP Frank b.27May1869-d.21Nov1935, "Father" n/t Louise, Charles J., George A. & Anna Koepp

SEC8 KOEPP Anna b.16May1872-d.29Jul1950, "Mother" n/t Louise, Charles J., George A. & Frank Koepp

SEC8 KOEPP Louise b.1871-d.1963, "Mother" w/ Charles J., n/t George A., Frank & Anna Koepp

SEC8 KOEPP Charles J. b.1868-d.1952, "Father" w/ Louise, n/t George A., Frank & Anna Koepp

SEC8 FEZER Laura J. b.1879-d.1953, w/ Lawrence S. Fezer
SEC8 FEZER Lawrence S. b.1869-d.1958, w/ Laura J. Fezer
SEC8 ESCH Clara b.1896-d.1974, w/ Frank Esch
SEC8 ESCH Frank b.1894-d.1953, w/ Clara Esch
SEC8 MAHN Lucille b.1896-d.1983, w/ Eric Mahn
SEC8 MAHN Eric b.1893-d.1977, w/ Lucille Mahn
SEC8 SZEKELY Caroline C. b.1910-d.19—, "Daughter" w/ Sari, Ernest &
George E. Szekely
SEC8 SZEKELY Sari b.1883-d.1971, "Mother" w/ Caroline C., Ernest &
George E. Szekely
SEC8 SZEKELY Ernest b.1888-d.1956, "Father" w/ Caroline C., Sari &
George E. Szekely
SEC8 SZEKELY George E. b.1912-d.1970, "Son" w/ Caroline C., Sari &
Ernest Szekely
SEC8 JACKSON Joan Louise b.1928-d.1964
SEC8 POST Anna Elsie b.1885-d.1967
SEC8 TREBILCOCK Elsie H. b.1891-d.1973, w/ Roy J. Trebilcock
SEC8 TREBILCOCK Roy J. b.1890-d.1958, w/ Elsie H. Trebilcock
SEC8 HALL Hazel L. b.1895-d.1962, "God Needed a Special Angel"
SEC8 JOHNSON Loretta M. b.29Nov1929-d.8Nov1998
SEC8 SCHNEIDER Patricia K. b.1Dec1936-d.no date, "Mother" w/ Mark
D. Schneider
SEC8 SCHNEIDER Mark D. b.7Mar1959-d.9Jan1999, "Son" w/ Patricia
K. Schneider
SEC8 BUCHANAN Thomas Boyd b.1924-d.1988, "SGT US ARMY
WWII"
SEC8 EPPSTAEDT Robert R. b.1937-d.1997, w/ Mary Jo Eppstaedt
SEC8 EPPSTAEDT Mary Jo b.1939-d.no date, w/ Robert R. Eppstaedt
SEC8 COLLISON Isabel Goin b.2Jul1914-d.no date, w/ Lewis H.
Collison & Mary L. Larsen
SEC8 COLLISON Lewis Henry b.27Jan1914-d.no date, w/ Isabel G.
Collison & Mary L. Larsen
SEC8 LARSEN Mary Lucy b.28Sep1938-d.8Aug1995, "Daughter" w/
Isabel G. & Lewis H. Collison
SEC8 WORM Luella b.1893-d.1972, w/ Edward Worm
SEC8 WORM Edward b.1888-d.1945, w/ Luella Worm
SEC8 KINDER Rose M. (WOELM) b.1887-d.1971, "Mother" n/t Charles
Kinder
SEC8 KINDER Charles b.1885-d.1947, "Father" n/t Rose M. W. Kinder
SEC8 BRENNAN Charles Coleman b.22Jan1939-d.4Jul1962, w/
Josephine W., Suzanne G. & John E. Brennan

SEC8 BRENNAN Josephine Wigdale b.4May1905-d.16Oct1958, w/ Charles C., Suzanne G. & John E. Brennan

SEC8 BRENNAN Suzanne Gardner b.27Dec1936-d.18Nov1965, w/ Charles C., Josephine W. & John E. Brennan

SEC8 BRENNAN John Emil b.25Nov1905-d.20Apr1993, w/ Charles C., Josephine W. & Suzanne G. Brennan

SEC8 ROCKENBACH Sylvia M. b.1910-d.1999, w/ Raymond F. Rockenbach

SEC8 ROCKENBACH Raymond F. b.1904-d.1968, w/ Sylvia M. Rockenbach

SEC8 BURK Alvina b.1886-d.1946, w/ George Burk

SEC8 BURK George b.1886-d.1965, w/ Alvina Burk

SEC8 HILL nothing else

SEC8 BUCHANAN nothing else

SEC8 KURTH Martha b.1880-d.1967, w/ Adolph & Marvin Kurth & Evelyn, Raymond, Kent K., Barbara H., Mary & Louis Krueger

SEC8 KURTH Adolph b.1881-d.1946, w/ Martha & Marvin Kurth & Evelyn, Raymond, Kent K., Barbara H., Mary & Louis Krueger

SEC8 KURTH Marvin d.1911, w/ Martha & Adolph Kurth & Evelyn, Raymond, Kent K., Barbara H., Mary & Louis Krueger; only one date

SEC8 KRUEGER Evelyn b.1907-d.1983, w/ Martha, Marvin & Adolph Kurth & Raymond, Kent K., Barbara H., Mary & Louis Krueger

SEC8 KRUEGER Raymond b.1908-d.1998, w/ Martha, Marvin & Adolph Kurth & Evelyn, Kent K., Barbara H., Mary & Louis Krueger

SEC8 KRUEGER Kent K. b.1938-d.no date, w/ Martha, Marvin & Adolph Kurth & Evelyn, Raymond, Barbara H., Mary & Louis Krueger

SEC8 KRUEGER Barbara H. b.1940-d.1990, w/ Martha, Marvin & Adolph Kurth & Evelyn, Raymond, Kent K., Mary & Louis Krueger

SEC8 KRUEGER Mary b.1879-d.1955, w/ Martha, Marvin & Adolph Kurth & Evelyn, Raymond, Kent K., Barbara H. & Louis Krueger

SEC8 KRUEGER Louis b.1877-d.1966, w/ Martha, Marvin & Adolph Kurth & Evelyn, Raymond, Kent K., Barbara H. & Mary Krueger

SEC8 TOFTE Florence M. b.1891-d.1990, w/ Paul M. Tofte

SEC8 TOFTE Paul M. b.1886-d.1964, w/ Florence M. Tofte

SEC8 PAIGE William F. b.1942-d.1985, w/ John H. & Ella R. Paige

SEC8 PAIGE John H. b.1908-d.1983, w/ William F. & Ella R. Paige

SEC8 PAIGE Ella R. b.1872-d.1976, w/ William F. & John H. Paige; she was about 104 years old

SEC8 WARREN Phillip Allan b.19Oct1937-d.2Nov1998

SEC8 KALKHOFF Rhea L. b.18Jan1934-d.no date, "Wife & Mother" w/ Dr. Ronald K. Kalkhoff

SEC8 KALKHOFF Ronald K., Dr. b.6Dec1933-d.20Dec1990, "Husband & Father" w/ Rhea L. Kalkhoff

SEC8 HAERTER Ann S. b.1925-d.1991, "Beloved" n/t Jack J. Haerter

SEC8 HAERTER Jack J. b.1951-d.1979, "Beloved" n/t Ann S. Haerter

SEC8 HAYES Hanlin J. b.1914-d.1994, w/ Virginia K. Hayes

SEC8 HAYES Virginia K. b.1916-d.no date, w/ Hanlin J. Hayes

SEC8 CORBETT Rose L. b.16Feb1892-d.28Feb1974, w/ Richard A. Corbett; dates completed from cemetery records

SEC8 CORBETT Richard A. b.1889-d.1964, w/ Rose L. Corbett

SEC8 PLETCHER Mabel E. b.1895-d.1985, "Beloved Mother" n/t John & Harold E. Pletcher

SEC8 PLETCHER John b.17Jul1890-d.6Feb1948, "Father" n/t Mabel E. & Harold E. Pletcher

SEC8 PLETCHER Harold E. b.31Jul1930-d.13Jun1972, "WIS CPL US MARINE CORPS KOREA", n/t Mabel E. & John Pletcher

SEC8 SIMROCK Frank Harold b.8Dec1919-d.11Jan1947, "WIS RM 3 US NAVY WWII"

SEC8 NOONAN Edward D. b.1891-d.1961, "Father" w/ Edith T. Noonan

SEC8 NOONAN Edith T. b.1892-d.1975, w/ Edward D. Noonan

SEC8 WANKOWSKI Edith R. b.1928-d.1983

SEC8 PROPP Cecilia b.1892-d.1978, w/ Laurence Propp

SEC8 PROPP Laurence b.1890-d.1937, w/ Cecilia Propp

SEC8 ZOBEL Kerstin b.1862-d.1940, "Mother" w/ William Zobel

SEC8 ZOBEL William b.1854-d.1933, "Father" w/ Kerstin Zobel

SEC8 MARQUARDT Fred b.1885-d.1951, "Father" w/ Minnie Marquardt

SEC8 MARQUARDT Minnie b.1888-d.1945, "Mother" w/ Fred Marquardt

SEC8 DAHNKE Bertha b.1891-d.1974, "Wife" w/ William Dahnke & Karen Hahn

SEC8 DAHNKE William b.1888-d.1970, "Husband" w/ Bertha Dahnke & Karen Hahn

SEC8 HAHN Karen d.1956, w/ William & Bertha Dahnke; only one date

SEC8 SCHEEL Amelia b.1864-d.1948, w/ William Scheel

SEC8 SCHEEL William b.1856-d.1944, w/ Amelia Scheel

SEC8 McNAIR Hugh b.1870-d.1934, w/ Nellie McNair

SEC8 McNAIR Nellie b.1870-d.1945, w/ Hugh McNair

SEC9 VANG Jua Yia b.1927-d.1994

SEC9 PETERSON Carroll D. b.1926-d.no date, w/ M. Harriette Peterson

SEC9 PETERSON M. Harriette b.1931-d.1985, w/ Carroll D. Peterson

SEC9 TENDLER Adeline L. b.1912-d.no date, w/ Lawrence M. Tendler

SEC9 TENDLER Lawrence M. b.1912-d.1996, w/ Adeline L. Tendler

SEC9 THOMPSON Dorothy b.10Oct1909-d.no date, w/ Chester Thompson

SEC9 THOMPSON Chester b.28Jul1915-d.1Mar1997, w/ Dorothy Thompson

SEC9 OLVEY Margaret Rice b.1951-d.1994, "Maggie" n/t Frank H. & Virginia K. Rice

SEC9 RICE Frank H. b.1928-d.no date, w/ Virginia K. Rice, n/t Margaret R. Olvey

SEC9 RICE Virginia K. b.1927-d.1991, w/ Frank H. Rice, n/t Margaret R. Olvey

SEC9 BECK John A. b.16Nov1899-d.12Jan1996, w/ Emma C. Beck

SEC9 BECK Emma C. b.6Nov1913-d.no date, w/ John A. Beck

SEC9 WILSON Kathryn b.15Jun1910-d.13Sep1992

SEC9 NEITZER Anah b.3Dec1920-d.8Nov1998

SEC9 JACKSON David Hernandez b.1985-d.1994, "Our Beloved Son"

SEC9 KANIS Warren b.25Aug1924-d.12Feb1998, "TEC 4 US ARMY WWII"

SEC9 COOPER Floyd Arthur b.1920-d.1992, "SP 2 US NAVY WWII" n/t Laverne O. Cooper

SEC9 COOPER Laverne Ochalek b.1921-d.1996, n/t Floyd A. Cooper

SEC9 BALTZLEY Larry A. b.8May1935-d.22Jul1994

SEC9 LINDNER Rebecca W. b.1905-d.1996, w/ Jacob Lindner

SEC9 LINDNER Jacob b.1904-d.1998, w/ Rebecca W. Lindner

SEC9 GARCIA Justina T. b.9Aug1934-d.no date, "Mami, Beloved Wife" w/ Jose M. Garcia

SEC9 GARCIA Jose M. b.29May1920-d.23Oct1996, "Papi, Beloved Husband; Estamos Con Dios" w/ Justina T. Garcia

SEC9 WITZKE Winifred R. b.1919-d.no date, "Married 28 Jul 1945" w/ Paul T. Witzke

SEC9 WITZKE Paul T. b.1919-d.1996, "Married 28 Jul 1945" w/ Winifred R. Witzke

SEC9 BRADY Lyle R. b.5Mar1942-d.10Dec1993, "Loving Father & Son; You Are Dearly Missed"

SEC9 BRAATZ Lorraine b.5Oct1910-d.28Feb1993, "Mom"

SEC9 POTTER Donald Herbert b.16Jul1909-d.26May1992, "COX US NAVY WWII"

SEC9 TESKA Stacy Lee b.5Sep1968-d.12Jul1994, "Loved By All Who Knew Him"

SEC9 FYRNYS Edward Lawrence b.27Mar1913-d.22Apr1997, "MAJ US ARMY WWII KOREA" w/ Leone K., Sarah J. & Edward L. Fyrnys; 2 stones

SEC9 FYRNYS Leone K. b.1912-d.no date, w/ Edward L., Sarah J. &
Edward L. Fyrnys
SEC9 FYRNYS Sarah J. b.1946-d.no date, w/ Edward L., Leone K. &
Edward L. Fyrnys
SEC9 FYRNYS Edward L. b.1943-d.no date, "Ned" w/ Edward L., Leone
K. & Sarah J. Fyrnys
SEC9 SAMPO Ruth G. b.1916-d.1996, "2 Sep 1939 (in a heart)" w/
Henry J. Sampo
SEC9 SAMPO Henry J. b.1914-d.1994, "2 Sep 1939 (in a heart)" w/ Ruth
G. Sampo
SEC9 REDDIN John N. b.1911-d.1977, n/t Marcia L. Reddin
SEC9 REDDIN Marcia L. b.1910-d.1997, n/t John N. Reddin
SEC9 DANEK Frank J. b.11May1927-d.no date, "PFC US ARMY WWII"
n/t Harriet Danek; US NAVY EMBLEM
SEC9 DANEK Harriet b.24Mar1928-d.22Jan1999, "Beloved Wife &
Mother" n/t Frank J. Danek
SEC9 ANDERSON Audrey E. b.1939-d.1996, n/t Malinda J. Anderson
SEC9 ANDERSON Malinda J. b.1959-d.1997, n/t Audrey E. Anderson
SEC9 HAMILL Robert D. b.1935-d.1996
SEC9 BRANGE Karlis b.10Sep1908-d.16Aug1994
SEC9 AMPARO Willie Alexander b.1964-d.1994, "f/o Willie, Jr.,
Anthony & Adam"
SEC9 JOHNSON Otis H. b.29Jul1924-d.10Sep1993, "TEC 5 US ARMY"
SEC9 INDVIK Julian Orville b.1912-d.1998, "2nd LT US ARMY WWII"
SEC9 HIEGEL Frieda I. b.1915-d.no date, w/ Andrew P. Hiegel
SEC9 HIEGEL Andrew P. b.1898-d.1993, w/ Frieda I. Hiegel
SEC9 PHALPHOUVONG Feuane b.1931-d.1993
SEC9 XIONG Joua b.8Aug1967-d.28Apr1997
SEC9 WEBER Curt H. b.4Feb1930-d.18Apr1998, "US ARMY KOREA"
SEC9 CHANG Nao Pheng-TSAB, Tub Rwg, b.5Feb1967-d.5Jul1996, the
inscription reads "NOM PHEEJ. YUG NYOB LUB ZOS LIS VAIS.
FOOS XAM LIS. NPLOG TEB. NIAM TXIV YUG. TXOOJ TUAM
TSAB. NWS TUAJ RAU ASMISLIKAS TEB XYOO 1986 NWS YAUV
POJ NIAM RAU XYOO 1987. NWS UA KAM NYOB RAU HAUV
RESTAURANTE (CHEF). NWS MUAJ VAJ TSE. MUAJ 4 TUG MI
NYUAM. TXOJ HMOO TSIS NCAU NWS TAU LOS TSO LUB NTIAJ
TEB TSEG RAU HNUB TIM 5 LUB 7 HLIS XYOO 1966"
SEC9 KROHN Ellen B. b.1912-d.1997, "Beloved Mother"
SEC9 MENZEL Louisa b.1857-d.1926, w/ Phillip Menzel & Emilie M.
Heumann; reinterred here from Fairview Mausoleum
SEC9 MENZEL Phillip b.1850-d.1935, w/ Louisa Menzel & Emilie M.
Heumann; reinterred here from Fairview Mausoleum

SEC9 HEUMANN Emilie Menzel b.14Oct1886-d.21Feb1919, w/ Louisa
& Phillip Menzel; reintered here from Fairview Mausoleum
SEC9 MAZUREK James H. b.23May1929-d.3Jan1995
SEC9 BRITTAIN James E., Jr. b.1925-d.1996, n/t Shirley Brittain
SEC9 BRITTAIN Shirley b.1926-d.no date, n/t James E. Brittain, Jr.
SEC9 FURST Darlean J. b.1927-d.no date, w/ Warren L. Furst
SEC9 FURST Warren L. b.1926-d.1995, w/ Darlean J. Furst
SEC9 LANGER Mary Louise b.12Jul1929-d.8Oct1996
SEC9 LY Youa Xiong b.1955-d.1996, "Beloved Wife & Mother", "KUV
ME NPLOOJ SIAB KOJ LUB NTSEJ MUAG QUAB ZIB LUAG NTXI
TSUAS YOG TSHAUV DAIM DUAB" is on the left side of her picture
and on the right side is: CAI RAU PEB COV TXIV TUB TAU SAIB
DAB MUAG NTAWM TAXOJ KEV NCO "
SEC9 REINERT Linda A. b.1956-d.1996, "m/o Adam, Beloved w/o John
Reinert" northwoods fishing scene on stone
SEC9 RYAN Margaret C. b.8Jun1912-d.no date, "m. 7 Sep 1940; (en-
twined rings)" w/ Frank E. Ryan
SEC9 RYAN Frank E. b.18Jun1910-d.17Dec1997, "m. 7 Sep 1940;
(entwined rings)" w/ Margaret C. Ryan
SEC9 SAVAGE Shirley Mae b.1929-d.1997, "Forever in the Hearts of
Twelve Little Angels"; w/ Millard D. Savage
SEC9 SAVAGE Millard D. b.1928-d.no date, "Forever in the Hearts of
Twelve Little Angels; Doc"; w/ Shirley M. Savage
SEC9 GIFFEN Elliott V. b.23Mar1928-d.26Oct1995
SEC9 WENTEN Henry W. b.11Nov1930-d.23May1996, "m. 21 Jan
1956" w/ Nancy R. Wenten
SEC9 WENTEN Nancy R. b.1Oct1934-d.no date, w/ Henry W. Wenten
SEC9 GANZER James b.4Jul1933-d.17Apr1998, "Grandpa"; dates from
cemetery records
SEC9 BREITLOW Dale H. b.1947-d.1993, "Loving Husband & Father;
Dedicated Educator & Sports Enthusiast"; w/ Susan M. Breitlow
SEC9 BREITLOW Susan M. b.1947-d.no date, w/ Dale H. Breitlow
SEC9 EDWARDS Ray C. b.1919-d.1999
SEC9 LINTOTT Arthur, Jr. b.1915-d.1994, "Father" w/ Pauline S. Lintott
SEC9 LINTOTT Pauline S. b.1925-d.no date, "Mother" w/ Arthur
Lintott, Jr.

AURIS Anna M. 184
AURIS Eric 49
AURIS Fred 49
AURIS Ida 49
AURIS Walter H. 184
AURIS William 49
AWE Clara 46
AWE Luella I. 46
AWE Mathilda 46
AWE Richard F. 46
AWE William 46

B

BAAS Anna 101
BAAS John 101
BAAS John, Jr. 101
BAAS Julius 101
BABICH Sam 3
BABICH Stephanie 3
BACH Gerry H. 129
BACKUS Gertrude 149
BAEHR Bertha 115
BAEHR Edward T. 115
BAEHR Theodore 115
BAEHR William 115
BAETZ Anna B. 131
BAGEMIHL Frank 50
BAGEMIHL Lydia 50
BAHLER Albertina (SCHMIDT) 147
BAHLER Ferdinand F. 147
BAHLER John 98
BAHR Amelia 166
BAHR Elmer R. 170
BAHR Emilie 131
BAHR Frederick 176
BAHR Martin 132
BAHR Mary 129
BAHR Tilly 168
BAHR William H. 129
BAIER Jeanette 190
BAIER Robert E. 190
BAILEY James 31
BAILEY Rebecca B. 31
BAKER Eliza S. 152
BALISTRERI Stephen A. 191
BALL Emma N. 183
BALL George W. 183
BALL Henrietta E. 183
BALL Lester R. 183
BALTES Clara 19
BALTES George 19
BALTZLEY Larry A. 197
BANSEMER Adelheid 174
BANSEMER Johann 174

BARBER Belle 64
BARBER Ben F. 64
BARBER Beulah 64
BARBER Eddie G. 64
BARBER Edward R. 64
BARBER Gertrude 64
BARBER Lottie M. 65
BARBER Martha Earls 64
BARBER Olive B. 64
BARBER Sara Olive 64
BARBER Wm. Gilbert 64
BARFORTH Dorothy (KRULL) 80
BARFORTH Ernst 80
BARG Frederick 48
BARG Fredricka 48
BARK Addie (NOLL) 118
BARK Bertha 188
BARK Dorothea (SIGGLOW) 118
BARK Ferdinand 59
BARK Frederich H. 118
BARK Gustav 188
BARK Harold 117
BARK John 117
BARK Laura 60
BARK Lydia 117
BARK Minnie 59
BARK Sophia 117
BARK William W. 152
BARK Wm. F. 59
BARNEKOW Augusta 81
BARNEKOW Charlotte 148
BARNEKOW Ernst 81
BARNEKOW Frank 148
BARNEKOW Frederick 81
BARNEKOW Hannah (MILLER) 81
BARNEKOW Harrison 148
BARNEKOW John 81
BARNEKOW Mary (HOLZ) 81
BARNEKOW Walter F. 44
BARNES Willie 40
BARRETT Benjamin 15
BARRETT Georgie C. 13
BARRETT Gladys Arline 13
BARRETT Julia Cain 13
BARRETT Marie A. 10, 13
BARRETT Mary 15
BARRETT none 14
BARRY Arthur R. 187
BARRY Sarah M. 186
BARRY Sidney Ferris 186
BARTEL Clair 177
BARTELS Bernard 85
BARTELS Meta 87
BARTELT Augusta A. 177

BARTELT Charles T. 177
BARTELT Ernestine 131
BARTELT Tillie 166
BARTH Alma 149
BARTH C. W. 55
BARTH John F. 55
BARTHOLOMEW Dorothy Brown 153
BARTHOLOMEW Henry 153
BARZDUKAS Albert C. 170
BARZDUKAS Vivian A. 170
BASSLER Phillip 1
BASSLER Soloma Frank 1
BAST Helene 174
BASTIAN Lillian Kumm 131
BATISTE John 63
BATISTE Marie 63
BAUER Fred 131
BAUER Geo. 112
BAUER George 112
BAUER Marie 178
BAUER Wilhelmina 112
BAUKAT John 177
BAUMGARTNER Chas. D. 146
BAUMGARTNER Olga Belle 146
BECHERER Amelia 154
BECHERER Frank 155
BECHERER Franz 154
BECHERER Lulu (WHEELER) 155
BECHTEL Alma 83
BECHTEL Annie 83
BECHTEL Edwin 81
BECHTEL Elizabeth 16
BECHTEL Ella 83
BECHTEL Erwin 83
BECHTEL Frank 83
BECHTEL Helena 16
BECHTEL Hilda 81
BECHTEL Ida 16
BECHTEL Jacob 16
BECHTEL Jacob Jr. 83
BECHTEL John 16
BECHTEL Margaretha 16
BECK Anna 61
BECK Emma C. 197
BECK John 61
BECK John A. 197
BECKER Adolph G. 152
BECKER Anna F. (FRANZ) 93
BECKER Donald J. 75
BECKER Emma 135
BECKER Erwin 93
BECKER Fay A. 151
BECKER G. Mortimer 152
BECKER Heinrich F. 93

BECKER Ida J. 177
BECKER Jennie 93
BECKER Jessie 152
BECKER Johanna (STEINGREBER) 53
BECKER John H. 135
BECKER Julius W. 93
BECKER Lucille M. 74
BECKER Maria (HEBEL) 93
BECKER Mary Jane 152
BECKER Otto H. 177
BECKER Wilhelm 93
BEECK Edwin 130
BEFI Anna (WEGNER) 181
BEHLING Armand A. 112
BEHLING Augusta 111
BEHLING Emilie 164
BEHLING Harold A. 150
BEHLING Herman 111
BEHLING John E. 150
BEHLING Mabel C. 150
BEHLING Mabel I. 150
BEHLING Norma K. 111
BEHLING Robert C. 150
BEHLING Roland 111
BEHNKE William 178
BELL August L. 178
BELL Clara L. 191
BELL Erwin J. 129
BELL Laura G. 48
BELL Orbie R. 191
BELNAR Anna R. (TONN) 117
BELTON Harry 39
BELTON Neva 39
BENDER Isabella M. 89
BENDER Otto J. 89
BENDINGER Phillip 134
BENEZIS John P. 83
BENKERT Kathrine 13
BENKERT Paula 13
BENNETT Babes 70
BENNETT Catherine 70
BENNETT Charlie 70
BENNETT Harry G. 71
BENNETT Henry D. 70
BENOY Ida L. 130
BENOY John R. 130
BERGMANN Gertrude 146
BERNDT Fred 167
BESECKE Gustav 176, 178
BESECKE Selma 178
BEUTLER Grace Mary 143
BEUTLER Howard 142
BEUTLER William F., Dr. 143
BEVIER Almira Cleveland 35

BRANDT Louisa 59
BRANDT Mary 54
BRANDT William C. 59
BRANGE Karlis 198
BRANT J. G. 71
BRANT John F. 71
BRANT Martha 72
BRAUN Friedrich W. 37
BRAUN Maria 37
BRAUNE August 73
BRAUNE Magdalina 73
BRAZEE Alice E. 25
BRAZEE Alvin C. 25
BREDE Frederick 95
BREDE Minnie 96
BREDE Theodore 96
BREDE Theodore, Jr. 96
BREDE Wilhelmine 95
BREED Catharine L. 25
BREED Gersham P. 25
BREED Henry A. 25
BREED Mary A. 25
BREEN Elizabeth 117
BREEN William 117
BREITLOW Dale H. 199
BREITLOW Susan M. 199
BRENDEMUEHL Elmer A. 153
BRENNAN Charles Coleman 194
BRENNAN John Emil 195
BRENNAN Josephine Wigdale 195
BRENNAN Suzanne Gardner 195
BREU Anna 167
BREU August 167
BREU Heinrich 115
BREU Marie 115
BREU Minnie 115
BRIGGS Franklin P. 9
BRIGGS Hosia F. 129
BRIL Allan 47
BRIL Clara A. 47
BRINKMAN Katherine 62
BRINKMAN Paul W. 62
BRITTAIN James E., Jr. 199
BRITTAIN Shirley 199
BROCKWAY Addie 4
BROCKWAY Arthur W. 5
BROCKWAY Bessie 4
BROCKWAY Beulah V. 5
BROCKWAY Gilbert H. 4
BROCKWAY Lafayette 4
BROCKWAY Mary B. 4
BROCKWAY Mary Francis 4
BROCKWAY Mildred 5
BROCKWAY Robert C. 5

BROCKWAY Walter H. 4
BROOKS Alma 113
BROUWER Elizabeth Ellis 175
BROUWER Roy 175
BROUWER Stephen John 175
BROWN Abbie A. 6
BROWN Abe 153
BROWN Albert 183
BROWN Amanda F. 6
BROWN Anna S. 111
BROWN C. Elmo 131
BROWN Carl Martin 99
BROWN Charles C. 76
BROWN Charles L. 131
BROWN Clarence Henry 10
BROWN Corolin C. 16
BROWN Daniel 187
BROWN David 187
BROWN David C. 76
BROWN E. H. 57
BROWN Elizabeth 31, 57, 183
BROWN Emma 31
BROWN Geo. W. 10
BROWN Grace May 153
BROWN Harris 31
BROWN Helen 31
BROWN Hiram M. 76
BROWN James 96
BROWN Janet 96
BROWN Jennie 96
BROWN Jonathan 6
BROWN Julia M. 10
BROWN Leonard 6
BROWN Lillian M. 131
BROWN Lincoln 6
BROWN Lorette Caemelt? 10
BROWN Lucy Minnie 6
BROWN Malcolm G. 16
BROWN Marie? 10
BROWN Martha J. 6
BROWN Mary 187
BROWN Mary Ann 6
BROWN Mathilda 6
BROWN Melvin E. 31
BROWN Mettra H. 149
BROWN Nellie Johnson 153
BROWN O. A. 31
BROWN Oscar 31
BROWN Oscar W. 6
BROWN Polly 187
BROWN Robert 96
BROWN Rodolph M. 58
BROWN S. M. 57
BROWN Sarah 31

BROWN Sarah M. 6
BROWN Scott C. 15
BROWN Silas I. 57
BROWN Susan M. 76
BROWN Sylvester 76
BROWN Theodore 31
BROWN Virginia 6
BROWN William 31
BROWN William M. 76
BROWNE Abbey Everts 12
BROWNE Charles E. 12
BROWNE Clarence Duane 12
BROWNE Edith Darrow 12
BROWNE Elizabeth M. 8
BROWNE Ella 8
BROWNE Henry W. 8
BROWNE Ida Isabel 12
BROWNE Jonathan 12
BROWNE Levi H. 8
BROWNE Maria L. 8
BROWNE Martha Everts 12
BRUDER Augusta 114
BRUDER Eliza 114
BRUDER Herman 114
BRUDER William 115
BRUINS Dirk 174
BRUINS Flora Belle 174
BRUINS Mother 174
BRUSS Mary Thiel 176
BUCHANAN 195
BUCHANAN Thomas Boyd 194
BUCHHOLTZ Amelia 47
BUCHHOLTZ Henry 47
BUCHHOLTZ Joseph 167
BUCHHOLZ Gasten A. 172
BUCHHOLZ Jennie 172
BUCHHOLZ Robert William 172
BUCHMANN August H. 149
BUCHMANN Fred 149
BUCHMANN Fredericka Joers 149
BUCHMANN Otto E. 149
BUCHMANN Wilhelmine 149
BUCHOLTZ Anton E. 96
BUCHOLTZ Roselle 96
BUCK Elfrieda 76
BUCKINGHAM Frank V. 18
BUCKINGHAM Viora V. 18
BUCKMAN C. Arthur 15
BUCKMAN Gertrude 15
BUEGE Charles 167
BUEGE Johann 100
BUEGE Martha M. 172
BUEGE Mary 167
BUEGE Robert 167

BUEGE Walter F. 168
BUEGE Walter G. 173
BUELL Bernice M. 11
BUELL Theodore W. 11
BULGRIN Anton Fred 193
BULGRIN Frank 189
BULGRIN Martha 189
BULGRIN Richard 189
BULTING Jacob 166
BUNKE Helen B. 13
BUNKE Matilda 116
BUNKE Paul F. 116
BUNKE Paul W. 13
BURK Alvina 195
BURK George 195
BURLINGAME Elizabeth M. 174
BURR Dexter 3
BURR Mary 3
BUSCHER Anna 15
BUSCHER Clarence 15
BUSCHER Gustav 15
BUSSE Lydia L. 130
BUSSE Walter A. 130
BUSZ August L. 183
BUSZ Charles F. 183
BUSZ Emelia H. 183
BUTCHER Grace Esther 146
BUTTERFIELD Anna M. 25
BUTTERFIELD Benjamin 44
BUTTERFIELD Sally 44

C

CABBOTT W. H. 2
CAIN Cornelia 29
CAIN Elmer Ellsworth 34
CAIN Eva Cleveland 34
CAIN Frederick G. 34
CAIN George F. 29
CAMERON Katharine (SOMMERS) 22
CANRIGHT Lillie 120
CARLSON Grace 20
CARON Minnie L. 176
CARPENTER Frank 117
CARPENTER John B. 68
CARPENTER Lilliam M. 117
CARRICK Christina 179
CARRICK James 179
CARRIGAN James 134
CARTER Karen Seitz 191
CARTER Lavinia Andrews 5
CARY Baby 146
CASE Bigelow 42
CASE Elizabeth 147
CASE Elvira H. 42

EGGERT Almond H. 182
EGGERT Anna 133
EGGERT Dorothea M. (JACH) 110
EGGERT Fred 59
EGGERT Fred W. 133
EGGERT Gertrude(HELLBERG) 132
EGGERT Ida 133
EGGERT Johann 118
EGGERT John 111, 118
EGGERT Lillian 188
EGGERT Mary 59
EGGERT Roland 111
EGGERT Theresa 118
EGGERT Viola 71
EGGERT William J. C. 132
EGGERT-RIEMER Clara 165
EHNERT Harry 112
EHNERT Lucille 112
EHNERT Lydia 112
EICHLER Lillian 60
EINFALT John 177
EINFALT Maria 177
EITENEIER Charles 4
EITENEIER Julia (NASS) 4
EITENEIER William 4
ELHART Clara E. 169
ELHART Infant 167
ELIAS John 184
ELIAS Rachel 184
ELLIS Clarissa 52
ELLIS Daisy Wilson 152
ELLIS Emma Wehr 150
ELLIS Helen Myers 135
ELLIS John A. 166
ELLIS Marion Elizabeth 135
Elsie 166
ENGEL August J. 89
ENGEL Clara A. 89
ENGEL Johann 131
ENGEL Otto H. 48
ENGEL Sophia 131
ENGELHARDT Ernst E. 115
ENGELHARDT Henry 35
ENGELHARDT Mary 115
ENGELHARDT Sophia 35
ENGELHART Clara 35
ENGSTAD Leonora J. 18
ENGSTROM Frank E. 19
ENGSTROM Irma S. 19
EPPSTAEDT Mary Jo 194
EPPSTAEDT Robert R. 194
ERDMAN Fred E. 166
ERDMANN Harry S. 131
ERIKSEN Claire Guequierre 189

ERIKSEN Elisabeth 147
ERIKSEN Fred Esbern 189
ERIKSEN Martin 147
ERKE John W. 20
ERKE Julius J. 20
ERWIN Maude Flory 22
ESCH Clara 194
ESCH Delores M. L. 131
ESCH Frank 194
ESCHENBERG Fred 193
ESCHENBERG Minnie 193
ESCHENBURG Caroline 99
ESCHENBURG John 100
ESCHENBURG William 100
EVANS Lona M. 190
EVANS William A. 190
EVERTS Mabel 7

F

FALBE Anton T. 114
FALBE Arrie B. 113
FALBE Arthur 114
FALBE Eugene 113
FALBE Latara 114
FALBE Otillie 156
FALBE Sophia 156
FALBE W. F. C. 114
FALK Adolph H. 50
FALK Anna 116
FALK Annie 156
FALK Arthur 68
FALK Arthur W. 146
FALK Berga A. 67
FALK Charles F. 147
FALK Charles W. 118
FALK Ella L. 119
FALK Erich A. 67
FALK Ernestina 131
FALK Fred 68
FALK Frederick Lee 145
FALK Fredrick 18
FALK Friedrich 117
FALK Hazel E. 145
FALK Henrietta 68
FALK Henry E. 119
FALK Hulda 146
FALK John A. 50
FALK Lillie 118
FALK Louise A. 147
FALK Martin 134
FALK Minie 50
FALK Minnie A. 147
FALK Norman F. 146
FALK Olga 118

215

MOORE Elsie M. 32
MOORE Harvel L. 35
MOORE Julia B. 32
MOORE Lamara 35
MOORE Lorenzo W. 35
MOORE Miranda I. 35
MOORE Nellie C. 35
MOORE Phyllis E. 117
MOORE William H. 32
MORGAN David 11
MORGAN Fanny C. 11
MORGAN James 11
MORRIS Ann 119
MORRIS David 119
MORSE Jessie E. Rhodes 120
MOSS Cornelia S. 135
MOSS Dorothy C. 135
MOSS John 135
MOSS Lillian C. 135
MOSS Roy M. 135
MOULTON Elsie 146
MOWER Arba B. 77
MOWER Augustus B. 77
MOWER Caroline B. 77
MOWER Caroline Rice 35
MOWER Edmund C. 77
MOWER Eunice 2
MOWER Harriet E. 77
MOWER Harry T. 32
MOWER Infant 77
MOWER Lydia C. 32
MOWER Margaret West 35
MOWER Mary A. 32
MOWER Timothy 2
MOWER Timothy B. 32
MUELLER Esther 44
MUELLNER Adolph 183
MUELLNER Clara 183
MUENCHOW August/Augusta W. 131
MUENCHOW Henry 169
MULHOLLAND Meta 116
MULHOLLAND Thompson 116
MULLER Albert 73
MULLER Bernhard 73
MULLER Emilie T. 72
MULLER Ernst J. 73
MULLER Herman A. 72
MULLER Louise M. 72
MULLER Minna F. 73
MULLER Wilhelmine (BRAUNE) 73
MUNDSTOCK Emily 35
MUNDSTOCK Frank 35
MUNDT Edgar 35
MUNDT Gretchen 35

MUNGER D. H. 40
MUNGER Elverton 40
MUNNINGHOFF August 192
MUNNINGHOFF Louise 192
MURKETT Jessie Y. 117
MURPHY Clara A. 87
MURPHY Johanna Lang 46
MURPHY John W. 87
MUSKAT Carl 75
MUSKAT Emma 75
MUSOLF Anna 120
MUTH Adam H. 131
MYERS Jacob Oliver 134
MYERS Laura Chapman 134

N

NAAB Adam 154
NAAB Amelia Keeler 154
NAAB Georgiana K. 155
NAESER Arthur 168
NAGEL Irma 193
NAGEL Margaret 176
NAGEL Paul 193
NAGEL William 176
NAHS Carl 99
NARWOLD Dorothy M. 14
NARWOLD Margaret J. 63
NARWOLD T. Josephine 63
NARWOLD William L. 15
NASS Caroline 86
NASS Catharina 4
NASS Charles 4
NASS Elizabeth 4
NASS Emilius 4
NASS Katherine 86
NASS Wm. 86
NEEDHAM Amelia 24
NEEDHAM Anna O. 24
NEEDHAM Arthur E. 23
NEEDHAM Edward Irving 24
NEEDHAM Emma Louise 24
NEEDHAM Enoch Gardner 24
NEEDHAM Esther Amelia 24
NEEDHAM Henry Martyn 24
NEEDHAM Mary Caroline 24
NEEDHAM William 24
NEHRING Anna H. 120
NEHRING Anne 120
NEHRING Emil 120
NEHRING Emma 120
NEHRING Emma M. H. 120
NEHRING Wilhelm G. 120
NEILS Florence J. 63
NEILS Walter L. 63

RADTKE Ernstine 171
RADTKE Gertrude 13
RADTKE Marie 164
RAGDALE Caroline B. 181
RAGDALE Edwin James 181
RAGDALE Helen Echols 181
RAGDALE Norman A. 181
RAGDALE Ralph S. 181
RAGSDALE Charles E. 26
RAGSDALE Elizabeth 26
RAGSDALE Elizabeth G. 26
RAGSDALE Virginia 26
RAKOS Mary 14
RAKOS Mike 14
RAMSTACK Amelia 171
RAMSTACK George 171
RANK Jeanie 152
RANK Robert 152
RANWICK Alfred 164
RANWICK Herdrikke 156
RANWICK Oswald 168
RASCHKA Charles 13
RASCHKA Frank C. 13
RASEY Lee C. 168
RASEY Mabel U. 168
RASMUSSEN Adler T. 134
RAWSON Elizabeth 164
READ Bessie Ferne 189
READ Victor A. 189
READER Sophia H. 4
READER Wm. J. 4
REBHOLZ Elizabeth Ann 10
REBHOLZ Richard A. 10
REBHOLZ Richard Andrew 10
REDDIN John N. 198
REDDIN Marcia L. 198
REDOEHL Christian 92
REDZINSKE Bertha 189
REDZINSKE Charles J. 189
REDZINSKE Paul 132
REDZINSKI Arthur 134
REDZINSKI Carl 134
REDZINSKI Caroline 134
REDZINSKI Martha 82
REDZINSKI Mathilda 134
REDZINSKI Rosette 134
REDZINSKI Wilhelmine (MARQUARDT) 82
REICH Eugene F. 63
REICH Frances M. 63
REICHE Carl H. 115
REICHE Minnie 115
REICHOW Adeline 135
REICHOW Michael 135
REICHOW Minnie 135

REIMER August F. 148
REIMER Christian 148
REIMER Lillian A. 148
REIMER Louisa 148
REIN Clarence E. 191
REINERT Linda A. 199
REINKE Adeline 117
REINKE Albert L. 117
REINKE Carol 117
REINKE Emilie (FALK) 117
REINKE Florence 117
REINKE Irene H. 135
REINKE Joyce B. 13
REINKE Robert F. 13
REINKE Russell 117
REINKE Wilbert 117
REIS Elizabeth 47
REIS Jacob 47
REMICK Laura C. 192
REMICK Wilson H. 192
RENNER Joseph J. 178
RENNER Marjorie Sullivan 178
RESEBURG Arwin 154
RESEBURG Arwin O. 154
RESEBURG Laura S. 154
RESEBURG Ruth L. 154
REUL Alma 142
REUL Emil Rev. 142
REYNOLDS Benjamin R. 41
RHODE Augusta H. 149
RHODE Otto R. 149
RICE Agnes M. 77
RICE Ann Fisher 36
RICE Cynthia Ann 36
RICE Frank H. 197
RICE Harriet 36
RICE Talitha 36
RICE Thomas J. 35
RICE Thos. J. 77
RICE Virginia K. 197
RICHARDS Clarence P. 18
RICHARDS Harry B. 135
RICHARDS Janet H. 135
RICHTER Paul 62
RICHTER Paula 62
RICKE Otto 166
RICKERT Christoph 69
RICKERT Edward J. 69
RICKERT Henry J. 66
RICKERT Mathilda 69
RIDDELL Clarissa 76
RIDDELL Samuel 76
RIDDLE Adaline 74
RIDDLE Samuel 74

229

RUSH Grace R. 191
RUSSELL Alice Wadsworth 114
RUSSLEY Adelaide M. 187
RUSSLEY John H. 187
RUTZ Alvina 120
RUTZ Eleanor 120
RUTZ Ella 119
RUTZ John 119
RYAN Elmer 148
RYAN Frank E. 199
RYAN George 148
RYAN Ida 148
RYAN Margaret C. 199

S

SACKETT Anna M. 51
SACKETT Edwin H. 51
SACKETT Sarah 51
SACKETT Squire 51
SADEWASSER Herman 178
SAMPO Henry J. 198
SAMPO Ruth G. 198
SANBORN Upham T. 165
SANTAIS M. A. Margaret (MELENDY) 4
SARGEANT Harry W. 76
SARGEANT Katherine M. 76
SAVAGE Millard D. 199
SAVAGE Shirley Mae 199
SCARRITT Eliza S. 54
SCHABLOW August 98
SCHABLOW Henrietta M. 176
SCHABLOW Louis H. 176
SCHABLOW Louisa 98
SCHABLOW Louisa (BARNDT) 98
SCHABLOW Louise 98
SCHABLOW Wilhelm 98
SCHABLOW Wilhelmine F. A. (KREULL) 98
SCHAFER Della H. 17
SCHAFER Gustave A. 18
SCHAFFER Alice M. 184
SCHAFFER Frank J. 184
SCHANING Melitta Raschig 183
SCHAPER A. A. 156
SCHAPER Louise 156
SCHARMER Amanda 135
SCHARMER August 135
SCHARMER Emilie 135
SCHAUER Alfred Fred 168
SCHAUER Catherine B. 168
SCHEEL Amelia 196
SCHEEL William 196
SCHEIBE Alfred 88
SCHEIBE Amelia 88
SCHEIBE Emilie A. 88

SCHEIBE Emma 88
SCHEIBE Gustav 88
SCHEIBE Wilhelmina 88
SCHEINBEIN Elimor M. 78
SCHEINER Adelle 19
SCHEINER Fred 19
SCHELLIN Karl 164
SCHEMBERGER Gladys 169
SCHEMBERGER Harold 166
SCHEMBERGER Micheal 169
SCHERNECK Rudolph 156
SCHERREIKS George 132
SCHETTER Julia 99
SCHICANTEK Frank 144
SCHICANTEK Mathilda 144
SCHICK Emilie 135
SCHILDT August 39
SCHILDT Dorathea 39
SCHLICHTING C. J. 50
SCHLIESKE Maria 100
SCHMAH August F. 130
SCHMAH Elsa I. 130
SCHMECHEL George F. 45
SCHMECHEL Irma M. 45
SCHMECHEL Wilma 45
SCHMELING Albert 168
SCHMELING Alvera 168
SCHMELING Anna 168
SCHMELING Arthur H. 168
SCHMELING Charles 169
SCHMELING Florence 169
SCHMELING Walter 168
SCHMID Nathalie B. 62
SCHMIDT Alfrieda A. 186
SCHMIDT Alma 171
SCHMIDT Anton 112
SCHMIDT Augusta 98
SCHMIDT Bernice 165
SCHMIDT Bertha 2
SCHMIDT Carl 98
SCHMIDT Edwin 171
SCHMIDT Ernestine 147
SCHMIDT Ferdinand 165
SCHMIDT Franz D. 186
SCHMIDT Franz Joseph 111
SCHMIDT Hugo E., Dr. 186
SCHMIDT Jessie R. 186
SCHMIDT John 2
SCHMIDT Laura Hemsing 111
SCHMIDT Lloyd 165
SCHMIDT Louise 111
SCHMIDT Maria 2
SCHMIDT Mathilda 186
SCHMIDT Michael 165

SEEMANN William 146
SEHLER Hazel 165
SEHLER Walter G. 165
SEIBERLICH Anita 184
SEIBERLICH Roy J. 184
SEIDER Cassandra K. 132
SEIFERT Richard H. 97
SELEY Edwin H. 1
SELEY Ellen M. 1
SELEY Harry R. 1
SELEY Lucinda 1
SEMROW Ferdenand 136
SEMROW Ferdinand 146
SEMROW Louise 136
SEMROW Wilhelm 164
SERCOMBE Selma 101
SETTE Isabel 68
SETTE James A. 68
SEUBERTH Lillian 79
SEUBERTH Lydia 79
SEVEDGE Dorothy (CARRIGAN) 134
SEVEDGE James Lewis 135
SEVEDGE Millie Loretta 134
SEVERIN Gustav 166
SEYBOLD Warren A. 66
SHAFER Clarence 131
SHANTZ Lucia Ragsdale 26
SHAPE Minnie 171
SHAW Charles 116
SHAW Enid C. 179
SHAW Eugene M. 179
SHAW Luella J. 116
SHAW Sandra Lee 179
SHELDON Carroll C. 36
SHELDON David S. 36
SHELDON Ida M. 11
SHELDON John 10
SHELDON Mary 11
SHELDON Roscoe 152
SHERKUS Blanche 178
SHIELLS Alexander E. 171
SHOEN Fred 156
SHOEN Maria 156
SHUBERT Herbert 155
SHULTIS Arthur H. 78
SHULTIS Dorothy E. 78
SHUMWAY Alfred 71
SHUMWAY Harriet E. 71
SHUMWAY Margaret 71
SHUMWAY Mary Gibson 71
SHUMWAY P. J. 71
SIEBERT Arnold W. 116
SIEBERT Mary 116
SIEBERT Mary F. 116

SIEBERT William 116
SIEBRECHT Emma 129
SIEBRECHT Max C. 50
SIEBRECHT Max J. 51
SIEBRECHT Minna 50
SIECKE A. P. 176
SIEGEL Alma 99
SIEGEL Caroline F. 168
SIEGEL Frank 99
SIEGEL Roland J. 168
SIEGER Ernest W. 133
SIEGERT Benjamin E. 82
SIEGERT Friederike 82
SIEGERT Herman E. 82
SIEGERT Willie 82
SIEGESMUND Albert 149
SIEGESMUND Ida 149
SIEGESMUND John 149
SIEMAN Elmer 131
SIGRIST Bert 49
SIGRIST Christine 49
SIGRIST Eleanor 49
SILVERNESS Harold O. 46
SILVERNESS Ruth Wadsworth 46
SIMMONS Dorothy Mae 169
SIMMONS Jerold G. 169
SIMON Isaac E. 131
SIMONS Elsie (ESCHENBURG) 99
SIMROCK Frank Harold 196
SKEPPER Dorothy 53
SKEPPER Edward C. 53
SKEPPER Ellen 53
SKEPPER Ellen A. 53
SKEPPER Jennie F. 53
SKEPPER Richard 53
SKINNER Isabel Elder 171
SKINNER James Martin 171
SKINNER Mary Low 171
SMITH Albert W. 38
SMITH Alice Field 112
SMITH Alson Arthur 112
SMITH Alson I. 112
SMITH Amanda E. 41
SMITH Catherine Garrett 38
SMITH Coley 41
SMITH Elisabeth S. 75
SMITH Erastus C. 76
SMITH Ethel H. 62
SMITH Evalina Wheeler? 8
SMITH Harriet B. W. 96
SMITH Helen M. 38
SMITH Henry H. 166
SMITH John M. 94
SMITH Lottie M. 112

233

STREHLOW Wilhelmina 132
STREHLOW William 166
STRENG Adam 165
STRENG Adam, Jr. 184
STRENG Anna 184
STRENG Caroline 165
STRENG Mayme 165
STRIKOWSKY Carl 100
STRONG Clara Jane 29
STRONG Gordon M. 171
STRONG Helen Adele 29
STRONG Henry 29
STRONG Henry F. 172
STRONG Jessie E. 172
STRONG Madelaine Freeman 171
STRONG Mary A. 172
STRONG Mary Eliza 29
STRONG Mary Ethel Freeman 172
STRONG Myron W. 172
STRONG Reuben Myron 172
STRONG Signe (FELLAND) 171
STUDEMANN Carl 110
STUDEMANN Ludwig 111
STUDEMANN Maria 111
SULLIVAN Bertha Kimball 179
SULLIVAN Edward C. 179
SULLIVAN Lois J. 44
SUTTON Jerry L. 191
SWAN Alvin H. 42
SWAN Betty James 44
SWAN Caroline M. 42
SWAN Clara E. 143
SWAN Clara May 43
SWAN Craydon McGill 44
SWAN David More 43
SWAN Edward U. 45
SWAN Emery 42
SWAN Emery A. 47
SWAN Frank E. 42
SWAN Hannah Gilbert 43
SWAN Ida M. 45
SWAN James 154
SWAN Jeanette S. 143
SWAN Julia A. 42
SWAN Julia E. 47
SWAN Lilly A. 42
SWAN Maria M. 44
SWAN Marion P. 42
SWAN Nathaniel J. 43, 143
SWAN Orlin J. 143
SWAN Seth B. 44
SWAN Virginia R. 143
SWAN Walter C. 45
SWEET Blanche 180

SWEET Charlotte M. 180
SWEET Hattie 184
SWEET Lucien S. 180
SWEET Ross 184
SYLLM Ad. Oscar 134
SYLVESTER Bertha 118
SYLVESTER Gustav A. 118
SYLVESTER Infant 118
SYLVESTER Pauline 118
SZEKELY Caroline C. 194
SZEKELY Ernest 194
SZEKELY George E. 194
SZEKELY Sari 194
SZUPPA Henry 169
SZUPPA Marie Fellows 168

T

TADDEY Anna 151
TADDEY Edward Walter 151
TADDEY Ferdinand 151
TANNER Charles M. 71
TANNER Lilah F. 71
TARASOFF Evelyn A. 87
TARASOFF Peter N. 87
TAYLOR Catherine 145
TAYLOR Cornelius 145
TAYLOR Dorothy (ROSE) 96
TAYLOR Elouise 145
TAYLOR Martin M. 145
TAYLOR Mary E. 75
TAYLOR Mary R. 145
TAYLOR William G. 75
TELFER Adam Ferguson 63
TELFER Eva Oliver 63
TEMPLE Anna M. 75
TEMPLE Henry S. 75
TENDLER Adeline L. 196
TENDLER Lawrence M. 196
TENGES Anna 172
TENGES Gottfried 164
TENGES Louisa 164
TENGES Sophie 164
TENNANT Agnes D. 117
TENNANT Agnes S. 117
TENNANT Cora L. 117
TENNANT Harriet D. 117
TENNANT Richard 117
TENNYSON Addie Erast 134
TENNYSON Esther A. 134
TESKA Stacy Lee 197
TETTING Elsie 192
TETZLAFF Bill 191
TETZLAFF Shirley M. 191
TETZLAFF William J. 191

235

WAGNER Paul C. 83
WAGNER Wm. 147
WALES Allen A. 7
WALES Arvine R. 7
WALES Gideon 7
WALES Mary C. 7
WALES Polly 7
WALKER Charles A. 97
WALKER Constance M. 181
WALKER Ella Mays 182
WALKER Emery L. 182
WALKER Gratia A. 12
WALKER James A. 12
WALKER Jesse M. 182
WALKER Mabelle Scott 182
WALKER Mary Jo Wolfe 18
WALKER Norma I. 97
WALKER Olive A. 18
WALKER Winefred 12
WALLMANN William 119
WALTER Adolph 114
WALTER August 61
WALTER Caroline 114
WALTER Katharina 113
WALTER Kathryn 114
WALTER Otto 114
WALTER Rebekka (BACH) 61
WALTER Wilhelm 113
WALTERS Fred H. 119
WALTERS Vera R. 118
WALTERS William A. 190
WANDSNIDER Alvin L. 92
WANDSNIDER Thressa H. 174
WANGELIN Anna 167
WANKOWSKI Edith R. 196
WARNECKE Henry 166
WARNECKE Herman K. 170
WARNECKE Olga M. 170
WARNECKE Ruth 170
WARREN Albert D. 134
WARREN Anna Hoppin 21
WARREN Clara B. 20
WARREN Delinda H. 134
WARREN Della M. 20
WARREN Harriet F. 26
WARREN Jon w Albert 20
WARREN Jonathan M. 20
WARREN Joseph Alonzo 26
WARREN Joseph Dennis 134
WARREN Kate C. 134
WARREN Lavinia D. 20
WARREN Luther A. 20
WARREN Paul C. 134
WARREN Phillip Allan 195

WARREN Roxena B. 134
WARREN Sarah B. 26
WARREN Sarah H. 26
WATKINS Edwin C. 72
WATKINS Estella M. 72
WATNER Emma C. 75
WATNER Harriet P. 75
WATNER Henry 75
WATNER Roy S. 37
WATNER Tillie 37
WATSON C. Dwight 112
WATSON George 7
WATSON Henry Eugene 7
WATSON Jennie M. 7
WATSON Mary Everts Browne 7
WATSON Mary J. 112
WATSON Thomas Courtney 112
WATSON Willis E. 7
WATT Russel C. Watt 90
WATTERS Patrick J. 193
WEATHERLY Frances 146
WEBB Jeanne 128
WEBB Wm. 128
WEBER Annie 80
WEBER Curt H. 198
WEBER Earl C. 71
WEBER Herman 80
WEBER Isabel M. 71
WEBER Olive F. 80
WEBER William H. 80
WEGNER Albert H. 146
WEGNER Alvina 166
WEGNER Carrie A. 146
WEGNER Charles 181
WEGNER Charles F. 181
WEGNER Earl A. 181
WEGNER Emma M. 181
WEGNER Frank P. 181
WEGNER Fred Wm. 193
WEGNER Gladys B. 146
WEGNER Helen J. 181
WEGNER Herman J. 179
WEGNER Howard 166
WEGNER Johanna 180
WEGNER Lottie L. 193
WEGNER Margaret M. 181
WEGNER Marie R. 179
WEGNER Mary 181
WEGNER Mary A. 181
WEGNER Roger W. 181
WEGNER William 180, 181
WEHE Edward C. 166
WEHR Georgia 150
WEHR Gustav 150

WILSON Charles E. 181
WILSON Cynthia M. 11
WILSON Edwin T. 11
WILSON Eugene 13
WILSON Kathryn 197
WILSON Mary A. 181
WILTERDING Ethel C. 78
WILTERDING Forest 78
WIMBLE James 50
WIMBLE Mary Jane 50
WINDING Ethel M. 185
WINDING Mary Jane 185
WINDING Walter G. 185
WINDING Walter Jr. 185
WINIGER Frederick J. 97
WINKEL Fred 97
WINTERS Caroline E. 167
WINTERS Emma H. 2
WINTERS John W. 2
WINTERS William 76
WINZENRIED John 89
WINZENRIED Samuel 89
WINZENRIED Sophia 89
WITTE Frances 29
WITTE George R. 51
WITTE Hedwig 115
WITTE Ida M. 51
WITTE Mabel W. 24
WITTE Richard 29
WITTE Richard S. 24
WITZKE Paul T. 197
WITZKE Winifred R. 197
WLETSCHAK Elsie C. 5
WLETSCHAK Faye 15
WLETSCHAK Frank 15
WLETSCHAK Frank E. 5
WLETSCHAK George 15
WLETSCHAK Horton S. 15
WLETSCHAK Joan 15
WLETSCHAK Maxine H. 15
WOLF Augusta 120
WOLF Clarence A. 120
WOLF John 120
WOLF Leonard 99
WOLF Mary 99
WOLFGRAM Bertha 119
WOLFGRAM Carl 119
WOLFGRAM Fred 120
WOLFGRAM Minnie 120
WOLFGRAM William 119
WOLLAEGER Amanda G. 115
WOLLERS Arthur 90
WOLLERS Louisa 90
WOLTER Anna 11

WOLTER Emil A. 11
WOOD Ben 167
WOOD Dorothy A. 78, 167
WOOD Emma Ivens 114
WOOD George L. 78
WOODMANSEE Leroy W. 119
WOODMANSEE Persis E. 119
WOODMANSEE William 119
WORCESTER George E. 89
WORCESTER Sarah W. 89
WORM Edward 194
WORM Luella 194
WORM Maria L. 57
WRASSE Harry H. 113
WRASSE Lulu F. 113
WRIGHT Frederick M. 8
WRIGHT Ione Turner 113
WRIGHT Irving F. 113
WRIGHT Tom G. 113
WRIGHT Walter H. 113
WRIGHT? Baby 113
WUNSCH Maria 135

X

XIONG Joua 198
XIONG Lee Hang 69

Y

YANG Chue Cha 69
YANG Xia 69
YOB Natalie 99
YONK Ewold J. 191
YONK Marietta E. 191
YORK Orpha 165
YOUNG Anna M. 146
YOUNG Lloyd E. 146
YOUNG Robert 146
YUNGKANS Bertha 169
YUNGKANS Fred 169
YUNK Frank X. 3
YUNK Theresa 3

Z

ZAHN Andrew 164
ZAHRTE Kenneth H. 184
ZAHRTE Lenore H. 184
ZELLER Casper 113
ZELLER Sophie 113
ZELLER Walter C. 113
ZELLMER Peter Ernest 73
ZEMKE Amelia 136
ZEMKE Augusta 80
ZEMKE Carl 79

240

ZEMKE Clara 111
ZEMKE Flora 80
ZEMKE Frank 136
ZEMKE Herman G. 83
ZEMKE Hermann 80
ZEMKE Lillian F. 83
ZEMKE Paul 136
ZEMKE Susie 80
ZEUNERT Ida M. 62
ZIEMER Amelia 146
ZIEMER Bertha 81
ZIEMER Clara 81
ZIEMER Frank 24
ZIEMER Henry 81
ZIEMER Herman 146
ZIEMER Theresa 24
ZIERHUT Joseph B. 169
ZILLMER August 89
ZILLMER Carl 90
ZILLMER Eric W. 40
ZILLMER Estelle M. 40
ZILLMER Josephina 89
ZILLMER Josephine 88
ZILLMER Louise 89
ZILLMER Magdalene 89
ZILLMER Michael 88, 90
ZILLMER Otto A. 40
ZIMDARS William 167
ZIMMERMAN George 90
ZIMMERMAN Minnie 90
ZIMMERMANN Emma 1
ZIMMERMANN Etta A. 133
ZIMMERMANN Franz 54
ZIMMERMANN Friedericke W.
    (SCHAPLOW) 54
ZIMMERMANN John 1
ZIMMERMANN John C. 1
ZIMMERMANN Margaretha 1
ZIMMERMANN Ph. W. 1
ZIMMERMANN Phillip 1
ZIMMERMANN Rosetta 2
ZIMMERMANN Stella L. H. 90
ZIMMERMANN Theodore E. 133
ZIMMERMANN Wilhelmina 1
ZIMMERMANN Winfield D. 133
ZINN Carl Walter 112
ZINN Viola L. 112
ZIRWES Jacob 14
ZIRWES Mabel 14
ZIVANOVIC Bora 134
ZIVANOVIC Virginia 134
ZOBEL Gustave 60
ZOBEL Henry 190
ZOBEL Irene 190

ZOBEL Kerstin 196
ZOBEL Mary Ann 190
ZOBEL Richard 131
ZOBEL Susan 60
ZOBEL William 196
ZOPHY Adelaid 39

www.ingramcontent.com/pod-product-compliance
Lightning Source LLC
Chambersburg PA
CBHW061726270326
41928CB00011B/2123